ANSWERING THE CALL

Answering the Call

Letters from the 2/4th Bn.
Somerset Light Infantry (PA) 1914–1919

With Best Wishes,

John Mackie.

RABY

First published privately in 1999
Copyright © John H. F. Mackie, 1999

Copyright © John H. F. Mackie, 2002

Published in 2002 by
Raby Books
The Coach House
Eggleston Old Hall
Eggleston
County Durham
DL12 0AG

British Library Cataloguing-in-Publication data
A catalogue record for this book is available from the British Library

ISBN 1-84410-005-7

Printed and bound by Bookcraft Ltd, Bath

This book is dedicated to the memory of my Grandparents, Hugh and Geraldine Mackie, who preserved all the letters for posterity. Also to the memory of my uncle, James R. Mackie, who wrote them and to his widow Sylvia, who after the untimely death of their own son, Richard, kindly gave and entrusted them to me — knowing my intrest in the Somerset Light Infantry (P.A.). Finally to all those who served in, gave their lives or were wounded whilst serving with the 2/4th Bn. during the 1914–18 war

Editor's Note

I t will be seen that within the text of the letters, many instances of incorrect spelling, incorrect grammar or crossings out have been printed. This has been deliberately done, in this form, on the advice of the Imperial War Museum, London. All the letters have therefore been transcribed authentically from the original hand-written pages. At the beginning of a year an occasional date appears to be wrong. Again, this has been accurately reproduced from the original script. Many of us have made this mistake ourselves, sometimes on cheques and important documents!

John Mackie

Contents

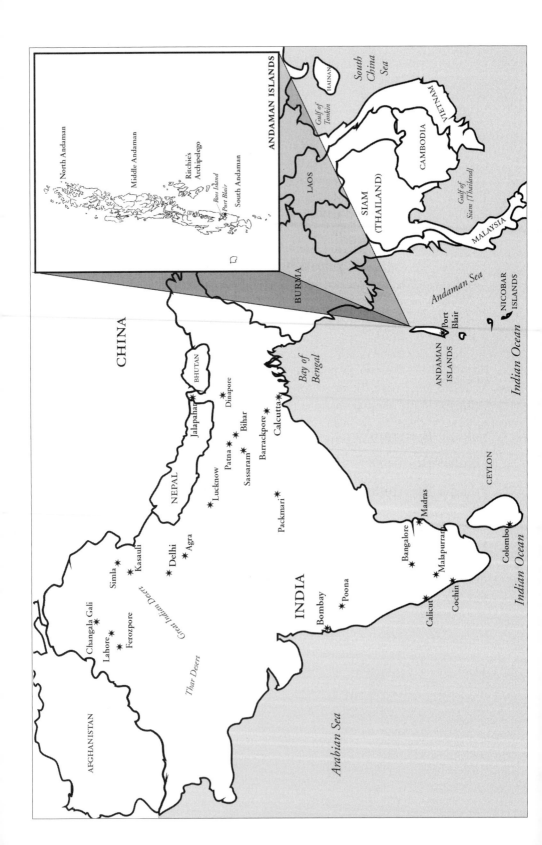

Foreword

In 1954 Lieutenant John Mackie of the Somerset Light Infantry was severely wounded while on anti-terrorist operations with his battalion in Malaya. The military career to which he had dedicated himself and for which he was already showing extraordinary promise was thus abruptly ended.

He left the Army and particularly his Regiment – in which seven of his family have served – with a deep and abiding regret, which passing years and events have not diminished. Unsurprisingly, he has always played an important part in Regimental affairs: his Regimental friends, ranging in age and rank, are legion.

Generously, but wrongly, John suggests, in his Acknowledgement, that I influenced his decision to produce this book. However, it was clear to me from the outset that his mind was set and publication inevitable!

John's love of the Regiment, especially its history, traditions and soldiers, together with his pride in his family's long association with it, were super-charged, when he was given by an Aunt, an old shoe box, tightly packed with letters bundled with red tape, together with documents and photographs, which now form the bulk of this book.

He immediately recognised their value as family and Regimental records and after taking professional advice, now accepts that they would probably be of interest to a much wider readership.

John has presented his material skilfully and through careful research has been able to set it in a wider context, linking documents together to make the book an easy, yet serious and fascinating read, of which he and his family can be justly proud.

Robert Waight
Colonel R.E. Waight O.B.E.

Acknowledgements

M any people have been most generous with their time, encouragement and hard work in helping me to collate these fascinating letters and photographs.

Firstly, I owe a great debt to my old friend and former brother Officer, Colonel R.E. Waight OBE, who encouraged me to get on with the job of collation, which I wanted to do but might not have done. Also to Nigel Steel of the Department of Documents at the Imperial War Museum in London, who gave me the most valuable advice on handling, preservation and transcription of the original letters, without which I would have gone astray.

Extracts from the Official Regimental History of the Somerset Light Infantry (PA) have been reproduced by kind permission of Brigadier A.I.H. Fyfe DL of Light Infantry Office (Somerset) and of his predecessor Lt Col R.G. Woodhouse M.B.E. I am most grateful.

I am, however, especially indebted to Mary Phillips, who has undertaken all the typing and layout of the letters into their present form. Coupled with Mary's huge input, is that of her husband, Mark, who despite ill health has undertaken all the computer and printing work. Without their help, this would never have come about.

Additionally, I am grateful to David Bolland, who with his intimate knowledge of India has helped with interpretation of the Indian names.

Finally, to my wife Jean, who has not only encouraged me, but together with Lt Col Tony Collyns and Elisabeth, has accompanied me to the Andaman Islands, in 1998, to follow in the footsteps of the Mackie brothers and the 2/4th Bn. The Somerset Light Infantry (PA), over eighty years later.

John Mackie
March 1998

Introduction

This is the story of one man's war. An Officer who served throughout that war in one Battalion. The 2/4th Battalion of The Somerset Light Infantry (P.A.). It is told through his delightful, interesting and affectionate letters, written almost every week of the First World War, to his mother and father, interspersed with occasional letters to his younger brothers and sisters who remained at home and at school.

It is also the story of three brothers who joined that Battalion at the outbreak of hostilities, a Territorial Volunteer Battalion, who sailed from Southampton to India in December 1914, who were seen off by their proud but sad parents, who, in their hearts, must have wondered if they would ever see their boys again. All three had distinguished war records, survived the war and went on to lead equally distinguished lives in Government and Military service until after the Second World War. Their medals and decorations are in their final resting place in the Regimental Museum of The Somerset Light Infantry (P.A.) "The Military Museum", The Castle, Taunton, Somerset.

The brothers served together for the first year after which, the eldest, John, moved to become a Political Officer, serving in India and Persia. The youngest, Andrew, transferred to the Indian Army, obtaining a Regular Commission, where he made his career until retiring in the rank of Brigadier in 1947 on the partition of India into India and Pakistan.

The middle one of the three, James (known as Jim) remained in the 2/4th Somersets throughout the war, serving in India, The Andaman Islands, Egypt, Palestine, France, Belgium and finally marched into Germany with the Battalion after the Armistice (November 1918) to be stationed in Bonn.

It is a story of excitement, of new places and experiences, of boredom, responsibility, of relationships and pride. The story of a great County Regiment, close-knit, proud, loyal to each other, cousins, brothers, friends, fellow townsmen and fellow villagers serving together, suffering, fighting, laughing and sadly, sometimes, dying together.

Through the letters of James R. Mackie we have an insight to both the pleasures and horrors of war. The brothers always keeping in touch with one another even when Jim is wounded and in hospital in Cairo he is visited by Andrew (now Indian Army) and also serving in Egypt. Receiving occasional truckles of Cheddar Cheese from Father (a cheese factor in Castle Cary, Somerset) and sharing round the Mess or Company. Twenty-first birthdays are remembered and gifts arranged, even birthdays and Christmas are remembered for all the family at home.

All were great men from a close family, Somerset born, bred and educated, though of Scottish descent. James Mackie was however an outstanding man, a wonderful letter writer, who after the war devoted his life to Agriculture in Nigeria, where he finally served as Director of Agriculture until his retirement in 1945.

We are indeed fortunate that the letters were so carefully kept and stored by his mother before being handed on to his wife Sylvia and ultimately to me, his nephew. They are a wonderful, possibly unique record from the perspective of a Junior Officer in the 1914–18 war.

John Mackie
September 1999

W 4355—491   5000   9/14   H W V $\frac{G. 14}{692}$

T. F. 1r.

Any further communication on this subject should be addressed to—
The Secretary,
War Office,
London, S.W.,
and the following number quoted.

WAR OFFICE,

LONDON, S.W.,

23 Sept 1914.

$\frac{9}{\text{——}}$ *Inf*. (T. F. 1.)

58no.

SIR,

    I am commanded by the Army Council to inform you that you will be gazetted as Second Lieutenant in the

4th Bn. Somerset Light Infantry Regiment, in the

London Gazette of *22 SEP.*

    You will receive instructions from the Officer Commanding the above unit as to your joining. You will receive a Railway Warrant, and should join your unit as soon as possible after receipt of those instructions.

    Please acknowledge receipt.

I am,

SIR,

Your obedient Servant,

R W Brade

J. R. Mackie
Castle Cary,
Somerset.

2/4th Battalion

By the end of October 1914 the 2/4th Somerset Light Infantry (Lieut-Col H. F. Clutterbuck) were 1,000 strong, being the first second-line Territorial Battalion in the West to reach strength. It was at that period located at Prior Park, where everything possible had been done to make all ranks comfortable.

On 12th December the second-line Wessex Division sailed for India, the 2/4th Somersets leaving Bath in the early hours of a foggy morning – 800 strong. They went out to India with the 2/4th Wilts aboard HMT *Saturnia*, and, on arrival at Bombay early in January, proceeded at once to Bangalore. From the latter station two detachments of the 2/4th were sent off, one to relieve a party of of the 1/4th at Malapuram and the other on a similar errand to Calicut. At Malapuram the Somerset men were twice called upon to send out a mobile column to quell risings by Moplahs, though the latter were actually taken by native police.

In August 1915 the 2/4th were suddenly mobilised and moved to Madras, where all sorts of rumours were afloat. Finally, the Battalion sailed for the Andaman Islands upon which a German raid was expected.

After several months spent in the Islands amidst somewhat novel surroundings, the Battalion, early in January 1916, embarked and sailed for Calcutta, proceeding to Dinapore where detachments were sent off to Barrackpore and Dum Dum.

Everard Wyrall
The Somerset Light Infantry 1914–19

LETTERS FROM THE 2/4TH BN. SOMERSET LIGHT INFANTRY (P.A.) 1914–19

VOLUME I: 1914–15

December 1914

The three Mackie brothers with their younger brother pictured prior to their departure to India on the SS Saturnia

Left to right: John; Andrew; James (Jim). *Front*: Malcolm (Duff)

Prior Park,
Bath.

1st Dec. 1914

My dear Pud,

I heard the Colonel saying this morning that he wanted one more subaltern so I at once approached him and said that I had a younger brother who would like to join. He jumped at the idea at once and said that he should be delighted to have a brother of mine in the Regiment. I told him that you were not very old & had no experience, but he said that if Father & Mother were willing & Doctor passed you he would take you.

We are going to India in about a fortnight so that you have not much time to spare and we shall have to move quickly.

I asked you to send your birth certificate & medical certificate to-night because the Colonel is sending to the War Office to-morrow & if your certificates are sent up you will be gazzetted more quickly. If however you were unable to get them don't worry but just get them as soon as you possibly can.

As the Colonel has definitely decided to take you, you need not wait till you are gazzetted before you get your uniform but can begin at once.

Come up to Bath the first day you possibly can, to-morrow (i e Wednesday) if you like, the sooner the better (don't come Thursday as shops will be shut) & I will help you get your uniform. All you have to do is to either phone or send me a wire before 10 o'clock in the morning & I will try & get off to meet you.

You will have £57–10–0 given you to get your kit so you will be quite well off. You see you will have the usual £30 like I had & then there is £20 which we get to fit ourselves up for India. Besides that you will get £7–10 to get a camp kit, but before you get that you will have to show your receipt.

You will be better off than I was because I will help you so that you will only get what you really want. Quite possibly if I am down in Bath I shall order your camp kit as soon as possible as it may take some little time before it is ready.

Uncle Will wired to Father & asked him if you could go & he said yes so that you will be able to get going at once. I hope Mother won't mind losing her And Pud for a little while, but it is an awfully good chance for us to see a bit of the world.

I am to have five days leave before I go & can have it either this Wednesday or next but I have decided to have it next week because I hope Father will be home then & John may aslo also be home.

I don't expect we shall be home for Christmas as we ought to be tossing on the ~~By~~ Bay of Biscay by then probably handing over the side feeding the fishes.

Well I can't stop to write any more now as no doubt I shall see you before long

your loving brother Jim

Prior Park,
Bath.

Dec. 10th 1914

Dear Mother

It did not take us long to get at it after we arrived to-day for there is heaps of work to be done. We are sending you a pair of gloves to wish you a very happy Xmas. As you know we were absolutely stumped as to what to get you so we got these gloves as a last resort. They are not going to keep us waiting about long for we are to be inspected by the General at 4 P M to-morrow (Friday) and then we leave Bath for Southampton at 3–45 A M ie Saturday morning, so that we shall not get much sleep to-morrow night I don't know when we shall sail but I expect we shall go straight on to the ship. Untill we sail ~~write to~~ after to-night write to

C/o Embarkation Officer
Southampton.

After we sail please write to C/o GPO
Bombay.

Please note that our Regt. is now 4th (*1st Reserve*) Bttn P.A.S.L.I.

Well Mother I am afraid it was rather an ordeal for you to part with all three of us this morning but cheer up for it wont be long before we are back again and you may depend upon it that we shall do our best to bring honour & respect to you & Father so that you will you will always be as proud of us as when we said good-bye this morning. Whatever you do have a very happy Xmas as it would vex us very much if we felt that your Xmas was spoilt because we have gone away.

We were able to get some very nice white shirts this morning at 2/11 each & I think we are have now almost completed our outfit.

I do hope Father will keep well & that you will take care of yourself this Winter.

> With very much love to all
> your affectionate son
> Jim

SS *Saturnia*
Bay of Biscay

Dear Mother & Father

By the time you have read letters from us all you will probably know more about our voyage than we do. There is one thing I can tell you & that is that the Sea Gulls & fish in the Bay are getting fat for I should think that they have had more food lately than they can eat. Now let me see, we left home on a Thursday morning & I believe that I wrote & told you all about what we did before I sailed. On Friday we had a very busy day getting all the packing done, and at 5'o'clock the General arrived to inspect us: but as it was pitch dark he contended himself by making a speech. After this I raced off down into Bath to get one or two small things which I had forgotten & returned just in time for dinner. This dinner was a very important meal because it was the last meal we had till lunch on board the following day. About 10 o'clock our uniforms arrived from Crooks & also our presents from Mr Pither.

John Andrew Royal & I managed to get a couple of hours sleep on the floor but at 2 o'clock A.M. we had a cup of tea & then went out to fall the men in. The whole Battalion marched out of Prior Park at about 3–15 AM headed by the band which played our own Regimental march. In spite of the earliness of the hour there was a good crowd of people to give us a send off at the station. We left by two trains one the first at five & the other at six. Most of the band are staying at home so as each train moved off they stood on the platform & played "Auld lang syne" It had a most remarkable effect. Imagine a train containing 400 men all crowding to the windows slowly steaming out with the strains of "Auld Lang Syne" gradually dying away in the distance mingled with the cheers of the people. On arriving at Southampton we proceeded straight to the ship & not since the day I arrived in London after travelling from Scotland without food have I been so much in want of food as I was when we had lunch on board.

Our boat is the "Saturnia" a twin screw steamer belonging to the Donaldson Line of Glasgow; most of the crew are Glasgow men. She is a

Post Card from Andrew to Mother and Father

fairly large boat & as we afterwards were glad to admit ~~uncommonly steady~~ uncommonly steady.

During Friday afternoon before we left I was delighted to see Drummond come to see me. He was very sick because at the last moment he had been left behind with the Home Battallion, but I was ever so pleased to see him. We left Southampton just as we were having dinner & some wag very tritely

S.S. SATVRNIA

Hands Across the Sea

Good Lucke

remarked that we ought to have a good meal for it might be our last for a few days: Some people found that the spoke very truly.

I have just read John's & Andrew's accounts & I find that both have given a graphic description of the journey down the Solent I did not see much of it for I was very tired and went to bed about nine & did not wake up till Sunday morning at breakfast time. I might mention that we are very crowded as besides the 4th Somersets there are the Wilts. & also a battery of Devon RFA & some Wessex Engineers. The men sleep in hammocks which I believe are quite comfortable but their quarters get very stuffy. ~~It is an awful shame that the Government War Office do all they can to get men to go & then treat them like so many cattle~~. I must say that the officers are awfully good to the men & have given up the whole of the promenade deck to them.

I had not been in to breakfast many minutes on Sunday morning before I had to leave to be followed quickly by John Andrew & several others. I was not sick, but only felt a ~~litt~~ bit queer. In about half an hour I was quite fit again & have not felt a bit sick since, in fact I am beginning to think I am quite a good sailor. After about an hour I plucked up courage to visit my men & the sight I saw was enough to turn anyone up. The poor fellows ~~would~~ were lying about on the floors & tables absolutely helpless. They were sick all over the place & the stench was terrible. I did what I could for them & did my best to cheer them up & I think they were very grateful for it. I can tell you that many times since this voyage commenced I have felt that I am ever so lucky to be an officer & not a private. We spent the rest of the day slacking about in our bunks & on the whole the sea was fairly smooth. I went down to the men again at night & saw them in bed & then we all three went to bed ourselves.

On Monday when we woke it was a beautiful morning and the men were looking much more cheerful on the whole although there was still plenty of sickness about.

John spent some time with his men & it about finished him for after lunch he was sick & he again repeated the performance later in the ~~after~~ evening. As a matter of fact the wind freshened up & the fine morning turned a veritable hurricane in the afternoon. The wind blew great guns & the waves got up to a tremendous size. Poor old Pud lay in his bunk & wished himself back in the saw mills but he was not sick till Tuesday morning when he had a good clear out. The storm continued all night & I stayed out on the top deck till quite late in the night for it was a magnificent sight to see the ~~hugh~~ huge waves smashing themselves against the vessel which pitched & tossed & rolled from side to side. Tuesday morning was still very rough but the rain had stopped & the wind was not quite so wild. The whole day was fine but the wind kept blowing so that the sea was rough. When we entered the Bay on Sunday everyone was saying how kind the Bay was but when we reached Cape Finnesterre on Tuesday night most people were glad to be out of it. The men were much better on Tuesday & we had a parade in the morning just to get them up on deck while it was well cleaned up below. They are really awfully cheerful & ~~when I~~ are greatly to be admired for people like Whitely ~~has~~ must find it very hard. Poor old Royal has had an awful time. I am writing on Tuesday night & so far he has not had a single full meal since the dinner we had the night we left Southampton. As ~~pud~~ Pud puts it he is as green as a cabbage.

Pud was very sick in the morning but was quite himself afterwards. John was not very fit all the morning but after tea he seemed quite recovered. As for me I am as fit as a fiddle & as hungry as a hunter. I left Southampton with a very bad cold which is considerably better now. I don't think there will be much more sickness now for we have experienced the Bay of Biscay at its worst & most of us are used to the motion by now.

(As I write at 6 PM. Tuesday) the light on Cape Finnesterre has just become visible).

There is not much to do on board because we are so crowded that there is very little room for anything. I bought a camera before we left Bath & I hope to be able to illustrate our voyage with a few photographs later on. It is a film camera so I shall have to take a dozen before they can be developed so that you will not get any for a bit. I am continuing this letter on Thursday afternoon sitting out on the deck with the sun blazing down just as if it were the middle of Summer. The only thing which reminds us that we are only a week from Christmas is a rather cold wind blowing off the land which is now visible.

When I stopped writing on Tuesday night we were just off Cape Finnesterre but we gave it a wide berth. On Wednesday we had a beautiful day and the sea went down till it was quite smooth. Everyone is beginning to feel the want of exercise and now that the first excitement is over it is getting a little monotonous. All the sick people appeared on ~~Tuesday~~ Wednesday morning & even Royal appeared on deck. I was orderly officer Thursday so I had to be up at six to turn the men out. It was quite dark at that hour but about 6–45 I went on deck & saw a beautiful sight. The sun was just beginning to rise colouring the sky & clouds a beautiful pink while away in the distance I could just make out Cape St Vincent. This is the first land we have seen since the Lizzard disappeared below the horizon.

I was very busy all the morning and had to accompany the Captain when he inspected the ship, after which I gave my men some physical drill for half an hour. Since we rounded St Vincent this morning we have been quite close to the shore and of course the day has been much more interesting as there has been something to see. There are quite a lot of ships about today & they cause quite a lot of excitement.

As I have said before the weather to-day is delightful just like a Spring day. The Mail boat has unexpectedly come alongside & we have to finish off at once.

Wishing you all a very happy Xmas
your affectionate son
Jim

On Board SS *Saturnia*

Dear Mother & Father

My last letter was despatched in great haste just off Gibraltar & I don't know if you will get it, at anyrate I hope so. I left off on Thursday afternoon I believe & will continue from there. We were in sight of land in beautiful weather expecting to reach Gibraltar before long. I woke up on Friday morning & looked out of my porthole & was surprised to find that the ship was stationary. On both sides land was so near that we could see the nature objects on the shore quite clearly, so that I knew we were in Straights of Gibraltar. Just a little way from us there was a little sailing ship and as I looked at her I saw the he masts waving about in an alarming fashion: then with a crash two of them snapped off & fell into the sea. Please don't think I had been drinking on Thursday night for that is not the case, I actually saw the masts break off. Next a boat was lowered from our ship & the men began to row towards the little vessel. At this stage I had my bath, for I have my cold bath every morning just about the same time as Father goes into his the only difference being that mine consists of salt water, and after dressing went on to the deck.

It was a glorious morning, the sun was just rising and the sea beautifully calm. In the distance on the left was the town of Tangiers & on the right Cape Tarifa while in the distance we could see Gibraltar. At first I could not make out what had happened for finding Africa on our left showed that we were facing the wrong direction. On inquiry I found that the little sailing vessel had run into us & that of course was the reason I saw her masts go overboard.

It was intended that our convoy should disperse at Gibraltar & that each troopship should go on at her own speed so that we were not going to stop at Gibraltar. This was a disappointment to both men & officers as we all wanted to send home letters just to wish you many a happy returns Xmas but owing to this slight accident we had to stop in the Straight Straits about three or four hours. During the parade about 10–30 in the morning a little gunboat came alongside to see what was the matter & she offered to take our letters. Thinking we should not stop I had none ready but I managed to seal up what I had written to you & sent if off & as I said I hope you will get it.

After a bit we got going again & passed Gibraltar about 12 o'clock so that we had a magnificent view of it. It is a sheer rock rising out of the sea & absolutely impregnable as the sides are like the roof of a house. In the distance we could see the mountains of Spain on our left & on our right those of Africa. The Spanish mountains, the Sierra Nevada Mountains were capped with snow & looked awfully pretty. Those on the African side were the Atlas Mountains.

The weather is grand here in the ~~Med~~ Mediterranean & the sunsets are marvellous: I can't imagine that we are so near Christmas as it is just like Spring.

Quite an interesting occupation is that of watching the porpoises which sport about in the water around the bows of the ship. The men & officers have quite recovered from sickness now, & it is a very difficult matter to satisfy their appetites. On Saturday, (i.e the day on which I write) when we got up Spain was quite out of sight & Africa was just visible, but during the morning we came in fairly close & could see the mountainous nature of the country. The mountains come right down to the sea & the shore is very wild & rocky. ~~We are managed~~ John & Andrew are very fit now & both are getting on very well: I think Pud will make quite a good soldier after a bit.

I am going to stop now & shall continue again in a day or two, as I am going to get ready for dinner.

Sunday was beautifully fine & the hottest day we have had, but towards evening it became dull & looked as if we were in for a storm which however passed off.

At 9 o'clock we Somersets had Divine Service which in the absence of a parson was conducted by the Colonel. He followed it up with a lecture to the men on India. The other Regiments also had services during the morning. During the afternoon we had Harry Marsh up to our cabin just to hear how he was getting. I think he was awfully pleased to come: he says he & the other Cary fellows are enjoying the voyage very much indeed.

It is now Monday morning (21st) & we hope to reach Malta by to-night. We are not going to stop but there is just a chance that we may be able to send letters if a boat comes out to meet us. I am therefore going to seal this one up, then if there is a rush to get letters off like we had at Gibraltar I shall not have to trouble about it.

We expect to spend Xmas day at Port Said and they tell us that there are plenty of Turkeys on board as we hope to spend it in the usual way.

It is not much good to wish you a happy Xmas with this letter for by the time it reaches you Xmas will be a thing of the past, but I sincerely hope that you will all have a jolly good time throughout the whole Christmas season. I also wish you all a very happy New Year. I hope Father will make a good start & quite regain his health & I hope the Mother will take care of herself & enjoy the best of health. Give my love to all the others I hope to ~~be a~~ write to all of them in turn after a bit.

The address to which I want those pictures sent is as follows.

R. A. Shell Esq.
Tillingham
Southminster
Essex

I shall not do any more writing to-day for we are going to be innoculated presently

your affectionate son
Jim

SS *Saturnia*

Christmas Eve

Dear Mother & Father

We did not stop at Malta so you will get my last letter with this one, so if you open this one first read the other one before this ~~one~~.

On Tuesday evening we passed Malta in the distance but as I have said did not stop there so we had no chance to post letters. The weather has been getting warmer all this week and to-day Christmas eve we are fairly sweltering under a cloudless sky. On Weds. & Thursday a very hot wind blew ~~with~~ very strongly & the sea got quite rough. I believe it is called the Sirrocco wind and it comes over the desert of Africa, hence it is very hot & dry.

We passed North of Malta and since then have not seen land but we hope to reach Port Said some time to-night so that when all of you at home are being awakened by the band we shall probably entering Port Said. It seems very likely that the officers will be allowed to go ashore therefore in all probability we shall spend Christmas day on land although we shall have to come on board to eat our Christmas dinner. I saw the turkeys being drawn up from the hold & they looked awfully nice. After all if it were not for the heat we might say with the old Song that "it's just like being at home".

All three of us were ~~innoc~~ innoculated against Typhoid last Wednesday: except for a slight stiffness on Thursday & a sleepy feeling we should not have known that we had been done. We shall have to have another dose in about ten days time. Today just before lunch we submitted our arms to the Dr for vaccination which will be fare more painful but not less necessary. I am very glad to be able to tell you that Weeks has been made a Sergt. I think he will get on very well, at any rate he will be very pleased.

I am writing this in diary form because one day has been as like another but in my las next letter I will try & give you an account of Port Said. We have been advised to lock up everything we posess as the natives are very expert thieves. The Colonel is going to spend about £50 to-morrow in order to get the men a supply of turkish delight, oranges & cigarettes: can you wonder that he is so popular.

I am enclosing a copy of our newspaper as I thought it would interest you. Untill two days ago the news came from London but now we only get a little from there most of it coming from Eiffel Tower. It is just enough to keep us in touch with things.

Andrew has just come up to me very pleased with himself for owing to his company officer being indisposed he has had to pay the company himself.

I can think of no more news now and I want to write one or two other letters. John is not writing to-day as he has two letters for you Park Cottage in this mail. I hope Bunna & Angus had a good time on Prize day & took some prizes.

We shall think of you all to-night when you the smaller ones are hanging up their stockings and while we should like to be with you we feel awfully pleased that we are doing our little bit so that the rest of you may spend a very happy Christmas at home. Personally from this point of view I feel more contented than I have since war broke out.

I sincerely hope that both Father & Mother will make a good start in the New Year & have good health throughout the whole of it.

With best wishes for a very very happy & prosperous New Year I remain

your affectionate son
Jim

P.S.

On board TSS *Saturnia*

Boxing Day 1914

Dear Mother & Father

While most of the children were hanging up their stockings on Christmas eve we were nearing port Said. When we got near the port we could see the lights all along the front & also the light from the lighthouse but it

Above: SS *Saturnia* coaling at Port Said, Boxing Day 1914

Right: Royal, Andrew, Bartlett, John

Left: A Port Said Tramcar

Below: The bungalow ("quite a good picture"), Bangalore

was too dark to see anything more. The anchor was dropped outside the breakwater about 10 PM.

On Christmas morning when we awoke we were still in the same position where we stayed till ꞵ 9–30. We had plenty to interest us for 10 huge liners came out of the canal and anchored in a line quite close to us the nearest being the Royal George, formerly of Bristol, but now painted steel grey she is being used to bring troops back to the front. All those 10 liners contained troops on their way from the front. The pilot came on board about 9–30 and we entered the Port keeping quite close to the breakwater till we anchored about 100 yards from the side. The statue of De Lessepps stands on the breakwater: he is de pointing to the Canal with his right hand.

Hundreds of boats came alongside with oranges, turkish delight, etc making a very animated scene with the bright coloured clothes so typical of the East.

The officers were allowed to go ashore about 12 o'clock so we made for the Eastern Telegraph office & sent you a cable. This office is just opposite the place where we are anchored. We felt quite at home as we steamed in for the first things we were able to read were Dewar's Whiskey, Pear's Soap, & Remmington Typewriters.

My first impression of Port Said was that it was unfinished. With the exception of one street which is quite a good one, the houses seem unfinished or very delapidated. The streets of the town itself are quite wide & the shops are excellent & as everyone can speak almost any language & will accept any kind of money we had no difficulty in getting on. We visited the original Arab village which is very squallid & smells most unpleasantly. It is not safe to be anywhere except in the main streets after dark unless you are well armed.

In the evening those of us who were not on duty had a Christmas dinner at the Eastern Exchange Hotel & they did us splendidly. We had among other things the usual turkey, plump pudding & mince pies. This morning I went on shore & drove right out of the town to the desert past the cemetery which seems to mark the outside of the town.

John & Andrew are on shore now The coaling is a marvellous sight for it is done by a continuous string of men who carry the coal in baskets on their shoulders up the from the barges up the a single plank to the entrance to the hold. There they empty the baskets & come back down another plank. The process is absolutely continuous the whole day & I am amazed at the endurance of the men.

Everything is absolutely black with coal dust; it will be no end of a job to clean the ship again. I have taken some photographs some of which are quite good. I had some films developed last night & I hope to have some printed by the time I write next Some of us have to be always on board so I came in at 3 o'clock and relieved John & Andrew.

I expect we shall leave here to-morrow morning & now that we have a good look at the place we shall be quite ready to move especially as the Suez Canal will be exceedingly interesting at this time.

I must close now with very much love to all

> your affectionate Son
> Jim

P. S We were able to get a little present for Janet: I hope she will get it alright.

Give my best love to little Duff.

SS *Saturnia*

31st Dec. 1914

Dear Mother & Father

I am starting this letter on the last day of the "Old Year": it will be finished by the time we reach Bombay & posted there.

Our coaling at Port Said was finished rather sooner than was expected and those who were on land had to be recalled. I think however that the boat actually left Port Said during the small hours of Sunday Morning. I must say that although our Christmas day was spent in a rather strange way it was full of interest to us all.

When we woke on Sunday Morning we were in the Suez Canal & if any of us had any fear of the Turks these fears were soon dispelled for one of the first things we saw was a large camp of the Camel Corps. The day we spent in the Canal was about the most interesting of the whole voyage, for there was something fresh to see the whole time. The country on the Egyptian side was much more attractive o than that on the Arabian side. On the former there were quite a lot of palm & other trees as well as rushes & scrub but the latter was for the most part absolutely barren & I realized for the first exactly what a desert is like: miles & miles of bare sand with not a thing to be seen while away in the distance you could make out a ridge of low hills. On the Egyptian side there were frequent stations which were very pretty for they were always situated in the midst of a clump of trees The Canal is jolly well guarded on both sides mostly by Indian troops & every time we passed one of their camps their English officers wished us good luck & a "Happy New Year"

We reached Ismailia about 10 o'clock & there in the little lake was a small French gunboat. It so happened that the Wilts' band had assembled to play some music so as ~~they~~ we passed the gunboat they played "La Marseillaise" The Frenchmen all stood at attention while the music was playing & took their hats off but as soon as it stopped every hat went into the air & they gave us a rousing cheer.

It was thought that we should get to Suez about four but we had to tie up to the bank & allow some homeward bound ships to pass so that we dropped anchor at Suez about seven being therefore unable to see anything of the town except the lights.

The stay at Suez was long enough to drop the pilot & then we moved out again into the Gulf of Suez.

For the next two or three days we were going down the Red Sea & about all that any of us can remember is that it was so frightfully hot: and yet those who have been here before say that it was remarkably cool for a strong head wind was blowing all the time. The fact is that it was cool enough on deck but our cabins, in fact anywhere below deck, were ~~frightfully~~ were absolutely unbearable. It was impossible to sleep at night for the heat was so great.

It is now the 2nd Jan. and we are in the Indian Ocean. Thank goodness it is much cooler for there is a beautifully cool wind blowing from over the ocean. We passed Perim Island on Thursday and about tea time on New Year's Day we were able to see Aden in the distance but did not stop. The last stage of the voyage has now started and we shall probably land a week to-day.

Andrew was not very well for

The Maharaja's elephants

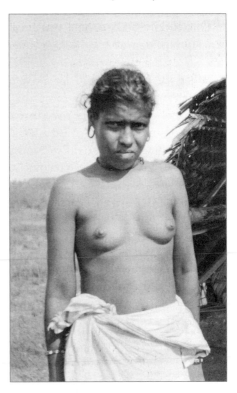

Typical native woman
("note how they mutilate their ears")

two days: his second innoculation gave him rather a rough time but he is quite himself. Both he and I have had bad arms from the vaccination. Mine reached its worst yesterday and I shall be very glad to get it well for it was easily the worst arm on the ship. When I went to bed last night it was swollen from my shoulder to my wrist but to-day it is certainly much better.

It is now Weds Jan 5th and I must finish this letter to-night for we reach Bombay to-morrow afternoon and we shall hardly have time for meals to-morrow.

Since I last left off we have been going steadily on across the Indian Ocean & have had beautiful weather for there has been a splendid breeze going the whole time.

My arm has reached its worst & is now getting better & we are all three very fit indeed as are all the other Cary men. Although things are very much the same every day we get a certain amount of diversion at times. For instance all the subalterns turn out at 7 o'clock in the morning to have sword drill on the deck under the Adjutant. We are all dressed in pyjamas over which is the sword belt so you can just imagine what a fine colour scheme there is – stripes of blue green, red & yellow in fact almost every colour of the rainbow.

I have just had a good present for Captain Foxcroft has just given me £5. He says that as I have been doing his work I am entitled to some of his pay & that I am to regard it as extra pay & not as a present.

When we land we shall have a 3 days train journey but we only travel by night going into resting camps by day. I had rather a surprise the other day when I opened one of my boxes for I found that the heat was making my truckle run a bit so I at once took it out & gave it to the chief Steward who is keeping it for me till we land in a cool room. The food on the boat has been so good that we have not wanted it during the voyage.

Well I shall soon have to stop to-night for I have to get my things packed up. I hope you are all keeping well at home & having a good time. We shall look forward to having some letters from you all when we land or soon afterwards.

Some of my first photographs came out quite well & I have printed out a few but when we are settled down in India I will send you home some.

I hope Father left his bad headaches behind with 1914 & I also hope that Mother is keeping strong this Winter.

> With much love to all
>> your affectionate son
>>> Jim

MAP II. SKETCH MAP OF BANGALORE c. 1895

Source: *Bangalore, Civil & Military Station & City* 1894, prepared under instruction from the Bangalore Municipality by Mr H. Todd reproduced the *Survey of India*, Calcutta; *Bangalore*, published by John Bartholomew & Co., Edinburgh

Devon Cottage
Ulson Road
Bangalore

Jan 13th 1914

Dear Mother & Father.

At last we are at Bangalore and although we have only been here two days we are already getting settled down. Since we landed at Bombay everything has been fresh and every day has brought new experiences.

The Saturnia arrived in Bombay harbour on Thursday night (Jan 7th) and anchored outside the docks. In the morning just after breakfast we went into the docks & were moored to the side. Bombay has tremendous docks & there were any amount of ships there so that it was awfully interesting to us watching from the ~~docks~~ deck.

On arrival one of our first duties was to post guards & sentries at all the entrances & then the work of unloading commenced. I was detailed to do duty all night so was allowed on shore in the afternoon but John & Andrew did not go on till the evening.

When we arrived we found that the reason we were so crowded was because one of the other ships only had about 500 on board so that we had far more than we really ought to have had.

The Wilts went off to Poona at 11 o'clock on Friday night and we left Bombay at 11 o'clock Saturday morning, the Artillery staying on board till Sunday. I was able to have a good look at Bombay while I was on shore & I must say that it is a really fine city. Of course everything was strange, but the English influence is very marked. The first thing which everyone notices is the bullock waggons. These are very rough carts without springs & drawn by two bullocks & they are absolutely one of the commonest sights in India. Hundreds of them were going down to the docks with bales of cotton.

The railway station is architecturally one of the finest in the world – it is so fine that at first I thought it was a cathedral. Just opposite it is the Town Hall which is also very fine. There is one long street which is very ~~fine~~ nice & nearly all the big firms of England have shops or agencies there. The residential part is up on a hill outside the City but I had no time to go up to it.

I had a pretty stiff time on the Friday night for as I said I was on duty and as the guards were very important owing to the fact that we had a large quantity of ammunition on the quay I had to keep on visiting all the sentries some of which were over a mile from the ship.

After a tremendous rush we got away punctually at 11 o'clock and the first thing I did was to go to sleep for some hours.

We entrained on ~~Friday~~ Saturday morning & reached Bangalore on the following Monday night so that we had three days & two nights in the train. I enjoyed the train journey ~~intensely~~ immensely for there was something fresh to see the whole time.

By the time it was dark ~~Mon~~ Saturday night we had reached the top of the Ghats & had supper a Poona about 10–30. The journey up the Ghats was splendid & the scenery was grand. The gradient was far steeper than anything in England; often the line ran along the side of the a precipice which dropped sheer to an enormous depth. We had to have two engines and we were surprised to find that most of the engines on the "Great Indian Peninsular" Railway are made at the works of the N. British Ry. at Glasgow.

I have no time to describe the rest of the journey fully as it is very late now. At a place called Gunstakel we changed to another railway which had a different guage so that we had to transfer all our baggage etc to another train. The guage was only 1 metre & the railway was quite a minature affair. Throughout the whole journey we stopped at appointed stations & had meals in the refreshment rooms and they did us very well indeed. On the small railway we had to go in two trains: I was in the first but John & Andrew came in the second.

My train arrived at Bangalore about 7–30 & we were met by the General & an officer of the Lancashire regiment who is stationed here. The Wesleyan minister also met us & gave us a welcolme He is a splendid fellow & is untiring in his efforts to help us to settle down.

I was not able to get in the same bungalow as John & Andrew but am quite close to them. The bungalows are absolute little palaces, beautifully furnished & fitted out.

We have all got our servants now & I can tell you that you will find we have been spoilt when we get home for the servants do absolutely everything for us.

When you dress for dinner you sit down in a chair & a servant ~~se~~ takes off your boots & stockings & pulls off your trousers while another lays out your clothes. Then much against my will they proceed to dress you. I ~~don't~~ would much sooner do things myself & I often send them off to do a job outside & then dress myself as quickly as possible.

We were delighted to find a letter from Mother awaiting us when we reached Bangalore & were awfully pleased to hear that Father was pretty well when it was sent off.

I am glad the photographs have turned out well & am quite looking forward to seeing them. They will be splendid to put up in our bungalows.

There seems to be a good deal of illness about Cary – poor old Mack I hope he is better again now. Have you both got fresh glasses as a result of your ~~visit~~ journey to Bristol – I hope you will both be better as a result of the visit. Please thank Duff for the kisses he sent: I am awfully glad that the soldiers give him some amusement.

Since we have been at Bangalore I have been awfully busy & did not get out to look about till this afternoon. I only had time to visit the English shops which are nearly all in one long street. The native part is ~~perhaps~~ the largest portion of the ~~comercial~~ commercial city and I hope to go there ~~this~~ to-morrow afternoon.

The Barracks are splendid. Each company has a separate bungalow: the sergeants each have a separate room & the men have very nice beds with sheets & blankets.

Just below ~~where~~ my bungalow there is a splendid building belonging to the Y.M.C.A. They provide the men with everything there free of cost. There are two billiard tables, magasines & papers of every kind, tennis courts & a football ground besides which they give the men a very good supper ~~at~~ for about 4^d. The money puzzled us a good deal at first, & even now we find it very difficult to think in rupees & annas. All three of us have started a banking account with Cox & it is very convenient to write out a cheque for everything.

The other 4th Bttn were partly at Madras & partly at Wellington but they have just been moved up North to start training as they have done practically nothing so far as that they are no better than we are so far.

We are all very well indeed except that my vaccination places do not heal up but the doctor dresses them every day & they should begin to form scabs before long.

I hope you are all well at Park Cottage & keeping clear of colds etc. Tell Duff that we sleep under a net just like he used to do in his crib but in our case it is to keep out the mosquitos & not to keep us in bed.

We are all looking forward to the next mail to hear what sort of a Christmas you had.

I really must stop now & go to bed.

With very much love to you all
your affectionate son
Jim

2nd/4th Bttn Somt. L.I.
2nd Wessex divn.
C/o GPO
London

Jan 20th 1914

Dear Mother & Father.

My stay in Bangalore was very short for we arrived there on a Tuesday & I left again on the following Sunday. I am now at a place called Malappurum which is 17 miles from the nearest railway station and which contains only two other white people besides ourselves.

I was very sorry to leave Bangalore because it is an awfully nice place but in spite of the fact that it is very lonely here I think we shall have a good time. A few days after we arrived we were told that we should have to send a garrison to this place & to Calicut; for although they are usually supplied from Madras there being no troops at the latter place the new garrison had to come from Bangalore. One Company was chosen to go consisting of 200 men & four officers. 50 men with two officers were sent to Calicut & three of us with the other ~~100~~ 150 men came on here.

I had to be transferred from my old Company to come here because only the most experienced officers were sent. We relieved a detachment of the 1st 4th Sommts. under Capt Baily and ~~that~~ for one night we were ~~altog~~ all together here.

Farwell is the Captain & Royal the other Subaltern which is very fortunate as he & I get on splendidly.

We left Bangalore on Sunday at 12 o'clock mid-day & reached Tirun (ie the Station for Malappuram) at 4-30 AM. Tuesday morning where we said goodbye to the party for Calicut. In spite of the early hour of our arrival we were met by the Brigade Major & the doctor who is stationed here. He had provided a makeshift breakfast consisting of hard boiled eggs bread butter & tea & the men had bread & jam & tea.

The baggage had to be sorted & loaded in bullock waggons & then we started at 7 AM. to march 17 miles which we did in six hours. Allowing 1½ hours for resting the actual time for marching was 4½ hours or nearly 4 miles per hour which was jolly good considering that we have done very little training since coming off the ship.

At half way we halted for an hour & I had some tea & bread just to keep us going & then marched on. Only 3 men dropped out but when we finished the Brigade Major was carrying two rifles & Royal & I one each. Tirun station is only half mile from the sea but to get to Malappurum the road goes inland right through the jungle gradually going up the whole time. We are right in the middle of the jungle in fact big game shooting can be had quite close here but most surprisingly it is very healthy the barracks being right at the top of a hill.

The natives are quite different to the ordinary Indian being very light in colour & very tall & strong. They are called Moplars and they will not mix with the other Indians keeping themselves very pure. As a matter of fact there is a good deal of Arab blood in their veins & they are all Moham-medans. Just at present they are very unrestful & trouble is feared. They do not fight the Europeans for whom they bear no ill will but they absolutely hate the Hindus & trouble always starts by a quarrel between the Moplars & Hindus. The duty of the garrison is to keep peace & ~~at the present time~~ & it is only called out to assist the police.

Malappuram is one of the prettiest spots in India. Being so near the coast & on the ~~winds~~ windward side of the mountains there is a very heavy rainfall which all comes during the three months of the monsoon. As much as 156′′ of rain falls here every year you so you can imagine that once the rain starts there is not much done.

We can get tennis & golf & the men play football besides plenty of shooting for us so that if we are able to provide a certain amount of sport, but I fear we shall get rather tired of each other if we are here 3 or 4 months. The heat is terible & we can do nothing but sleep after 10 each day till 4 in the afternoon when we play tennis.

Enclosed are some more photographs which we have taken & some of which are quite good, in fact I am very pleased with my camera.

I can't go on much longer to-night but will write again next week.

To-morrow ~~ws~~ is Janet's birthday & I felt just like sending her a card almost forgetting that she would not receive it for 3 weeks or more.

I suppose they are all back at school again now working hard.

I hope you are all well & that Father is keeping fit.

With very much love to you all

      I remain
          your affectionate son
            Jim

2nd/4th Battn Somt. L.I.
Malappurum
South Malabar

Jan 27th 1914

Dear Mother & Father

I have just finished dinner and gone to my bungalow to write a few letters before going to bed.

My letters from the last home mail which the boys sent on from Bangalore reached me to-night and I received so the photographs. The one of you two is absolutely splendid and little Duff looks first class in the one of we three.

I was delighted to hear that you are had quite a good Xmas time this season & also that Father is keeping fairly well. What sort of a calf did you get? I should think you would get a good price for it as I should think that all cattle were dear owing to the war.

There are plenty of cattle out here of a sort but mostly bullocks which draw the carts & also buffalo. The latter are very fierce in fact they always charge straight at a motor bicycle. I am just beginning to get settled down here now and we are doing some serious work. It is very nice to feel that we are at last more or less settled after so much moving about & this is a delightful spot. Every week either Royal or I has to go to a place called Minijesi seven miles away to get the money to pay the troops from the treasury. Last week we both went together: & after a motor our method of travelling was not very fast for we were stretched out on the bottom of a bullock cart. As this is the only method of going except walking we have to put up with it & after all it is not a bad way if only you are content to sleep & don't mind a considerable amount of jolting.

On Sunday we all went to Church. This was the first time we entered a Church since we left England. The Church belongs to the Barracks and the Officer Commandg the station has to take the service except once a month when the chaplain for the district comes to the rescue.

I am afraid you will find my letters get shorter now for of course we do nearly the same kind of thing every day.

We start parade at 6–30 AM & have breakfast at 8. At 9 we start again and work in the shade of the verandahs till 11 when it is too hot for work of any kind. We usually sleep all the afternoon & then after tea the men play football & we usually have a good game of tennis.

Nothing at all is done on Thursdays because it is a holiday all over India. I believe the reason is that Queen Victoria was made Empress of India on a Thursday. I am glad to say that my arm is now quite well. I took the last dressing off to-day & it is beautifully healed & the scabs gone.

John has gone to Satara to do a course in musketry so Andrew is the only one of us left at Bangalore. He is however quite alright there & has got one or two excellent pals. I get one or more letters each week from him just to make sure that he is getting on alright.

Just at present we have another white man staying here. He is an officer in one of the Indian Regiments who has come down here to recruit the natives of this district. They hope to be able to raise several companies & put them among the other Regiments.

We have just heard of the Naval success in the North Sea. Considering that the fleets were both about equal it was not very dignified on their part to run away Mother would not make a fortune with fowls if she were keeping them out here for eggs are 3 a 1^d everywhere & we eat chicken at nearly every meal.

Well I must close for this week as I have no more to write about.

Once more thank you very much indeed for the photos with which I am delighted. I hope you are all well & hope Father is taking things steady. How is the business going this year – is there much doing & what sort of a year did 1914 prove to be.

> With best love to all
> I remain
> Your affectionate son
> Jim

Please thank Ted for her letter. I will write her one next week if possible.

2nd/4th Bttn Somerset L.I.
Malappuram
South Malabar

Feb. 3rd 1915

My dear Mother & Father

I said last week that my letters would begin to get shorter & the fact is I can hardly think of anything to say this week. We have settled down to the usual routine of barrack life and one day is very like another.

I am rather busy at present for besides my usual work I am trying to learn a little gunnery. We have at this station two little field guns belonging to a mountain battery & an expert has been sent down from Madras to teach us how to use them as I have taken the matter in hand & am doing my best to learn something about them. I have also to ~~keep~~ be responsible for the Company accounts such as pay etc & although the colour sergeant does the actual work I have to check them all & be responsible for mistakes.

I play tennis nearly every evening & am beginning to get hold of the idea of the game but I am afraid I don't pick it up very quickly. The men play football but the number of accidents are very bad. The pitch is not a turf one like we use at home but just bare sand or rock so that when a man falls down he always skins his knees & often smashes his wrist or puts his knee out.

We had an amusing incident one ~~even~~ night ~~when the~~ with one of the sentries. He saw something coming towards him & challenged. Getting no answer he repeated his challenge twice more & then still getting no reply fired a round of buckshot. The Guard turned out & went forth with lanterns to find the intruder which proved to be a cow.

The Territorials have made a very good impression in India & the authorities are amazed at the rate by which we improve. The natives at once found out the difference between Territorials & Regulars & in the bazaars the men are known as the ~~Gen~~ gentleman soldiers while the officers are all supposed to be the sons of noblemen & the elite of England.

I never came across such artful beggars as natives: they will rook you right & left if you don't keep your eyes open & they are infernal thieves. The worst of it is you never know what they are thinking about & yet after about two days they know your habits & fancies exactly.

As I told you in a previous letter there are two sorts here Hindus & Moplahs. The Hindus are very light coloured & are easily distinguished because they shave the head except for a tuft on the top. The Moplahs are fine fellows, very fierce & well built. They shave their heads all over & the men are not allowed to wear trousers so they wear a sort of skirt.

There is a Hindu temple in the ~~town~~ village quite close to our bungalows & it is an awful nuisance for they go there nearly every night & make a row with their tom-toms.

Besides these two classes of natives there are the Cherumars or sweepers – the lowest of all the natives. They are really the serfs or slaves & are bought or sold with the land on which they live. They are looked down upon by everyone & are very dirty & foul in their habits.

Royal & I make our ~~usual~~ journey to Manjeri every Thursday to fetch the pay for the men in a bullock cart. I shall have to go ~~with~~ by myself to-morrow because Royal is going to the station to meet the Colonel who is coming to see us. He has wanted to come ever since we came here for he was awfully sorry to see us go.

Andrew tells me that he has finished his recruit drills on the ~~sq~~ Barrack square, so I think he must be getting on very well indeed.

Did you ever get the letters we sent from Gibraltar? It was quite a chance whether they ever reached you.

I have had the photographs framed : they look splendid & quite improve the appearance of my bungalow.

I wrote to Chell & thanked him for the photograph : there is no need for you to send it on for I shall see it when I come home.

Poor Foxcroft is having a rotten time in a hospital in Bombay. He left England with water on his knee & it does not get any better. I had an awfully nice letter from him when I was transferred to this company & he thanked me for the work I have done for him & said I had done excellently.

I will close for this week now & hope to get hold of some news for next week

I hope you are all well. How is Father keeping – I hope is is not doing too much work again. I also hope that Mother is taking care of herself this Winter.

With very much love to all

       Your loving son
        Jim ..

Tell Duff he looks quite a man in that photograph with we three.

Malappuram
South Malabar

Feb. 3rd 1915

My dear Ted

Thanks awfully for your last letter – we were jolly pleased to hear from you. I was delighted to hear that you had a good time at Christmas & I have no doubt that in the capacity of eldest of the family you rose to the occasion in fine style.

Your effort in getting the holly was very smart – you must be be getting very hardened & brave to be able to say that you had permission without blushing. There is one thing about living out here & that is you can't blush if you try, for in my case it is impossible for my face to get much redder it is so sunburnt.

I hope Mary & you had a good time at Frome – although I don't suppose there is much doubt about it. Of course you did not treat Ron so badly when he kissed you as you did on one other occasion at Scotland House.

You would think I looked rather funny if you saw me now for I have had my hair cut very short all over so much so that I can't get a parting.

You must do something of the sort out here as it is much cooler with short hair.

We never wear tunics except Sundays for Church, always going about in shirt sleeves. There is a nice little Church here which we attend every Sunday & as the Chaplain only visits us once a month the Captain or senior officer present has to take the service. Needless to say we only have a sermon once a month.

I was awfully surprised to hear about Aunt Janet's engagement – but still one must not be surprised at anything in these days. Do you know if she is still going to live in Japan of if she is coming home?

I have told all the news in my other letter so I will write to you again another week.

I hope you are getting on well at school & doing your best to help mother

> With love to all
> From Jim

2nd/4th Bttn Somt. L.I.
Malappuram
South Malabar

Feb. 10th 1915

Dear Mother & Father

The mail this week has not yet arrived as the boat was more than a day late at Bombay so I have not yet seen your letter for this ~~wek~~ week. The boat usually reaches Bombay on Saturday & then I get my letters here on the following Tuesday or Wednesday night in time for me to read before I write to you. I have to get mine posted Wednesday night for the mail leaves here about five Wednesday morning I was sorry to hear last week that Mary was not well & I hope it was nothing serious. I was very glad to hear that Father & Uncle had a satisfactory year in the business & I hope that in spite of the war 1915 will be a better one still. I don't know if I shall be back to help this year but if not Father must be careful not to work too hard & make himself ill again. How much is the war affecting the cheese trade? I this new move on the part of Germany in waging war on all shipping will tend to send the price up as I imagine it will make Canadian dearer.

We had a visit from the Colonel last week & he was very pleased with the way in which we are carrying on here. He stayed two nights & left us in style in a bullock cart before it was light last Friday morning. I asked him about Andrew & he said that he (Andrew) was getting on very well.

33

The Bangalore people have been woried by two inspections by Generals, ~~but~~ and the advantage of being right away here is that so far at anyrate we have been let alone. The Colonel says that these Generals have found a new toy in the Territorials & they come just to see what we are like & each one decides that we want certain things ~~so that~~ & instructors so each sends them quite independantly of the other. The result is that instructors etc are coming from all over the place.

~~Take~~ I think I said that one of the other white men here was an inspector of the police. He is now camping about twelve miles from here & last week he had the extraordinary good fortune to shoot two tigers in one evening & his native attendant shot a rhino. It is a jolly good fortune for him as besides the skins etc he gets a reward of 75 rupees for each from the Government.

Those ~~photos~~ photos which I sent of the camps on the Suez Canal have a new interest in view of the recent operations along there. ~~Canal.~~ I have not taken many lately but before long I shall have another dozen to be developed.

Enclosed are a few stamps which I thought would interest Bunna & Angus. If they want more I will get hold of some for them.

There is not much other news this week as things are going steadily. I am quite fit & as brown as a berry. I hope you are all well

With much love to all

Your affectne son
Jim

P. S. I should very much like a photo of we three sent to Passmore. If you have one to spare I should like him to have a large one. 3 Queen's Crescent Exeter will find him.

2nd/4th Bttn Somerset L.I.
Malappuram
South Malabar
India

Dear Mother & Father

I have on the table in front of me ~~seven~~ six letters which John sent on to me last week & last night I sent him one from Father which came this week. Thank you both very much for the ones you sent & will you please thank the others for theirs – I was delighted to hear from them all. I am glad our letters & cards from Port Said arrived safely, but I can't think why they were so late. The postman must have wondered what was the matter having so many at once.

I have a bit of news for you this week for I have just received orders to move on again. A telegram arrived yesterday to say that I was to proceed to Calicut to take command of the station. It will be a jolly good experience for me for I shall be all on my own but it is a great responsibility. However I shall do my best & shall try to take Janet's advice & "not be rash"

Since I have been here I have been in charge of a platoon consisting of Radstock miners whom no one has ever been able to manage properly. I was delighted this week to find that they have at last become tractable & they are now drilling as well as if not better than any other men of the company. It was rather stormy at first but they have given in at last.

It is very hot indeed here now – up to 90° in the shade in the day time but I am getting used to it & don't feel the heat now as much as when I came here although it was much cooler then. I was very sorry indeed to hear that Mother has again been suffering from neuritis. She must be very careful & just try & rest a little more. I suppose the excessively wet weather has had something to do with it.

I am awfully pleased however that Father is keeping fairly fit & if he doesn't work too hard I have every hope that he will remain so.

It is very funny answering a letter from home out here for you forget that it will take three weeks to reach its destination. For instance I was just going to say that I hoped you had a good calf, but by the time you get this letter the calf will probably sold & forgotten.

What a splendid effort on the part of Janet four teeth & no fuss – marvellous! I am beginning to think she might be able to live here without dying with fright the first night.

I had an awful fright one night. We sleep on the verandahs of our bungalows & there is only a narrow road & a low hedge between mine & the jungle. One night I was almost asleep when I heard a noise in the bushes & looking up I saw a huge white dog leap over the hedge & run up to the bed where he stood looking at me. I managed to frighten him away but it gave me a bit of a start. The jackals often run up to our beds & start howling about three yards from our heads but we are quite used to it ~~&~~ by now.

I agree with mother that it is best for Mary to wait a little before having her teeth out if they are not already drawn. I also shall have to have some out when I come home.

I see the food prices in England are getting very high : it must be very serious for the poor people although those who have men in the army will do pretty well. Many of the men here hardly ~~save~~ have enough to live on, for they allot their mothers & wives 6^d & 9^d a day out of their pay of 1/-. It is awfully good of them because they have to out themselves frightfully to do it, because all sorts of stoppages have to be taken out of what is left.

I leave here for Calicut to-morrow & I suppose shall be very busy for the next few days till I have settled down again.

I can't answer all the letters to-day but I hope to write to them all in turn.

Hoping you are all quite fit

I remain
Your affectionate son
Jim

2/4th Somerset L.I.
Calicut
India

My dear Mother & Father

I have been awfully sorry to read in the last two letters that mother has been so poorly. Knowing as I do that it must be something pretty bad to make mother stay in bed I was rather anxious about her & was awfully glad to hear that she is better. She must be very very careful & not work to hard for a bit. It is awfully pleasing to hear that Janet is able to look after her & make the poultices etc & I do hope she will do her best to take care of mother for the rest of the Winter.

I was jolly glad to know that Father is feeling better after his journey & I hope he will continue to keep fit. 90/- is a tremendous price for cheese & as you say the poor people will have hard times. If Father has a fairly good stock they ought to do well out of it for a time at anyrate.

When I wrote last week I had just heard that I should have to go to Calicut & take over the command. My train left the station at 11–15 AM but I had to go seventeen miles & to do so in time to catch a train when the only means of conveyance was a bullock cart meant leaving Malappuram at five in the morning.

I stole away like a thief in the night for the men did not know I was going & I went round & woke up Farwell & Royal to say good bye.

For the next two days after arriving at Calicut I was awfully busy taking over the place & settling down.

To-day I can really feel that I have got straight & have got a grip of things. There is tons of work to do but it is awfully nice to feel independant again. I make my own orders & decide what punishments to give : for the officer commanding a detatchment has exactly the same powers as the O.C. Battalion. Besides O C detatchment I am Station Staff officer & Cantonment Magistrate. In the latter capacity I have to deal out justice to the natives in the Cantonment. Bartlett is here with me & we get on splendidly together.

The men are getting very fit indeed & in spite of hard training most of them are getting very fat.

Douglas Milton & Goodland the insurance man are here at Calicut. The former has had a bad attack of Rheumatic fever but he is now out of the hospital although he is not yet allowed to do duty. I am going to keep my eye on him to see that he takes care of himself.

Calicut is a small port on the West Coast & no doubt Janet can give you any information you require about the geography of the place & about the connection between Calicut & calico. The town itself is a ~~fow~~ foul hole. There are no European shops the whole town being one large native bazaar, in which one sees the foulest sights it is possible to imagine. The amount of disease is appalling, cholera & smallpox are always more or less there & wherever you go you see leprosy, syphillis & elephantisis.

Our barracks are however in a beautiful situation & we are quite safe from disease. They are at the top of a fairly high hill overlooking the sea three miles out of the town. In front of us we have the sea & behind in the distance the mountains rise up their tops always covered with clouds.

Needless to say the town is out of bounds to the men & all our water is specially boiled & placed in cisterns which are locked so that the water can only be drawn out through a tap.

There is a nice little club in the place which is most useful for we can go there & play tennis, billiards & cards, read the papers, use the library & meet the few other English people in the place. There are a few more of the latter than there were at Malappuram and Bartlett & I shall have to call on them all next week.

I think we ought to be able to save a little here for we are sharing a bungalow & our messing is being done very cheaply. Besides that I get 30 rupees a month extra for being in command of the station.

It is very hot here but just at the hottest part of the day a good sea breeze gets up & this makes it much more bearable. Being so near the sea the air is always very moist so that in spite of the heat it is always a bit damp.

Thank you very much of the papers you are sending out – they are very welcome indeed. The January visitor came last evening & I see that Cathy mentioned the fact that we had left for India. John has finished his musketry course & I see from Battalion orders that he is now very busy teaching recruits. There seems to be quite a chance that Andrew may have to go to Wellington for the hot months. It will be awfully nice for him if he does go for Wellington is right in the hills & has a beautifully cool climate.

I hope to be able to send back some more photographs next week. They ~~they~~ are not nearly so good as the last lot as the light out here is very funny & I have got them all under exposed. But I hope to profit by experience & get better ones next time.

I have just about exhausted my stock of news for this week so I will now end with the usual "to be continued in our next".

You all seem to have had bad colds but I hope all of you are well again now. Once more I hope mother is better & that both she & Father will remain well.

With very much love to all

From your affectionate son
Jim

2/4th Bttn Somerset L.I.
Calicut
South Malabar

March 2nd 1915

My dear Mother & Father

We received your letters dated Feb. 3rd this week and it was awfully good news to hear that Father's health is so much better & I only wish we could have an equally good report of Mother's. Of course we were awfully sorry to hear about Father's accident, but the fact that he is so much better in himself almost made us forget the sprained wrist. I sincerely hope the latter is not very serious & will very soon be right again.

I have had a very busy week as there is a great deal to do but it keeps me occupied & except for the Club where we can get tennis there is not much to do here outside the barracks.

I am afraid the men find it very dull although we do our best to provide amusement. They are however an awfully nice lot of men if you happen to rub them the ~~wrong~~ right way. I found to-night that there are several Evercreech men here which was quite a surprise because I thought they all came from Radstock & Paulton district.

Douglas Milton has had to go back to hospital with another attack of rheumatic fever. The poor boy has had a very bad time & I am afraid that India does not suit him. When he gets well again we shall send him to Bangalore & then if he is no better there he will be invalided home.

During last week we had quite a lot of rain. This is very unusual for the time of year and I have never seen such rain – one inch fell in $\frac{3}{4}$ of an hour. Of course it all comes with thunderstorms which are particularly heavy.

It is very noticable the way the grass grows after a storm of rain. A perfectly bare patch of ground becomes quite green in a day after we have had a storm.

That massacre in Singapore was a terrible affair – it is almost incredible that such a thing can happen in 1915. It is sure to have its effect in India where all is not easy now. There are no very open signs of restlessness but they are there. There is a certain lawlessness – natives murder each other & robberies are getting very frequent. Of course these things are not seen in a town like Bangalore but in places like this one sees more of the natives & gets hold of the bazaar gossip.

My opionion of the natives steadily goes down. When I came out I thought people out here were rather unfair to them but the more I see of them the more hopeless they become. They are the worst liars you can get & you have to be continually watching them. We can go round these barracks fifty times a day & every time there is something wrong somewhere – they seem to know the wrong way of doing everything.

Last Sunday afternoon Bartlett went out to call on the few white residents but luckily we did not stay anywhere. The fact is we worked it so that we arrived at the houses just at times when we knew that the people would not see visitors so we just left cards & in that way got out of the ordeal of official calls.

~~Tell Duf~~ Tell Duff I am glad to hear he is being such a good boy & I hope he is taking great care of Mother for us.

I have been writing scores of letters to-day & have been working hard since 6–30 this morning so I will stop now & go to bed.

With very best love to you all

> I remain
> Your affectionate son
> Jim

Calicut
South Malabar

March 3rd 1915

My dear Ted.

It is awfully good of you to write us such nice long letters – we are delighted to get them.

You have been awfully brave to have so many teeth out & I fear you have had a very bad time. Never mind you will have no more trouble with them & false teeth will look much better than those decayed front ones. As soon as I get a chance I shall have to follow your example & have some of mine out.

I am having quite a good time in Calicut but the climate is awfully trying.

You never wake up with a nice fresh feeling in the morning. Instead you just feel as if you had never been to bed. The hardest thing I have to do here is combat that awful languid feeling which makes we want to sit down & slack all day. ~~When it~~ On a very bad when it is thundery the only thing to do is to work all the harder & then have a good hard game of tennis.

One thing I have at Calicut is a really good bed. It is the first time I have had a decent bed since I joined the Regiment except of course the few nights I was at home.

The poor old pony cart will be completely done for some day I suppose. It will soon be difficult to find the original car among the patches. It has had new shafts, new wheels, a new bottom & now I suppose it will want new springs.

I think there must have been too many boys in the cart to make the springs break like they did – Father will have to make a surprise visit to the Cole road again just to see what really goes on.

I hope you are quite fit & to use your own expression "don't be rash".

> With much love from
> Jim

Calicut

March 10th 1915

My dear Mother & Father.

The English mail for this week has not yet arrived, being very late, probably owing to the recent operations in the Suez; but I think we shall get our letters to-morrow.

The week that has just gone by has not been without its excitement for the Moplah rising we have expected ever since I have been here has taken place. It was however nipped in the bud and came to nothing.

The affair started by an attempt to shoot the collector of Malabar as he was cycling along & he was only saved by the fact that the rifle misfired. After that the Moplahs began to collect but the Special police force which is a military organization were on the spot very quickly & after shooting five troops at Malappuram were called out but they were unfortunate so did not have a look in. We did not move off, although they had a special train in Calicut station for a few days in order that there might be no delay if we should be called away.

If the riot had lasted another day they would have been out in thousands so quickly do they collect if there is any chance of success. However they are quiet now for a time at anyrate I am carrying on here in a quiet way :

there is nothing very exciting to do but always plenty of work in connection with the detatchment.

I am quite surprising myself in some ways. To start with I give the men about three lectures every week a thing I should never have dreamed of doing a short time ago. Again I always said I was no good in the office but here I write scores & scores of letters every week & do the accounts as well, in fact I spend two or three hours in the office every day – jolly good experience.

I attended the first real service I have had since I left England last Sunday. The chaplain of Calicut comes up & holds a service once a month in the Schoolroom. The men never go to service in Calicut except on Easter Sunday & Christmas day as it is too far to make them march on a Sunday.

I suppose it will be just about Easter when this letter reaches you & I sincerely hope that Father will be better this year than he was at the corresponding time last year. I remember it was very funny spending Easter without you both last year & I hope that this year you will be able to spend it at home both enjoying the best of health.

I was very sorry indeed to see the name of P Rossiter among the killed when I was reading the casualty lists one day. He was in the 2nd VIII last year & I slept in the same tent with him at Stobbs. He took a commission the Special Reserve of the Berkshires just before war broke out & now he is killed. He was only about 20 years old.

The Russians are a marvellous race. They are absolutely beaten one day & then they manage to take the offensive the next. This last effort of theirs is absolutely marvellous for they seem to be recovering all the ground they lost a few weeks ago.

The bombardment of the Dardenelles is a good move & if only they can get them open it will do something to reduce the price of bread. Out here the prices are not greatly affected except for imported goods which have gone up considerably.

I hear that Andrew is not quite so fit as he ought to be : I think the hot weather tries him & he will be better if can get away to the hills. I hear from him every week & he seems to be happy enough.

I hope you are all well by now & have got rid of your colds & I hope that Mother is fit again.

With very best love to you all

     I remain
        Yours affectionate son
          Jim

Calicut

March 17th 1915

My dear Mother & Father

Owing to delay in the post I did not get any letters for nearly three weeks but yesterday they all turned up & I had quite a task (pleasant enough) to read them all through. I thank you all very much indeed for your letters and birthday wishes. As Father remarked I shall not forget my 19th birthday very quickly: at the corresponding date last year I had no idea that I should spend my next birthday in Calicut.

It is awfully cheering to hear that you are all well again & especially so to hear that Father is quite himself once more : it was just about a year ago that he was taken ill

I am glad that Mother is better but should like to hear that Angus was stronger. I am afraid the Winter tries him very much & hope that when the warm fine weather comes on he will get fit again.

I have carried on for another week & feel quite satisfied with the result I have at last come back to a little civilzation for I have been out to lunch & out to a tennis party this week. I went to lunch on Sunday with the engineer & this was the first time I had been to a private bungalow since my arrival in India it was my first meal away from mess since I left England.

On Tuesday I went to a tennis party given by the judge & there I broke another record for I had a talk with English ladies for the first time since I left home near three & a half months ago.

Thursday is always a holiday in India & last week Bartlett, the Doctor & I went sh snipe shooting. It was splendid sport wading about in water up to our knees down on the paddy flats. I had the satisfaction of getting my first snipe with my first shot.

Did I ever tell you that or Ted one of the Appleby's is here in this detachment I think it is the second one. He has smartened up wonderfully & I think he is the smartest man for drill in the detachment, but unfortunately he has no authority with the men & is therefore no use at all for an N.C.O. I hear that Andrew is going up to Wellington next week for a few days. I am awfully glad, because it will do him good : I think the heat tries him a good deal at Bangalore so I don't know how he would get on here

The Moplahs seem to have settled down again for a bit : but the German influence has been working very deeply & they were told all sorts of queer tales about the war. The government has now taken steps to have the official bulletin printed in Malayarum & distributed among the people everyday so that they will get the truth. The Germans have got a big influence on this coast because they have a big missionary institution called the Bassel Mission.

under cover of this missionary work they have been gradually working for years to stir up the natives against the English.

I am awfully delighted that the photographs are giving you so much pleasure & I am this week sending fifteen more. I will try & get more of this district as soon as possible & you shall have them as soon I as I can get them ready. Bartlett has taken some very good ones & he has promised to give me some so I will send back those as well.

I don't often get a sleep in the afternoon like I did at Malappuram for I have to work up lectures for the men & master the ten volumes of Indian Army Regulations. Bartlett has not had much experience & I have to try & teach him as well as the men. He is not very fit here the heat is almost too much for him & if he is not very careful I am afraid that he too will have to go to the hills for a change.

Thanks very much for the papers you send us. I get them on from Bangalore when John & Andrew have finished with them. Then I read them & the "Visitor" goes to Douglas Milton in the Hospital who finds is rather dull lying in bed with himself. The "Times" & "Western Gazette" I give to the men so that you see they go nearly as large a round as our letters

I am glad that mine go to Passmore & Withers because I find that I can't write to the same person very often.

Father made quite a good price for the calf & I hope he will get an equally good one for the calf

It is an awfully good scheme building a fowls' house inside the gate of the lower orchard as it will be much easier to get at, & the ground just there is not very valuable. Also I think Mother's idea of planting bushes between the fir poles along the drive is splendid – they will be very nice indeed in a few years time.

I don't Will you please thank Janet for her letter birthday wishes. I hope she will get on with her buttermaking: but tell her to be sure to screw on the top of the churn before she begins to turn it or else the same thing will happen as I have seen in the Dairy at College you should just see Miss Little on those occasions.

It was awfully funny that Father should have met old Pennington's sister in the train – I wonder if she was anything like her brother?

I have quite exhausted my supply by now so this must suffice for this week. With very best love to you all

I remain

Your affectionate son

Jim

P. S. I thought you might be interested to see the enclosed petition. fro It is from some section boys who were sacked. I get several of these each week & some of them are awfully funny. They are written by professional petition writers in the bazzaar.

West Hill
9" March 1915.

The Officer Commanding
Somerset Regt-
West Hill of Barracks
Calcut-

Most Respected Sir,

We the undermentioned Section boys beg to bring the following few lines to your honors kind consideration & favorable order :-

We were ordered by the Captain who left Barracks lately that our services are not required at present and we are of no work for the past month. We are therefore put to greatest difficulties - Sir, now there are no work of any kind for us & We are actually starving for the present. We therefore require of your honor graciously pleased to take our case into your kind consideration and to reinstate us for our work.

For which act of kindness a Charity we shall as in duty bound

Ever Pray

Francis.
Ryan.
Francis.

West Hill

9th March 1915

The Officer Commanding
   Somerset Regt
      West Hill of Barracks
         Calicut

Most Respected Sir,

We the undermentioned Section boys beg to bring the following few lines to your honors kind considerating favourable orders:-

   We were ordered by the Captain who left Barracks lately that our Services are not required at present and we are of having no work for the past month. We are therefore put to greatest difficulties – Sir, now there are no work of any kind for us & we are actually starving for the present. We therefore request your honor graciously pleasure to take our case into your kind consideration and to reinstate us for our work.

   For which act of kindness Charity we shall be in duty bound.

                          Sur Bray
            Francio
            Rayan
            Francio

Bangalore

24/3/15

My dear Mother & Father

I have come to the conclusion that I must be the rolling stone of the Battalion. First I came to Bangalore, then I was sent to Malappuram, from there to Calicut, now back again to Bangalore & on Saturday start again for the Andaman Islands.

   Last Thursday, my birthday we spent very quietly at Calicut, but on Friday my boy woke me from a sleep with a telegram saying "come back to Bangalore at once". At first I wondered what I had done wrong that I should be recalled but reading further I saw that I was to proceed to the Andaman Islands this week. Another wire from Capt Farwell told me that Royal was relieving me at Calicut & that John was going to Malappuram.

   I think John was rather disappointed that he did not go to the Andaman's because they almost promised that he should, but the Colonel told me that he wanted John to teach musketry at both Malappuram & Calicut.

I ~~was~~ had a great rush after receiving those two telegrams, but Royal arrived on Sunday & I left about midday Monday.

I was very sorry to leave Calicut in some ways. I had just begun to know the men & settle down to the work, and Bartlett & I got on splendidly to-gether. The men seemed very sorry to see me depart & one man was heard to remark to another "There! that's what I call an officer".

Andrew has gone to Wellington in charge of a detachment of convalescents & young soldiers. I was very disappointed that I was unable to see him especially as we were within arm's length of each other at one station. He left Bangalore at about the same time as I left Calicut & our trains crossed at a little station about 9–15 PM. His train was waiting for mine to come in : as soon as the latter arrived his moved out. I know he was in it & looked out. When his carriage passed mine I shouted to him but he had the shutters down & did not hear.

John & I also missed each other for he came down to Malappuram the ~~same~~ day before I left Calicut.

I asked Major Bunting about Andrew & I was delighted at his reply. He told me that Andrew was getting on splendidly & only wanted age & experience to make a really good officer. He was also very pleased ~~wh~~ with John who he said was making great progress with his Hindustani. Hindustani will not be much good to him at Malappuram because the natives there talk a language called Malayarum which is quite different.

I must say it is nice to feel cool again. Bangalore is much cooler than Calicut & when I arrived in the early morning I really felt quite chilly. John will feel the heat at Malappuram at first as it is hotter there than at Calicut I miss John & Andrew at Bangalore and shall be glad to move off again. You see I have been away from the Battalion ~~that~~ so long that I don't feel quite at home yet.

The Colonel has just had a splendid report from General Hamilton who inspected the Bttn after they had been here six weeks. He said that we were making excellent progress & although not yet fit for active service we were rapidly attaining a high state of efficiency.

Last week's letters were waiting for me when I got here Tuesday. I am awfully sorry that Mother is still unwell, & I do hope that the warmer weather will do her good. She must go away for another change with Father if it does not.

I am glad Father is still fit & was delighted to hear that he has been to see Passmore at Bath.

I saw the names of two more Reading men in recent casualty lists namely Hogan of the Berkshires & Shacklock of the Sherwood Forresters. The number of officers killed in the last fight at Neuve Chappelle is simply appalling. The sinking of the two ships in the Dardenelles was jolly bad luck but the capture of Prezemsyl by the Russians will do be something to make up for it. Things are fairly quiet out here now although there are rumours of trouble in the North. I think it is very doubtful if any of the troops now in India will come back to the front as I think their presence in India is absolutely necessary to keep things quiet.

The 1st/4th Hants Regt. were sent to the Persian Gulf the other day being the first Territorial Regt. to be sent out of India. The 4th Shropshires who were at Rangoon are gone to Singapore & that is why we have to send a detachment to the Andamans. The troops there are usually supplied from Rangoon.

My name has been sent up for my second star & I ought to be gazetted Lieut in a few more days. Royal's has also gone up.

Young Duff seems to be getting a bit of a rascal. He sent John a splendid letter saying that he had cut off the cat's whiskers. It will do him good to go to school a little.

I think we shall sail from Madras on Sunday & I will try & drop a line from there & after that if you don't hear for a week or two don't be anxious because there is only a mail boat about once in ten days & it a wil letter from the Andamans will take fully a week longer to reach you than one from Bangalore as the passage takes just over three days. I shall of course write a good letter for every mail & then when they once start coming they will follow on regularly.

I hope you are all well at home now & also that when this letter reaches you : you will be having better weather

With much love to all

Your affectionate son
Jim

Bangalore

27/3/15

My dear Mother & Father

I wrote my last letter on Wednesday & it is now only Saturday so I have not much news for you but I am writing to-day because we leave here for the Andaman Islands to-morrow morning & I may not be able to send off another letter for a week or two.

We thought we were going yesterday but owing to the boat being late at Madras we were unable to start. The train leaves the station at 7–15 AM to-morrow & we shall reach Madras in about twelve hours. I believe it is

Palm Sunday to-morrow but we shall spend it in the train. Our first Sunday in the Andamans will be Easter Sunday – do you remember being in the Channel Islands this time last year.

We have been rather busy getting ready but the men are quite fitted out now. They have all had a new outfit completely & can turn out very smartly. You must be very busy indeed working for both Mr Brown's & Mr Thompson's regiments. I don't think our men are in need of anything now although socks are always acceptable to them. I don't think it is worth sending them out however as I believe the duty is rather high.

On Thursday evening the ~~three~~ four of us who are going the Andaman Islands were the guests of the other members of the mess & I must say they gave us a really good time.

Our English mail arrived last night about 11 PM & we were all waiting up for it. When the postman arrived he threw all the letters on the floor & we just picked our own. I ~~had a~~ was glad to hear that you are all well & also that Duff likes going to school. I don't think he will take long to learn. I expect he will soon be the terror of the rest of the school.

I am enclosing half a dozen more photographs this week some of which are quite good. One or two are slightly over exposed but show quite a good picture.

It is very funny ~~to-day~~ that the colour sergeant who is going with us is the schoolmaster under Mr Lewis at Radstock & he ~~was~~ is able to tell me all about Lewis who as you probably know went to the front & was invalided home. I only found it out to-day while in conversation with him.

I have not yet heard from John or Andrew ~~yet~~ so I don't know how they like their new stations.

I hope all who are entering from Park Cottage will do well in the S.S. exam – shall expect to hear of five 1st prizes – nothing else will do. We get the papers you send us quite regularly & are delighted to ~~get~~ have them. ~~You can if~~ There is not much in any of them that we don't read.

I really can't think of anything else now, but will write again at the first opportunity & tell you all about the Andaman Islands.

Hope you are all quite fit

With love to you all

Your affectionate son
Jim

R.I.M.S. *"Mayo"*
Bay of Bengal

1st April 1915

Dear Mother & Father.

You will see from the above address that we are at sea again on the Royal Indian Marine Ship "Mayo". We hope to reach the Andaman Islands early to-morrow morning and when you are all eating your hot cross buns we shall probably unloading our baggage & getting the men off the boat.

We left Bangalore at 7–30 AM last Sunday morning and I was very glad to get away. I have been away from the Regiment so long that I did not feel quite at home at Bangalore & I missed John & Andrew there. Also I if I had stayed there much longer I should have been obliged to make a good many calls & I detest that sort of thing.

On the Saturday night i e the night before we left, I saw a real tropical thunderstorm & I am not likely to forget it. For For several days previously the weather had been getting hotter & hotter till on Saturday afternoon black clouds began to collect on the horizon. They gradually rolled up & the storm got nearer & nearer. The lightening was very vivid long before the storm was near enough for us to hear the thunder. About 10–30 PM it broke over Bangalore & it was a marvellous sight. The lightening was far more vivid than anything I have ever seen before – you could see things half a mile away quite clearly & the thunder was absolutely deafening. The rain came down in sheets washing away all the dust & rubbish lying about. As a result of the storm it was beautifully cool when we left Bangalore but after we crossed the Ghats & began to get down into the coastal plain the heat became almost unbearable.

It is a twelve hour journey from Bangalore to Madras & I was awfully interested in comparing the West coast with the East.

I have now been almost across India in two places namely from Bombay to Madras & from Calicut almost to Madras. The Western Ghats are high mountains & you have to ascend in order to cross them wh from either direction while the Eastern Ghats are practically only hills from the Coast side. Approaching them from the Deccan there is very little ascent. I think the West Coast is more wooded than the East as of course the rainfall on the West is greater than that on the East.

Around Calicut for instance there are miles & miles of coconut forest with stretches of paddy flat on the in the clearings, but on the Madras side the paddy flats seem to predominate while the coconut trees take a second place. The coastal plain is much wider on the East coast & the natives are not so distinct as they are on the other side.

As As soon as you get over the crest of the Ghats going towards Calicut the appearance of the native changes. The Deccan natives are very dark coloured & their women wear bright coloured clothing, blue & red being the predominating colours. The West Coast natives (at least those of Malabar) are very light in colour some of them being almost white. The men are tall fine men & well built while the women wear no clothes except a short skirt which is almost always white. You very rarely see the Malabar native wearing bright coloured clothes.

Of course around Malappuram & Calicut you have the Moplah, but he is not a native of the district. He has come there from other countries & is quite different from the ordinary native.

Judging from the natives I saw from the plain there is very little difference between the native on the Deccan & the native on the Madras Coast. Anyhow there is no sharp change in colour or clothing.

As we came down on to the plain it got very hot indeed & the nearer we got came to the sea the damper the air was so we arrived at Madras about 7 O'clock in the evening feeling very hot & sticky. We did not go on board till 4 pm next day so we stayed at Fort St George with the Devon 2/4th Devons. Our Pt 4th Somersets sta were stationed at the Fort when they came to India first. It is rather a fine set of buildings & contains a church & various civil buildings so that if there were a riot most of the white people could shelter there.

The climate at Madras is about the same as, or worse than that of Calicut you can't move a muscle sweating in streams. We spent the next morning driving round the City & I must say that it is a beautiful place It is rightly called the "Garden City" for none of the large shops stand in rows along the streets. They all stand in large gardens quite detached, & you hardly know whether you are going to a shop or a private gardens house. There are a great many open places with statues & monuments & the whole place is beautifully laid out with flowers & trees.

When we marched down to the docks in the afternoon we saw the municipal buildings & the gap in the boundary wall made by one of the Emden's shells. We went on board in the afternoon but did not sail till 6 O'clock next morning. When we got out of the harbour it was quite rough & there was a very heavy cross swell which made the boat roll & pitch awfully badly. I could not stand that & like most of the others had an attack of sea sickness which however soon passed off.

To-day is Thursday, the third day on the boat & as I said before we shall land early to-morrow

it is very very hot to-day, hardly a breath of air moving & the sea like a mill pond. I should not like to be in a sailing vessel on a day like this: it would be almost unbearable. Every now & then the smooth surface of the water is ruffled by a shoal of flying fishes trying to get away from the porpoises which leap out of the water to try & get at them.

The Captain of the ship has promised to post this letter at Rangoon so I don't know how long it will be before you get it. I don't expect I shall hear from you for a few weeks but I shall write whenever there is an opportunity of getting a letter off. I am fairly busy on board because I am ships Adjutant & have to get out the orders & see that things ~~go~~ generally go on well.

~~You~~ You will all have to have a good walk to-morrow & try & find the early cowslips. It did not seem right last year to go off on Good Friday without Father. I hope he will be quite fit this year & I also hope that Mother is quite well now.

I have no more to say ~~next~~ now & I am just off to see if the men have got a good tea.

With much love to you all

    I remain
        Your affectionate son
        Jim

Tell Duffy I had a letter from him a few days ago & will write one to him as soon as we get on shore.

Port Blair
Andaman Islands

April 8th 1915

My dear Mother & Father.

I posted my last letter on the boat the night before we arrived at Port Blair & I promised I would tell you about the Andaman Islands in the next.

We arrived at Port Blair on Good Friday & spent the whole day disembarking & taking over from Shropshires who left here the same day.

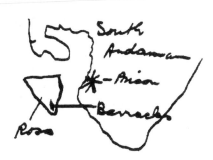

When I awoke about 5–30 AM on Good Friday we were in sight of land & were running parallel to the coast which we continued to do till we came in sight of Port Blair. South Andaman is a huge Island about 300 miles long & Port Blair is at its South end. As a

Barracks on Ross Island

matter of fact there is no real place called Port Blair the whole penal settlement Ross being known by that name

The prison is on the Mainland as the large island is called & it is consists of a central building from which seven long arms radiate The barracks, club, post office & all the stores are on a little island called Ross separated from the mainland by a stretch of water which takes about five minutes to cross in a steam launch. Ross is very small indeed being only about a mile long & half a mile wide. It is very steep & well wooded. The barracks are right

Marching towards the Barracks

Convicts in chains, loading wood

on the crest at the po one of the points of the islands. They are like look like an old castle & are quite picturesque in the distance.

My bungalow is also on the crest & I can look out to see on both sides. This makes it nice & cool for I am able to get all the breeze possible, as it blows through the bungalow from whichever side it comes. We do not mess in our bungalows but go down to the Club. It is a Service Club & there is a regular mess there. It is one of the nicest Clubs I have seen & it has the greatest advantage of being one of the coolest spots on the Island owing to the fact that it is supplied with electric fans. There is no room on Ross for us to drill & we have to cross over to the other side every day. The men all get into boats which are towed across by a steam launch.

The large Island is divided into counties the one opposite to us in which the prison stands is called Aberdeen. The names you will notice are all Scotch. There are about 15000 convicts on the settlement & to look after them there are 800 military police, 200 500 Native troops & 140 British Infantry. Most of the convicts are allowed after a short time to have a pass & become self supporting. Only the worst cases are kept in the prison & these are brought out to work with chains on their legs. The chains are arranged so that they can walk but cannot move freely.

My servant is a convict who has become self supporting owing to on account of good conduct. He is a murderer but I believe he is quite harmless. The worst part is that he cannot talk English & I cannot talk Hindustani. We manage to understand each other fairly well on the whole.

These islands are one of the most beautiful spots on the earth. Set down right in the middle of the sea they are beautifully wooded & covered with *green* grass. The latter is a fine sight after the burnt brown plains of India. There are grass tennis courts here besides grass hockey pitches & cricket field. At present is is almost too hot for games but we manage to play most evenings either tennis hockey or cricket The nights are fairly cool which is a great blessing after Calicut, but the sun in the day time is terrible. The Andamanese live mostly away in the jungle but there is a sort of home for them on one of the islands which I hope to be able to visit before very long. Just at present they are out hunting down escaped convicts.

I have had rather a strenuous time since we arrived here because I have been appointed adjutant to the detachment & that means a good deal of work. It will however ease off very soon when we have really settled down.

On Easter Sunday we had a Church Parade & attended the little Church on Ross Island. It was the first full service I have attended in Church since I left home.

One of the attractions of coming here was that we were free from Generals but as luck would have it we found on arrival that a General was due here by the next boat. He arrived yesterday & inspected us to-day. He is General Johnstone, commanding the Rangoon division.

There is a mail boat leaving here nearly every ~~mont~~ week but we only get English letters about three times a month. I hope we shall be able to get some next week.

There are some awfully pretty views about here & I am taking a good many photographs which I will send home as soon as they are developed. We get a certain amount of news by wireless when the weather conditions are good enough & the club provides English papers & magasines which however are very late when they arrive here. If I write any more this week I shall have nothing to say in my next few letters.

I hope you all had a good time at Easter & hope that Mother & Father are both very fit now. I suppose you are all glad that the warmer weather is coming on but I would give a good deal to be really cold & to see a good hard frost.

~~Andrew~~ I heard from Andrew by this week's mail & he seems to be having a very good time at Wellington. I expect he will be better up there than at Bangalore which is not really a healthy place.

Once more I hope Mother & Father & all the others are quite well again With very much love to all

Your affectionate son
Jim

Port Blair
Andaman Islands

17th April 1915

My dear Mother & Father

This weeks mail brought me some English letters which were very welcome as I had not had any for three weeks. I was very glad to hear that you are all well now & I hope that Father had a safe journey to & from the Channel Islands. What ⅄ luck did he get with the new agentcy?

We are getting on very well indeed here but shoud like it very much better if it were not so hot. Yesterday was by far the hottest day I have ever experienced & I am told that we shall have several more as hot but none hotter. The sky was cloudless & there was not a breath of wind so you can imagine what it was like. ⅄ It is cooler to-day there being quite a nice breeze.

I tried to tell you all about Ross last week & during this week I have been able to see a little more of Aberdeen, It is awfully pretty being very hilly & well wooded. Sometimes instead of woods you come out on open downs which look quite like those we get in England.

There are two temples for the convicts one for the Hindus & one for the Mohommedans. I have not yet been inside of either but they are very pretty from outside. The outside of Hindu temple is covered all over with fantastic carvings & paintings of various gods. I think I know most of the people here now as we meet nearly all of them at the Club. Last Tuesday we went to a dinner at the club given as a farewell dinner to several people who are leaving here shortly & last night we dined at Government House. It was quite a good evening but I must admit I am not fond of such functions & feel am not in very good form after having spent nearly three months away at Malappuram & Calicut.

I have had a couple of games of cricket & some very good tennis. It awfully nice playing on grass again after the bare sand which we used to have in India.

I am hoping to have a few days leave before very long & then I shall be able to have a look round. The convicts are awfully clever with their hands & some of their carving & beaten brass work is marvellous. They also make very pretty things with tortishell & mother of pearl. I daresay I shall be able to get hold of some things before I come away.

The men seem very pleased with the place & they spend most of their time fishing & bathing. I am afraid however that they will find it rather dull when the rains come on.

There is an Andamanese Home over on Aberdeen where the original natives live in a sort of preserve. I have not yet seen them but am told that they are very interesting. The really wild ones live out in the jungle & just at present they are rather troublesome because they are getting short of water & are coming in to the villages & shooting the inhabitants. For this purpose they use bows & arrows with which weapons they are very expert. The arrows have poisoned ends so that it is one ~~not~~ advisable to be shot by one of the aboriginees. Each convict has a wire ring round his neck to which a label bearing his number is attached. The wild natives are awfully keen on these wire rings & in order to obtain them they often shoot the convicts.

I heard from both Andrew & John this week & both seem to be getting on very well. Andrew says he is having the best time he ever had in his life & from what he said Colonel Waddy is giving him an awfully good time.

You ought to get some eggs now with all those new fowls. Personally I am getting tired of eggs for we get them ~~at~~ every day without fail, & chicken in some form or other appears on the menu nearly every day.

I hope they will all do well in the Scripture exam just to keep up the reputation of the house

I suppose Father saw Bow Wow when he was in the Channel Islands – to which of our girls did he send back the kisses?

I don't think I can manage any more this week for I have just exhausted my supply of news etc.

With very much love to all

Your affectionat son
Jim

P. S. I was as glad to hear in Mother's last letter that ~~she~~ her rheumatic has quite gone & I hope that Father is still keeping fit

Port Blair
Andaman Islands

22/4/15

Dear Father

Very many happy returns of your birthday. Now that you are better I sincerely hope that this year you will enjoy really good health again & that you will be quite yourself once more. We hope that ~~we shall be~~ the war will be over & we shall be back again with you before your next birthday but it is absolutely useless to speculate on how long the war will last.

I do hope that you will not work too hard this year & knock yourself up again because I often wonder how ~~whether~~ long before I shall be able to help you. I thought when I left college last Summer that I should be well into the business by this time but the war quite upset our calculations. Anyhow I think the experience we are all gaining out here will make us more efficient when we come back.

The mail boat came in to-day but she had no English mail on board The latter was late at Calcutta so our mail boat left Rangoon before the boat from Calcutta, (which brings the mail English mail) arrived there. We do not get another mail of any sort for nearly three weeks so that it will be a big one when it does come & you can imagine how pleased we shall be to see it. Luckily I received letters from Andrew & John which enclosed some of their last week's letters so I am not entirely without news.

I have had quite a busy week, & in spite of the heat am very fit indeed & not much fat left now it has all melted away.

Flower & I dined at Government House last Friday evening & I suppose we must have made a fairly good impression for we were invited again on Tuesday night. Besides these two dinners we have twice been invited up to play tennis there.

The Chief Commissioner as the Governor is called is Colonel Douglas. He is the most pessimistic man I ever met, in fact he is most depressing. He is not at all popular here & people will be glad when he is relieved although from the point of view of the Government he is considered very efficient.

It is almost too hot for cricket but I have played two matches this week. The first one was the Somersets v the Andaman volunteers & the second was between two scratch sides. The Regiment was badly beaten in the first the scores being Volunteers 208 Somersets 71. I managed to get 192 19 which was easily top score for us & strange to say they were nearly all from boundaries. We should have done better only we had to field all the afternoon when the heat was terrible.

It is Thursday to-day & of course we have a holiday so we started at seven this morning & went up the harbour in a launch. It was a glorious trip & we got back to breakfast about 11–30 AM. We saw the government workshops on Viper island & were awfully interested in seeing the natives working. They are awfully clever with their hands & make awfully pretty things out of tortishell & mother of pearl. I hope to get mother some things before I leave here. Their brass work & carving is also marvellous.

I also saw some of the Andamanese to-day. They are very funny little people – quite naked & absolutely coal black. They are only about five feet high & have short thick woolly hair. They never go about without their weapons, which consist of bows & arrows in the use of which they are very clever indeed.

The gun has just gone off & we are have all set our watches & clocks because it is the signal that the right time is 8–0 PM. It also means that I shall soon have to dress for dinner because we have our evening meal at

Andaman Islands: the people

8–30 PM. This ~~with~~ breakfast at 10 AM are the only large meals we have in the day & at first I found great difficulty in getting used to the two meal system but now I am beginning to realize that it is the arrangement most suitable for this climate.

I am so glad to hear that you are able to go & see Passmore sometimes & I hope he will be able to spend a few days with you before he leaves Bath. ~~as I~~ Do you know where Johnny Withers is stationed now? – I have not heard from him for a long time.

It is not much good for me to discuss the present state of the war with you because my ~~present~~ knowledge of events is regulated by telegrams received at the wireless station which needless to say are not very full. We get the papers at the Club but they are of course very late & the next lot will be ~~very of~~ a very ancient date.

I see that in your letter to Andrew you said that you had not seen his gazette but I his name appears in the army list as having been gazetted on Jan 20th (I think)

I hoped to send you a dozen photographs to-day but I sent them to a local photographer to develop & he has spoilt all the films. It is rather disappointing because some of them I ~~rath~~ are rather interesting

The forerunner of the monsoon has arrived in the shape of ⱥ cyclonic disturbances & thunderstorms. They are not very big yet but are a sure ~~sigh~~ sign that the monsoon is not far off.

Once more I will wish you very many happy returns of the ~~20th~~ 27th of May.

I hope Mother is keeping well & also all the others
With much love to all

Your affectionate son
Jim

Port Blair
Andaman islands

29th April 1915

My dear Mother & Father

There is not much for me to write about this week as it was only four days ago that I last wrote. The mail goes out early this week & we don't get an inward mail.

For five days we were completely cut off as far as news was concerned owing to some very severe thunderstorms which prevented the wireless messages from getting through. Last night however some news got through

& we learned that the Germans had been having another go at the British & that the Canadians had been forced to retire slightly. When the news was out off we all thought Italy was going to join in but there was no mention of her in last night's telegrams.

We have had a severe thunderstorm every day for the last six days with unfailing regularity. The lightening is really magnificent & when the rain comes you can hardly hear yourself speak it makes such a noise.

Last night I was asleep on the verandah when I suddenly awoke to find my sheets blowing about all over the place & everything inside blown over. The next thing was a blinding flash of lightening & then the rain came down in sheets. Of course we had to get up & shut the windows & move our beds inside or we should have been almost blown away.

In our bungalow it always sounds as if there were a storm blowing owing to the roar of the sea on the rocks. We are right on the crest of the island & the sea is only about 100 yards away on either side.

We are hoping to get a game of cricket to-day & after the rain it will be just like playing at home. It is marvellous how quickly the grass grows after the first rain. ~~You leaving~~ The ground is quite brown one day while on the next it is covered in green grass.

We have a tremendous number of men ill just at present with what is called Rangoon fever. It is not very serious, and an attack lasts about seven days, but it has fairly got hold of our men. Over thirty paraded sick yesterday & the day before there were forty. Another thing that troubles them here is that if they get a scratch it does not heal up but festers & then they get blood poisoning. Lots of men are going about with festers & sores that started with a tiny scratch.

Ross, fortunately, is free from malaria but it is very bad on Aberdeen & that is ~~why~~ one reason why most of the white people live here instead of on the mainland.

The sea around these islands is absolutely splendid for bathing & is so warm that you can stay in for hours without feeling any ill effects. Our bathing however is very restricted owing to the prevalence of sharks & also the danger of sunstroke. The latter makes it impossible to bathe before five in the evening. Sharks are very common in these waters & they seem to know when & where the men bathe & gather such places so that we have to be very careful ~~about~~ not to go out of our depth. A very favourite sport about here is that of boat sailing. I have not yet tried it but if I have time I think I shall go out a few times for it may be useful to know the way to sail a boat.

I suppose Park Cottage is just beginning to look pretty again after the Winter; with the fruit trees in blossom & the flowers all coming out. I can just imagine what it looks like. What sort of a year will it be for fruit? I hope there will be plenty because it will be jolly useful with all other food so dear.

The May cheese will fetch a high price this year if the new season starts anywhere near the figure at which it left off & the farmers will be making a good thing out of it. The government have a very large dairy farm here & they are trying experiments with the various breeds of cattle. The man who looks after it told me that they have almost every breed in India represented. He also said that they have imported some shorthorns from Australia to see the effect of crossing them with the native breeds. I have not had a chance of seeing them yet but he has promised to take me out on the first opportunity. They have also started sheep & goat farms which I am anxious to see.

I sincerely hope you are all well now & that Father will take things steadily in order that he will not knock up again.

Are you all going away for a holiday this year? It would do you all good if you could manage it.

With love to all

> I remain
> Your affectionate son
> Jim

**Port Blair
Andaman Islands**

13/5/15

Dear Ted.

I meant to write to Mary this week as it is her turn but I really must let you have this one to congratulate you on winning that buttermaking prize. I now begin to have hopes that so in the near future I may see my sister making butter at the dairy show surrounded by a crowd of admiring spectators. In any case you will now be a great asset to the old & established firm of "James Mackie & Sons".

I must also thank you for the nice long letters you write me – they are always very interesting & very welcome. You asked me in your last one to tell you something about the women of India & I will just give you my impression of them (I have just been away to mount the Guard & do a few other jobs but will now continue). The native women of India are on the whole absolutely foul & filthy. Of course some are better than others but that is what I think of them taken all round.

Down on the West Coast there were women of several types or castes.

The Moplah is a Mohommedan & his women are therefore covered. Unlike most Mohommedan women they do not cover their face completely but they always wear a cloth on their heads. The rest of their clothing consists of a loose fitting sort of coat & a skirt which nearly always has a blue edge to it. The coat or blouse is characteristic of the Moplah women & is what one might call a badge of office. I noticed that on the whole they were not very good looking & had very prominent teeth. They are also not very clean although for natives the Moplah women are supposed to be fairly moral.

The Hindus are divided into castes. ~~The namely~~ The highest are Bhramins, then Nains, then Taens & lastly the Cherumas who have no caste at all. The Bhramin women are well dressed in clean white clothes which seem to consist of yards & yards of muslin in loose folds They wear lots of jewellery, such as anklets, bracelets, ear-rings & nose-rings. Bhramin women are not allowed to marry into any other caste although the men may do so without losing caste.

The Nains & Taens ~~& other~~ are not allowed by their religion to wear any clothes of any sort above the waist, in fact it is considered immodest for a woman to wear clothes above her waist in the presence of a man. Both are very similar in appearance, very light in colour, rather small & with the hair done up in a peculiar knob on the head. The Nains being a higher caste are much cleaner than the Taens. The children are very pretty but the older ones go off badly but some of them are quite pretty for natives.

The women of the Deccan are very dark, much bigger than the women of the West coast & they wear coloured clothing. They also wear a sort of shawl over ~~the~~ one shoulder.

The Cheruma women are mere slaves & are bought & sold with the land. They are naked to the waist and the foulest creatures you ever saw. They wear long strings of cheap beads, & their voices are absolutely terrible.

Most of the women in the gaol here are murderers having murdered their children, but it is not considered a very serious offence out here.

The last lot of women are those of the Andamanese who are very small & absolutely coal black. They are quite naked & have short wooly hair.

I have noticed that natives are either young or old; there seems to be no middle age. They ~~are~~ look fairly decent up to about eighteen & then they get old all of a sudden. I am sure this is quite enough about the women for this time at anyrate. I have not seen very much of the ~~white la~~ English ladies since I came out so will leave them out & make the most of them when I come home again.

Please thank Bunna & Angus for their letters of last week. I am glad Angus is getting on well at school & also with his violin.

Also please thank Duffy for his note. I am so glad he likes it at school & is getting on well. He will do something big when he is older & he will not have to work till two o'clock in the morning to get a mere pass B.A. or B.Sc. – nothing but 1st class honours at Cambridge will do for him.

And who is it now? Have you captured Marcel yet or does Margy still hold him captivated by that beautiful (? – don't laugh) face of hers. I am just going to dress for dinner & my servant (Moses I have named him) is patiently waiting to for me to finish this.

With very best love to you all

> I remain
>> your affectionate brother
>> Jim

2/4th Somerset L.I.
Port Blair
Andaman Islands

May 13th 1915

My dear Mother & Father.

When I last wrote you a letter a fortnight ago & we had then received no English letters for three weeks. A mail arrived a week ago to-day bringing crowds of letters which had accumulated during those three weeks & you can imagine how pleased we were to see them. There was no outward mail last week so I telegraphed to the postmaster Bombay & asked him to send you the wire which I hope you received. This week we had another inward mail & there is also an outward one so I have four weeks letters to answer.

The last fortnight has not been very eventful for now that you know what the place is like there is not a great deal to write about from week to week. The chief interest has been in watching the monsoon coming up. First of all we had very violent thunderstorms which brought torrents of rain but which did not make the weather any cooler. For the last few days we have had no thunderstorms but the wind has been fairly strong – it is gradually working away to the S W Yesterday & to-day have been two of the hottest days we have had for the wind has quite dropped & after the rain you can almost see the steam rising off the ground. This is the lull before the storm which is due to break in a very few days now & when it does I am told that the rain is almost continuous till the middle of September.

The rain has made the burnt grass beautifully green & the trees are all coming out into leaf. it is really quite like Spring at home but the seasons are not the hot & cold but the wet & dry. One tree in particular has attracted my attention. A few days weeks ago it was quite bare except for some long black seed pods hanging from the branches. Now it is one mass

The Cellular Jail

of huge orange red flowers with just a trace of the young green leaves between. The flowers are so brilliant that you can pick out one of these trees fully a mile away. One tree, whose name I don't know seems to prefer the hot dry weather to the wet for it was quite green in the hot weather but the leaves are now turning yellow & falling off.

The men are still getting fever & lots of them go to the hospital every day. I have not had it yet & the doctor told me that the only thing to keep it off was plenty of exercise, so he & I play football & hockey alternately nearly every one on one day & the other the next. To this We vary this with a little tennis. The Doctor is an awfully nice fellow. He comes from Devonshire, went to school at Blundells & has played cricket for the Devon & Somerset Wanderers & has therefore met Will Donne about whom he made the remark "once seen never forgotten". Flower is also an old Blundelian & one the first night soon after we got here we went to a dinner at which, the Doctor & he & another old Blundelian sat at one table. It was rather strange that the three of them should have accidentally met in that way.

A very sad thing happened here last week – the wife of the Senior Medical Officer died of malaria after having been only just over a day. I had to take a party of men to the funeral to carry the coffin & I think it was one of the saddest sights I have ever seen.

I received a letter from Colonel Waddy last week & I was delighted with what he said about Andrew in fact I don't know if anything lately has pleased me more. I quote the extract in the exact words of the letter; "We all enjoy this lovely spot & climate; and his own big brother won't know

The landing of the Andaman Expeditionary Force

2/4th Bn. Somerset L.I. (P.A.)

the little soldier when you meet again. He is a good sub., keen, & useful
& tries to learn & do all he can". From that I should think that soldiering
will is going to make a man of Andrew.

I am very glad Father had a good trip to the Channel Islands – rather a
risky journey in these times – I am pleased to hear that he found Tom
Warren quite fit. I was delighted with those two little snapshots which were
quite good.

I was very sorry indeed to hear this week that Aunt Emma is dead &
shall write to them by this mail. Is Cecil going to keep on the Farm & if
so what will John do?.

Another bit of bad news which came by wireless was a short telegram
saying that the Lusitania had been sunk by a submarine with 190 over 1900
people on board. A later wire stated that about 600 had been saved. Of
course the usual note followed to the effect that it had aroused great
indignation in America but of no-one take any notice of that story now.
We have heard nothing further about the it so far.

This is about all I can manage this week in the way of news but before
I forget it I should like to have another pair of stockings or perhaps two
pairs if they could be sent out. I only brought one pair & they are nearly
worn out. Also I if it could be sent I should like my best suit of clothes.
It is almost too hot for English clothes but I believe it is cooler in the
monsoon & it is convenient to have a dark suit on certain occasions.

Janet says that mother had to have a few days in bed at Easter but I hope it was nothing serious & I do hope she will be quite fit by the time this letter arrives home. I hope Father is keeping well & also all the others

ꭓ With much love to all

> I remain
> > Your affectionate son
> > > Jim

2/4th Somerset L.I.
Port Blair
Andaman Islands

19th May 1915

Dear Mother & Father.

There is not much to write about this week as it is a very short week the mail going out on Thursday instead of Saturday.

It has been much cooler on the whole although even now we have to change our shirts every time we come in. There have been some exceedingly hard storms & the rainfall has been very heavy but the monsoon has not yet started in real earnest: in fact I am told that now it has missed the usual date it may quite possibly be a fortnight or even a month late.

I have had some games of football & hockey which although very strenuous in a climate like this are awfully enjoyable, & which keep one very fit. Fever is still very bad on in the settlement: it is one of the worst

Burt and Flower

The officer's Mess
Flower, Burt and Hartford

years they have ever known since the settlement was started as both Malaria & Rangoon fever are rife. The hospital is still full of men, but luckily only one of them has had malaria. Flower had a slight touch earlier in the week but it was nothing much & he soon got fit again. A very bad trouble with the men is that their skin does not heal. The slightest scratch turns to blood poisoning & some of them have had very bad places. The doctor thought that they scratched themselves with dirty finger nails so we now have the pleasant job of making an inspection of feet & hands every other day.

I have been down for a swim to-night & have been learning to dive. I think if you ~~would~~ had seen the first effort you would have laughed nearly as much as when we were standing on the brink at ~~St~~ Bournemouth. I got on the edge & after shivering there for a few minutes prepared to jump but my pluck failed. I thought that would not do so I set my teeth stuck out my chin & jumped ... (bubbles). It was an awful flop flat on my stomach & my head hardly went under, but the next time although my knees were very bent I got well under. After several more tries I believe I at last got one which might have been called a dive – (with a little exaggeration) so I decided to "continue in our next".

Life in a place like this is very monotonous for there is so little room to move about. ~~but~~ I manage to find plenty to do but Capt. Harford gets very bored at times so do the others, owing to the fact that they do not go in for games.

The Englishman in India is not like he is at home. He seems to have a swollen head & there is no esprit de corps. I suppose coming straight from school & college you miss ~~it more~~ the latter more than if you had been out in the world for several years, but it is very noticeable. Everyone, although apparently friendly on the surface, ~~is~~ in reality despises & backbites everyone else, & everyone seems to try to be far too superior. The men notice this very much – they are treated quite like ordinary tommies who in India are very much looked ~~looke~~ down upon & ~~every~~ except in a few ~~exceptional~~ isolated cases no-one takes any notice of them. The people out here don't seem to realize a bit that we are at war ~~& make no~~ except that they read war news in the papers: ~~&~~ they carry on just the same as in peace time ~~he als~~ and as long as there are troops to protect them they don't seem to care. The war has not touched them yet & I don't think that on the whole they ~~realy~~ realize a bit the condition of things in ~~India~~ England.

The Territorial in India is not having a pleasure trip by any means. We have been training hard ~~alth~~ all through the hot season a thing which regular troops never think of doing. The men are badly paid & can afford very few luxuries. It is not that the pay is any worse out here than in England but many of the men are married & send home half of it & most of the single men also make allotments to their mothers & Fathers. I am sure

Captain Hartford

many of the latter would not ask for allotments if they knew what it meant to their boys. The usual conversation on pay day is as follows: "Your mother has applied for an allotment from you – are you willing to give it? The answer is alway yes 6^d or 4^d per day. ~~Hens Hence for~~ Henceforward instead of taking 5 rupees per week the man takes two or at most three. Out of this he has to buy himself a supper every day, tobacco & cigarettes & any little extras he may want. The point is that at home the men have all these things given to them by the people who are only too pleased to ~~helf~~ help the soldiers, out here no one ever thinks of giving anything to the men & they have to buy all these things themselves Also at home the government pay for all sorts of things which the men have to pay for themselves out here such as reparing boots, damages to barracks etc. ~~Also~~ Further at home the men are getting service rations while out here they are having peace rations which have to be supplemented with extras which they have to pay for themselves. Every day we stop ~~2½~~ 2½d out of each man's pay to provide butter jam etc to go with his ration which is just the plain 1lb of bread & 1lb of meat with tea & sugar & vegetables I am afraid this is very dull & uninteresting but it will give you an idea of the conditions of things in India & it just shows how much the men are putting up with in order to do their country a good turn at this time. I know these facts are true because I have been responsible for the pay sheets & feeding of the men in my ~~co~~ company ever since I came out here.

20th May. The mail has just arrived & we have got a big rush for the boat goes out again to-night It is Father's birthday to-day & I have mentally wished him very very many happy returns of the day but of course the letter bearing those wishes left here weeks ago.

I am sorry that father will be obliged to get rid of some of the animals but of course if they don't pay it is no good to keep them & I suppose the price of feeding stuffs is very high now.

I wrote to Shepton Montague last week but I am afraid that it was a very poor effort for I did not know quite what to say. I was awfully sorry to hear ~~of~~ that Aunt had died & I feel very ~~for~~ deeply for the rest of the family. She was exceeingly good to me & was one of the kindest women it is possible to find.

I enclose a few photographs which only returned from being developed to-day, so I am wasting no time in sending them off.

I am going to write to Mary if I have time, but have to attend to several official letters as well as my own, so will write next week if I can't manage to-day.

John & Andrew both seem very fit, but John like myself has had rather a trying time with the heat. Mother's attack of influenza about Easter seems to have been very severe, and doubtless she is very weak after it. I do hope she is fit again now & will take great care of herself.

Please thank Bunna for his letter : I am glad he liked his dressing gown.

With very best love to you all

      I remain
        Your affectionate Son
        Jim.

2/4th Somerset LI
Port Blair
Andaman Islands

May 28th 1915

My dear Mother & Father.

We shall have a great rush again to-day as the mail boat only arrived this afternoon & leaves again to-morrow afternoon. It came direct from Madras this week instead of from Rangoon so that we have two lots of English letters, which I have been reading for the last hour. We don't have to wait long for our letters once the boat drops anchor, for the bags are at once sent ashore & some of our men go the to the post office where they are allowed to sort out our letters. They are taken to the barracks & sorted again & an orderly runs down to our bungalow with ours. The rush for me in my case will be greater than usual this week for I hoped to write most of my letters to-night but I have to dine at Government House. Until I came here I had not dined out of the mess on a single occasion, but now I have been out on several occasions. Last Sunday evening I had dinner with the Harbour Master & his wife over on the mainland and afterwards came back in a rowing boat. It was a splendid moonlight night (we never get such moonlight in England) & the water was as still as a duckpond. It was awfully interesting watching the fish swimming about for they all left a phosphorescent trail. The oars looked as though they were on fire & each little splash looked just like a spark.

I had a my first experience of at a fresh kind of sport last Monday – the Padre took me out sailing with him & I have now become very keen on it. This is a specially good place for sailing & most of the people who are more or less permanent keep a boat. It is awfully good fun especially when there is a good breeze on & the boat is tilted up on one side with the sail nearly touching the water. Under such circam circumstances the yachts cut through the water at a tremendous pace.

The last few days have been very hot indeed & there has hardly been any breeze so that we have had to slack off our work to a minimum as the men absolutely can't stand it. There is still a good deal of fever, several new cases have occurred among the men including a couple of cases of Malaria. Burt ha is now in bed with it so Flower & I are rather busy as we have to do his work as well as our own.

My sisters have become awfully brave to have so many teeth out & I fear poor little Mary is having rather a bad time. I hope that by now she has had them all seen to & has finished with the dentist & is feeling quite fit again.

I don't wonder that Janet & Mary enjoyed their motor ride to Swanage for it is a splendid run & of course Swanage is always worth going to visit. I remember going there with Father & Brainem when we first had the motor – we fairly moved along in places. it is quite a wonder that the Colonel did not come here for a visit. He has had a rather serious illness but is now convalescent & has been ordered to go away for a change. He ~~N~~ practically decided to come here for a few weeks & looked up a boat but being very weak he feared that he would have a rough passage which he could not stand, so he has decided to go the Ceylon ~~insted~~ instead. I should very much have liked to see him & I think that he ~~my~~ may come on here even yet. It is a great relief to know that he is better for I don't know what this Bttn would do without him.

There seem to have been some big changes in the Cabinet this week, which must have caused a good deal of excitement at home. I am rather sorry that Winston Churchill has left the Admiralty for he was a good man for the job, but I suppose he has been interfering too much. Balfour will probably be a great help ~~for~~ he is very clever & the best man in the Conservative party, but Bonar Law is a useless sort of person. I should think that on the whole the Cabinet is very representative but where is Redmond? He surely should have represented the Irish party because the Irishmen have fought well & are doing their best in this war ~~like~~ & ~~any~~ have a perfect right to have a say in the management of affairs.

The people at Port Blair are rather interested in the doings of the 1ˢᵗ Munster Fusiliers who are at the Dardenelles because ~~they~~ the ~~ho~~ Irishmen were stationed here last year, only being moved when the territorials arrived here.

I am awfully glad that Mother is so much better but very sorry indeed to hear that Father has been having a bad time again. After having been free from those bad headaches ~~it is~~ for the last few months it is a great pity that they should have come on again & I ~~am~~ sincerely hope that Father will soon be quite himself again.

Please congratulate Bunna for getting a prize in the SS exam. I am sorry the others did not manage to get one but no doubt they all did their best.

I With very much love to all

> I remain
> Your affectionate Son
> Jim

P.S.Enclosed is a better photo of ~~thos~~ some of the men waiting for breakfast. They ~~have~~ had all just had a good wash after a long march & were feeling quite happy at the prospect of a good breakfast. The barracks are just at the back.

Port Blair
Andaman Islands

May 29th 1915

Dear Angus

Thank you very much indeed for all the letters you have sent me. Unfortunately I have been unable to answer them all but I always look forward to yours.

I am very glad indeed you are getting on so well with your violin : I suppose you will be able to play anything by the time we get back again. I was also glad to hear that you are getting on well at school. You did very well indeed last term but you must try & be 1st this term & then we shall see your name in the Magazine.

It is very sad news about the poor old pony for he has been a jolly good old fellow all these years, but I suppose you are all looking forward to getting a fresh one which will go rather faster. I shall never forget the night the old pony arrived – George, Andrew, Rapson & I went out in the orchard with a lamp to inspect him. Af Ask father if he remembers driving him to Ditcheat?

We are now in great hopes that the cooler weather is really coming for it has been raining hard this afternoon & it looks as if the rains were coming on in ern as earnest, although it may clear up again for a few days.

I have been hobbling about with a stick the last few days owing to an injured ankle. I had a smack on it while playing hockey & for a few days was rather painful but it is practically well now

Give my love & some kisses to Duff & tell him not to play too many tricks on the little girls as at school. I expect they find him a bit of a terror.

I hope you are quite well now – with love

from your affect. brother
Jim

P. S. Sorry to hear you did not get a prize in the Scripture exam – did you get a 1st class certificate?

2/4th Somerset L.I.
Port Blair
Andaman Islands

4th June 1915

Dear Mother & Father.

We are now patiently waiting for the rains, not because we like wet weather but because we hope that ᴉ it will be cooler when the monsoon starts. The latter is very late this year, for it has not yet arrived & it usually breaks with great regularity on May 16th. Things are already getting serious & we are running short of water. The men have been forced to use sea water for washing purposes for some time & the pool from which our bath water is fetched is almost a mud pool. All our drinking water is boiled, although on these islands the water is supposed to be fairly ~~dry~~. good.

You would be very amused if you could see us going out in stormy weather. A few paces in our rear a mullah (the name given to our convict servants) laden with umbrellas & coats walks along & as soon as there is a spot of rain he rushes up & tries to force us into our coats, partly because he wants to get rid of them & partly because he is afraid that his sahib will get wet in which case he gets into a row from the head servant. We all have a bearer or butler just as in India & then we are supplied with a certain number of Mullahs, the number varying with rank. A 2nd Lieut has one, a full Lieut has two, a captain 4 a Major 6 ~~six~~ & so on. The chief commissioner has about sixty & as we have to pay each one Rs 2 per month his servants' bill must be fairly considerable. As I told you in a previous letter my butler is a murderer. He has done two murders but in his country is is a very small offence. He is a great big Baluchi from the province of Sind & up there if a man is offended he at once tries to kill the offender & makes a feud against all his friends & ~~real~~ relations, just as they used to do in Scotland at the time of the clan feuds.

In a place of this sort you get a unique opportunity of seeing representatives of ~~practly~~ almost every tribe in India & there is a wonderful difference between the various races. I like the Pathans best of all. They are very fine looking, tall, bearded men & with their proud bearing you can always pick them out. They are not good workers but they ~~are a~~ have a marvellous way of making other people work. I am very friendly with one old fellow who is a billiard marker at the club & although he is a convict he practically runs the whole place. He used to be a soldier & is very keen to have a go at the Germans but I believe he is here because he tried to steal rifles in order to carry out a family feud.

There are a great many Burmese here but I don't like them at all. They are very light coloured & their features are very like those of a Chinaman They are very short & thick set & look absolute villains. They are however very clever indeed with their hands & do most beautiful carving & brass work & also work with mother of pearl & tortishell.

It is rather a difficult job to feed all the 1500 convicts for each caste & race eats different food. The authorities do their best for them & as far as possible they get their own class of food. The amount of rice which they eat is enormous & some of them eat of a good deal of meat & stuff called "ghi" made from rancid butter.

I have played a few games of tennis this week & on Monday evening I played at Government House. I have not been able to play hockey or football for my foot is still tender from a knock which I took last week while playing hockey.

Burt has been in bed with fever all the week, but he is better again now. There are still a few men down with it, and I think they will all have it before it is over. The sick parade is reduced from 46 to 25 as you can see there is a good deal of improvement.

There was no English mail for us this week as we had two week's letters from Madras last time, and we shall not get another for a fortnight as it will be a three weeks break. What a huge mail the next will be!!

I hope Mary is quite fit again & quite rec recovered from the effects of the dentist. I am awfully sorry she had such a bad time.

Andrew still seems to be very fit except for a graze on his leg. The climate at Wellington just suits him & has pulled him together – I think he found Bangalore very trying.

I was glad to hear last week that Mother is so much better & I hope Father is keeping fit. I didn't like to hear that he had been getting headaches again & I fear that he must have overdone it a little.

I suppose Duffy is getting very clever indeed by this time & I expect he will soon be able to look over Margaret's head if she does not make haste & grow. It was no surprise to hear that Ted is getting fat as we all know that she has a tendancy in that direction. What a man Bunna must be getting – I hope he will get through the Junior Oxford with 1st class Honours this year & also get his cricket colours. Angus must try & play a little cricket too for he was getting on quite well with it last year. I don't know if he will have time though, as I have no doubt that the violin takes up a good deal of his time.

With best love to all

I remain

Your affectionate son

Jim

P. S. I was glancing through the casualty lists in the Rangoon gazette & saw

the names of five Reading men who were at College with me, Two were killed, two wounded & one missing. One of the killed was Whittington who stroked our eight at Henley two years ago & he was without exception one of the finest fellows I ever met The missing one H. W. Hyde used to live almost next door to me at Wantage Hall & two years ago he was a colour sergt. in the O.T.C. The others were D Rosling & Huskinson wounded, & D Rich killed

2/4th Somerset LI
Port Blair
Andaman Islands

June 10th 1915

My dear Mother & Father.

There will boat which takes out these letters does not come back again till next week & she does not go out again for three weeks so do there will be no outward mail next week, but you will get a letter for the week after next. We are now in the middle of one of those periods when we get no mail for three weeks. For a fortnight no letters have arrived but next Thursday we shall get some more

I sh had some awfully good sport last Monday when I sailed in a race. The yacht club at Port Blair has a race every Monday afternoon & last time one of the fellows took me out in his boat. When we started it was blowing hard & a squall came up making the boats fairly rush through the water. It is marvellous to me how they can lean so far over without upsetting they seem to be travelling along on one side. After the squall had passed the wind dropped completely & all the boats were becalmed & with the exception of two had to be towed home. It is very remarkable how quickly the storms come up : you may be fairly sweltering away & longing for a breeze when suddenly without any warning it begins to blow quite hard.

We thought two days ago that the rains were coming up : the sky began to cloud over & the sea although apparently as smooth as a duck pond had a tremendous ground swell which made huge waves dash in on the rocks. This swell seemed to be coming up in advance of the wind, but it has gone again now & the weather is as hot as ever. When the sea is rough & the waves begin to get big you can hardly hear yourself speak in this bungalow owing to the noise they make on dashing in on the rocks just below.

We are doing very little work now for the men absolutely can't stand being out in the sun. I took them for a march one day last week & I thought I had killed one man. When we got back to the boat he went down like a log & for a time was very bad indeed. He was taken to the hospital & after a time got better but I have not taken them very far since for it gave me a bit of a fright. The fever is nearly all gone, no fresh cases having occurred for the last four or five days, & the men are generally much fitter than they were a month ago.

The Italians have made quite a good start in their campaign & if they get to work quickly the Russians will be on~~ on~~ the forward move again. I see that the latter have already taken the offensive again. They are marvellous people for sticking to their job & when they seem quite beaten off they come on harder than ever. Last night's telegrams said that the Russian fleet had done some damage to the German Baltic fleet but this remains to be confirmed – anyhow we all hope that it is true. I was ~~very~~ rather surprised when I saw the complete list of names ~~in~~ included in the Cabinet to see the name of Sir Edward Carson. In some ways it ~~shows~~ is a good choice & shows how completely party politics are put aside but in view of some of his speeches & actions ~~in~~ during the recent Irish question one almost felt inclined to doubt his loyalty. I suppose those responsible for his choice known best & the Cabinet as a whole is certainly very representative.

Away in this quiet spot it is difficult to realize that there is a war going on & it is only when you see the names of your own friends in the casualty lists that the seriousness of it comes home to you. I told you that W J Whittington has been killed & I am awfully sorry about it for he was a splendid fellow, one of the very best I have ever met. ~~I find~~ It is difficult to find much to write about for I have tried to describe the place & we do the same sort of things nearly every day.

I hoped to have had some photographs this week but they have not yet come back from the man who develops them so I will try & send some next time if they are any good.

I will try & write a letter to Duffy next time – tell him I hope he is getting on well up at School & is not too mischevious.

I hope you are all very well & feeling the benefit of the warmer weather. I am sure Mother will be better when it gets warm & dry & I think Father will also be better again if he does not do too much through the busy season.

With very best love to all

I remain
                    Your affectionate son
                              Jim

2/4th Somerset L.I.
Port Blair
Andaman Islands

June 22nd 1915

My dear Mother & Father.

As there was no outward mail last week I was unable to get off a letter so I suppose you are expecting a long one this week. There was a mail in last Saturday & we are expecting another to-night but the sea is so rough that ~~she~~ the boat will probably be very late & it is doubtful if she will be able to land the mail.

The monsoon has come at last & it is much cooler : in fact we can ~~sh~~ sleep with one sheet over us at night & ~~there is no~~ if we go for a walk it is possible to come in with a dry shirt if the pace has been fairly slow. This is a great improvement because formerly we could not stand a sheet at night & the slightest exertion made us sweat in streams.

The monsoon broke with a series of very violent thunderstorms – real tropical ones – & then yesterday the wind began to blow hard & the rain came down in sheets. The rain is not absolutely continuous but comes on in storms. These sweep across the sea & you can see them coming long long before they reach here for there is always a great wave in front of them which is heaped up by the wind. When the storms reach the land the roar of the wind & water is absolutely deafening & I like to go out to the point & watch them come up.

June 23rd I started this letter yesterday & left the sheets lying on the table with the result that two of them were missing this morning. A violent storm came on during the night & swept them out of the window. Last night we had a very big dinner party at the Club, & our noble selves being the hosts. We were entertaining all the people who have entertained us & our guests included the Chief Commissioner & his wife so we felt particularly honoured. I am going to Government House to-morrow to a birthday party in honour of Miss Douglas the Commissioner's daughter, & Flower & I are staying to dinner after the party is over.

One day last week I had an opportunity of seeing over the prison : I am glad to have been but it is not exactly a great treat. It consists of a central tower from which radiate seven long wings each three storeys high. The whole is surrounded by a big wall & at one end is the big gateway & the Suprintendant's house. There are cells for over 1000 prisoners but it is not quite full at present. The most remarkable thing about ~~the pr~~ it is, that with the exception of two white men the ~~who~~ place is managed by convicts.

All the assistants & gaolers are convicts and I am told that the system is remarkable efficient – the old saying "Set a thief to catch a thief". The spaces between the wings are occupied ~~wit~~ by workshops, baths, cookhouses, latrines & not least the gallows. I went into the latter & had a look at the apparatus but needless to say did not ~~try~~ test its ~~efficientcy~~ efficiency.

The prisoners were mostly engaged in manufacturing rope, matting, oil etc from coconuts, but some were making wickerwork furniture at which they are remarkably clever. Each convict has to do so much work ~~each~~ per day & if it is not done he is punished. One fellow undergoing punishment for refusing to work was handcuffed to a wall with his hands above his head so that he was obliged to stand & he was unable to move his feet because they were ~~fra~~ fixed by an iron bar. He was sentenced to stand in this position for ten days doing eight hours a day. They have a splendid device for stretching a man out previous to having a flogging but I did not see it in use (and I am not sorry for we saw some men recovering from this form of punishment).

The names of the convicts are sent up every six months & if they have behaved they are let out & are more or less free, but in spite of this some of them spend most of their lives in prison. One old man has spent the greater part of thirty years in solitary confinement & still seems very cheerful.

Such then is the prison : & having seen it I have no desire to become a convict either at Port Blair or elsewhere.

One very sad incident has happened since I wrote last namely one of our men died of malarial fever & blood poisoning. The poor fellow was only ill about three days & during that time his ~~tem~~ temperature twice reached 110°. We gave him a military funeral & did all that we could but it was very sad so far away from his home. The other men were very upset & for a few days were very unsettled & discontented with the place but they have somewhat settled down again by now.

Capt. Harford has been in bed the last few days but will be out again to-day. He first of all had an attack of ptomaine poisoning & this was followed by fever. Flower has also had a touch of fever but was only in bed three days. I am still very fit but am ~~wo~~ rather worried with prickly heat. It is a sort of rash which everyone gets in this climate owing to the excessive perspiration & its characteristic is that as soon as you begin to get hot it begins to prick just like thousands of needles. This is most annoying & decidedly painful & I have had rather a bad dose as my skin is naturally rather tender, but it will go away now that the cool weather has come.

Capt Harford Flower & I thought we would like to see what the country was like further inland so one day we had a carriage & drove inland for about seven miles. The country beyond the settlement is very pretty indeed & in places reminds one very much of England. ~~althoug~~ It is quite hilly & thickly wooded & the road such as it is runs between an avenue of ~~aca~~

accacia trees which give splendid shade. Every now & again there is a swamp ~~which~~ in which coconut trees grow but we hurried past these for they are very unhealthy.

The letters could not be landed last night but we have had them to-day & I have now got letters from Mother, Janet & Father in front of me. ~~for which~~ I am glad to hear that you are all well now for the whole family seems to have been poorly during the Winter.

I was very interested with ~~fa~~ Father's letter from Scotland & as I read it I followed him about from place to place in my mind. I hope the change did him a lot of good & that he will keep very fit all the Summer.

Will you please thank Janet for her letter & Angus for the one which was beautifully typewritten. Fancy Janet leaving school – I can hardly realize that she is so old. Mother will hardly know herself with three sons & a daughter more or less self supporting.

I don't know how the prices are running now but I should think Mother had a fairly good price for the lamb – It was very hard luck for poor little Duffy having to part with his lamb.

I heard from Andrew & John this week : both seem very fit especially Andrew who says he may have to return to Bangalore before long.

Enclosed you will find a petition I received from a native & which I thought would amuse you : it is about the funniest I have ever seen. Also I have enclosed a few photographs which are not very good. It is very difficult to get good ones here for the damp spoils the films & it is rather expensive having to send away for everything so I shall not take many while the rains last.

I see that for some reason the price of wheat has dropped suddenly, but can find nothing in the papers to explain it. However mother must be pleased to see it for I expect her housekeeping is rather expensive with such tremendous prices for everything. I also read this morning that they have ~~dec~~ at last decided to raise our pay. 2nd Lieuts. are to have an extra 2 rupees a day & Lieuts an extra rupee per day (ie 16^d) while the men are going to have 3^d per day more. As this increased rate is to take effect from the date of our landing we shall have a nice little sum to come.

Once more I hope you are all quite fit

With love to all

> from your affectionate Son
> Jim

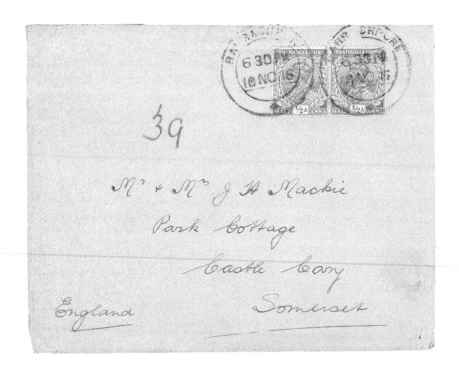

An envelope used by James Mackie to post correspondence home

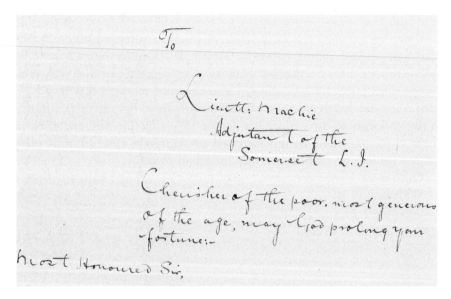

Enlarged view of letter address [opposite]

To

Lieutt: Mackie
Adjutant of the
Somerset L.I.

Cherisher of the poor, most generous
of the age, may God prolong your
fortune:-

Most Honoured Sir,

I most humbly, and respect-
-fully beg to submit the following lines
of my woe-begone condition before your
gracious honor for favourable consideration
and kind justice orders:-

That I was supplying eggs, and Bananas to
the men in the detachment barrack since less
1½ years, i.e eversince the manager stopped
The supply of the eggs, and was carrying
on the business without any complaint,
and by this source I was supporting myself,
childrens, wife and aged mother, as I had
no other either a temporary or a permanent
source of income:-

That your honor without finding
fault cancelled my pass and grant a
fresh pass to To.Sri Ram who was a contractor
of the Coffee-shop long ago but removed
for bringing a false civil suit against
the Sergtt: mess for Rs 200/- or 300/- and
eversince messrs: Dyer & Co: was addressed
to manage the Coffee-shop business:-

Sir, It would not be out of way
to mention that T. Sri Ram has no right
according to the recent order of the C.C and
Superintendent to get the egg supply-
-ing job when he is already employed
in the Drill Hall and drawing Rs 40/-

a month and also has a shop in the Ross market.

Sir, That the main object of my present-ing this petetion to your honor is because that my living was solely dependent only on the above trade which you may find out by perusing my petetion presented to Capt. Litt 4th H.S.L.I. together with the remarks of the Subdivisional Officer Ross and the Dy: Superintendent about my straitened circumstances who very kindly considering my case provided me with a pass as I was the first man applied for the job.

That your honour without giving any notice cancelled my pass and granted fresh passes to the wealthy men who can afford their maintenance by sitting in their shops and many other sources through their wealth but your honor I have given no cause about my being thrown in such a deepest sorrow that I cannot get rid of it without presenting the same before your honor for redressing. Sir I invoke your honors benevolence to rid us of it.

That I have got some food materials left back which I hope you would kindly allow me to dispose of in the barrack till Tuesday evening or I shall be put into a great loss as I cannot dispose them of no where else.

Under the above circumstances I most respectfully knock at the door of your honors mercy and solicit the favour of your indulgent mind to consider over my case favourably and extend your mercy and clemency by granting a fresh pass to me for starting the business or permit me to dispose of the food materials left back on account of passes being taken away without receiving any notice till Tuesday evening:—

And for which act of kindness I shall ever and ever pray that may God your age and fortune:-

I beg to remain
Honoured Sir,
Your most obedient Servant

Moula Baksh
O/13th June 1915

Moula Baksh
O/13th June 1915

To
Lieutt: Machie
Adjutant of the
Somerset L.I.

Cherisher of the poor, most generous of the age, may God prolong your fortune:-

Most Honoured Sir,

I most humbly and respectfully beg to submit the following lines of my woe-begone condition before your gracious honor for favourable consideration and kind justice orders:-

That I was supplying eggs and Bananas to the men in the detachment barrack since last 1½ years, i.e. eversince the manager stopped The supply of The eggs, and was carrying on the business without any complaint and by This source I was Supporting myself, childrens, wife and aged mother, as I had no other either a temporary or a permanent source of income:-

That your honor without finding fault cancelled my pass and grant a fresh pass to. T. Sri Rana who was a Contractor of the Coffee shop long ago but removed for bringing a false Civil Suit against the Sergtt: Mess for Ro 200\- or 300\- and eversince Messrs: Dyer & Co: was addressed to manage the Coffee shop business:-

Sir, It would not be out of way to mention that T. Sri Rana has no right according to the recent order of the C.C. and Superintendent to get the egg supplying job when he is already employed in the Drill Hall and drawing Ro 40\- a month and also has a shop in the Ross market.

Sir, That the main object of my presenting this petition to your honor is because that my living was solely dependent only on the above trade which you may find out by perusing my petetion presented to Captt. Litt 4th K.S.L.I. together with the remarks of the Sub Divisional Officer Ross and the Day: Superintendent about my straitened circumstances who very kindly considering my case provided me with a pass as I was the first man applied for the job.

That your honour without giving any notice cancelled my pass and granted fresh passes to the wealthy men who can afford their maintenance by sitting in their shops and many other sources through their wealth but your honor I have given no cause about my being thrown in such a deepest sorrow that I cannot get rid of it without my presenting the same before your honor for redressing. Sir I invoke your honors' benevolence to rid us of it.

That I have got some food materials left back which I hope you would kindly allow me to dispose of in the barrack till Tuesday evening or I shall be put into a great loss as I cannot dispose them of no where else.

Under the above circumstances I most respectfully knock at the door of your honor's mercy and policit the favour of your indulgent mind to consider over my case favourably and extend your mercy and clemency by granting a fresh pass to me for starting the business or permit me to dispose of the food materials left back on account of passes being taken away without receiving any notice till Tuesday evening:-

And for which act of kindness I shall ever and ever pray that may God your age and fortune:-

> I beg to remain
> Honoured Sir,
> Your most obedient servant
> Moular Baklish   Moular Baklish
> of 13th June 1915   of 13th June 1915

2/4th Somerset L.I.
Port Blair
Andaman Islands

July 3rd 1915

Dear Mother & Father.

There is so little happening here just at present that I hardly know what to write about this week. We were very lucky this week for the mail boat arrived without an English mail; but as we got ours because owing to having ones sent on from Bangalore they are a week later and therefore independant of the direct English mail to Rangoon.

The excitement of the week was centred around a concert which was given last night. It was run by the Government House people but several of our men took part. The whole thing has been kept very quiet & came as a pleasant surprise. You will probably think it funny to start a concert at half past nine nine in the evening but when one only gets two meals a day it is very important that dinner should not be interfered with. It did not finish till 12 O'clock so those men who attended th did not have to parade till 7–30 AM this morning, and as they were present to a man the officers did not turn out till 7–30.

The weather is quite nice now & much cooler. There are two or three hard storms every day but the intervals are very nice indeed owing to the breeze which blows strongly almost the whole time. Of course it is not cool like we get it at home but it is a great improvement on the hot weather.

The change is very marked on the men who have become much more cheerful & active. The sick parades are getting smaller & altogether they are already beginning to look better.

I received the papers Father sent me one giving a photo of Poulton & the other ~~giving~~ an account of the train disaster at Gretna.

The latter was an awfully bad business – it must have been very near Aitchinson Bank. It is rather strange that on the same page as that on which the account of the disaster is given ~~that~~ there should be one of the best pieces of news we have had lately namely the declaration of war by ~~Germany.~~ Italy. This should have a some tendency to bring the war to a close : but it looks at present as if it were ~~als~~ going to be a very long struggle. With things almost stationary in the West & the Russians retreating it does not look as hopeful as we all thought it would when the Spring campaign started. However I believe that the Russians have a definite end in ~~wie~~ view & that their retirement is part of a plan : also the case in the West is not so bad as it looks for the Allies are doing a ~~good~~ lot deal of good work, straightening the line & pushing back the German salients.

If only Greece would come in we should ~~make~~ get along faster in the Dardenelles – I think she will before long & may bring Rommania with her. It was very bad luck on the North Somersets getting as knocked about but they seem to have made a splendid fight. I am awfully sorry about poor Harry Warr & glad that Douglas Sims, Alec Clothier etc are only wounded.

I hope Bunna will manage to get into the School eleven & keep up the traditions of the family. His bowling seems to be quite effective but he must try & do something with his bat & not ~~allowed~~ the whole of West House to be bowled out for three. I am very fit indeed now & in excellent condition. All the soft fat disappeared months ago & I don't think I have ever been so thin in my life; but I am none the worse for that.

Capt. Harford's attack of fever gave him rather a bad time & he does not seem to be able to get fit again easily. I expect he will take a trip up to Rangoon next week just for a change of air.

I hope Father is quite well (– I fancy those headaches seem rather more frequent lately) & I hope that Mother is taking great care of herself & feeling quite ~~herself~~ well now.

With very much love to all

> I remain
> Your affectionate son
> Jim

2/4th Somerset L.I.
Port Blair
Andaman Islands

9/7/15

My dear Mother & Father

The most interesting event of last week was a field day we had on Tuesday. After weeks of almost total inactivity we thought we would take advantage of the cooler weather & go out to do some field work.

We started at 6–30 in the morning & crossed over to Aberdeen & then marched for five miles to a place we had previously decided upon. We The transport was in charge of the quarter master sergeant who had three bullock carts & a water cart. The plan was to halt for breakfast at the above mentioned place & then after a rest to do some field work returning for dinners about three. Then after a short rest we intended to march home & have tea at the barracks. As it happened events did not quite turn out like we anticipated.

The Q M Sergeant misunderstood where we were to halt & he pitched his things about two miles from the proper place & prepared a jolly good hot breakfast for the men. In the meantime we were waiting for our breakfasts & finding that they did not arrive sent a man back to see what happened to the transport. About two hours later we saw a procession of men carrying boilers & pans by hand & on hw we found when they got near that they were carrying the breakfast which had been cooked at the other place.

Instead of getting breakfast at 9–30 we had it at twelve which does not say much for the Army Service Corps of the "Andaman Expeditionary Force". However they provided a good feed & later in the day turned out a first class dinner consisting of stew & vegetables with rice pudding. It is an ill wind which blows no-one any good says the proverb & we found it quite true. It was fairly cool when we started & looked like being cloudy all day, but about 10 the clouds parted & the sun came out making it terribly hot, so that we did not mind waiting for breakfast as an alternative to working all day in the sun.

After breakfast we did a little field work in which the men put up a very good show & then returned to the bivouac for dinner; a short rest followed & then we marched home As I say it turned out to be very hot but it was a welcome change from what we have been doing lately.

The monsoon so far has been quite a failure in these islands & we have not had half the usual amount of rain. ꞮA most unusual thing has taken place the last few days for the weather suddenly cleared up & became frightfully hot. I am glad to say that we have had a heavy thunderstorm to-day which I hope will break up the weather again.

I was very pleased with your letters which arrived to-day but was very sorry to hear that german measles has entered the house, especially in the case of Rob who ~~wa~~ has an exam coming off soon. Tell him that I sincerely hope he will get through & if he does it will be all the more credit after having missed three weeks school. As a matter of fact I fully expect he will get 1st class honours & several distinctions if only to keep up the family reputation.

Several more men have got malaria so I have started to take precautions myself & am taking a little quinnine & sleeping under a net. So far I am awfully fit & don't want to get ill if I can help it.

This mail brought us some news from Bangalore which is very interesting although I don't know if it is strictly official. First of all the detachment at ~~Bangalore is~~ Malappuram is going to be relieved so John will be going back to Bangalore to ~~jon~~ join Andrew who has probably arrived there by this time. Then there is a report which says that 40000 troops are coming to India to relieve the Territorials gradually. It says that the 1st Wessex Division are to go home in September to go either to France or the Dardenelles & that the 2nd Wessex Division are to move up North to replace them & to do Brigade & Divisional training ~~so~~ in order that they may be relieved in the Spring say about February. This means that our detachments will be recalled to headquarters in ~~ab~~ two or three months & that we shall go to the North which will be quite a nice change.

Tell Edith that I am glad to hear that her young man has decided to enlist for it will do him ever so much good & I don't suppose she will carry out that awful threat – – Please thank Angus for his ~~ty~~ newspaper which was beautifully typewritten & will be very useful for information & reference.

I was very interested in ~~N~~ "Henry's" letter giving an account of the accident – she seems to have found a rather unexpected outlet for all her Red Cross knowledge.

I shall have to stop now but will carry on again next week.

I hope the measles people are all better by this time & hope that ~~Fa~~ you are both quite fit

With love to all

> Your affectionate son
> Jim

2/4th Somerset L.I.
Port Blair
Andaman Islands

16/7/15

My dear Mother & Father

For the first time since I came to Port Blair I have slept a night off Ross Island, & although I was only away one night it made a very welcome change.

I arranged to go and spend last Wednesday ~~on~~ night on ~~V~~ an island called "Viper" which is about the same size as Ross but much further up the harbour. It so happened that we had another field day on Wednesday so ~~I met the~~ when I came back from the march I met the fellow with whom I was staying Chitham by name on the hockey field & we went across together.

The field day was not very enjoyable owing to the weather. We marched out five miles as before, & had our breakfasts. Then it started to rain & we all got wet through so we were unable to do much work. It was frightfully hot – not a breath of air going – and we were all thoroughly uncomfortable. As soon therefore as the men had finished their dinner we marched back again. As I said before I did not cross to Ross but played hockey & then walked another two miles to a pretty little harbour where we were met by a boat which took us to Viper. By that time I was very tired but a good dinner put things right & I went to bed feeling very fit.

We were up early in the morning and from the bungalow where I was staying I saw some of the finest views I have ever seen. Unlike Ross which is triangular Viper is almost round & rises very steeply to a point on which the bungalow stands. It is the only large bungalow on the island & with the exception of a couple of subordinate officers the accupant is the only white man living on the island. From the windows ~~of~~ whichever way you looked there was a magnificent view the one down the harbour being exceptionally fine. As soon as we had ~~our~~ finished our ~~tea~~ early ~~morning tea~~ we set off to the Andamanese home, & we were very fortunate because there were a great many in. They had returned from a hunting expedition & were resting a few days before going out again. The head man of the tribe had come in from North Andaman to visit the home & he was delighted when we gave him a cheeroot. I have described ~~them~~ these little people before so will not trouble to do so again. They gave us a shooting exhibition with their bows & arrows & it ~~was~~ is marvellous ~~the way~~ how accurate they are with them & also the distance they can shoot. Considering how small they are they are wonderfully strong for I had great difficulty in drawing back the arrow ~~when on the bow~~ in order to shoot but they do it with the utmost ease.

After the shooting they danced for us but I am afraid we did not understand what they were trying to do. The music was provided by the women who sat down in a row & sung, or rather, wailed & clapped their hands keeping perfect time. All the performers were rewarded ~~by~~ with a cheeroot which pleased them very much for they are very fond of tobacco. Before we left by way of a finale they had some races. They run quite well considering their size but seem to have no idea of starting. After the signal to start has been given th it takes a second or two for them to realize it & then one starts. The others then seem to wake up ~~with a st~~ and another will go off & so on.

After we left the Andamanese we went back to viper & had a look at the workshops where they make things out of mother of pearl & tortishell & then went back to the bungalow for breakfast.

We received no letters this week as the English mail was very late at Rangoon & shall not have another mail for the next fortnight. I don't like these long gaps at all, but am getting used to them now. It is much better to have letters regularly once a week than to have a whole lot after a break of three weeks.

This is a most remarkable year as far as the monsoon is concerned & people who have been here 30 years ۸ cannot remember a similar one. Instead of rough cool weather with a great deal of rain we are having very still weather & it is frightfully hot. We have had some storms lately but they have not really been very severe & the rainfall is already 50′′ below the average. I daresay we shall get more than enough a little later on.

The men on the whole are much better now but there are still a few cases of malaria. Starting next week they are all going to be dosed with quinnine every Monday & Tuesday which I hope will prevent any further cases.

I have just returned from dinner at Government House & Flower & I have promised to go for a picnic to-morrow. ~~We.~~ We are to go to the top of Mount Harriet which is the highest point in South Andaman being 1200 feet high. I am told that it is ۸ glorious up at the top & always several degrees cooler than down below on Ross.

I hope that when I get another letter that I shall hear that the Germans have retreated from Park Cottage taking the measles with them. I do hope Bunna will ~~not~~ find that he has not lost much ground while away from school & that he will get through the Oxford with 1st class honours.

I hope ~~you~~ all are ~~all~~ well again & both ~~of y~~ Father & Mother keeping very fit. As it is nearly 12 midnight & I have to be up at 5–15 AM. I will stop for to-night

With very best love to you all

Your affectionate son
Jim

2/4th Somerset L.I.
Port Blair
Andaman Islands

22/7/15

My dear Mother & Father.

Do not expect a letter next week as there will be no outward mail. The mail boat comes in bringing three weeks letters but she does not go out till the following week when I will try & write a long letter to make up.

I have had rather a good time the last few days for there have been some visitors up staying up at Government House & Flower & I have been requisitioned nearly every day for purposes of ammusement. One one or two days we dined there, on another day we went to an "at Home" & yesterday & to-day there have been picnics. You see Flower & I are the only reasonably young fellows in the settlement so we hence the sudden demand.

Our picnic yesterday was rather exciting. We were going to a place called Corbyn's Cove, an awfully pretty little bay about three miles down the coast. The Chief Commissioner had his launch ready & we started off. At this time of the year there is always a very heavy monsoon sea running but yesterday it was particularly bad owing to a heavy storm which had passed over. As soon as we got outside the harbour we were fairly in for it. I have never seen a boat so tot tossed about for at one minute her bows were right out of the water & then she suddenly dipped into a huge trough & a great ten foot wave crashed down on the deck. Two or three of the people were soon jolly bad & as it got worse & worse we turned back. I was awfully pleased because that I did not feel the least bit sick & was able to laugh at the unfortunates the whole time. We did not go home but went to the pavillion in the Gymkhana ground where we had tea after which rounders etc we played rounders etc till dark.

This afternoon we are going up the harbour & land the other end & then I don't quite know where we are going but I probably shall not finish this letter till we come back & will add a note at the end.

Last Sunday Flower & I spent the day with Capt Rowlandson who is the in command of the Police here. In the evening we walked to Corbyn's Cove by over the land & had a bathe. It is a delightful spot reminding me very much indeed of the little bay to which Tom Warren took Father & I when we were in Guernsey. The walk was awfully nice : we crossed quite a steep ridge of hills & then came down a long steep valley to the sea. It was very nice going down but it was a different matter when we had to go up again.

I am awfully glad to say that we are all jolly fit now: there are only two men left in the hospital and I hope they will be out again in a few days. Capt Harford thinks of taking a trip to Rangoon before long so if he does I shall be left here in charge : but when he returns I am hoping to be able to go up & have a look at the place ~~as one or two people have~~

23rd July We had quite a nice trip yesterday to the tea gardens. First of all we went up the harbour in a launch & then got ~~out~~ into a smaller one which took us a long way up a long winding creek. Each side of us there was a big mangrove swamp : but just beyond the steep wooded hills seemed to close us right in. At the end of the creek we landed on a little jetty & found some little trollys waiting for us. There was room for two in each trolly & each was pushed by two two convicts. The trollys ran on an awfully well laid little railway & down hill we travelled at a great speed, but I felt awfully sorry for the poor unfortunate convicts who had to push us up hill & along the level.

The country was glorious – I can hardly describe it. Along the railway there were rows of bamboos which grow to a great ~~hight~~ height but are beautifully graceful. Beyond, the hills ran along each side & wooded gullies ran down into the valley in which there is a rubber plantation. The whole is as green as can be & now that we have had some rain the little streams have all got plenty of water & look awfully fresh & cool.

We went about five miles on the trollys & then got off to have tea, after which it was too late to go any further because the place is infested with snakes & malaria so we wanted to get back before dark. The tea gardens were about a mile further on so we did not see the tea growing but I hope to go there again later on. The monsoon was very strong early in the week & we had some very rough weather indeed but it is much finer again to-day & it looks as if it is clearing up again.

I have not heard from John or Andrew lately owing to there being no mail but I suppose that both are quite fit.

I hope you are all well at home now – am fairly looking forward to next Friday to get a letter again. I expect Father & Uncle are very busy now for this ~~us~~ is usually the busy time but I don't ~~se~~ suppose there will any shows again this year & that will make things easier.

This is quite a long letter so I will stop till next time & just write a line to John.

With best love to all

Your affectionate son
Jim

I hope Mother is keeping very fit this Summer.

2/4th Somerset L.I.
Port Blair
Andaman Islands

July 31st 1915

My dear Mother & Father.

I am starting this letter to-day but as there is no outward mail this week, shall add to it during next week & send it off a week to-day. Since my last letter the monsoon has been blowing at full strength & I am just beginning to realize what people mean when they say that they don't like travelling by sea during the monsoon. We have had torrents of rain & the wind has been blowing a gale the whole time. The sea is a fine sight now for after all this wind the waves are enormous & it is a magnificent sight watching them roll in on the rocks.

The mails should have arrived two days ago but according to the latest information the boat has not left yet left Rangoon owing to the rough weather, & this means that she will not reach here for at least another two days. I thought therefore I had better start writing some letters or else I shall have so to answer four weeks' mail in about two days.

It is much cooler with this wind blowing & we the men seem ever so much better. They were in very good spirits yesterday for I paid them each of them just over 20 rupees, this being the extra 3^d per day which has just been granted & which is due from the 1st of April.

Flower & I thought we would practice revolver shooting last night so we fitted up a very novel range. We went down to the rocks & fic fixed up a target & shot out to sea, so that there was no possible danger of shooting anything but sharks. Neither of us were very brilliant but we managed to get a few bulls & with a bit more practice I daresay we could make sure of a German twenty five yards away. We might have done a good deal better only Miss Douglas & her cousin turned up soon after we started & as both wanted to shoot we had to give them a lesson & that rather put us off.

Aug. 4th Imagine how pleased I was when, on looking out of over the harbour this morning just as I woke up, I saw the mail boat lying at anchor. She had arrived during the night after a very bad voyage & was just a week late, so that it was just a month ago that we had our last mail. She had two English mails on board & there is another boat due in from Calcutta the day after to-morrow which will bring two more. I enjoyed reading your letters very much indeed & was awfully glad to hear that the measles patients are all well again. When me I read in Mo all about how nice Park Cottage is looking I could just imagine you all strolling round the garden in the dusk on a cool August evening, & then coming in to a good sa supper of bread & cheese & salad. And then some other sentence made me think of it in the morning withthesun just rising over the Hill & pouring into your bedroom : The the lawn covered with dew & the ramblers, & the fresh flowers in the beds all came into the picture & made it seem so beautifully cool. This is a lovely spot & I think it prettier every time I go out but one never has that splendid fresh, vigourous feeling which you have when you come downstairs in the morning at home.

All the letters this week seem to agree that you are having a very dry time & want rain badly. Of course if the rain drought continues the cheese will be very short : but I am glad that they you are busy at the stores & hope you are having a really good season

Monday was August Bank Holiday and although it is not recognised as a military holiday we gave our men a day off. We secured a special launch & I took them over to the Andamanese home. Unfortunately most of the Andamanese were away in the jungle but those who were left seemed to amuse the men very much. They showed us a live turtle which they had captured & were keeping for some reason or other. He was a huge fellow : I had no idea that a turtle was such a big beast.

Acting under instruction from Rangoon, instead of parades to-day the troops & in fact the whole Settlement attended divine service owing to the fact that the war has lasted just a year. It was rather an impressive service & especially so when we think of all the splendid fellows who have been killed. I saw in one of the casualty lists yesterday the name of A. N. Scott of the Berkshires. He was a great friend of mine at Reading & rowed three in the eight last year – you wil find him in the photo of the eight which is in the dining room.

Aug 7th. The Calcutta mail arrived yesterday but something seems to have gone wrong with our letters for none came through from Bangalore. Flower had none at all but I got one which Father sent straight here dated July 15th. The latest letter I had by the other mail was one from Janet dated June 16th & now I have one from Father dated July 15th, so that all the intervening ones have still to come.

Janet says that Mother sen has sent off my suit of clothes & some stockings & Fathers letter says that another parcel contains shirts & soft collars. Thank you for sending both; but they have neither arrived yet but no doubt will do so next week. I shall be glad of all the things for my clothes begin to want some renewing.

I am delighted to hear that Father has at last found a doctor who is really doing him good & shall hope to hear in a few weeks that he had effected a complete cure.

I have only had five days leave since I joined this Bttn so Capt. Harford & I are going up to Rangoon in the same boat as this letter just to have a few days change. We leave here to-morrow evening (Sunday) & arrive in Rangoon Tuesday morning. The boat leaves again early on Thursday morning so we shall have to do all our sight seeing as quickly as possible. I will tell you all about it when I write next & hope to be able to get some postcards for you all in Rangoon. I ~~expect~~ don't expect I shall enjoy the voyage very much for the sea is very rough now but I am very keen on having a look at Rangoon.

I think this is almost enough for to-day for if I write much more you will tired of reading it. Please thank Janet for her letter. I hope you are all very well indeed now : I ~~af~~ am afraid that Mother must have been very busy when the measles were in the house, & I hope that she will not work too hard now that the fruit perserving is in progress. I am still quite fit & enjoying life much as usual.

With best love to all

> I remain
>> Your affectionate son
>> Jim

2/4th Somerset L.I.
Port Blair
Andaman Islands

Aug 12th 1915

My dear Mother & Father

At last I have got my letters from home up to date. ~~They~~ There was no English Mail for most of the people but all our back ones turned up & I have got over twenty letters including four from ✗ you which have been lying about in the post for the last few weeks. It is awfully nice to get some news from you again for it is rather disappointing when the boat comes in week after week & brings no letters. The effect is very marked in the case of the men : if they get their letters they are as happy & cheerful as possible but if the✗ mail does not come they go on parade in a very half-hearted sort of way & for the whole week ~~it~~ you can get very little out of them.

I told you last week that I was going to take a trip to Rangoon : I have been & returned to-day. We left port Blair at noon last Sunday & were moored to the ~~warfe~~ wharf at Rangoon early Tuesday morning. I was awfully interested in everything I saw going up the river. I did not wake till we were about 10 miles up the river when we were stopped by the officials of the examination boat who examine all boats to see that there are no Germans on board. After waking I went on deck to look round & was amazed at the size of the river. The Thames is the biggest river I have ever seen but this was a broad waste of yellow water probably two miles wide fringed on each side with mango swamps & low lying paddy ~~swamps~~ fields

As we went up the city gradually emerged out of the mist & we could make out the golden top of the pagoda ~~shingn~~ shining splendidly as the rising sun struck it.

Just below Rangoon the Pegu river joins the Irrawaddy & at the junction there is a big bar. The officers of our boat were afraid that we should be too late to get across before the tide went out in which case we should have had to wait till the next tide but luckily we were just in time & so were able to pass up to our moorings which we reached about ~~6.3~~ 7 AM. There is a tremendous lot of shipping on the river at Rangoon: some of the ships are moored to the side but ~~som~~ many of them are tied to buoys in mid stream so that you have to pass up between two lines of big ships.

We happened to know ~~a man~~ the suprintendent of the telegraphs of Burma (because he came to Port Blair a few weeks ago & lived at the mess) who lives in Rangoon & he met us & took us all round in his motor before breakfast. It was very lucky for us that he did so for our stay in Rangoon was unexpectedly cut very short. We were supposed to wait for the English mail which was due to arrive on Thursday afternoon, but late Tuesday night a message came to the Post Office to say that Port Blair M mails had gone to Madras. It was therefore useless ~~to~~ for our boat to remain in Rangoon so we received a telephone message from the chief officer early Wednesday morning to say that the boat would sail at noon. Of course we were very annoyed but had to make the best of it.

After breakfast ~~we~~ Tuesday morning we went into the city & bought some things which we wanted & then had a look round. In the afternoon we ~~hav~~ went over the Shwe Dagon Pagoda which is the most famous sight in Rangoon. It is a marvellous affair but Burma is the land of pagodas & I believe there are even finer ones at Mandalay & other Burman cities. It stands on a hill about 160' high which rises out of the centre of the city & you get up to it by means of flights of broad steps. ~~Up~~ Thousands upon thousands of people pass up & down these steps every day as they go up & come away from their worship of Buddah. It is marvellous to stand & watch them all passing up & down & it is an awfully picturesque sight. The Burmans both male & female wear very bright clothes which are made mostly of silk. The priests are easily distinguished because they wear the characteristic yellow robes. Besides Burmans however there are crowds of Chinese & ~~Japa~~ a few Japanese who also go up to worship Budda

The pagoda consists of a tall central tower terminating in a bellshaped dome & all around the base are hundreds of shrines each of which contain an image of Budda. The shrines & the lower part of the central tower are all covered with gold leaf but the upper part of the tower is covered with plates of pure gold & studded with marvellous jewels which are supposed to be without value.

The images in the shrines are are also very wonderful – some are of gold, some are of silver, some of brass & others of marble, ~~while~~ some are of a huge size, while others are quite small. The people choose out their own particular favourite & pray to it & make offerings & burn candles etc & there seems to be room for everyone.

Away in one corner fenced in are the graves of the British officers who were killed while storming the pagoda when the British took Rangoon & in – I forget the date – ~~ak~~ ask Janet!

~~To contin~~ We went to see some pictures on Tuesday evening & intended going out round the town on Wednesday but our hurried departure prevented this.

I rushed off to the dentist to have a tooth out before leaving & I am still suffering from the effects of that extraction. It was a huge thing like the one I had out at Swanage but I had cocaine this time. It did not pain much coming out but I have had an awfully bad time since. My face, throat & neck have all been swollen & the first day I could hardly swallow or speak while the pain was very bad. ~~This~~ It is now three days ago since I had it our & although the pain & swelling are nearly gone it is still giving me trouble but I hope that to-morrow I shall be quite fit again. I seem to have bad luck when I have my teeth out but I don't think this was the fault of the dentist for the tooth came out fairly well.

I never realized till I left Rangoon ~~how~~ the power of a big river. We left Rangoon at noon and at six o'clock when it began to get dark the water was still yellow & I was told that the sea was not properly blue again till we were about 90 miles from the mouth of the river. Although our stay was so short I was very glad to get a bit of a change for one gets a little stale after living many months in a place like this. I see in Janet's letter that she wants to know something about the monsoon. This is probably the most critical monsoon India has ever had for if it is a failure the agitators will get to work & tell the people that God is angry with the English & has therefore stopped the monsoon thereby causing a famine : this will mean very serious trouble in India. So far the rainfall has been fairly average in many places but the Punjab is very short & people out here are ~~all~~ already getting afraid that there will be trouble up there in a month or two if the rain does not come.

I am awfully glad to hear that you are all quite well & hope that the Birmingham doctor will be able to cure those bad headaches which ~~father~~ Father gets.

I received my parcel containing a suit of clothes & two pairs of ~~socks~~ stockings yesterday. Thank you very much indeed for sending them on.

Except for the tooth trouble I am very fit & the men are also better although there are just a few cases of malaria in the hospital.

If the war does not go on faster in the near future I doubt if we shall be home to help eat all that jam which mother is making : it looks at present as if we shall spend another Xmas in India.

With love to all

> I remain
>> Your affectionate son
>> Jim

2/4th Somerset L.I.
Port Blair
Andaman Islands

Aug 21st 1915

My dear Mother & Father

Although the clock has just struck II. P.M. I must make a start with this letter to-night or I shall not be able to get it off to-morrow. I am rather busy just at present for Flower is in bed with fever & I am doing his work for him. ~~All of~~ If he had not been ill we should be very busy for we are making arrangements for the reception of the rest of the Battalion which will be coming here in a few days. The fact is they were expecting a bit of trouble here so ~~they~~ the others are coming ~~by se~~ to reinforce us, but do not be alarmed for precautions have been taken which most probably have stopped any trouble there might have been before it had time to develop. There is a little man of war lying at anchor in the bay which makes us feel very secure : & which provides us all with someone fresh to talk to.

I shall be very glad to see John & Andrew again for I have seen neither for seven months : but in one way I would sooner the whole Battalion were not coming for it does away with our independence Instead of being a separate unit we shall be only a small part of a larger unit & there will be all the senior officers to order us about. ~~The~~ However it will be good to see them all again & hear about what they have all been doing. Beyond the fact that we have had plenty to do there ~~is~~ has not been much of interest that I can tell you about this week. On Thursday evening we had a very grand concert to which the whole settlement turned out. Several of our men took part & it really was an awfully good show. The people in a place like this have not much to do so they can spend plenty of time rehearsing etc & we therefore have some really good entertainments from time to time.

We have been saying all along that the rainfall has been remarkably short this year but it now seems to be making a determined effort to pull up. Yesterday it rained almost unceasingly the whole day & to-day although not quite so incessant it has been very ~~hae~~ heavy. It simply comes down in sheets when it does come & if you happen to be out in it you are wet through in a very few minutes. We are not doing many parades now for most of the men are doing guards : it will be a good thing when the others arrive in this respect for of course the men are now getting very little sleep at night.

I received the parcel containing my suit & the stockings quite safely last week & I expect the other on will be here by this mail, but I shall not know till after this letter has gone.

Aug 22ⁿᵈ The mail has just arrived & brought me a letter from Mother which I was delighted to receive. It is awfully good of the Cary people to get up the fete at Florida for our men & I know that they will appreciate it ⟍ very much indeed. As a matter of fact they are rather better off now for they are getting 3ᵈ a day extra & it is a great help to them.

I am afraid this is not a very long letter but there is no more news this week, ~~and~~ I Andrew sent me on a letter from Father & I am so pleased to hear that he really is getting quite well. I hope you are all keeping well & have not found the hot weather too trying. I shall not know if the other parcel has come till to-morrow.

With very best love to all

    Your affectne son
     Jim

**Port Blair
Andaman Islands**

27/8/15

My dear Mother & Father

Once more ~~I~~ the mail boat has arrived without an English mail which means no letters for three weeks as there is no inward mail next week. I have therefore no letter to answer & shall have to content myself by giving you what little news there is about Port Blair. To-day I saw John & Andrew for the first time since the middle of January & as you can imagine we were all exceedingly pleased to see each other. Both were looking very fit ~~es~~ especially Andrew:- I don't think I have ever seen him looking so well for he ~~is~~ has got a good colour & ~~is in~~ has filled out quite a lot. John has not grown fatter but he is looking very well.

Of course, we knew they were coming about three weeks ago, but they turned up unexpectedly this morning. The Port Officer at Madras did not wire to say that they had left Madras so we naturally concluded that they were still there. We were therefore very surprised when we saw a large liner coming in this morning. We have had a tremendous rush the last fortnight getting ready to receive them & we were not quite ready to-day : so they are staying on board for a day to enable us to put the ~~fin~~ finishing touches to their ~~improverased~~ improvised barracks. Port Blair is not like other stations for you can't get things at a moments' notice : It takes at least a week to get anything from Rangoon, & when they arrived to-day there was no food in the place for them. However this difficulty was solved by the appearance of the boat from Rangoon loaded with supplies. There has never been such a large number of troops in Port Blair before & I don't know how we shall manage to get enough milk butter etc : which supplies are only sufficient for the usual population of the place.

They had a very rough passage from Madras owing to the very heavy monsoon sea which was ~~sk~~ striking the ship broadside on. No doubt they will tell you all about it in their letters.

I have a bit of good news to tell you, namely that I was gazetted Lieut on July 27th. I did not know it till two days ago when I came across ~~the~~ my name in the ~~time~~ "Times" quite accidentally. I was having breakfast with the deputy Suprintendent, & after breakfast he gave me some papers to read in one of which I came across the London Gazette with my name in it. Royal has also got his second star dated from the same day.

29th Aug. The troops all landed yesterday, except B Company who stayed on board to clear up, & we had a very strenuous day getting them into barracks. Andrew's Company is stationed on Aberdeen so he will live over there in a big bungalow with the rest of the officer's of his Coy. & those of D Coy. John's & my Companies are both stationed on Ross but we are not living in the same bungalow.

The parcel containing shirts collars & chocolate arrived by the last mail quite safely. I was rather surprised to find the chocolate in such splendid condition for I thought the heat would have spoiled it. Thank you very much for all the things : I am going to get ~~the~~ John & Andrew up to my bungalow presently to share the ~~chola~~ chocolate.

Enclosed are some photographs of the Andamanese which ~~N~~ Flower took when we went over to visit them. They are awfully good & give you a good idea of what they are like.

Later. My bungalow is no full of officers who absolutely refuse to let me write any more (one of them is my brother John). Having eaten all the food & drunk all the liquid in the bungalow they are now very pleased with life & quite content with Port Blair.

I hope you are all quite well at Park Cottage : I ~~also hope~~ expect that the cheese business has almost doubled it profits since Janet was installed in the office.

With best love to you all

Your affectionate son
Jim

2/4th Somerset L.I.
2nd Wessex Division
C/o Port Blair
India

1/9/15

My dear Mother & Father

There is something wrong with the mails lately : the letters are getting through very badly. India had one from Father to-day written from B'ham, but John had none at all & as I have not seen Andrew to-day I don't quite know how many he had. We are not the only ones who have suffered however for all the officers & al men are complaining that they have had practically no letters for the last three weeks : they will come through in a lump some time or other.

There is not much news this week for nearly every day has been occupied in watching the rain which has been torrential. Two nights ago we had eight inches of rain during the night so you can just imagine what it was like. The storm is now passing away & I expect it will be fine to-morrow. We have not seen much of Andrew for the rain has kept him on Ross but John & I have been out for a run or something of the sort nearly every day just to keep fit & in good condition.

The telegrams have been awfully good this week – the British seem to have made a very good progress in the West & the Russians have at last started to come back again. I hope this is the beginning of great things for the allies so that the war may be finished off before long.

We hear to-day that there is some trouble with the Moplahs over on the West coast again – it shows that they want the "Somersets" back there again to keep them quiet.

Last Tuesday I had my first experience of being on guard as an officer. Most guards are commanded by a sergeant but we have a very big guard over the wireless station & they have decided that it is to be an officer's guard in future. It was not a very good night for a start as it was raining in torrents & we we all wet through in a very short making it decidedly uncomfortable during the rest of the night. We are not allowed to take off anything not even our belts & swords.

I am glad to hear that you have got such a fine litter of pigs – if they all do well they ought to make a jolly good price. I should think the little farm was paying fairly well now with a good price for eggs & a good price for pigs, butter etc, but I agree with you that it will be rather expensive to have to buy fodder for two cows all through the Winter. I hope little Duffy has quite recovered from his accident & is now as active as ever. I should like to hear one of his sermons – no doubt he is quite a rival to Mr Parsons.

Hoping you are all well

>   With much love
>   From your affectionate son
>   Jim

2/4th Somerset L.I.
Port Blair
Andaman Islands

2/9/15

My dear Mother & Father

Although there is no mail this week we have not missed it as much as usual, for ~~hav~~ we have had all the other fellows to talk to & all their news to listen to. Of course we three have had lots to talk about & many experiences to relate. It seems so funny that last year at this time we had seen only a very small part of England, yet now we meet after being separated for eight months & we have all travelled many thousands of miles & seen things which only a short time ago we read about in books & never hoped to see. It is awfully nice to have Andrew & John here again : they come up to my bungalow nearly every afternoon & proceed to eat everything I ~~have~~ can produce & then we sit round & talk. I am just going to begin to get my own back & this afternoon am going to have tea with John while to-morrow I hope to demolish some of Andrew's supplies.

Andrew has become a great man having spent the hot weather at Wellington among the élite of Southern India : I must say he has improved wonderfully in every way

The advent of the ~~bat~~ Battalion at Port Blair has not been ~~an~~ an unmixed blessing however from our point of view at anyrate. Among other inconveniences we have to turn out of our barracks & bungalows which we have occupied for five months & go over to the mainland in order to let another company take our place. The men have felt it very keenly because they took a great pride in their barracks & it goes against the grain to see another company come in & take them over while they have to go over the other side where they have not even got beds to lie on. Of course there are reasons for the move & things will settle down again but just at present they are rather sore about it.

Since the others arrived we have been bathing ~~every~~ every day & John & Andrew are learning to swim in great style. I can swim quite well now & they are getting on splendidly. On Wednesday there was an "At Home" at Government House which was attended by all of us : in fact it was arranged in order to save everyone from making the usual call. I think the above event comprises the whole of Port Blair news for the week that is it was the only event out of the ordinary run of things.

John & I have just been playing tennis but Andrew is orderly officer & could not come out. We were stopped by a storm of rain which I think marks the end of the ~~few~~ fine weather which we have had during the last few days.

I really ought to write to Janet & Mary this week for both have written letters, which are unanswered but I am rather busy just now & I really have nothing to write about except what I put in this letter.

I have seen several of the Cary fellows about but have not yet come across ~~we~~ Weeks. Douglas Milton is much better than when I saw him last at Calicut – he is fairly fit now.

I hope we shall hear next mail how Bunna got on in his exam & we are all expecting great things from him. Of course Sunny Hill School will be re-opening just about now and I suppose Janet will be found wanting her place in the pony trap being taken by little Tibbie. I very well remember driving Teddy along the Cole road on her first morning at school. I don't think she has grown much in height since then but no doubt she has become very wise (& also very rotund).

I hope you are all keeping well & I hope Father is quite fit again now. ⸲ Now that the cooler weather is coming on again Mother will have to be very careful we don't like her to be as poorly as she was last Winter : ~~But~~ but then of course Janet is home now

With much love to you all

        Your affectionate son
          Jim

Port Blair
Andamans

8/9/15

My dear Mother

Very many happy returns of your birthday & every good wish for another year.

I sincerely hope that you will keep free from sickness & have a much better Winter than you did last year.

We cannot get presents very well in Port Blair so a week or two ago we asked Father to get you a nice thick warm motoring coat so that you will not catch cold when you go our motoring. I hope you will be able to get one that you like & one that will be really useful to you.

Well Mother! w I wonder when we shall be back to see you again. The war does not seem to be over yet & there is a good deal of fighting still to be done, but still I think when we get back again we shall find that our soldiering has done us a great deal of good in many ways.

I am sending you some regimental buttons which you will be able to have made up into broaches. They have travelled round with me & have been in every station to which I have been sent.

Once more many happy returns of Nov 10th

from your affectionate son
Jim

2/4th Somerset L.I.
Port Blair
Andaman Islands

8/9/15

My dear Mother & Father

I think to-day has been the wettest ↓ day I have ever experienced. It started to rain at 3 a.M. this morning & went on unceasingly till about half past five this evening : the whole time it simply came down in sheets as if we had had no rain for months. As a matter of fact for the last fortnight our sole occupation seems to have been watching the rain. The rainfall for the month of September was 25′′ but for the whole year we are still about 40′′ below the average.

John is out to-night being on guard at the wireless station. ~~The w~~ An officer is on guard up there every night with the men & it has been anything but pleasant lately. I had my turn about a week ago & Andrew will be on to-morrow night. Your letters arrived to-day and we were very pleased indeed to see them. I can imagine how anxiously you waited to hear where we had gone & I should have wired to let you know but the censor would not let it pass. For all we know our letters are censored every week now – at anyrate we have to put them in a separate bag & are not allowed to post them at the post office.

I am awfully glad to hear that little Duffy is better. He must have had a very bad time but we knew that would be very brave & patient – a real Mackie in fact.

I have just come in from a ride which I took as soon as the rain stopped. I have hired a pony off the police for Rs 15 i.e. 1£ £1 per month and I get a for that amount the pony is fed & I get the use of a syce. It is rather a good opportunity to improve my riding especially as the pony is rather a lively fellow & takes quite a lot of managing. Every time I go out on him I think of old Bunna for strangely enough the pony's name is Robin.

Father seems tho to have had quite a good price for the pigs – if only you could get 2/6 per dozen for eggs you would be doing a great business. it seems so funny that while they are such a price at home out here the usual price of eggs is 3 for a penny.

The wet weather has rather interfered with our work & also with our exercise because the ground is too wet for games. We therefore have been going in for cross country runs. We set off about 4–30 & go for a good long run getting covered in mud from head to foot & absolutely wet through. A good hot bath removes the dirt & we then feel very much fitter & I believe the exercise keeps off fever.

Now that we are together again we should be delighted with the truckle which Father has promised to send us. The only cheese we can get is pink Dutch cheese in tins & sometimes we would give anything for a good bread & cheese supper.

I am afraid this is all the news I have this week but will you please thank Janet & Rob for their nice long letters.

I We are all three very fit indeed & I hope that all at Park Cottage are equally fit.

With love to all

I remain
Your affectionate Son
Jim

2/4th Somerset L.I.
Port Blair
Andamans

16/9/15

My dear Mother & Father.

There was no outwards mail last week so I could not write to you : & I don't know how much of this letter will reach you for we have been told that our letters will in all probability be censored.

Since I wrote last I have made my exit from Ross & am now living on Aberdeen. John is also over here but Andrew has gone to Ross & is living with the Padre In some ways it is an advantage being over here for instance there is ~~noo~~ no need to have to rush to catch a boat if you want to go for a walk or have a game of footer etc. Our bungalow stands right on the golf links so we have no difficulty in filling up our odd hours with a club & a ball.

I have quite as much as I can do now for I am 2nd in command of A Company & John is also very busy being acting adjutant for the Aberdeen wing. A Company are doing their musketry on the range which is two miles away so we have to get up at 4–30 every morning in order to start shooting as soon as it gets light. it is too hot to shoot after 9–30 AM and we have therefore to get as much as possible done before then. We have had tremendous rain the last fortnight & the ground is now very soft indeed & very suitable for rugger which we have just started. We played the first game last Saturday & it was a great success although I was very stiff across the neck & shoulders afterwards. To-morrow we are going to play Ross or Aberdeen – it will probably be a very hard tussle. Among the players last week were Weeks & James so that one felt quite at home playing rugger with Cary men again.

I had three weeks' letters from you last week & was very pleased to hear that you are all well It is the very best of news to hear that Father is so much better under the new treatment. I sincerely hope that he will quite regain his old form again. I am sorry that Mother can't throw off here rhumatic & sciatica especially now that Winter is coming on again. I suppose the days are beginning to get short again & you are having fires in the evening. How nice to sit down in a big armchair & see a good fire blazing in the grate. I wish it was cool enough for fires out here.

Mother asked in here last letter what I size shoes I took – my best size is 9½. A big 9 or a small 10 is a trifle too large. I am getting short of marching boots & should be very glad if you would ~~se~~ please send me out a pair. Good ones are difficult to get out here & when they begin to wear out you cannot get them nicely mended for they use Indian leather which is very soft & wears out very quickly indeed.

Royal made a rather bad start in Port Blair for he went down with malaria last week. Luckily it was a very mild attack & he is nearly well now. We are all taking 30 grains of quinnine every week & the men call it their extra ration. It is taken on two consecutive days each week – 15 grains at each dose & there is always a run on the coffee shop for chocolates etc before quinnine parade.

I was sorry that you had such a wet day for the fête at Florida on August Bank Holiday but it was very good of Cary people to get it up & I can assure you that whatever is sent out here to the men will be fully appreciated.

Douglas Milton is in A Company now & I see a good bit of him again – he is looking much better than when I left him at Calicut.

Please thank Duff very much indeed for his letter which was awfully well written. As soon as I can get anything I will send him a present as I promised to do when he wrote me a letter all by himself.

All three of us are very fit & so far John & Andrew have found that Port Blair agrees with them very well indeed.

With much love to all

> I remain
> > Your affectionate son
> > Jim

2/4th Somerset L.I.
~~Pot~~ Port Blair
~~India~~
Andaman Islands

Sept 24th 1915

My dear Mother & Father

A year ago yesterday I was gazetted to the 4th Somersets & we little knew then what an eventful year was to follow. Six months of that year I have spent here at Port Blair but I was not so stationary during the first six months for I was stationed at Bath, Bangalore Malappuram & Calicut.

I don't know what has happened to our letters lately – they are very irregular indeed. I got a few from Calcutta a fortnight ago but since then although the mail has come in twice I have not had a letter of any sort. Luckily Andrew had one letter from home last week so we are not quite without news.

I am awfully sorry that poor little Duff has hurt himself so badly & I sincerely hope that by the time you get this letter his little leg will be quite

The trucks on which we travelled after landing from the boat. They are pushed along by the convicts standing behind

well again & that all the pain will be gone. I have just been looking at the photo of him which John has received – he makes a fine little Scotch laddie & his sword makes him look quite a soldier. He has altered since we have been away & I fancy he looks thinner. John has just come back from the club and he says that the new ~~buget~~ taxes etc are in to-nights telegrams.

This was taken from one of the windows of the club and shows Flower (in white) with Captain Hartford walking across the lawn

Fancy having no half penny post in future – it will make a great difference to business firms who send out receipts & invoices in half penny packets. The extra tax on petrol will also make a big difference to business men, but the increased super-tax will hit the rich people rather hard. It seems to me that it will be rather difficult to live at all in England after the war is

Miss Douglas (the Chief Commissioner's daughter) sitting on one of the trucks with Flower standing behind. Notice the police orderly stood behind. No lady ever goes out in Port Blair without being followed by a police orderly

over if it goes on much longer & yet the people out here hardly feel the effect of the war at all.

General Raitt arrived here to-day to inspect us. He inspected the barracks to-day & we are to have an inspection parade to-morrow morning. I expect there will be some funny sights when the mounted officers draw their swords for all the ponies are very nervous at the best of times so you can just

Having tea at the gardens. The men are Harvey, a settlement officer on the left and Flower on the right. The ladies from left to right are: Miss Douglas; her cousin Miss Lucie Smith and two ladies from Rangoon staying at Rangoon

picture the scene when the swords are waving about & the bugle band suddenly starts to play the general salute.

The weather is very hot again now, owing to a break in the monsoon. The wind is trying hard to change from the S W to the N E monsoon with the result that there is no breeze at all & it is very hot. I think the S W will win this time but the N E will soon have another try & will probably get the best of it some time in October.

(Contd)

It is fairly making the people who have come down from Bangalore lose weight in great style & the fat & portly sergeant major is simply one mass of prickly heat.

There is to big be a big dance at Government House to-morrow night to at which all officers have to attend in order to meet the General & his wife. I shall not be sorry when it is over for I am not a great success at these big functions;

I was not quite without a mail this week – a g the Guernsey Cattle breeder's journal has just arrived for which many thanks. It is awfully interesting to me for I like to keep in touch with my agriculture & dairying.

Heartiest congratulations to Bunna for getting 3rd Class honours in the Oxford. I think he did quite well considering how he was handicapped by those wretched measles & I am sure he will do great things in the Senior next year after which he will go straight for a S Scolarshi Scholarship to Cambridge.

I hardly know what to write now for all our letters are kept separate so that they can be censored. The reason for this no one seems to know but those in authority seem to think it necessary.

We are all delighted to hear that Father is keeping so well & I hope that Mother will be able to keep fit this Winter.

With much love to you all

      I remain
        Your affectionate son
          Jim

2/4th Somerset L.I.
Port Blair
~~India~~
Andaman Islands

Oct. 28th 1915

My dear Mother & Father.

We received your letters dated Sept. 29th last week & there is another mail due to-day from Calcutta which ought to bring us some more. The papers which you sent were very interesting indeed & we have now more or less mastered the details of the new ~~buget~~ budget.

We have had some very hot fine weather the last few days but the wind has been gradually working round to the NE and last night we had the first storm of the NE monsoon. It was not very heavy but we have had more rain to-day & for the next fortnight it will probably get gradually rougher. Being on the ~~West~~ East side of the Islands the S W monsoon never gives us a very rough sea but the harbour opens to the N E & people say that it gets very rough indeed about the middle of ~~December~~ November.

I had three days on the patrol boat during the early part of the week : the weather was very fine & still & we had a most enjoyable time. I had ten men on board & could go just where I liked so I cruised about among the islands & saw as much as possible in the time.

We landed whenever we saw a nice sandy beach, which was very rarely, for the islands are covered with thick jungle ~~wh~~ reaching down to the water's edge at which it becomes a mangrove swamp. ~~Even~~ These little sandy stretches have all been made use of in the past for forest camps so there was usually a little clearing behind with a few disused huts & the men thoroughly enjoyed rambling about trying to find any little thing which may have been left lying about. We bathed every evening but had to be very careful indeed to keep together & splash about a good deal in order to keep off the sharks which absolutely infest the sea in these parts. The men caught one or two, but they are no good to eat & we just ~~kl~~ killed them & threw them overboard again.

We spent several hours one day paddling about in the shallow water of a coral shore looking for shells & nice bits of coral. ~~It is~~ The sea is so clear that you can see everything on the sea floor at quite a considerable depth & I could have spent days merely watching the fish, ~~etc~~ & other animals which we could see swimming about The coral is awfully pretty when you see it under the water just where it was made. It forms beautiful patterns; some is white, some red & some pink & the fish dart about here there & everywhere taking shelter under the ledges of coral.

~~The~~ I was rather impressed with the jungle for it was the first time I had really been into a really thick tropical jungle. It was so thick that you could only go a few yards in, & the ~~mystery~~ mystery to me is how so many plants can find room to live being so thickly crowded. The trees were covered with creepers & orchids (but unfortunately the latter were not in flower) & the whole formed a barrier which was absolutely impassable. There seemed to be very few birds about except where the jungle had been cleared a little & the silence was remarkable. Except for our own voices & the roar of the sea on the beach there did not seem to be a sound of any sort.

I can now understand ~~how~~ how in the old days the pirates could run their vessels into creeks & remain absolutely hidden from the sea. Some of the creeks go inland for miles & wind about in a most bewildering way & a whole navy could be hidden in them if only the water were deep enough for the ships to enter.

Among the men who went with me was Frank Martin a Cary boy & a former member of the Boys Brigade. He was at Malappuram & I had not seen him since I left there, but during that time he has improved wonderfully & although young is an excellent soldier. Last Sunday I spent the day at the top of Mount Harriet, the hill station of Port Blair, (1100′ high). it is much cooler up there than it is down below & I was very sorry to have to come down, but some of us are going to try & get some leave shortly & spend a few days up there.

Colonel Clutterbuck has been very ill again, but is now decidedly better, although the doctors have decided that he must not stay in India any longer. He is leaving here next week & is I believe going to Italy to try & recuperate before going back to England. I am awfully sorry that he has to go but he has not been the same man since he came to India & I don't think he will live long if he does not return to Europe.

Oct 29th The mail has just come in bringing your letters of Oct. 7th. We are very lucky to get them for very few people have had any this week, in fact the post office ~~are~~ is treating us very badly here. There has been no proper mail since the Bttn came here & several of the men have not had a letter for seven weeks although the boat has come in several times : the letters seem to be held up somewhere but we cannot find out where.

I am awfully sorry to ~~heare~~ hear that poor little Duffy has had to have his leg broken especially after having had about six weeks in bed already; but I hope now that it will go on well & that he will soon be able to run about again. We often wonder how he is getting on & should awfully like to be able to look into his room & play with him ~~just~~ to help pass the hours away. I expect it has made Mother very busy indeed & I hope that she will not overdo it.

I was sorry to hear that Rex Lewin has been wounded & also to hear that Andrew of the Bank is so ill. I am afraid that this war is taking all the best fellows & I often feel that we are hardly doing our fair share: ~~had~~ but I suppose our presence here in this ~~our~~ outpost of the Empire is very necessary.

This is rather a long letter & I must now stop to get some others written. We are all as fit as can be & I hope everyone at Park Cottage is equally well

With love to all

    Your affectionate son Jim

2/4th Somerset LI
2nd Wessex Division
~~C/o GPO~~
C/o Cox & Co
Bombay

5/11/15

My dear Mother & Father.

I have no letter from home to answer this week for the mail was late at Rangoon and therefore the boat left without the letters. We have all got a good many letters however, because, owing to some gross slackness on the part of the Post Office our letters have been held up and the greater part of the Regiment have had no letters for eight weeks : a good many of them were sent on this week and everyone is rejoicing at having some news again. I doubt if they would have come through even now, only Colonel Waddy cabled to the Postmaster General in London & the director of post offices at Bombay reporting the matter last week the result being a good mail this week.

I have practically no news this week : we have been getting on quite well & doing a good deal of hard work. Colonel Waddy is O.C. now that Colonel Clutterbuck is ill & he is waking us all up. The latter is leaving Port Blair to-morrow on his way back to Europe. I hope he will soon get fit again when he leaves India, but at present he is very bad indeed.

Capt Harford has gone up to Rangoon for three weeks & I tried to go with him to go to a dentist but I was unable to get leave, as the O.C Troops cannot spare more than two officers away at once.

The men are still getting malaria very badly & the number we get on parade is gradually diminishing. Flower & Royal are the only officers who have had it so far and for that reason they are taking sixty of the worst cases away to Wellington to-morrow. They are awfully lucky to get the chance of going up there where it is nice & cool & I should very much like to go myself.

I heard from Passmore to-day, but his letter had been delayed for a long time. When he wrote he was just going off to the front so I suppose he is out there now, & I suppose Withers is also out there. I rather envy them in some ways for one does not like to be left behind when all the others are going out.

I am awfully glad that Mary & Janet both took prizes at Sunny Hill – Mary did very well indeed to get two. No doubt next year the little Pussy will also have her name in the prize list.

If the ladies in Cary have not quite worn out their fingers making things for the soldiers we should be awfully glad if they would knit us some socks for our men. In a climate like this where we sweat excessively the number of socks the men wear out is tremendous & they would all be glad of some new ones from home.

How is little Duffy getting on? I hope his leg is setting well & that all the pain is gone. Give him lots of kisses from us all & tell him to cheer up & make haste & get well.

Are you all having some fireworks to-night? We intended to have a big bon fire but the rain has been so hard this week that we cannot get enough dry wood.

Enclosed are some photographs which I took when we were out in the patrol boat.

We are all very fit & I hope you are all equally well.

With very best love to all

> I remain
> Your affectionate son
> Jim

2/4th Somerset LI
2nd Port Blair
Andaman Islands

14/11/15

My dear Mother & Father.

At Port Blair really seems very like England to-day for I am writing on the verandah on a Sunday morning and there is a nice cool breeze blowing in from the N E which makes the air feel very much like it does on a Summer morning at home. It is considerably cooler now compared with what it was a few months ago & we all feel very grateful for the breeze which is fairly continuous & which keeps us at a comfortable temperature.

We have not had a very eventful week but we have been rather busy owing to the fact that we are rather short of officers. Capt Harford is away on leave & several others are on the sick list so those of us who are fit have rather a lot to do. ~~The~~ I am sending ~~off~~ you a box this week containing an inlaid table & I hope it will arrive safely. The top of the table is inlaid with mother of pearl & tortishell & the wood work is all made of marble wood. The table is is pieces which are numbered & Arthur or Pither's people could soon put it together. In addition there is a small box made of tortishell and a few pieces of unpolished tortishell which I took off the back of a dead turtle when I was out in the "Nancowrie".

We shall have to send off our Xmas letters next week in order that they may reach you by Xmas day, but as the mails are ~~st~~ very irregular they may not arrive quite up to date, in which case you ~~will~~ can depend upon it that they have been written & will arrive sooner or later. The mail is due in from Madras now – we are all keeping one eye on the harbour as we write our letters – and we hope that there will be a very big mail indeed. Most of the men have had no letters ~~from~~ for six weeks : apparently they have been held up at Madras and have been put on board this week's boat so that ~~these~~ Port Blair post office will have a bit of work to do to-day for once in a way.

The men are still going down with malaria and we are all taking 45 grains of quinnine every week. I believe it does a good deal of good in fact if it had not been for the quinnine I am sure we should have lost several men by now. I often think when I go up to the hospital & see it absolutely full of men with fever that our men deserve quite as much credit as those who go & sit in the trenches for a fortnight & then get a week's leave.

We have been very busy this week trying to arrange to give the men a big dinner on Christmas day. Wills father has given the money for it & we have to make the arrangements – not an easy job for we have to get everything down from Rangoon. I think we have now settled it all up & the order is to go up this week – you would have been amused to see us pouring over grocery catalogues etc to find the price of currents or how many rasins are required to make plumpu pudding for 160 men & so on. I think they will have quite a good dinner for Mr Wills has given ~~quite~~ a good sum for each man. On New Year's day I believe the Settlement are going to hold sports for them & provide them with a tea. John, Andrew & I were invited to spend Xmas day at Government House but we were unable to do so because the Regiment are going to entertain all the white people in the Settlement at dinner on Xmas night. ~~In return~~ On New Year's even everyone is going to a fancy dress dance at Government House.

How is Duffy getting on? I should think by this time his leg must be getting fairly strong again unless any other complications have set in. Has he started counting the days till Xmas yet? I hope you are all quite well &

in case this letter reaches you nearer Xmas day than next week's I will wish
you all a very happy Xmas.

With love to all

I remain
Your affectionate son
Jim

2/4th Somerset L.I.
2nd
Port Blair
Andaman Islands

21/11/15

My dear Mother & Father.

I will start my letter this week by wishing you all a very merry Xmas & a
happy New Year. it seems rather funny to have to send these wishes so long
before Christmas, but then, the Andaman Islands are a long way from Castle
Cary. We thought we were a long way from home when we wrote from
Port Said last year, and I remember how we speculated on where we should
be this Christmas, and now we find ourselves at Port Blair wondering where
we shall spend Christmas day 1916.

Any letters which we forget to post this week will be ꞵ pretty useless for
there will be no boat either in or out for the next three weeks during which
time, ꞟo except for the wireless we shall be cut off from civilization I suppose
it is because we have been seeing so many fresh things & fresh places, but
this year seems to have slipped away remarkably quickly & one can hardly
realize that it is getting near to the end of November.

We three have been very lucky in the matter of health for we have been in
India nearly a year and except for Andrew's illness at Bangalore neither of us
have ever had to report sick. John & I have both had very trying stations &
we have both been unable to get any leave in a cool hill station so that we
really ought to consider ourselves very lucky indeed that we have kept fit.

I am very glad indeed that Father has been able to find a doctor who
could cure him & new that he is better I hope he will keep well all through
the Winter. I also hope that Mother will have a better Winter this year
than she did last & keep clear of rheumatic & neuritis. We did not get our
mails this week so that by the time we hear from you again I sincerely hope
that we shall hear that Duffy a is quite well & strong again.

We are very sorry that we cannot get Christmas presents for you all but
there is nothing here to buy much as we should like to get ꞵ something,

so we are going to continue to give everyone a good ~~Christmas~~ birthday present & Andrew is just sending 2/6 each by way of pocket money.

I suppose the war will rather cut down the usual Christmas festivities but I hope you will all have a jolly good time together – we shall just picture you all sitting round the turkey & plum pudding on Christmas day & shall think of Duffy searching for his stocking very early in the morning when the band wakes him up. I am afraid there is no news from here. The weather has been very rough the last ~~few~~ three days owing to a cyclone which has been blowing. The sea is very rough indeed & we thought the launches from Ross to Aberdeen would have to stop running, but they have managed to keep going so far & ~~I think~~ the worst of the storm is now over.

It is much cooler now & we have been ~~do~~ taking advantage of this to do some rather strenuous field training. I went up to Mount Harriet for the day last Thursday & it was really quite chilly up there.

The photo which mother mentioned last week was a group we had taken before we left Prior Park. I ordered one, but it had not arrived when we left England, & appar`k`ently it lay about at the depot : I am very glad you took it because it will be rather interesting. Enclosed are two photos of the officers of the Regiment which we had taken about two days before Colonel Clutterbuck sailed for Europe They were taken on the steps leading up to Government House.

I have just been granted 12 days leave to go up to Rangoon to get my teeth done. I shall leave Port Blair on Dec. 11th & return on the 24th. I expect it will be rather an expensive job for my ~~th~~ teeth have got very bad since I have been here & I ~~wand~~ they want some attention very badly.

> Once more every good wish for Christmas & the New
> Year from your affectionate son
> Jim

2/4th Somerset L.I.
Port Blair
Andaman Islands

10/12/15

My dear Mother & Father.

No boat has come into or out of Port Blair for three weeks ~~unit~~ until to-day when the usual mail boat arrived bringing three English mails. Alas! however the mails were for everyone except the Regiment, ours having been delayed again for some reason or other. I don't know why they are so careless with our letters – we have only had two really good mails in the last thirteen weeks.

~~There~~ Not much has occurred worth writing about since we last ~~wot~~ wrote, and every day being very much like the one before it.

Last week we were practically confined to the bungalow for four days on account of a very severe storm. The sea was exceptionally rough, the usual service of launches being completely stopped & the rain was absolutely marvellous. We had 12′′ of rain on Aberdeen in 48 hours which is as much as ½ the average yearly rainfall in many parts of England. At the beginning of September the rainfall in Port Blair was over thirty inches below the average but we have had so much rain that we are now within three inches of the usual yearly average.

Unless we get some stormy weather about Christmas we shall probably get no more rain till next March for the NE monsoon is now blowing

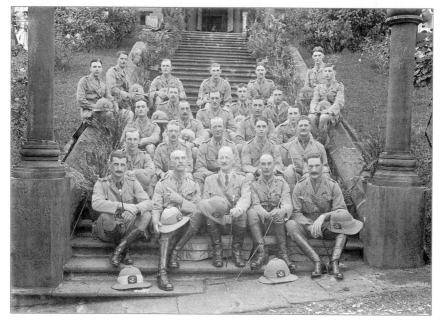

Taken on the steps of Government House, Port Blair.

Back row: 2nd Lt Buckley, Lt Ingram, Lt Wills, Lt J.R. Mackie, 2nd Lt Thatcher, 2nd Lt J.B. Mackie

4th Row: 2nd Lt Clutterbuck, 2nd Lt Philpot, 2nd Lt A.K. Lee, 2nd Lt A.H. Mackie

3rd Row: 2nd Lt Davis, 2nd Lt Burtt, Lt Miles, 2nd Lt Royal, 2nd Lt Elliott

2nd Row: Lt Stevenson, Captain Farwell, Captain Harford, Captain Bartlett, Lt Gilmour (Quartermaster)

Front row: Captain Maclaren (Adjutant), Colonel Waddy, Colonel Clutterbuck, Major Bunting, Captain Bealy steadily. It is beautifully cool now; even in the middle of the day you can go out for a walk & the mornings are really quite chilly.

~~The~~ One eats a good many strange dishes out here but I never thought I should ever eat parrots. I have however made the attempt & they are awfully good. ~~They are~~ There are flocks of them all over the paddy fields, which are now being harvested, and it is awfully good sport shooting them. Two of us went out one day last week & we got seven between us in about an hour. Others have brought in some at various times & parrot pie is becomming quite a ~~fav~~ favourite course.

I am glad to say that the malaria seems to have slackened off a little. Not nearly so many men have had it the last fortnight, chiefly because the cooler weather has stopped the mosquitos from breeding. To make up for the malaria we are all covered with a sort of ring worm, which, if not very serious is most annoying and uncomfortable.

The only letter which came through was one from Aunt Ethel & she said that Duffy was not quite well even yet. I do hope that by this time he is able to move about again and use his leg.

John has had rather a bad cold the last day or two otherwise we are all very well

I will now resume after having dashed out to take a photo of one of the forest elephants which has just passed the bungalow. There are several elephants kept here & they are used by the forest department to carry about the timber at the forest camps.

Our news telegrams have been very scanty the last week or two and we hardly know what is going on. Reading between the lines however it looks as if things were none too bright in Servia : but on the other hand it was reported one night that the ~~Run~~ Russians had been allowed to pass through Rumania, which is certainly rather good news.

Luckily nearly all our papers have arrived even if the letters have been delayed, so we shall have something to read for the next few days.

I ~~was~~ should be going up to Rangoon for a fortnights leave this week only ~~al~~ for ~~so~~ various reasons all leave from Port Blair has been cancelled for a time, and I shall have to wait a bit. I want to go rather badly for I had the bad luck to have another tooth knocked out while playing rugger, and my teeth now want some attention.

I hope you all had a jolly good Christmas & will all have a very happy New Year.

Hoping you are all very well

> With much love to all
> Your affectionate son
> Jim

2/4th Somerset L.I.
Port Blair
Andaman Islands

♉ 18/12/15

My dear Mother & Father

Going North at last – hurrah ! T̶o̶ Two nights ago Colonel Waddy came into the mess with a telegram in his hand which stated that we should be relieved shortly by the 18th City of London Rifles and should proceed to Dinapur. We don't know quite what the word "shortly" means but I expect we shall be on the move about the middle of January. The relieving troops are coming straight here from England and I s̶e̶ really feel quite sorry for them for they have had no chance to become acclimatised and the hot weather will soon be coming on.

Dinapur is on the Ganges about 300 miles from Calcutta & not far from Patna so that we are going right into civilization again. Just fancy seeing a railway train again & getting our letters every week regularly – it will be splendid : w̶e̶ ̶h̶ This weeks mail brought us letters from home dated October 20th this being the latest we have so far had.

As far as climate is concerned I believe we shall be out of the frying pan into the fire for I believe in the hot weather it is hotter there than it is here. But still it will be a change and in India one does not want to stay long̶e̶r̶ in one place – it is much better to move about. There is one advantage about the new place, I don't think there is any malaria there although when we get there we shall probably find i̶t̶ something else equally bad.

I expect we shall be allowed to take it fairly easily for a bit after leaving here for since the trouble started here all of us, men & officers, have had rather a strenuous & trying time.

We have just come in from an inspection parade. Brigadier General Young came down yesterday from Rangoon & inspected us this morning. He has just gone up to the wireless station to see the big guns fired & inspect the defences & then he will come back here to breakfast with us. The Battalion did awfully well on parade to-day & I think the General is very pleased with us.

Thank you very much indeed for sending me out a pair of boots for Xmas. There is nothing I am more in need of for all mine are now worn out & it is difficult to get b̶o̶ good boots out here. They have not yet arrived but will probably come down next week, in which case they will arrive on Christmas eve.

We started cricket again last Thursday, the Regiment playing the Gymkhana. The Regiment won by about 20 runs. John did quite well, getting six wickets & about 20 runs but I made the usual duck being given out L.B.W. before I had a chance to get going.

I have enclosed the photographs of the elephant which I took last week – I think Duffy would like to see them. I hope his leg is now quite well & that he is quite himself again.

I can't think of much else to write for we are all speculating & wondering what our new station ~~is~~ will be like & that is all we have been talking about ~~sinc~~ for the last two days.

I hope you are all quite well

With love to you all

> I remain
>> Your affectionate son
>>> Jim

2/4th Somerset L.I.
Port Blair
Andaman Islands

Christmas Day 1915

Mr dear Mother & Father.

As you see above it is Christmas day to-day but a very strange one for us. When Duffy got out of bed at 4 aM to have a look at his stocking this morning we were all standing to arms at the barracks & pickets & patrols were sent out, being recalled again at day break.

~~W~~ John was at the wireless station, Andrew at Ross & I was sleeping in a tent on the barrack square & when I turned out at 4 a m feeling very sleepy I went to the signallers and got them to signal Christmas greetings to John at the wireless station & in a few minutes the reply was flashed back wishing the same to me. Then we repeated the message to Andrew on Ross. This is the first time we have ever wished each other a merry Xmas ~~x~~ by means of a heliograph. Neither John or I will be able to eat our Xmas dinner to-night for we shall both sleep out under the stars. John will be in charge of a picket at the wireless ~~x~~ station and I shall have one at Corbyns Cove about three miles out, and I don't expect there will be much sleep for either of us. For about a week now we have been standing to arms at 4 pm remaining out till daybreak, but it will not last much longer for ~~the attack~~ we were to be attacked on Christmas night, when ~~at~~ the enemy no doubt thought we should all be feasting. However they will not catch us napping this time if they come, but it is very unlikely that they will get here for we are surrounded by a huge fleet of warships. The mails came in yesterday and brought your letters for Nov 18th but we have had none of the letters between this Oct 20th & Nov 18th. Thank you very much indeed for all you have sent out to us – I hope some of it has arrived this week (parcels have not yet been dilivered) but it may be late as parcels usually take longer than letters to arrive.

Fancy George joining the army – things ought to push ahead now – he seems to have chosen a pretty soft job anyhow.

I am going up to Barracks in a few minutes to see that the men's Christmas dinner is alright. The money for it has been provided by Wills, but besides this the people of Bath have very kindly sent out about £50 for the same purpose so the men will not do at all badly. We have got turkeys for them locally & green vegetables & oranges came down from Rangoon yesterday. Owing to the trouble no man is allowed more than two pints of beer but I don't think this restriction is very necessary for there have only been about three cases of drunkenness since the Regiment came to Port Blair.

The news that we are going to Dinapur has been confirmed and we are now playing the Settlement a final set of hockey & cricket matches before we go. Last week they beat us rather badly at cricket and we drew the hockey match, but I think we shall beat them this week.

I think Janet may be amused by the following funny incident which occurred to me yesterday morning :- When I got up I tried to put on my shoe but found I could not get my foot into it so I put my hand in to see what was there. I felt something mey very cold & clammy & drew my hand back about as quickly as I did when the owl flew out of the tree on the day were birdnesting in the orchard at Cockhill. On turning the shoe up I found that it contained a huge toad which sat grinning at me in great style.

The other night when I had a picket at Corbyn's Cove I rode out on a horse & told the syce to come out & look after him during the night. About 12 o'clock the syce came to me in great trouble to say that the horse had run away. In a few minutes a message came through by signal to say that the he horse had just reached the stables. The result was the syce had to walk home about four miles in order to bring the horse back for me in the morning.

I am very sorry indeed to hear that Edith is going and I am afraid Mother will miss her very much : but I hope here successor will make a good servant.

We are delighted to hear that Duffy is able to have the splints taken off & I hope he will thoroughly enjoy his Christmas day. I hope you have all had lots of Xmas presents and are all quite well so that you can make the most of the goose & plum pudding.

With very much love to you all & very many thanks for all you have sent out to us

Your affectionate son
Jim

Extracted from:
The Somerset Light Infantry 1914–19

15th December

On the morning of 15th at 5 a.m. the party, back in its billeting area, practised the attack for the last time. Officers and men then rested for the remainder of the day, moving forward at night to The Mushroom, from which the attack was to take place.

16th December

At 12.15 a.m. a patrol under 2/Lt. Wallis was sent out to see if the enemy's listening post was occupied and to see if the enemy were on the alert. After spending about twenty minutes in No Man's Land the patrol returned and reported the listening post still unoccupied, and from the sounds of shouting and talking coming from the enemy's trenches it was evident he was all unconscious of the impending attack.

By 2.15 a.m. the concentration of the attacking party was complete, and the order was given for the bridging ladders and mats to be taken over the parapet. This was done, the men following them and laying down behind the knife rests in the correct order of advance. At 3 a.m. the knife rests were removed noiselessly and the signal given for the advance. Slowly and quietly the men, led by their officers, crept towards the enemy's trenches. The officer leading the advance carried a roll of broad white tape, the end of which was left behind (in Bay 13). Unrolling the tape as he advanced, he left behind him a white path from his own trenches to that point in the German wire through which a path had been cut. He then passed the tape through the German wire and secured it. The advance across No Man's Land was perilous, for on the flanks of the positions to be attacked Véry lights burst in the air. The men, however, were very steady and remained motionless whenever a light went up.

The first party to reach the enemy's wire was that under 2/Lt. Withers. Putting down their mats over the broken knife rests, the whole assaulting party then crossed the wire and ditch by the mats without the slightest noise. Officers and men then extended along the German parapet, crawling up to the top of it. Taking a careful look over 2/Lt. Withers saw three

Germans talking together in the trench. He shot one and then jumped into the trench followed closely by his party. The other two men tried to run away, but were bayoneted. The enemy was completely surprised, and the assaulting troops were into the trenches before any alarm was given; indeed, it was about 3.16 a.m. when 2/Lt. Withers jumped into the German trench and the last man of the party was in by 3.20 a.m., just as the guns opened fire on the enemy's flanking and support trenches. This artillery fire was supplemented by trench-mortar fire and rifle grenades on the flank of the position assaulted. The majority of the garrison of the trench were in their deep dug-outs and were all put out of action. Of the few men encountered in the trenches some showed fight. Three Germans tried to rush Sergeant Coxon, but he shot two with his revolver and took the third man prisoner. An officer who would not surrender had to be shot. Lieut Shepherd, RE, who had been ordered to search for and blow up a supposed mineshaft could not find it, he therefore exploded his charge inside a steel machine-gun emplacement; the gun being too heavy to bring away was abandoned. At the end of 20 minutes the attacking party heard a whistle, it was the signal for the return. Bringing seven German prisoners with them, and carrying such trophies as gas masks, oxygen apparatus, grenades, Véry lights and other items, the men filed regularly out of the trenches and, following the white tape line, reached The Mushroom in safety, though the latter was by now under heavy hostile shell fire. Not a man of the attacking party had been killed or wounded, but 48 dead Germans had been left behind in the enemy's trench.

The success of the undertaking was not only due to the splendid co-operation of all arms (also the Royal Art Royal Engineers), but to the enthusiasm shown by the C.O. of the 8th Somersets:

"From the moment that he was told that the enterprise was to be entrusted to his Battalion he worked with the greatest energy to ensure its success. He impressed all ranks with his enthusiasm and confidence, and the success of the operation owes much to his example both before the day and on the night of the enterprise when he organized the advance from, and the retirement to, The Mushroom, the latter under heavy shell fire, with much skill and with complete indifference to personal danger."

For about an hour and a half after the return The Mushroom was heavily shelled by the enemy and three other ranks were killed and four wounded. A little later the attacking party marched off to billets, "and," records the Battalion Diary, "had a day's sleep." They deserved it.

Letter from 2nd Lt Withers, to J.R. Mackie, describing how in the above incident he, Withers, won his MC.

8 Somerset L I
B.E.F. France

Dec 31st 1915

Dear Jim,

I am writing this on New Years Eve & as you see above it comes from the front. I received your letter of Nov 22 safely in the trenches. I can imagine what you feel like being left out of this war but really you are a lucky beggar, – you only want a month of it to get bored stiff. I came out here just after the Battle of Loos in which the 8th Somersets were badly knocked about I found them resting in one of the typically dirty Flemish villages just on the French border. After staying there a fortnight we trekked by easy stages into the line arriving one night in a big town only 1½ miles from the firing line. Our division took of this line under very favourable conditions. The trenches were good & only half a dozen shells had fallen onto the town for months. Sad to say its mighty different now. We have straffed & the Huns have replied until our line is Hell on earth. The town has hardly a whole house in it & the trenches are something awful. Owing to the low level of the country trenches are impossible – the whole thing being breastwork. The water has risen steadily until the whole thing is more or less under water. The Huns are anything from 50 – 400 yards away. We are well provided for – each man has long gum boots which come right up to the thighs, a fur coat & a long mackintosh cape besides the usual kit. I won't bore you with a long description of the life as it merely consists of hiding behind a parapet & doing as many underhand tricks as possible to upset the Hun. The 8th have made a name for themselves & are considered by the Corps Commander the best battalion in the Corps, & as such were selected a few weeks ago to do a small night attack. Volunteers were called for & we picked a Hundred men & 6 of us officers were chosen. The scheme was to visit the Hun trenches at 3 A M stay for twenty minutes kill & loot & then return. We all had our faces blackened & wore respirators on our head like turbans. I had charge of 32 men, 24 carrying twelve mats rolled up like blinds & 8 carrying two long bridges. All had wire cutters Then there were 5 squads of bombers & 10 over to look after prisoners. Punctually at 3 I got out & we all lay down ready by our wire. Then we moved two or three rows of our wire & moved forward across No Mans land. We soon reached the Huns wire which had previously been blown about by our artillery & carefully placed the mats over the worse places. Then I went on with a sergeant (the Huns still asleep!) expecting to be spotted every second, eventually reaching a deep ditch half full of water with the german parapet over the other side We got over this & lay down under the parapet, where we could hear Huns talking quite plainly. However they didn't spot us I don't know. Here we waited until most of our men had come up & bridged the ditch. At last th It was most exciting expecting to see a Hun look over every minute. Suddenly the artillery started & then I gave the signal to rush! There were three Huns down in the trench & we shot one with the first shot & killed another later. The Bombers bolted each way & blocked the trenches to start a counter attack. We got going now & started looting. We entered several dugouts & took prisoners or killed as necessary. One Prisoner was very funny. I heard a scuffle in a dug out so went in followed by my young hoard, only to find my Hun with his hands up all ready, fairly babbling "Kamarade" & weeping like a child. I tried to persuade him by gentle taps of the revolver to "lead on" but my men frightened him so much with their bayonet drill that the poor bounder was too fri terrified to move. Eventually one man took his hand & led him like a lamb to the slaughter. He was a fat beggar & couldn't get over his own parapet so we hove him out – one man hoisted him out with the point of his bayonet & handed him over to our policemen. One dugout was fitted with electric light! This place we looted & afterwards blew up with a bomb. The time was all too short for us & we had to clear out on a given signal. Eventually we got back into our own trenches & then the Hun artillery got to work & fairly poured shells into us. I never hope to get another such a half an hour. The whole sky was ablaze with light & the air was full of falling earth & bits of shell. Several men were buried & most of us got small hits but there were very few casualties fortunately. Eventually we got back to the town to hot food & gallons of rum. Altogether we got about a dozen prisoners & killed about ten more to say nothing of the damage done by our artillery & bombs.

It was a glorious scrap! The loot was extremely valuable & some of the papers & letters have revealed things which the Army has been wanting to know for months.

I brought back a gas apparatus, an oxygen apparatus & a range finder myself (it was a weight! & among other things we got a Machine Gun, 5 kinds of bombs & 2 dead Officers diaries.

The Huns were wild next day & weren't long in retaliating. This they did by blowing up two mines which are however landed short. We have been fighting for these ever since & now we sit down opposite one another about 30 yards apart & grind our teeth like old bulldogs.

Excuse me saying so much about myself but I can't help it.

Home news is as usual.

Reading:- College does nothing but War Work. (you know all this no doubt.

Street. Just awoke fearing Conscription – which has come at last.

Bruton. H Crowther tried to enlist & there was nothing doing. All enrolled under Lord Derby's Scheme. Tucknel is ASC?

France Oh Hell.

We are just off now to a pub to feed through the night:- I'm nearly intoxicated now.

Excuse me being the teller but I was awarded the Military Cross for sharing in our scrap. Lucky dog. I've been in for promotion for weeks but have to wait for the wounded ones to be put off the strength.

Kind regards to John & Andrew

Yours every
Johnnie Withers

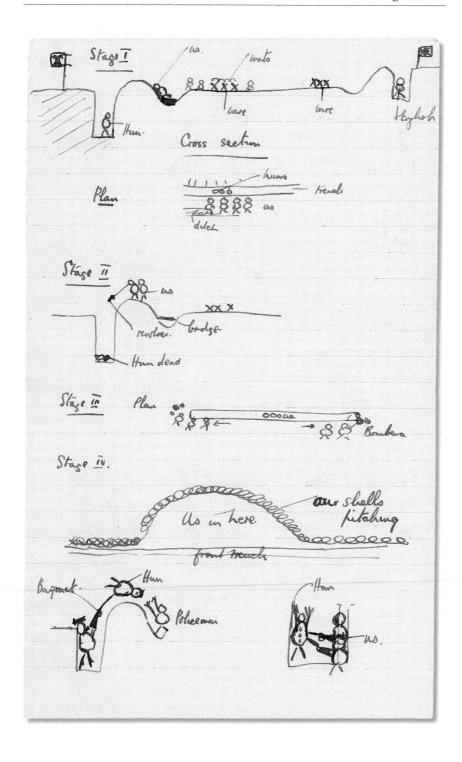

LETTERS FROM THE 2/4TH BN. SOMERSET

LIGHT INFANTRY (P.A.) 1914–19

VOLUME II: 1916

Extracted from:
The Somerset Light Infantry 1914–19

After the 2/4th Somersets (Lieut-Colonel H. F. Clutterbuck) had arrived in Dinapore, India, from the Andaman Islands early in January 1916, the Battalion led the usual life of an Indian garrison. The "Kitchener Test" was passed successfully. About the middle of the year-in July-the 2/4th, with a number of men of the 1/4th, marched through Bankipore and Patna, then seething with unrest, but before the column returned to Dinapore cholera broke out and some deaths occurred. At Dinapore the men of the 1/4th who had returned sick from Mesopotamia were formed into a depôt, commanded first by Major Graves-Knyfton and later by Captain T. B. Timmins. As men became fit they were drafted back to their Battalion in "Mespot," the 2/4th also providing drafts for its first-line Battalion. In this way, during 1916, some six officers and more than 800 other ranks were sent to Mesopotamia as reinforcements. In May 1917 orders were received by the 2/4th to proceed to Egypt, but just as the Battalion was ready to move to Bombay for embarkation, it was ordered to the Lahore District owing to the riots at Amritsar. Later the Battalion was to have moved to the Waziristan frontier owing to a rising of the Mahsuds, but this order was cancelled. Next came a move to Poona on the 1st August, and in September the Battalion at last entrained for Bombay and there embarked for Egypt. Disembarking at Suez the 2/4th Somersets moved up in cattle trucks to Kantara, whence the Battalion began its long trek across the desert to the British line in front of Gaza. On arrival at Belah in the XXI Corps area the Battalion was allotted to the 232nd Brigade of the 75th Division, and on the 24th October took over trenches from the 2/4th Hants in the Mansura East sub-sector. When the operations against Gaza opened, however, the 232nd Brigade, as already mentioned, was in Corps Reserve.

2/1/16.

My dear Mother & Father.

The last day of the Old Year brought us some really good luck for the mail came in & brought us all our back letters and the parcels you sent us out for Christmas. It was delightful to have some news of you again & we are nearly up to date now although we have not yet had Christmas letters from anyone by but you. Thank you very much indeed for all the things you sent us out. The boots are splendid & fit very well indeed. The cheese is a real beauty: it travelled quite well and has turned out splendidly now that it is cut. We produced it at Mess the last night of the year and everyone was delighted with it. I am sure that if Aunt Tabor had heard all the things which were said about it she would ask a very high price for her next lot of cheese. I can assure you that it was a real treat to be able to eat bread & cheese again & I thought of you having a bread & cheese supper at Prank Park Cottage. The plum pudding also arrived quite safely but we have not yet opened the tin Our trouble here is now over & we are going back to the ordinary routine to-morrow. We were far too well prepared for the enemy whose plans seem to have failed completely. Anyhow they managed to stop us enjoying our Christmas & have given is a very trying & strenuous time, with pickets, guards etc. For some little time the men only slept in their beds one night in four sometimes five, so that even if the fighting was rather a wash out we have had the experience which will not easily be forgotten.

We are leaving Port Blair on Jan 11th for Calcutta. On arriving there A & B Coys will go to Dinapore, C Coy to Dum Dum & D Coy to Barrackpore. As I am in A & John in B we shall be together again. and Andrew will be with us for sometime time at anyrate as he is taking up the duties of signalling officer & will have to stay at headquarters till he can go w away for a course of instruction.

La Last Thursday the Settlement arranged a sports meeting for the men by way of a farewell effort, and they were very well got up indeed. Everyone se had a thoroughly good time. I had a go at the pillow fight just for the fun of it but I did not get very far. After knocking off one man I was knocked off myself and fell into the bath of coloured water underneath. The pole was thoroughly well greased with some very foul smelling grease & it took me about half an hour to get myself clean again.

A great event was the officer's race in which all the officers started. The handicap was one yard start for every year of age eighteen being scratch. The Colonel won amid great applause which was even greater when he took his prize.

Yesterday was New Year's day but we were not allowed to have any festivities. We played a cricket match however – (married v Single) – in which the married beat the single quite easily. John did very well with both bat & ball – he seems to be in great form at cricket.

I am very glad indeed to hear that Duffy has now got his splints off and I expect that by this time he is now running about again. Also I am very glad that you are all so well. Of course colds will come whatever precautions are taken, I but I do hope that all of you will enjoy really good health during 1916.

Whatever induced George to join the army? I expect you will miss him, but still with men like Rob & Angus to fall back upon things ought to go ahead quite well. Who is looking after the motor? Father seems to have made quite a good price for the cow and it was lucky that she went before the foot & mouth disease broke out.

We are having beautiful weather now & the nights are quite cold & during the day the breeze keeps it nice & cool, although it is quite hot in the sun.

Please thank Mary, Angus & Rob for their letters which I will answer some time or other.

With much love to you all

      I remain
          Your affectionate Son
          Jim

2/4th Somerset L.I.
Port Blair
Andaman Islands

7/1/16

My dear Mother & Father.

I hope that by this time next week we shall have reached Calcutta on our way to our new station. The boat which will take us away is due here in a day or two, and we shall not take very long getting on board for nearly everything is already packed up. The men are awfully keen to get away for with fever heat & one thing & another they have not had a very good time here.

We are rather busy getting ready for the move so that there are not many parades now as most of the work consists of fatigues of one sort & another. Of course all the people here want to have farewell picnics & dinner parties before we go & as everyone is trying to have them in about three days you can just imagine how the invitations ~~clash~~ clash. We had an awfully good day yesterday – the Regiment ~~provided~~ played a cricket match against the Settlement in which we made 91 & they made 170 for about eight wickets. John made 55 not out & took several wickets. I only made four. We had lunch in the pavillion & in the evening the ℞ ladies of the Regiment were "At Home" & provided us with a jolly good tea. To finish up the day there was a concert for the men which was awfully good. Andrew came over from Ross for the concert & stayed with us for supper after which he was rowed back again. It is not very ~~off~~ often that one has to go by boat to get home from a dinner party but it is quite a usual occurrence here.

To-morrow we are going to a party at Govt. House & the next day I believe it is a picnic to Corbyn's Cove after which I expect we shall be too busy to have any more festivities before we go away.

I think perhaps we shall reach Calcutta quite as quickly as this letter, in which case there is no need to write to-day, but if we are delayed we shall not be in time to catch the mail & I ~~am~~ in order to be sure I thought I would just write to-day, although there is really nothing to write about. I hope our letters will be more interesting again when we leave here for we shall be able to write ~~al~~ about all the fresh things & places we see.

I was very interested to hear that Ted Drewett had managed to get into the R.A.M.C. – he was awfully plucky to keep on trying after he had been refused so many times & I hope that now he is in he will get on well.

I really cannot think of anything more to write about to-day and I ~~mus~~ must get up to the barracks as soon as possible.

I hope are all well

With much love to all

> I remain
> > Your affectionate son
>
> > Jim

2/4th Somerset L.I.
Dinapore Cantonments
Dinapore
India

20th Jan 1916

My dear Mother & Father.

We have left Port Blair at last & are now in Northern India living under very different conditions of climate etc.

When I last wrote we had just heard that we were to leave Port Blair on Jan 12th & as I said then everyone wanted us to go out on picnics & dinner parties etc as by way of farewell efforts. Well! we had a very festive time for two or three days – two picnics to Corbyns Cove in two days – & then it was all spoilt by the arrival of the troopship which was to take us away. We knew that her name was the "Sutley" so we looked her up in a shipping list & found that the only boat of that name was the very newest P & O boat so we thought we were going up to Calcutta in state. Imagine our disappointment when on her arrival we found that she was an old emigrant ship belonging to the Nourse line, & only 4000 tons instead of 12000 as we had expected. We were relieved by the 18th Bttn of the London Rifle Brigade (& not the London Irish) i e the national reserve Bttn. The officers are all elderly men, the youngest subaltern being thirty five, and the men are all well over thirty. Most of the men are old soldiers wearing strings of medal ribbons & several of them had been stationed at Port Blair before. It was really awfully funny to see our boys beside ~~one~~ these veterans & it really did not flatter us when we considered that the old men of the national reserve had been sent to do the same work as we had been doing. Of course all the trouble at Port Blair is over now & it is not likely that it will ever occur again.

The embarkation was rather hampered by a rather rough sea which caused several lighters to break loose, ~~thu~~ & thus wasting a great deal of time; but we eventually got away about 8 AM on the 13th.

I shall never forget my last night at Port Blair . "A" Coy was the ~~first~~ last company to embark and the orders we received were that all troops were to be on board ~~on bef~~ on the night of the 12th. We fell the men at ~~3=30~~ 3 o'clock in the afternoon & received orders to prepare to embark at once. Owing to the rough sea they could not get us on board before dark & orders were sent to "A" Coy to sleep the night in barracks. ~~Unfort~~ Unfortunately we did not get these orders till about 9–30 PM as they miscarried somewhere or other so we were standing on the jetty in full marching order from 3 PM till 9–30 PM. We took the men back to barracks & then had to find some food for them. We managed to fix them up & then had to look about for ourselves. We could not go back to Ross as there was no boat at that time ~~at~~ of night so we did the next best thing & presented ourselves at the various bungalows of the inhabitants & begged a bed & a dinner. Having survived the night we went on board early next morning.

The "Sutley" in peace times is used for carrying Coolie emigrants from Calcutta to Singapore so you can just imagine what an old tub she was. There was plenty of room for the men but the officers hardly had room to move. Before she arrived a wire came saying that officers wives would be able to go up in her, but we eventually found that there was no room for them so the poor wives had to stand & wave their handkerchiefs from the

jetty when we steamed out. It was a beautiful morning when we left &
although Port Blair is always a ~~bea del~~ beautiful place I don't think I ever
saw ~~her~~ it look so delightful as when we steamed out As soon as we got
under way the bugle band came on deck & played our Regimental march
which was answered by thundering cheers from the warships in the harbour,
answered again by cheers from our own men : it really felt good to be a
British soldier that morning even if we often thought otherwise when we
had to work hard back in the hot weather.

The people left behind in port Blair were all on the jetty waving handkerchiefs etc but they ~~K~~ soon faded from view & before long ~~Pt~~ Port Blair,
~~were~~ where we spent ten months ~~of~~ of the year we have had in India was
just a blur on the horizon.

You would have been amused to see us on the "Sutley" – six in one cabin
all trying to dress at once. The cabins were full of luggage – there was not
an inch of room to stand in & yet we all used to try & wash shave & dress
at once. The saloon was far to small for us all so we had our meals from
tables placed out on the boat deck. As soon as dinner was over in the
evening the tables were moved back & what had been our ~~dinningro~~ room
became changed into a ~~doir~~ dormitory the beds being brought up & laid
in a long row all down the deck.

We picked up the pilot during ~~dinnerti~~ time on the evening of the 15th
& anchored at the mouth of the river a little later in the evening in order
to wait for daylight before proceeding.

The voyage was absolutely delightful – there was a nice breeze the whole
time but ~~the~~ the boat was very steady indeed & I don't think anyone was
sick. We went up the river to Calcutta in daylight but none of us were very
impressed with the scenery of the delta. Perhaps it is hardly fair to say much
about it for we were all perished with the cold, but it was absolutely flat
& frightfully monotonous. As we came North it gradually became colder.
When we left Port Blair we went about in shirtsleeves, but the next day
several of us found the benefit of a tunic. The third day tunics were absolutely
necessary & as we went up the river on the last day ~~the co~~ as many of us
as had them were wearing great coats & the others were perished with the
cold. I think when we woke up on a cold raw morning in Calcutta a good
many men rather wished for the sun of Port Blair. We reached Calcutta
about 2–30 in the afternoon but it was about an hour later before we were
finally drawn up alongside the wharfe in Kidderpore docks. As we got nearer
Calcutta the river became more interesting & there were plenty of strange
things for us to see & talk about : but perhaps the strangest of all ~~was~~ were
a railway train & a daily paper. You should have heard the remarks of the
men when they saw a train for the first time for ten months.

Very little disembarkation was done that night & the officers were allowed
to go ashore so ~~we~~ John Andrew, myself & several others went to a hotel

& had dinner & a bath. We went back to the ship for the night and in the morning the disembarkation was carried on as quickly as possible. There was no need for us all to stay in the docks at the same time as "too many cooks spoil the broth" so we took it in turns to go out into Calcutta & see the city by daylight.

Calcutta is a magnificent City – at least as much as I saw of it – beautiful great ♮ buildings, magnificent & open spaces & splendid roads. It is the season in Calcutta now and it ~~was~~ is full of people – quite a sight ~~of~~ for sore eyes after living so long in Port Blair.

I could write reams about Calcutta but I have written a very long letter already & will reserve the rest till I have been there on leave.

We ~~left~~ ♮ left Calcutta on the evening of the 17th arriving at Dinapore station at 2 PM on the 18th. As we travelled along the line we dropped "C" Company at Dum Dum & "D" Company at Barrackpore; "A & B" Coys are therefore the only ones left at headquarters.

We were met by the band of the 1/9th Middlesex Regt. (who we are relieving) who played us into Dinapore. it is three miles from the station to the Cantonments along one of the dustiest roads I have ever seen; I believe the dust is very bad here in the dry weather.

The Middlesex men are all in camp in order that we can have the barracks. They are leaving here to-morrow for Rawal Pindi – I wish we were going with them for they will probably get some fighting up on the frontier. Since we arrived we have ~~very~~ been very busy taking over the barracks & settling down again, & I have therefore seen very little of the place but I think we shall have a good time here if we don't have to stay too long. The country is very very flat and monotonous as we are very near the Ganges, but it has not yet become burnt & brown as it will do later on and therefore does not look so bad as it might do.

The climate here is very different from that of Port Blair : the nights & early mornings are very cold indeed & even ~~in~~ at midday it is not uncomfortably hot. In the evenings it is quite cold enough to require a fire and we have had to turn out our thick flannel shirts to use before breakfast.

I shall have to tell you all ♮ about the place next ~~week~~ when we have had a chance of seeing more of it.

When we arrived at Calcutta we sent up to the post Office & fetched our letters. There were crowds of them ~~to be so~~ waiting for us – among which were our Christmas letters – and we had them sorted & delivered at the docks. We received a splendid box of shortbread from Aunt Agnes at Dornock Mains & the Portishead people sent us out some very nice ties & socks. it was awfully good of Aunt Agnes to think of sending us a Christmas present & I am writing to thank her for it to-day. It is Janet's birthday to-morrow – fancy Janet ~~no~~ nearly grown up. I can hardly ~~really~~ realize now that she has left school & is at home working in the office & helping

Mother. I hope she will have a very happy year & will get on well with her work & at the same time thoroughly enjoy herself.

I am so glad that Duffy's leg is well at last : it is quite time that he ~~was~~ should be able to run about again & tease everyone in the house. I should just like to have seen him make his first attempt to walk after lying so long in bed.

I hope Mother & Father are both keeping quite well & that the rest are getting on well at school

With very best love to you all

> I remain
> > Your affectionate son
> > > Jim

2/4th Somerset L.I.
Dinapore Cantonments

Jan 26th 1915*

My dear Mother & Father

I have just seen Rowe & two other of our sergeants off to Bombay en route for England. Two days ago we heard that they had been granted commissions & to-day about 3 PM a telegram arrived saying that they were to leave Dinapore to-night. They had an awful rush to get ready but they managed to get their things together & then they dined in the mess with us; & a few minutes ago they drove away. Rowe has promised to call & see you & tell you all about us if he is allowed to come down to Cary so he will probably call soon after you get this letter.

We have now had time to settle down here and have had some chance of seeing the place. it is very different from Port Blair or any other part of India that I ~~had~~ have previously seen but I think we shall like it here if we don't have to stay too long – which is very unlikely.

Just at this time of the year the climate is delightful. It is already beginning to get quite warm in the middle of the day, but the mornings and nights are very cold indeed. We have to wear thick clothes at night & in the early morning & at night we are ~~x~~ quite glad of two or three blankets, while the fire in the mess is really delightful. it seems rather funny but until we arrived here we had not seen a fire in a room for over a year. I am sure we shall feel the cold when we get back to England for when the temperature goes down to about 56° it seems bitterly cold.

---

* Should be 1916

The country is absolutely flat – not a hill to be seen anywhere; but luckily all round Dinapore there are plenty of trees which relieve the monotony. At this time of the year the country is fairly green, although it is beginning to get brown already, and in a few weeks time it will become quite bare.

The barracks overlook the river "Sone" (a tributary of the Ganges) and so does the club – in fact the whole of Dinapore is built along the river. About three miles along the road to Patna the Sone joins the Ganges and the road then runs along the banks right into Patna which is six miles away.

We were always told that the Ganges valley was ~~mo~~ one of the most thickly populated regions in the world but I never realized what it ~~ment~~ meant till now. It is six miles from Dinapore to Patna but there are native bazaars the whole way along while Patna itself is one huge bazaar ~~abso~~ absolutely swarming with natives. I have not been far the other way but I am told that it is just the same for miles. Of course to keep up a population like this the ground has to be cultivated to its utmost and in fact all round Dinapore is like one huge garden in which the chief crop is rice. As a matter of fact immediately round here there is not quite so much rice owing to the fact that vegetables for the Calcutta market are grown & it looks very home-like to see onions, potatoes, carrots etc growing instead of coconuts ~~etc~~. You can imagine how good it is to be able to get good fresh vegetables again for at Port Blair practically the only vegetables we had were potatoes & onions.

The soil seems to be very fertile. It is not the light brown soil of the Deccan but a deep black soil which is renewed every year when the river is in flood. The Ganges is a huge river & the only one I have ever seen which can compare with it is the Irrawaddy at Rangoon. I am afraid our poor little Thames would look very small if brought out & placed down beside these great rivers.

John, Andrew, & I are all in the same bungalow & we are quite comfortable. it is a very good bungalow & like all the others in Dinapore has a good large rose garden attached to it. The roses ʰ are absolutely magnificent – as good as we get in England & besides these lots of other English flowers grow well here such as crysanthemums & marigolds.

The great feature of Dinapore is the dust, the like of which I have never seen. The roads are inches deep with it and every vehicle which passes along leaves a cloud of dust behind it.

The men are very pleased with the place so far, and although they have to work harder than at Port Blair they are quite happy for they are getting good food & the climate is nice & cool. There is not a great deal for them to do but they ʸ can have hockey & footer & the recreation ʸ rooms are first class.

John & I have both taken over horses to try & improve ~~his~~ our riding. I have got one of the Colonel's which he lets me have provided I feed it

& take care of it & John has got another spare one on the same terms. I am very anxious to try my hand at polo as there is quite a good ground here. I shan't be able to play the game but I want to be able to take a stick & practice hitting the ball about as it is an awfully good thing to make one ride well. I shall have to improve a good deal yet before I can do this for only yesterday I took a toss while I was cantering round the race course.

I had a letter from Johnnie Withers to-day & he gave me an account of how he won his Military Cross. I al always thought he would do something big & I shall be surprised if he does not finish up with the V.C. He is a splendid little fellow – I sincerely hope he will come through the whole war unwounded.

I am awfully glad the tortishell table reached home safely as I was rather afraid that it would get broken.

We shall have plenty to tell you about next week for on Thursday the Viceroy is coming down to open the new High Court of Justice at Patna & our regiment has to provide the guard of honour for the occasion & also the guard over his person during his stay. Those of us who are not on duty have been invited to the function & also to the a garden party at Government House afterwards to meet the Viceroy.

There is always plenty to tell when we come into a new station & I could write lots more but I think this enough for this week.

W I hope you are all well

With much love to all

> Your affectionate son
> Jim

Dinapore Cantonments
India

4th Feb 1916

My dear Mother & Father.

We have had a very busy time during the last week, and Andrew & I have had the unique distinction of being part of the be guard of honour to H.E. The Viceroy.

Last Monday we had a field day against the Bihar Light Horse for the benefit of the General who wanted to see us both regiments at work.

On Tuesday morning early the guard of honour (3 officers, 4 Sergts. & 100 men) together with a guard of 1 officer, 32 men & 1 sergt. as a o for Govt. House marched to Bankipore a distance of about eight miles. The new High Court which was opened by the Viceroy is in Bankipore but the latter place is really the European end of Patna.

As soon as the transport arrived we pitched our camp & then had to go off to a dress rehearsal which was very tiring & uninteresting. The next day we had nothing to do except drive round & see what sort of a place it was. The precautions taken to prevent an attempt on ~~his life~~ the Viceroy's life were most elaborate, & I realized for the first time what a strain such an office must be to a man.

For days before he arrived the place was filled with detectives & police & the railway was patrolled by police. He arrived about 2 PM on Wednesday but during the morning several pilot engines ran over the line to make sure that all was clear. ~~The~~ I am told that when the King was out here they used to run dummy trains in order to be more certain.

Before he arrived, the station & the roads leading to Government House, were all closed & police lined the route one for every 10 yards on either side.

Our men on Guard at Government House had to take care of him while he was there & two of them were always on the roof above his head while the others were on sentry in the passages & all round the house.

The ~~ve~~ Viceroy left Govt. house for the ceremony at 10–15 AM on Thursday morning to a salute of 31 guns. We formed the Guard of Honour at the ~~Ent~~ entrance to the High Court our own men being on the right & an equal number on of the 89th Punjabis on the left X Following the troops were light natives in scarlet & gold carrying the regalia which was mostly of silver & then ~~wa~~ there was a procession of various important personages of the district.

The Lieut Governor~~ent~~ of the province arrived first & we had to give him a general salute; & the Viceroy arrived shortly afterwards escorted by the Bihar Light Horse & accompanied by his aides-de-camp. When he had alighted from his carriage he inspected the Guard of honour, but before doing so we gave him a royal salute. After the inspection he went into a large tent which contained all the people of note from miles around including the local Maharajas etc. Just as he came to the tent the trumpeters blew a fanfare & then he proceeded to take a seat on the throne. I don't quite know what happened in the tent for I was not inside but I believe speeches were made & the judjes were ~~introdued~~ introduced to him.

The next thing was the actual opening of the building, for which ~~porp~~ purpose he was presented with a golden key. He looked over the building & then drove away while we gave him another royal salute. it was rather an interesting ceremony, & well worth seeing, & of course we were lucky to have formed part of the Guard of Honour.

The same afternoon we were invited to a party at Govt. House to meet the Viceroy but when we arrived there we found that ~~the~~ His Excellency had an attack of fever & could not appear. He is supposed to have left Bankipore at 10–30 the same night but the general opinion is that he left privately soon after the ceremony – hence his absence at the Garden Party.

Our camp was struck early this morning & we reached Dinapore in time for lunch : but we are all feeling rather tired.

While we were away the General inspected our barracks & went through the books etc : we have every reason to think that he was quite satisfied. He decided that we are to do Kitchener's test at the end of this month so we shall have to work hard to get into good training or else we shall not be able to do very well.

The nights are still quite cold but it is beginning to get hot in the daytime now. it is already getting very obvious that we shall have it a good deal hotter than we want a little later on.

The mail is late this week so we have no letters to answer. They will probably arrive some time to-morrow.

I hope everyone at home is quite well

> With much love
> from your affectionate son
> Jim

P. S. Andrew & I are giving John a leather suit case for his 21st birthday

Extract from:

The Beharee, *Saturday 5 February 1916*

The Opening Ceremony of the Patna High Court

The ceremony of opening the Patna High Court last Thursday by Lord Hardinge was really an epoch making function in more than one respect. It marks the achievement of one of the most important factors that go to make a self-sufficient and self-contained province; the attainment by the province what his Excellency Lord Hardinge in his speech at the ceremony characterised "the outward and visible sign of the full development of a province-a development to which other provinces of India have aspirations, but which you are now about to see realised." There could hardly have been anybody in the vast assemblage in the pavilion, of members of the landed aristocracy, nobility and gentry of the province, on Thursday, who, looking at the imposing and stately structure, would not have felt that peculiar sense of gratification that comes only through the satisfaction of one's heart's ambition. And, we may be sure, to not a few of them as they went about inspecting the interior of the edifice, must have come instinctively memories of the days anterior to the creation of the province when this humble journal, then a weekly, under its founder editor, the late lamented Babu Mahesh Narain, agitated for separation of Behar and Orissa and Chota Nagpore from Bengal and the creation of them into an independent administrative unit; how prophetic has proved the pronouncement made by the late Babu Mahesh Narayan in 1896, when the agitation was set down as a "silly season" effusion by the then Lieutenant-Governor of Bengal, that sooner or later some such administrative reform was bound to be effected; and the untold benefits that should accrue from it to these parts. Few could then have seen that the prophecy was to come true so soon as it actually did. Most happily Providence sent over to us a Viceroy possessing in an uncommon degree the natural bene-volence of head and heart, who not long after assuming the reins of Indian administration realised the reasonableness of the wants and aspirations of the people of these parts; and, realising, had the courage to assist at the birth of this province, as his Excellency modestly puts it. One can well appreciate the "feeling of immense pleasure," to which his Excellency gave expression in the opening sentences of his speech, at the opportunity the opening ceremony of the High Court afforded him "of revisiting Bankipore, and to be able to leave India with the feeling and knowledge that all is well in this young but sturdy and loyal province, and that its progress and development are assured under the able and sympathetic guidance of Sir Edward Gait." His Excellency's gratification must quite naturally be very great at having seen before his retirement the foundation of this province well and truly laid and some of the essentials of a self-contained province realised. That sense of gratification is equally shared by the people. Nay, their gratification is far keener, their sense ef gratefulness to his Excellency profound; and with the progress of time, as the province makes headway and the administrative reform bears more and better fruits, that sense will strengthen and grow deeper and deeper still. There, however, comes over the mind at the present moment a feeling of disappointment and regret that his Excellency's term of office should not have been further extended, at least until sometime after the war. But the ways of the India office are times inexplicable; and this is not, perhaps, the time or place to enlarge on this aspect of the question.

Thursday's ceremony was an epoch-making one from another point of view. The performance of such a ceremony had not "fallen to the lot of any previous Viceroy". His Excellency considered it an "almost unique duty" to perform the ceremony. He said: "It is, therefore, my peculiar privilege to stand alone among those who have represented the Crown in the Indian Empire, in presiding at the opening ceremony of a building which is to house a new Chartered High Court". And his Excellency added;: "This is particularly gratifying to me, as it permits me to witness the final step, I may say, the placing of the coping stone of a great administration reform which, I am happy to say, has been brought to its frnition before the close of my term of office." No doubt, the people of this province may well congratulate themselves, as his Excellency observed "in many ways, on their new institution." But it is his Excellency himself to whose wise statesmanship and generous benevolence they owe the institution and, of course with it, their self-gratulation

From time to time since the outbreak of war, critics in the Bengal Press have been strongly assailing the wisdom of the Government in proceeding with the construction of the High Court buildings. His Honour Sir Edward Gait, in his speech inviting Lord Hardinge to open the court, referred to the fact that the construction of the Secretariat and other buildings had been postponed, but it was recognised that whatever else might suffer, nothing should be allowed to delay the establishment of the provincial High Court. In this to be sure, the Government carried with themselves the people of the province, whatever captious critics of Bengal might say. His Excellency very happily suggested that our enemies, might find a lesson in the establishment of the High Court under the distractions of this troubled time-The lesson "that the British Government, even under the distractions of this troubled time, persues with unfailing vigour the aim which it has always proposed to itself as one of the fundamental objects of all good government-the desire to facilitate the administration of justice to all its subjects."

His Excellency very considerately took occasion to refer to some other ambitions of the people of this province, which remained to be gratified, -viz., their own University and their own Engineering and Medical colleges. "These are very proper aspirations," observed his Excellency, "and will no doubt be fulfilled in due course of time and you need have no fear that your ambition will suffer from any lack of sympathy on the part of the Government of India." The materialisation of the University, as we know, has been put back owing to the financial stringency resulting from the war. The want of an Engineering College and Medical College is very keenly felt. Time and again has the demand been made through the local press for raising the status of the local Engineering and Medical schools to the status of colleges, and the question raised in the local Council. But no definite hope has been held out of the demand being met in the near future. It is, however, very gratifying to be assured by his Excellency that our ambition will not suffer from lack of syampathy on the part of the Government of India.

2/4th Somerset L.I.
Dinapore Cantonments
Bihar
India

Feb 11th 1916

My dear Mother & Father.

It is John's 21st birthday to-day & of course we are feeling somewhat elated but there is very little to ~~do~~ be done by way of celebration except hard work. We gave ~~to~~ him a leather suit case this morning & your wire was waiting for him when he came in for breakfast. I am very busy indeed now, being acting Adjutant for the Bttn. McLaren who has been the adjutant ~~is~~ has just joined the R.A.M.C. & the man who is to succeed him is still at Port Blair so I am carrying on till he can come on to Dinapore. It is rather hard work at first but I am very glad to have had the ~~ch~~ opportunity of gaining a little more experience.

We are now working hard for Kitchener's test which starts on Feb. 28th. Every morning we do a long route march & practice every conceivable military manouvre so that in a week or two we ought to be fit for anything. Andrew is getting on very well indeed as signalling officer – he will probably go away to the hills early in March for a course of instruction, & I also hope to go away to the school of Musketry for a course about the middle of March. John makes a splendid Station Staff Officer – he is getting on splendidly.

Last week I told you that it was getting very warm but during the last week we have had some very cold weather again. For about three days it was bitterly cold owing to a very cold NW wind which blew down from the hills: – it was very ~~dry~~ dry & made our skin crack & peel just like an East wind at home. I was awfully glad to hear that the table I sent from Port Blair arrived in good condition as I was rather afraid that it would get damaged on the journey.

I hope you had a good time at Portishead and feel better for the change. I was delighted to hear that Duffy was enjoying himself & hope that he has become really strong again now.

I suppose the "Compulsion Bill" came into force yesterday for I see in to-day's paper that all the classes up to thirty have been called up. In peace time I strongly object to conscription but I think it is about time that the slackers were compelled to join. Our own men are much keener & much more contented now that they know that their pals at home have been forced to join. Previously they were very annoyed ~~that~~ over the fact that while they were out here doing their best the fellows at home were drawing increased wages & having a good time.

I suppose Jim of Dornock Mains will be called up – what will Aunt Agnes think about that? We have not yet got tired of Dinapore, but we have seen nearly everything there is to be seen in the place & in the neighbourhood. The roads are very monotonous indeed being very straight & exceedingly dusty. On each side the native huts are almost continuous & the absolutely dead level of the country is rather wearisome. It would be quite a relief to see a good steep hill even if it was hard work getting to the top.

The natives are not nearly so clean & nice looking as those of the West Coast. Their clothes always seems dirty & the smell of the villages is absolutely disgusting. There is a great deal of plague in this neighbourhood, but of course it does not affect us at all.

So far we have not played much hockey or footer : – tennis has been our pastime, but we started hockey last week & I expect we shall soon get the games going again.

The health of the men has improved wonderfully & the effects of the malaria are gradually working off.

Flower & Royal returned from Wellington ⲭ two days ago looking very fit indeed – they at any rate seem to have quite got over ~~thier~~ their attacks of malaria.

My news is quite exhausted so I will stop at once.

I hope you are all quite well

With much love to all

> Your affectionate son
> Jim

2/4th Somerset L.I.
Dinapore
Bihar

17/2/16

My dear Mother & Father.

As I told you last week McLaren has joined the R.A.M.C. and I have been adjutant for the last ten days. I have had a very busy time for with Kitchener's test coming off shortly there has been a lot of extra work to do. I found it rather difficult at first but now I have got into the routine things are much more simple, & take less time. We have quite settled down here now and there is not so much to write about, but I should not be surprised ~~it~~ if we were moved on again very shortly. There is a good deal of moving of troops going on just at present & our 1/4ᵗʰ are on their way to the Gulf. It would be very stupid of me to spread silly rumours, but there is a persistent rumour that we shall shortly be moved to Rawal-Pindi up on the frontier. Yesterday we received a wire from the Brigade telling us to remain mobilized so that it looks as if there is some truth in the rumour.

We are glad that the 1/4ᵗʰ have at last got their chance of ~~seeing~~ active service & there is every reason to think that they will do really well for there is no doubt that they are one of the finest territoral units in India. I heard from Ronald Vallis last week, & he says that he is taking out a draft to the 1/4ᵗʰ Hants Regt. who ~~were~~ had such heavy losses last year.

We have had a little rain this week which has freshened everything up splendidly. The grass has started to shoot again & there is a delightful fresh smell in the air. It is raining slightly now, ~~but~~ and there is a very strong cold wind blowing, which makes one turn out all the thickest clothes he posesses.

I don't know if I ever told you what really took place at Port Blair but as I have nothing better to write about this week I will just tell you a little about it. When I returned from Rangoon last August I found Port Blair in a state of great excitement. The intelligence department reported that two ships had been fitted out in America, & loaded with rifles & ammunition and manned by a scalliwag crew of Europeans & Indians. When this was reported at Port Blair it was known that they had ~~proceeded~~ left America but they had been lost sight of somewhere near Java. The object in view was to arm the convicts in Port Blair & with this assistance to release certain important political prisoners now confined ~~their~~ there. Then they intended to go on to Rangoon & try & cause as much trouble as possible there.

This was all found out by the intelligence department & every precaution was accordingly taken – among others the rest of our Regt. was sent to Port Blair.

Towards the middle of November we heard that the attack on Port Blair was definitely planned for Christmas Day, when ~~it was~~ no doubt they thought we should be off our ~~Gua~~ guard. We took every possible precaution & a strong fleet of ~~war~~ cruisers were in the Bay of Bengal but on Christmas Eve we had an urgent wire to say that one of the ships had broken through the cordon of cruisers & was making for Port Blair. Needless to say Christmas day & night we stood to arms nearly the whole time.

The enemy did not succeeded in reaching Port Blair but she evaded our ships for several days. A day or two after the New Year we heard firing at sea & it was subsequently reported that she had been fired at & captured by one of our ships. The plan ~~was~~ to attack on Christmas day was part of a general plan for the whole of India but it was of course discovered & practically every garrison stood to arms on Christmas night. We saw more of the Navy during those few weeks than I have ever seen before for the various ships were constantly looking in & going away again.

18ᵗʰ Feb. I received your letter of Jan 19ᵗʰ to-day but John received one dated Jan 26ᵗʰ so I expect ours of the corresponding date will arrive to-morrow. We did not get a mail last week as a truck load of bags missed the boat at Marseilles & that truck contained last week's letters. They came on by ~~bo~~ this week's boat & I ~~x~~ suppose we shall have the full mail to-morrow.

Two days ago I received quite a lot of letters dated December 9ᵗʰ so that they took ~~tw~~ over two months to reach me.

I am ~~x~~ very glad that you had a good holiday at Portishead & that it did Duffy & Margaret so much good.

We are all very fit – playing the Devon Battery at rugger this afternoon as the rain has softened the ground a little.

I am enclosing one or two photos which are rather interesting.

Hoping you are all quite well

With best love to all

   I remain

     your affectionate son

     Jim

2/4ᵗʰ Somerset L.I.
Dinapore
Bihar

23/2/16

My dear Mother & Father.

There is very little to write about this week as we have had time for little ~~by~~ but training for Kitchener's Test. Ingram arrived from Port Blair last Monday and took over the Adjutantcy from me so I have not been quite as busy this week as I was last. As soon as the test is over I am going off to Lucknow for a week's leave and I have just written to a dentist to try & fix an appointment as I want my teeth thoroughly overhauled. As soon as the leave is over I am going off to a ~~Place~~ place called Pachmari for a course of musketry similar to the one John took at Satara last year. Andrew is leaving here for Kasauli on Sunday morning & he is very excited about it. He has worked very hard indeed to learn as much as possible about signalling before he goes on his course & you would be quite surprised at the way he sticks to his books – not a bit like the Andrew who used to go to Sexey's.

Last Sunday after Church Parade Mʳˢ Waddy & Mʳˢ Burt distributed to the men Princess Mary's Xmas Gifts which have only just arrived here. They consist of a very ornamental box containing a card & a pencil case made ~~like~~ of a ~~h~~ cartridge case from the front with a silver bullet. I daresay you have seen some of them at home. Of course the men were very pleased indeed and I expect some of those boxes will be handed down to future generations as family heirlooms.

Four more of our men left here this week for Bombay in order to go home to take commissions. It is rather bad luck on the Battalion to have to be continually losing ~~so~~ its best men but of course it is only fair to ~~h~~ them as most of them are far more suitable for officers that lots of the fellows who are getting commissions now. Stephens, one of the men who went back with Rowe was the Coy. Quartermaster Sergt. of our company & he has promised to come & see you to tell you all about us. He was a schoolmaster at Radstock under Mr Lewin before war broke out so I used to hear all about Lewin when he was here. I heard from Passmore last week – he is now at Salonika waiting for the ~~Turks wh~~ enemy who won't come on.

We are going to be the depôt for the 1/4th & all those who were not allowed to go to the Gulf ~~were sent back~~ are coming here next Tuesday. I suppose before long we shall have their sick & wounded sent back here.

I should think it must be very strange ~~at~~ in England in these days of conscription – I am extremely thankful that neither of us waited to be conscripted. The full mail has not yet arrived this week but stray letters have got through for some fellows, & it seems from them that you are still getting air raids each one of which seems to go farther westwards than the one before it. I wonder if something will be invented which will effectively stop the zepplins from coming over.

We have had some very rough wind this week but it is no longer very cold. The middle of the day is now too warm to be comfortable while the evenings & mornings are much warmer than when we came here. On the days when the wind was blowing there was so much dust in the air that it quite obscured the sun & it ~~seemed~~ got quite dark just as if the sky was full of heavy clouds.

I hope you are all very well at Park Cottage & I also hope that Aunty Susan is now much better.

With love to you all

        I remain

            Your affectionate son

                Jim

2/4th Somerset L I
Dinapore
Bihar

⚡ 3/2/16*

My dear Mother & Father

At 6–15 A M this morning we marched into the barracks after having completed Kitchener's test & as I have been busy a good part of the day I am just about tired out & shall not be long getting into bed as soon as mess is over.

I will just give you an account of of the Test & tell you what the General thought of us. On Tuesday morning we had to get up at 3 o'clock at and at 5 o'clock the head of the column marched out of the barracks. I was in charge of the advanced guard, then followed the remainder of the regiment, behind which was a battery of artillery & the rear guard. We marched about twelve miles to a place called Anandapur & then halted for an hour to have breakfast. As soon as the latter was finished we started an attack with ball ammunition on a position about 3 miles away. The enemy were represented by earthenware pots raised on little sticks which the men proceeded to knock down in five fine style. There were three lines of them representing three successive positions of the enemy & we had to assault each position with the bayonet as we came up to it. By the time the last position was captured it was about 1–30 P M & very hot the sun was very hot so you can imagine we were glad to get into camp bivouac again to get our dinners. During the afternoon the General inspected the bivouac & held a pow wow for officers & NCO^s – he was quite pleased with the attack & said that the marching & spirit of the men was magnificent. Only two men fell out the first day & both were went down with malaria.

We rolled up in our blankets very early indeed & even if we had no beds or mattrasses we all slept very soundly indeed.

The second day the various platoons did field firing, bayonet fighting, bridge building & physical drill for the General's benefit during the morning & at 4 o'clock in the afternoon we started the most strenuous series of operations I have ever experienced & which finished this morning when we marched into barracks. We were At 4 PM we put outposts which had to stay out all night. They were withdrawn at 5–30 AM & then we were able to have a cup & tea & a bus biscuit before the transport left at 7 AM. We left the bivouac at 8 AM to march about 7 miles to the next camping ground were where the cooks had ou who went with the transport had our

---

* Should read 3/3/16

breakfast ready. We represented the rearguard of a brigade & on the way we were attacked by a skeleton enemy of Sepoys. This meant that we had to fight a rearguard action for about 2½ miles before we beat off the enemy & could go on to our camp which we reached about mid-day very hungry & tired having had practically no food since 3–30 PM the day before. We rested at this place till 8–30 in the evening & then did a night march of about four miles. We then deployed & advanced on a prepared position over very difficult ground. On reaching a point about five two hundred yards from the position we were ordered to dig ourselves in. The men were digging nearly the whole night but they were so tired that the very minute they stopped work they dropped off to sleep where they stood. We had a very hard job keeping them at it for we were just about done tired out ourselves & it was a bitterly cold night. At 5 AM this morning the we manned the trenches we had dug during the night, fixed our bayonets & assaulted the enemy's position. We then marched back to barracks & were dismissed.

During the whole of the operations only 24 men dropped out, & of of these only two were suffering from exhaustion : the remainder of the cases were mostly fever.

The General was quite pleased with us on the whole – of course he had lots of criticisms to make but he was delighted with the spirit & endurence of the men who did their very best the whole time.

It is a very strenuous test & very trying owing to lack of sleep especially the last two days & nights. The nights were frightfully cold & the days very hot; conditions which are not the very best for manouvres.

Neither John or Andrew were out the former being on duty as SS Station Staff Officer & the latter being away at Kasauli.

I am going away on leave the day after to-morrow & then I am going to Packmari for a musketry course. John also has secured three days leave so he is coming with me.

I am afraid I am too tired to write any more now as I can hardly keep my eyes open.

W I hope you are all very well

With much love to all

> from your affectionate son
> Jim

2/4th Somerset L.I.
Royal Hotel
Lucknow

10th March 1916

My dear Mother & Father.

Thank you very much indeed for your letters containing birthday wishes :
I don't think any letters were ever more ~~well~~ welcome for they arrived
while I was recovering from an excessive dose of cocaine as I will explain
later.

The cheese has not yet arrived, but parcels always take longer than letters
and it will probably turn up this week. I can assure you that when it does
come it will be greatly appreciated as we can't get any really good cheese
out here, and it is delightful to be able to eat a really good piece of bread
& cheese again.

As you see from the above address I am now staying at Lucknow. As
soon as Kitchener's test was over John & I secured some leave – he had
about 4 days & I had rather over a week. I came straight to Lucknow
because I wanted to see a dentist but John spent a day at Benares on his
way up. The railway journey from ~~X~~ Dinapore to Lucknow was most
uninteresting. The line runs up the Ganges valley ~~where~~ and it is perfectly
flat ~~ever~~ everywhere : in fact anyone who had ever moved out of the district
would be perfectly justified in supposing the surface of the world to be
quite flat. Lucknow is ~~so~~ very much like most Indian cities – there is the
English part & the Native part, the former being characterised by large
bungalows surrounded by gardens, large open spaces & public gardens.
Yesterday we went down into the old Native City & ~~so~~ saw a bit of real
India. We had to walk down through streets as they were too narrow for
carriages, & the people were so thick that we could hardly get along. The
filth & stench were terrible & I can't imagine how the natives manage to
exist at all in such a place. It is was such a contrast from the English city
where each bungalow is quite separate from the next one & where space
& distance seem unlimited.

Of course, ~~the~~ as soon as we arrived here we went off to see the old
Residency where the handful of English under Sir Henry Lawrence held out
during the mutiny. The old building is now almost in ruins but it is awfully
picturesque as it is surrounded by beautifully kept lawns & gardens. The
Union Jack still waves over the tower & it is about the only one in the world
which is not lowered at night. ~~A new~~ The flag is renewed every year but it is
never lowered, because during the whole of the ~~munist~~ mutiny the British
never lowered their colours & therefore they do not let it down now. ~~We~~

The Residency

Dilcusta Palace: Held by the rebels during the Mutiny. Sir Henry Havelock died here

Bailey Giuard Gate at the entrance to the Residency. Holes in the masonry caused by the cannon balls of the mutineers

~~were shown~~ The guide ~~to~~ who took us round ~~sh~~ pointed out the place where Jessie Brown was lying when she dreamed that she could hear the pipers playing in the distance & also the house where Sir Henry Lawrence died. It seemed at first as if the mutiny was in the far distant past but ~~it was how~~ one realized that it was not so many years ago when the guide pointed to a house & told us that from the top of it Lieut Roberts (~~afters~~ afterwards Lord Roberts) signalled to the people in the Residency to let them know that the relieving force was coming.

I have spent a good deal of my time with the dentist since I came here, & I now have a very sore mouth but a much better set of teeth. This is a very bad climate for teeth & mine got very bad down at Port Blair so I made up my mind to have them properly seen to when I came here.

So far I have had five out, four stopped & ~~fo~~ three crowned, & before I have finished this letter I shall have had one more crowned. ~~The day I had~~ He had an awful job to pull my teeth out, they were tremendous things: & he gave me too much coccaine which made me pretty rotten for a time.

I have just returned from my last visit to the dentist and my mouth is fairly well fixed up. I shall have to get a plate put in below when I get a chance but at present the gums are too sore. The whole thing has cost me about £14 but I saved a good deal of money at Port Blair and I still have quite a useful reserve. I ought to have no more real trouble with my teeth for some years. i heard from Andrew a few days ago & was pleased to hear that he is getting on quite well : he says that Kasauli is the best place he has yet seen in India.

I am very glad you had such a nice party on John's 21st birthday : I think John is awfully pleased about it.

It seems that there will be lots of faces missing when we come back to Cary again & I am very sorry that Mrs S Parsons is gone for she used to be awfully good to us when we were kiddies.

I am very glad that Duffie is quite well again & has suffered no permanent harm & I hope that you are all keeping quite well.

With very much love to you all

> I remain
>> your affectionate son
>> Jim

I have enclosed a few photographs which I have taken since I have been here.

School of Musketry
Packmari

March 17th 1916

My dear Mother & Father.

Thank you very much indeed for the cheese which you sent me out & ~~all~~ the letters with birthday wishes. Janet's & Mothers letters of Feb 17th reached me to-day so they could hardly have been better timed. The cheese arrived last week, ~~but~~ and unfortunately I was away from Dinapore, being on my way up here from Lucknow, so I told John he had better open & eat it. it is so hot out here now that it would be impossible to have it sent on to me, but John says it was a real beauty better even than the other one & every one at the mess who had any of it were absolutely delighted.

I wrote last week from Lucknow but now I am at Packmari doing a musketry course. Packmari is in the ~~Vyn~~ Vindhya Hills & is almost exactly in the centre of India – a little South of Jubblepore. It was rather a long railway journey from Lucknow & I arrived at the railway station for Packmari at 2–30 AM in the morning feeling rather tired. I found Lee who had come from Dinapore fast asleep at the station, he having arrived rather earlier. At 6 AM we started to motor up to Packmari, 32 miles away, & ~~X~~ it really was a delightful ~~de~~ ride. The road, an awfully good one, runs right up through the hills which are beautifully wooded and the scenery is magnificent. I have never seen such gorges as there are in these hills. At one place we passed, the cliffs on each side of a little stream were 1000 feet high & it made one feel giddy to look over the edge. It must be very similar to the cannons of North America Packmari is a delightful spot being situated in a basin right on the crest of the hills which here are 3500′ high. I hoped that it would be nice & cool but in this latitude 3000′ is not sufficient to make much difference and it is already very hot indeed here. I don't know what the temperature actually is now but just below us at Nagpur it was over 100° in the shade yesterday & the hot season has not really started yet. It is awfully nice to see some hills again, for we get very tired of the absolutely ⟨×⟩ dead level of the Ganges valley, & before I go away from here I want to go to the top of some of the peaks around here. At present they are working us very hard indeed in order to cram a six weeks course into three weeks. What with lectures, notes etc it is just like being back at school again, but I am enjoying it because it is a change from our usual work.

Lee & I were the first arrivals & ~~we go~~ our first impression of the place was very funny : it was just like a place out of a fairy story. There was a big club, with servants all ready, there ~~were~~ tennis courts & hockey pitch were all marked out, bungalows were all furnished, & gardens beautifully kept, in fact the whole place was ready but there was no one to occupy it. When we arrived there was hardly a person to be seen in the place, as the season here has hardly started yet but during the last day or two several people have come up & there are already signs of life in the "deserted city."

It seems rather strange that ten months of last year were spent at Port Blair — a place we had hardly heard of before. ~~The~~ A year ago to-morrow I was told to return from Calicut to go to the Andamans & I certainly did ~~kn~~ not know then that I should be there so long.

I am awfully sorry to hear about poor old Johnny Withers — it is awfully bad luck after doing so well at the front & I sincerely hope that he will pull through all right in the end. I ~~am~~ have quite recovered from the effects of the dentist by this time & my mouth is hardly at all sore now. John & Andrew both seem very fit — the latter is having rather a strenuous time on his course.

I am very glad to hear that everything on the "farm" is doing well & I hope the calf will fetch a good big price.

I hope you are all quite well

With very much love to all

> Your affectionate son
> Jim

Packmari

17th March 1916

My dear Ted.

Thank you very much indeed for your letter containing birthday wishes, also thank you all very much indeed for getting me some books for a present. I have read neither of them before & am now looking forward to their arrival. It is awfully kind of all of you to get them for me & books are always welcome.

I am afraid I have very little news for you as I have put it all into the other letter. The longer I stay out here the more I wish that some of the rest of you could just come out & have a look at India for it really is a wonderful country. i have been particularly fortunate ~~for~~ in seeing all parts of India. We started from Bombay & I have been to Bangalore, Calicut & Malappuram, Madras, Port Blair, Rangoon, Calcutta, Dinapore, Patna, Lucknow & now I am up here at Packmari which is a delightful spot.

It seems rather funny to be harvesting in March but the harvest is now in full swing out here. All through Northern India there are thousands of square miles of splendid wheat & barley crops which are now being harvested. They are the Winter crops out here & are harvested just as the hot season is coming in & before very long you will probably be eating bread from Indian wheat.

This is a wonderful country for game all round here. Panther & bear are quite plentiful about three miles away, while buck often run across the road as you are going along., Several of the students of the last course shot panther while they were up here.

March 18th I have had a fine birthday present to-day in the form of a telegram from John congratulating me on getting my captaincy. ~~So~~ This is the first I have heard of it so you can imagine how pleased I am feeling. Isn't it strange that I should have received the news on my birthday. I knew that my name had gone up & I also know that John's went up at the same time for his second star so I suppose he has heard about his as well.

This will mean an extra 100 rupees a month to my pay so I shall now be quite well off (R100 =£6–13–4) We have had a very strenuous time since we have been up here & I am very glad that it is Sunday to-morrow to get a rest

I hope you are all quite well

With very much love to all

> I remain
> > your affectre brother
> > > Jim

School of Musketry
Packmari

24/3/16

My dear Mother & Father.

I have not a great deal to write about this week for we are being worked so hard at the musketry that we have had very little time for anything else.

We start work at 7 & go straight on to till 1 o'clock except for an hour at breakfast time & the afternoon & evening are spent writing up notes & reading up work for the next day.

I have played Hockey for the School once or twice & had a few games of tennis otherwise there has been no time for games etc. We finished the 1st stage of the course to-day & had an oral exam which I passed. It consisted of instructing a squad of men in various things. The men although trained represented recruits and of course were instructed beforehand to be as foolish as possible & some of the things they said & did were awfully amusing.

I went for an awfully fine walk last Sunday to a place called "Waters Meet" or Fuller's Khud. It is a place where two gorges meet & just where the rivers run into each other there is a deep pool in which we bathed. it is absolutely impossible for me to describe what the place was like for I have never seen anything quite like it before. The tw The rivers, or at this time of the year they are mere streams, both come flowing down narrow gorges with the cliffs on both sides 50 500–600 feet high & meet in a beautifully clear deep pool just below an enormous cliff. The sides of the rocks are all lined with tree ferns and the sides are so high & steep that the sun never shines full on the water except when it is shining straight up the gorge. The water in the pool was awfully cold & we could only stay in for a few minutes. it was very difficult getting down to it & worse still getting up again. The path was very narrow & ran along the side of the gorge gradually getting lower & nearer to the bottom. The scenery all the way along was magnificent & I took some photographs which I will send back to you if they come out well, but I am afraid photographs will hardly give much idea of the height of the cliffs.

For some reason or other Andrew & I did not get our letters from home last week but I suppose they will come on this week – the mail arrived at Bombay to-day so we shall probably get them the day after to-morrow. Wasn't it strange that I heard that about my promotion on my birthday. I received a wire from John in the morning & after that I had sev two or three others & several letters of congratulation so that it was somewhat of an exciting day.

It is very strange how one meets people out here : one of the fellows doing the course is the course is was the Captain of the Sidney Sussex cricket XI the year John played for them. He spotted me at once, as he said that I was exactly like John. Another thing which I heard a week or two ago is that Drummond who lived in the next room to mine at Wantage Hall is in India with the 1/5th Hants. He is now at Fyzabad & I hope we shall come across each other sooner or later.

Have you heard if Johnny Withers is any better yet? I do hope he will get fit again, but if he has enteric it will be a very long business.

I am awfully fit again now, my mouth has quite healed up and the crowns which he put on are quite comfortable.

I hope you are all quite well – I suppose Duffy has gone back to school again now.

With much love to you all

> I remain
> > Your affectionate son
> > > Jim

School of Musketry
Packmari

✗ 31/3/16

My dear Mother & Father.

I received this week your letters for Feb 24th & March 2nd & also the book which the girls sent for my birthday. I was delighted with it for ✗ it is an awfully nice story & I was just wanting a good book when it arrived. I am awfully sorry to hear that Margaret is ill & I hope she will soon get fit again. As Father said in his letter the Doctor does not seem to stay out of Park Cottage for long at a time; and I feel very thankful that we all three keep so fit for it is not very pleasant to be ill out here. The week has slipped along very quickly & we are getting on very well with our Course. it is much more interesting than it was at first and we have done a good deal of firing this week.

Yesterday they gave us a much needed rest so three of us went out for the day to a place called Fairy pool which is even more beautiful than Waters Meet.

To get to it we went down the side of the Khud till we came to the stream & then we followed it down till it came to a fall of about 100 feet. Below the fall in a little basin is one of the most delightful pools I have ever seen. The water is as clear as crystal & fish dart about all over the place while the water coming down over the fall is awfully pretty. The basin is surrounded by fern covered cliffs & at one end there is an outlet through which the water runs away.

About 200 yards below the pool is what is called ~~bi~~ Big Fall where the stream falls over a precipice into a pool 600 feet below. ⟩ It made me giddy to look down but it is really a magnificent sight. Of course what is now a stream is a raging torrent during the rains and I should like to see it falling over when there is plenty of water.

We had a bathe first before lunch and another just before tea – the water was beautifully cool and we should have liked to stay in all day. After lunch we lay down & read or slept just as we felt inclined, & about half past six we started home. We ought to have started earlier for it was quite dark before we reached the top of the Khud and it was very difficult climbing up a steep path in the dark.

I read in to-day's telegrams that you have been having a very severe blizzard in England & that the whole country is covered in snow. it seems funny that we are ~~comp~~ complaining of the heat in a place higher than Mount Snowdon & you are snowed up & shivering with cold.

It is getting hotter & hotter out here, & everyone who can possibly get off is going up to the Hills for the hot weather.

M I hope Mother is quite well again ; she said in her last letter that she had been obliged to stay in bed : I am afraid the cold weather will not do her any good.

I think this is all I can find to write about this week so I will get off to bed as we have to be up early in the morning.

With best love to all

>> I remain
>>> Your affectionate son
>>> Jim

Packmari

1/4/16

My dear Pussy.

I am awfully sorry to hear that you are unwell & I do hope that you will soon be quite fit again.

I was delighted with the book you three sent me for my birthday. I was feeling very tired when it arrived on Wednesday afternoon & and was just wanting a good book. On Thursday I went to Fairy pool & while lying in the shade just beside the pool I read it nearly all through. it is an awfully good story & I thoroughly enjoyed reading it.

Enclosed you will find a P. O. for 5/- with ~~wit~~ which I hope you will buy something to play or amuse yourself with for if you have to stay in bed I am sure the time must go very slowly.

I think this letter will reach you just as you are breaking up for the Easter holidays and I hope you will be quite well by then so as to enjoy the holidays as much as possible. We shall be thinking about you all when you are eating the hot cross buns on Good Friday & when you are out looking for primroses & violets later in the morning.

Give my love to Duffy and all the others & make haste & get well.

> With love from your affectionate brother
> Jim

School of Musketry
Packmari

April 8th 1916

My dear Mother & Father.

We finished our musketry course by a written exam this morning & now we have nothing more to do but await the result. I am staying here to-night to play in a hockey ~~mat~~ match & shall go down early to-morrow morning.

We have had to work rather hard, but I am not sure that it wasn't a very good thing to have an opportunity of working my brain again, & I shall be sorry to have to go down on to the plains again. I ~~hate~~ don't like the monotonous dead level of the plains at all : it is much nicer to be among the hills.

The weather has been unsettled this week : the heat has caused thunderstorms which have somewhat cleared the air & made it a little cooler. ~~&~~ As a rule you can be absolutely sure that it will be fine day after day at this time of the year.

This has been a very fortunate week for we have had two mails one dated March 8th & the other dated March 15th.

I am awfully pleased that Margaret is better again & I hope her birthday present will turn up safely – if not we will get her another. The news from the Persian Gulf is rather cheering to-day : the telegram only states that we have driven the Turks out of their trenches, but it is a far more important matter than that. The Commandant here has just come back from the Gulf & he explained the situation to us & from his account the position just captured ~~has~~ is ~~been~~ the one which has been stopping our progress so long. ~~There~~ Unless the Turks take up another position while retiring there is only one more Turkish position between General ~~Tons~~ Townsend & the relieving force The interest of the whole of India has been centred on the ~~N~~ new

Viceroy this week & judging from the press comments he has made a very good impression by his opening speeches. I don't envy him his position for he will have some serious difficulties to face when the war is over. I enclose some photographs which were taken with a small camera that I bought in Lucknow. It is an awfully neat little fellow & I can carry it about in my pocket everywhere I go. My other one is inclined to let the light in for the dry air has caused the wood to shrink a little.

I am afraid this is a rather short letter but it is all I can think of this week : I have not had much time for getting about.

Hoping you are all well with very much love to all

> I remain
> Your affectionate son
> Jim

Dinapore

13/4/16

My dear Mother & Father.

I have finished my musketry course & am back at Dinapore again, but I ~am~ was not very pleased to have to come down to the plains again. We finished the course last Saturday and I came down on Sunday. The train journey was not very enjoyable for it was very hot & dusty & there were not enough first class carriages on the train so we were packed in much too tightly to be comfortable. We had to change at 2 o'clock in the morning which was very annoying for it spoilt our night's sleep.

For the first time since I joined the Regiment I have been placed on the sick list. I was having some fielding practice with John two days ago & I missed a catch & put my foot on the ball, the result being a sprained ankle. It was very painful at first but now it only hurts when I try to walk on it. John bandages it up for me every four hours & puts fresh lotion on – he is quite expert at the job now. I don't like having to stay in at all & I hope it will soon be fit again. John is going with the first detachment to our hill depót on Sunday. Six officers are going up this time and they will come down again for the rest of us to go up in about six weeks time.

I went down to the riding school one morning & I was quite surprised to see how John has come on since I have been away. He was taking the jumps in great style & has now got quite a good seat. My pony seems to have had a great time while I have been at Packmari – nearly everyone who has tried to ride her has taken a toss so I am looking forward to trying her myself as soon as my Ẍankle is well enough. The mail is due in to-morrow

& I am hoping the book which the boys are sending will arrive by it : I liked the other one very much indeed.

The country is very burnt up now : everything is brown & dusty & all the crops have been gathered in. The only place where there is are is anything green on the ground is right down close to the big rivers. We had to cross three of these coming back from Pachmari : the Nerabudda, the Jumna & the Ganges. The railways run across on magnificent bridges which are of course much bigger than anything I have ever seen in England.

I hope you are getting better weather again now, for I am sure the cold & snow are not very good for Mother.

With love to all & hoping you are all quite fit

> I remain
> > Your affectre. son
> > > Jim

2/4th Somerset L.I.
Dinapore

20/4/16

My dear Mother & Father.

I am afraid there is nothing very interesting to write about this week for it is very quiet here now that so many people have gone away to the Hills. I have not been able to do very much owing to my ankle, which is now however decidedly better : the Doctor told me to-day that I could try to walk about a little & I shall try to go over to the mess for dinner to-night. I have just taken charge of a pony & trap for a R.A.M.C. captain who has gone to the Gulf & it has been most useful to me this week. I have been able to drive about in the evenings & get to the barracks in the mornings & just have a look round so that it has helped to pass the time away splendidly. The trap is quite a good one & the pony is quite a smart looking animal but he has a very bad habit of rearing when he starts or if he is stopped : but still he is very useful to me & I only have to pay for the cost of his food.

I shall be able to ride again in another week which will be a great help for I love riding about, & my pony.

John went up to the Hills last Saturday & I expect he found it rather hot in the train during the 1st part of the journey. Sunday was one of the hottest days I have ever experienced – there was not a breath of wind & the sun seemed to scorch everything. In the evening I drove over & had tea with Mrs Burt & about after tea we sat on the verandah trying to keep as as cool as possible. About six o'clock a faint breeze began to stir so we got up & had a look round. We could see that there was something coming for there was a great yellow cloud in the distance in front of which a flock of birds were being driven. We just had time to go inside & shut the doors when we were suddenly plunged into absolutely darkness & were surrounded by a howling dust storm. It sw was an amazing sight : the wind was so strong that it blew down trees & the dust was so thick that it completely made we were in complete darkness. After about ten minutes it cleared a little but the storm lasted for about half an hour in all, and was then followed by a violent thunderstorm which fortunately cleared some of the dust away. The dust storm seems to have followed the Ganges dow starting from somewhere just above Benares, & although similar storms are quite frequent in these parts the one on Sunday was supposed to be the most violent for over seventy years. The next morning was beautifully cool, but it has been getting hotter all again all the week, and at the present time another heavy thunderstorm is going on outside.

I have had a nice little job this week namely auditing the Regimental accounts. Three of us forming an audit board had to audit the whole of the accounts for the last quarter, & I really think now that we have finished that I know a little more about balance sheets etc than when we started.

We did not get a very big mail last week as a good many of the letters went down with the "Sussex." John & Andrew both received your letters from home but mine apparently were lost : but I had one or two others to make up for it.

It will be Good Friday to-morrow & I as can assure you that we shall be thinking about you all when you sit down to the hot cross buns. We landed at Port Blair last Good Friday. I heard from Andrew yesterday – he is doing great things up at Kasauli. He says that he has taken "specials" in all his exams so far & is keeping very fit : but I think he is having to work very hard.

It was is very sad news that Ken Lewin has been killed. I did not know him so well as Rex for he was before my time at School but he was an awfully nice fellow. Mr Lewin has now lost his wife & two sons in about four months.

I heard from lots of news about the College at Reading last week : apparently the men have almost entirely disappeared & the whole place is overrun with women students. I believe however that the latter look forward to the time when they will have some men to take them to dances etc again.

I hope you are all quite fit

With love to all

from your affectionate son
Jim

Dinapore

21/4/16

My dear little Duffy.

To day is Good Friday & I expect you are just starting out for a walk to find cowslips & violets. As there are no cowslips & violets here & it is too hot to go out for a walk I thought I would spend the time by writing to wish you very many happy returns of the day your birthday. you are getting such a man that you will soon be going to a big boys' school & I am afraid we shall hardly know you when we come back again.

I hope your leg is quite strong now for you will want to be able to play cricket with Rob & Angus this year Did you have plenty of snob snowballing the other day when there was so much snow on the ground? I should rather like to see some snow now for it is ever so hot out here in India.

I hope you are taking care of Mother & doing all you can to help her, for we want to see her looking fit & well when we come home.

We could not find a good present for you so we are sending back some money with which you can buy just what you like, & then you can write & tell us what what you bought.

With very best love to you all & many happy returns of your birthday

        I remain
           your affectre brother
           Jim

Dinapore

29th April 1916

My dear Father & Mother.

I think you would think there was something the matter if you could see us now for we have sh closed every door & window in the bungalow & the doors are again protected by wooden doors with louvred panels. It certainly looks as if we feared an attack of some sort ; but as a matter of fact we are only trying to keep cool. There is punkah going in every room & we just sit under them & try & imagine what it is like to be really cool. Outside there is a strong wind blowing which is just like a blast furnace & it is simply laden with dust which is so thick that sun is already partially obscured. The only way to keep cool is to keep out the hot air from the outside & that is why we ha we are shut up as if for a siege.

The wind is as dry as it can be & it is absolutely impossible to drink enough to quench your thirst. The evenings & the first part of the nights are very hot but it gradually gets cooler towards mornings. We all sleep out in the gardens & it is quite amusing if you happen to be out particularly early to see beds in ~ev~ all the gardens with sleepers in every sort of posture.

A rather amusing incident happened the other day in this connection. A gunner sergt. was ~tak~ riding along the road with a party of men & just as he passed the his Major's bungalow the latter ~was~ ~sitt~ with his wife was sitting up in bed drinking early tea. The sergt. told the Major afterwards that he had never been in such a fix before for he did not know whether to give "Eyes right" & salute or "Eyes left" in order to prevent the men from looking into the garden or just ride on & say nothing. Like a sensible fellow he ~di~ did the last of these.

My ankle is much better now and I am able to get about again but of course I ~ha~ shall not be able to play any games for a week or two. Our parades are all over by 9 o'clock after which the men are not allowed out again till four except to go from one bungalow to another.

I am afraid you will miss Heathman for ~yo~ with Garland gone & no man outside you will be very short handed. I suppose Janet is delighted to have the opportunity of milking, feeding the pigs etc – we shall expect to see her photograph in the Sketch or the Tatler in a long coat & ~bt~ leather leggings : and the remark "Women & the war" or "Women in war time" underneath, It seems to be nearly as fashionable as marriage now-adays.

We are shortly going to have a shooting competition against the Bihar Light Horse so we had a practice shoot on the range last Thursday morning. None of us shot very well but I managed to do fairly well at some of the ranges. ~It~ Shooting is rather difficult at this time of the year owing to the haze caused by the heat rising off the ground.

I am now making a really serious attempt to learn Hindustani & I have a "mumshi" or native tutor for an hour every day. John is going to Calcutta for the Higher Standard exam next week – he has picked it up awfully quickly.

I hope you all had a good time at Easter & are quite fit.

With very much love to all

from your affectionate son
Jim

Dinapore

4th May 1916

My dear Mother & Father

This has been the hottest week that I have ever experienced. It has steadily been getting hotter for some weeks but the last few days have been the worst of all. The temperature during the day has been 107° in the shade & during the night it usually drops to about 86°; but during the ~~48~~ 24 hours ending last Friday morning the minimum temperature ~~wa~~ night or day was 97° which is ~~abt~~ about the same temperature as the hottest summer day in England.

Everything is hot, the chairs you sit on, your bed & your clothes all feel as if they had been held in front of a fire. If you a ride a bicycle after about 10–30 in the morning the metal becomes almost too hot to touch.

Last ~~Sun~~ Thursday we had a shooting competition Officers ~~v~~& Sergeants in which the Officers won. The idea of it was to pick a team of eight to shoot in the big competition which came off to-day. ~~The Somersets~~ In to-days match the Somersets, Bihar Light Horse & the R F A all competed, & the Somersets were the winners. The scores were Somersets 209. B.L.H. 179. ~~R~~R.F.A. 172. I was fortunate enough to be the top scorer of the match – 35 out of 50. The targets were very difficult indeed, but I managed to get a possible at the silhoutte target at 200; 4 plates out of five in a minute at 300 & eight out of 20 at 500. The target at 500 was so small that we could hardly see the bull & there was a nasty wind blowing across the ~~wind~~ range.

We shall fire a return match on the B.L.H. range in a few days time & then ~~the winners of the~~ each member of the winning team of the whole thing will I believe get a silver cup or something of the sort. I have been obliged to have two days in my bungalow again this week owing to my ~~ak~~ ankle, which was very swollen again. I suppose~~d~~ I must have used it a little too much, but it is going on very well again now & I am going to take care of it this time.

The last day or two have brought us some very strange news. First of all came the news of the fall of "Kut" which was rather expected, but then followed the news of the rebellion in Ireland. The latter as far as we can judge from the telegrams seems to have been quite a serious affair, but apparently it is nothing to do with the Nationalists or Ulsterites. I suppose the business is a deeply laid German scheme but when one thinks of it, it is a wonder that Ireland has been so loyal all along, for it she had little enough to thank England for.

The fall of Kut became inevitable as soon as the ~~Trig~~ Tigris became

James R. Mackie (Jim) – 1916
India

flooded, but the moral result will not be good even if the material loss is not very great. A set back of this sort is not good for India, although I have no reason to suppose that any direct effect has as yet been felt out here.

We have had no mails this week : for some reason they are very late but the boat will reach Bombay on the 6th & we shall have the letters about the eighth.

I am sending ~~one~~ some photographs of myself this which which I had taken while I was in Lucknow about a week before my birthday. I should like one to be given to Grandma Mackie & one to Uncle Will. I am ~~sen~~ also sending one to Portishead & one to St Alban's – do you think there is ~~anywhere~~ anyone else to whom I ought to send one? If I send to Scotland I suppose I ought to send one to each place up there.

I heard this week that I passed the exams at the School of Musketry & shall now get an instructor's certificate. John has passed the Higher Standard Hindustani exam : the result was published in the "Statesman" to-day. It is splendid achievement because he practically taught himself.

I shall have to be Adjutant again for a time for the proper Adjutant has just been taken ill with a touch of sun & will have to go to the Hills for a rest.

I hope you are all quite fit
With much love to all

Your affectionate son
~~So~~ Jim

Dinapore

𝔁 12th May 1916

My dear Mother & Father.

Thank goodness! it is a little cooler now. Two days ago we had a heavy thunderstorm which cleared the air a little and made it cooler, but it is already getting as hot as ever again. We received two mails this week, one of which was a fortnight overdue, & we should have received another ~~this week~~ to-day but mine did not turn up. I expect it will be here to-morrow.

Last Saturday night after dinner we all drove over to Bankipore to attend an evening party given 𝔁 by the Raja Harihar Narayan Sinha of Amawan (to give him his full title) to celebrate his daughter's Churakarna. The latter I believe is a ceremony which takes place when 𝔁 the child first has her hair cut but we did not see the ceremony. It seems rather strange 𝔁 for a party to commence at 9.30 in the evening but it is the ~~Custom~~ custom out here as by that time it is ~~us~~ usually getting cool.

His gardens were beautifully laid out & lighted with japanese lanterns and little tables were dotted all over the place, ~~where you sa~~ absolutely loaded with food. ⅄ We had quite a jolly time for he gave us plenty to eat & drink & by way of entertainment native girls danced & sang to us. The singing was very weird but after a but you seemed to be able to pick out quite a tune to it. The Raja himself was magnificently dressed and wore round his neck ~~the m~~ a priceless rope of pearls. ~~On~~ You can get quite a lot of amusement out of these sort of shows by just watching the people & seeing their costumes.

I am now acting adjutant again & my ankle is ever so much better. I was able to go for a ride for the first time yesterday, and ~~no I~~ now that I can ride again I shall be able to get plenty of exercise.

Please congratulate Janet & Rob ~~for~~ on getting prizes in the Scripture exam – they did very well indeed. ~~Poor~~ Angus had jolly bad luck but he must just do a little better next time & then he will be certain of a prize. Cary did very well to get 8 prizes & I should have thought that they would have won the shield.

I am glad Bunna likes his cricket bat & I hope he will make some big scores with it this season.

I was pleased to hear that the "farm" is still going well & I hope the latest arrivals in the pig world will do well & fetch a good big price. Father said in his letter that if we went on service we need not be anxious on your account; we were very glad to hear this for after all we might have to go & we would not like to think that ~~you~~ we had gone without you consent. Of course we have offered to go on every occasion when there has been a chance of service but so far we have not been sent.

~~It was~~ am glad Mother was pleased with Col Clutterbuck's letter – it was very good of him to give such a good account of us. I am also very glad that he is so much better but I doubt if the doctors will ever allow him to come to India again.

We are all looking forward to the arrival of the truckle which Father said he was sending out: it is awfully good of you to send us another & I can assure you that we thoroughly appreciate them. The "Harvester" has not arrived yet but I expect it will turn up before long. It would be nice to be able to do a bit of harvesting again.

I hope you mare all quite well

With very much love

From your affectionate son
Jim

Dinapore

19th May 1916

My dear Mother & Father.

We have not done very much this week that is worth writing about and I hardly know how to set about writing this letter. I have been able to get some exercise again this week & am feeling much better for it : I cannot run yet but I have been out riding every day and that is quite good exercise.

It is frightfully hot again and the worst of it is the nights are getting very hot, which of course spoils our sleep. You can form no idea what it is like out of doors about one o'clock when it is 107° in the shade. The wind seems just like the blast of a furnace & the rims of your dark glasses get so hot that they burn your face. The day before yesterday it reached 113° in the shade The Major has been unwell the last two days & I have had to carry on by myself so I have had quite enough to do. Office work is not so bad in the cold weather but it rather goes against the grain now that it is so hot.

Everything is quite burnt up but a good many of the trees are in flower and in the evenings the air is quite heavy with the scent which they give off. This makes the evenings very pleasant & quite takes away the horrible smell of the bazaar, which is so unpleasant in Indian towns.

I have just had a sleep for about half an hour as I was feeling very tired after a rather strenuous mornings work. I went to the Range at five o'clock this morning and then worked in the office from 9–30 AM till quarter to one allowing only half an hour for breakfast.

I have been obliged to send my pony away, as a we were told that we had too many horses in the Battalion, but this apparently was a mistake so I hope to get her back again. I was very sorry indeed to see her go : she was awfully pretty and she all always whinnied whenever I went anywhere near her stable.

I expect I shall have to go to Packmari again before long for a machine gun course. John & I have both been recommended for it so we may go up together : which would be rather nice. I received Janet's letter dated 19th April last week, also and letters from Mary & Bunna. Please thank them all for them – I would write to each separately if I could think of anything to write about. I enclose a postal order & stamps to the value of 15/- which we are sending by way of pocket money to those who did so well in the scripture exam. I think it had better be divided so that the prize winners, Janet & Rob, get 5/- each & the other two Mary & Angus, get 2/6 each. I did not suppose Margaret & Duffy did not enter but never mind we will send them something as soon as we can find an excuse.

We X had a most amusing time down at the riding school last Thursday when we were learning to take high jumps. I invariably lost my stirrups & found myself sitting on the horse's neck, but I don't think I was any funnier than than the others. Riding without stirrups was also rather amusing to the spectators, but rather trying to those who were riding.

I think the riding school is some of the best training we have for we learn absolutely everything about a horse, and a good deal about ourselves as well. For instance, we learnt quite a lot about one fellow, who always told us what a great horseman he was, when he funked the jumps and said he would try them another time – he has never tried them yet.

I have just reached the end of my teather and can think of absolutely nothing else.

The last letters from home said that you were all quite well. I sincerely hope that that is still the case With much love to all

> I remain
> your affectionate son
> Jim

Dinapore

May 26th 1916

My dear Mother & Father.

Since I wrote last week we have had rather a surprise in the shape of an order to send off a further draft of 200 men to the Gulf on the 10th June to join the 1/4th. This will practically wash out over Battalion for we shall then have 300 in the Gulf and about 100 unfit owing to malaria & the other 400 are away on detachment. We You will be pleased to hear that no officers are allowed to go with the men, but I am we are very disappointed about it and so are the men, who will now have no-one to look after them. It looks as if we are to be made into a depót for training drafts, and I believe that all the officers not required for this will be used for Staff jobs and similar kinds of employment.

We have 241 recruits who came out about 2 months ago, and who were intended for the 1/4th but it is quite impossible to send them off for they are little more than school boys – lots of them have had their fifteenth birthday since they have been in India. They certainly should never have been recruited & why they were ever sent out to India is a mystery. The little fellows are as keen as mustard, but they can't stand the heat & several of them X have already gone to hospital with heat stroke.

Andrew finishes his course to-day and under ordinary circumstances would have had a fortnights' leave but we have received a wire from Wellington instructing him to report there at once. He will come down here to pick up his kit & then we shall have to say goodbye to him. John is due here on Monday also so I hope we shall all be here together.

I think Andrew has done quite the right thing & I believe he has accepted a real chance but I am very sorry he is leaving the Regiment. He is an awfully good officer and the men are very fond indeed of him – his signallers are very disappointed that he is leaving them, for he nothing he could for them was ever too much trouble for him to try.

John and I are both going up to Packmari next week for a machine gun course – we have to report there on June 1st.

Thank you ever so much for the cheese you sent me – much to my surprise it turned up in perfect condition, for it travelled across India in an ordinary train the temperature of which is usually about 130° at this time of the year. it had not even lost its flavour and I was only sorry that I could not save some for John & Andrew, but of course once it was out it had to be eaten quickly.

Yesterday was the hottest day we have had this year but I believe it is even hotter to-day. The temperature on the verandah of the hospital, which is as cool as anywhere in Dinapore reached 111° – this is in the shade so you can imagine what it was like in the sun. Fortunately it has been very very dry the last two or three days and we have not therefore felt the heat quite so much. I expect John & Andrew will feel it when they come down from the Hills.

I enclose a few photographs which I have just had developed – they are not very well printed as there is no good pot photographer here.

Thank you for the School magazine which also turned up this t last mail : it is quite a good one this time & I see that Bunna has managed to get his name into the Excelsior

I sincerely hope that you are all quite well

With very much love to all

> I remain
> > your affectionate son
> > Jim

Dinapore

2nd June 1916

My dear Mother & Father.

This has been a very eventful week & I could write a very long letter but

I am so tired that I shall have to cut it short & write a long one next week. It is just midnight & I have to be up at ~~four~~ 4 AM to catch a train for Rawal Pindi. Two of us are going to a place called Changla Galai for a machine gun course. It is right up on the frontier just beyond Rawal Pindi, so we ought ~~really~~ to have quite a good look at North India before we get there. We shall have a rotten journey as it is frightfully hot now and everything gets covered with dust when you are travelling.

Andrew came down from Kasauli on Monday & left here Wednesday evening for ~~Pindi~~ Wellington. Of course I was very sorry to see him go but I ~~was very glad to~~ think he is doing the very best thing for himself. He is looking wonderfully fit & I believe he has grown a bit since he went to Kasauli.

John goes off on service on Monday & I shall have to say goodbye to-morrow morning. I am awfully disappointed that I was not allowed to go with him, but although I tried ~~every way~~ everything I possibly could I was not allowed to go. I think he will do great things if he gets the chance and Mother may even yet have a V.C. brought back to her when we all come home.

I went over to Mirzaffapur yesterday to shoot off the return match of the shooting competition against the Bihar Light Horse & the R F A. We won the match, & all of us were presented with an awfully nice silver cup. We had a very jolly time but I had to come back early to get ready to go away to-morrow. They gave us a concert & then a dance and we did not get to bed till the small hours of the morning. ~~Whe~~ We had to be up at five to get the shooting done before the heat of the day and as we have been busy ever since you can imagine we are now very tired.

I think this will have to do to-night but will write longer next week.

I hope you are all quite well

With much love to all

from your affectne son
Jim

School of Musketry
Changala Gali

June 6th 1916

My dear Mother & Father.

I had very little time to ~~tell~~ write you a long letter last week but will try to make up for it this week.

Sunday week John came back from Jalapahar to get ready to go off on a machine gun course, but when he arrived he found that he was to go with our draft to the Gulf instead. We were allowed to send one senior & one junior subaltern, but no captains. I did everything I could to be allowed to go with John, for it would have been much nicer if we could have gone together, ~~by~~ and I am awfully disappointed that we ~~were~~ I was not allowed to go; I daresay I shall get my turn someday if the war lasts long enough.

Andrew came down from Kasauli the next day & we all met at Dinapore, but he went off to Wellington the next day on the Wednesday. Now that Andrew & John have both gone off I am the sole survivor of the family in the Regiment, but I can assure you that the other two will be greatly missed – they both had a jolly good send off from the mess & were paid some very high compliments

After saying goodbye to Andrew I went over the river to Mozafferpore for the shooting competition. I stayed with the Chief Commissioner and had a splendid time but unfortunately I had to leave directly the shooting was over in order to get back to Dinapore to pack my kit for the ~~musketry cour~~ machine gun course. We won the match and each one of us in the team was presented with a very pretty silver cup.

I got back to Dinapore & found that our machine gun course had been changed from Packmari to Changli Gali and we therefore had to catch the 6 AM Punjab Mail next morning.

Changali Gali is 40 miles beyond Rawal Pindi so we had to travel right up through the plains – not a very pleasant journey in the hot weather. It took two days to reach Pindi from Dinapore and we had to pass through all the big cities – Allahabad, Delhi, Agra, Jullundur, Amritsar & Lahore – and crossed a good many big rivers. We got to Delhi at midnight, and I woke up & looked out at the station which was absolutely crowded, as our train brought the mails up from Calcutta.

The country is very similar all the way up till within about 50 miles of Pindi where it suddenly becomes rocky & mountainous. Elsewhere it is absolutely flat just like the country round Dinapore.

As we went up the type of people completely changed, & I must say that the Punjabis, Pathans and the North country people generally are far superior to the Bengalis. I was very amused to find that the native women up here all ~~where~~ wear trousers, and if they can afford them they like to get hold of a waistcoat. They are all very pale in colour – some are almost white We reached Pindi about 6–30 PM & slept the night at the station. You can't think how pleased we were to get a bath & get really clean, for one gets covered with dust from head to foot when travelling in the hot weather. In the morning we motored up to Murree which is 40 miles from Pindi. it is 7000' high and is the Hill station for Pindi, Peshawar, Nowshera etc. The first ten miles were fairly flat, Pindi being situated on a big plateau, but after that we started going up into the mountains. The road was quite good but I almost held my breath in places when we found ourselves driving along the edge of a Khud which dropped sheer for 1000′ feet. At about 3000′ feet the pines began to appear & this fresh smell reminded me very much of Bournemouth.

We had our lunch & then in Murree & then set out for Changali Gali, twelve miles away. The only way of getting across was is by means of little hill ponies so we each hired one & rode across. It is marvellous how the little beasts get over the ground without falling. They gallop up & down the Khuds no matter how steep, & never make a false step. The other fellow from our Regiment, Williams, had rather a rough time for he cannot ride properly & when he reached Changali he was sore from head to foot. I simply roared with laughter to see him just hanging on by the skin of his teeth but it was hardly fair for he really had quite a bad time.

Changali Gali is the highest hill station (for troops) in India being 9000′ feet high. It is very isolated & there is no one here except those connected with the School of Musketry, but it is a delightful spot and beautifully cool. We found it very difficult indeed to breathe when we first arrived here – the least effort made us puff & blow as if we had run a mile, but we are beginning to get over that now.

It is very like England up here now for it is beautifully green & all the plants & trees are the same as we get in England. The cuckoos are very numerous : you can hear them calling the whole day long.

All the buildings are more or less in a row along the top of the ridge and from the verandahs you look straight down into a Khud 600′ deep. There is absolutely no flat ground, except the parade ground & the tennis courts : the former is about as big as the Store garden & there is just room for the squads to work. The tennis courts have been cut out of the hillside and we have to climb up 400′ feet to get to them.

The air is simply magnificent and I am already feeling much better than when I came up. The last two days have been rather exceptionally warm and we have not needed fires, but when it rains it gets very cold indeed and then I believe we shall be only too glad of a fire.

The course started strenuous yesterday, but the first three days are more or less preliminary, the real machine gun work starting the day after to-morrow. As far as I can see it is going to be quite as strennous as the musketry course, but up here it is quite easy to work.

I forgot to thank the boys last week for the "Harvester" which John brought down from Jalapahar with him. I read it coming up in the train & thoroughly enjoyed it : both it and "Freckles" are two jolly good books. I left Dinapore before last weeks mail arrived and as It it has not yet been sent on I have no letters top answer.

June 8th The news of the naval battle of May 31st reached India yesterday causing great excitement. The general opinion at present is that we did fairly well, and there is no doubt that our ships put up a very fine show but our losses were very ~~heasy~~ heavy. None of the papers out here have yet given us a full account of the German losses, ~~bu~~ but they seem to have suffered quite as severely as we did.

I suppose Father is very busy again – I hope he will have a really good season in spite of the high prices, & I also hope that he will not work too hard & so knock himself up.

I hope Mother & all the others are quite well

With much love to all

    I remain
      Your affectionate son
       Jim

School of Musketry
Changala Gali

7th June 1916

My dear Bunna.

I forgot to thank you last week for the "Harvester", which John gave me when he came down from Jalapahar : I believe it came out in a parcel of socks addressed to him. Please thank Angus & Duffie as well for I have no time to write to them both this week. I read the book in the train on my way up here & thoroughly enjoyed it : it is something different from the ordinary novel & intensely interesting.

As I came up here I noticed several things which may be of interest to you in your work, & the one which struck me most was the change of vegetation as we came up the mountains. Of course down on the plains everything is quite burnt up except where the land is artificially irrigated, but as you get higher there is more rain & things are much greener. At about 1000′ stunted trees & small bushes began to appear (that is trees other than the tropical ones which always grow in the plains). At 3000′ the pines begun to get quite numerous, but were not very big till we got up to about 5000′ where they were the predominating feature of the vegetation. Beyond 6000′ the plants ~~were~~ are all ~~of~~ practically the same as we get in England. This place is about 9000′ high and besides the pines there are lots of horse-chestnuts, sycamores, & a few elms. The common English grasses & white clover are all here also wild strawberries, Figwort, Violets, primroses, Cranesbill, Salvia, Veronica etc etc.

We did not notice much change in temperature till we were over 3000′ up & then it gradually became cooler. Even up here the sun is very powerful in the day time but the nights are very cold and if it is cloudy it is cold in the daytime. The air is very rare indeed and at first it is very difficult to breathe, so much so that people with weak hearts are not allowed to go to the hills.

Just before we came to Pindi I saw the most magnificent escarpment I have ever seen. The railway for the most part runs across the escarpment but in the valleys between the outcrops there are usually streams. As far as I could see all the great rivers of the Punjab run along the the transverse valleys in their upper waters & only turn South when they can find a gap to break through the escarpment.

The Monsoon has just broken in Calcutta, but it broke in the Andamans about three weeks ago. The Bay of Bengal current will now turn Westwards & follow the line of the Himalayas. The Arabian Sea current follows the line of the Ghats & has now reached Poona which is just South of Bombay. As the Monsoon was rather a failure last year everyone is hoping for an extra special one this year. You ha can form now idea how important it is to India to have a good strong monsoon. It is rather early this year probably on account of the abnormal heat which we have been having.

I think I shall have to stop now & get to bed for we are working very hard and are you get very tired at first when you first come up from the plains.

I hope you are getting on well & keeping fit

> I remain
>> your affectne brother
>>> Jim

School of Musketry
Changla Gali

14th June 1916

My dear Mother & Father.

By this time we are getting well on with our course, and we are finding it quite interesting but very strenuous. ha At the musketry courses you only have to carry a rifle but at a machine gun course you have to dash about with a machine gun and it begins to get very hard work when you have to carry the gun up & down the Khuds We are working very long hours, but of course it is not nearly so trying to work all day up here as it is to work for a couple of hours down on the plains.

The changes of temperature which we get up here are quite extraordinary.

When the sun is out it gets quite hot and we then take off our tunics & work in shirt sleeves, but in a few minutes if a storm comes up or if a fog comes on the temperature drops about 20°. We had some very heavy thunderstorms at the beginning of the week and it was very cold indeed – I had a fire every day. For two days we were absolutely in the clouds and could see nothing and then the clouds became lower & we came out above them. It was a very pretty sight to see the tops of the hills sticking out of the white fog which looked like just like snow. The last two days have been quite clear & warm again but I think we are going to get some more rain because my ankle is rather painful. It is quite strong now but it always gets painful when the air is damp and there is rain about. The news that Lord Kitchener has been drowned is about the worst we have had since the outbreak of war, for he was the one man who could least be spared. A memorial service was held in every station in India and we have all been wearing mourning. We had a memorial service up here on Tuesday and it was very impressive to hear the minute guns booming out all round the hills. We could hear four separate lots of guns and the echos seemed to go round & round the hills.

We are only 10 miles from the Kashmir country and on a clear day we can see it quite plainly. I am sending Mother a Kas scarf which was made in the Kashmir & it is quite a good one & I know it is genuine. I sent Lizzie (Calvertsholm) a magnificent shawl made of the same stuff for a wedding present.

We see lots of camels up here for nearly all the transport is done by mules or camels. It is rather a funny sight to see strings of mules laden with meat & other stores start out from here to all the camps. They leave here in time to issue rations at the camps at 2–30 PM. The camels go about in long strings : each one has a little wooden peg fixed into his nose, as and a string is attached to this peg & the camel in front, so that they cannot possibly break loose.

I was very sorry to hear that Aunty Dolly has been so ill and I hope she is better again now. I heard from Aunty Ethel this week & she said that Grandma Mullins had be also been ill having had rather a bad fall. I expect anything of that sort would shake her up rather badly.

Your letters dated 23rd May have just arrived & I am glad to hear that you are all well. The poultry farm suffered rather badly as a result of the visit of M.M. Renard – it was awfully bad luck especially as the hens were all laying well.

I suppose all the farmers are busy haymaking now & I expect they are in difficulties with their labour

John had a very good send off from Dinapore, but I think he must have had a very rough passage. I heard from Andrew this week – he has arrived at Wellington and has settled down to his work in good style.

Please thank Bunna & Pussy for their letters – W̶ what date does Bunna take the Oxford Senior – nothing short of 1st class honours will do this time.

It is Thursday to-day & norminally we are having a holiday, but I have to go off now to a mekometer class s̶o̶ in a few minutes, and shall have to stop this letter.

With much love to you all

I remain

  Your affectne son

   Jim

School of Musketry
Changla Gali

June 22nd 1916

My dear Mother & Father.

We have had another very strenuous week, but we have nearly finished now. As far as I can make out at present the course will end on the 28th, and then I hope to get three days leave, so that I can visit Agra & see the Taj Mahal on my way back. The journey from here to Dinapore takes three days, and I shall have three days leave, which will not include Sunday & Thursday as these are already holidays making in all eight days.

We have been doing field schemes this week up & down the Khuds and we usually finish up absolutely dead beat, but it has been very interesting and we m̶a̶n̶g̶ usually manage to get a good deal of fun out of it. Ɨ̶ You would roar with laughter if you could see us dashing about with the guns, sometimes we run, sometimes crawl, and very often we f̶a̶l̶l̶ slide down the Khud side much to the ammusement of those who are looking on. We get simply covered from head to foot in oil & grease, but that only adds to the fun of the show.

We start at 8–30 AM & go on without a stop till two when we dash off to lunch. By that time we are quite ready for it and we show quite a lot of zeal when the food comes along. After lunch we usually go down again to voluntary classes and then after tea we have our notes to write up. I usually try to squeeze in a game of tennis after tea but sometimes I have to l̶i̶t̶ let it slip.

The 9th Middlesex who a̶s̶s̶u̶r̶e̶d̶ we relieved at Dinapore are only four miles from here and I went over to a guest night at their mess last week. We had an awfully jolly evening, and after sleeping the night there rode back in time for parade next morning.

This afternoon I am going to ride over to a place called Barian to play hockey against the 4th Royal West Kents. it will be the first game I have played since I sprained my ankle and I am going to make a start by playing in goal. I have never played in goal before and I ~~do~~ shall not do so again if I can help it.

I hope we shall be able to get some rugger when we get back to Dinapore for now that the rains have broken ~~&~~ the ground ~~begins to~~ will soon be soft again. The temperature is still about 98° but that won't matter, ~~&~~ as we play hockey all through the hot weather. In England we say it is too hot to play footer etc in the Summer but out here we just go on playing all the year round.

There was rather a scare up here yesterday, and we thought we should all have to stay here for another three weeks, owing to an outbreak of plague among the native troops. one of them died and several more are in hospital all suspected of plague but a specialist was sent for & he said that it was not plague at all.

~~I have~~ We have had some tremendous thunderstorms the last few days and it has been very foggy at times. Last night we were playing tennis and quite suddenly we found ourselves right in the middle of a cloud & could hardly see our way across the courts. When the clouds settle down like that it gets very cold indeed, ~~&~~ & then when the sun comes out it is very warm again so that we always have to keep a warm waistcoat or sweater near at hand, ~~to~~ ready to put on as soon as it gets cold.

I have just had a long letter from Andrew telling me all about the Cadet College. He is working very hard, but he knows quite a lot of people up there and in his spare time I think he is having quite a good time. I shall be very sorry indeed ~~to~~ have to go back down to the plains for the climate up here just suits me to and ~~a nice~~ I am feeling awfully fit.

The mails have not yet arrived – it takes them four days to come up from Bombay and they will not get here till to-morrow evening. Bunna asked in his letter ~~its~~ last week if a man called Charles Hunt was in this Regiment. Will you please tell him that as far as I know he is not – at least I have never come across him.

I had a letter from Ron Vallis last week and was surprised to hear that he is spending two months sick leave at Kasauli. I hoped at first to get some leave & go up to see him but unfortunately he has to leave there just about the same time as our course ends, so we shall not be able to see each other. I told him to look out for John when he goes through Basra on his way to rejoin.

I hope you are all quite well
With much love to all

    Your affectne son
     Jim

School of Musketry
Changla Gali

June 29th 1916

My dear Mother & Father.

In three days time I shall be down in the plains again which is rather a terrible thought for I see from the papers that they are as hot as ever. We have now finished the course except for the final paper which comes in two days time. I have passed all the oral tests quite well and I hope to do a good paper.

As soon as we have finished I am going over to Murree where I shall spend a day & then down to Pindi. I have obtained three days leave and intend to have a look at Agra & Delhi on my way back.

It ought to be my turn to go up to Darjeeling as soon as after I get back to Dinapore, but I am afraid they will probably count the time I have been up here as my turn in the Hills.

I heard from Dinapore yesterday and much to my surprise I heard that I should probably find Col Clutterbuck there on my return. Of course I shall be very pleased to see him because as a man I am very fond of him, but as a Colonel I greatly prefer Col Waddy. I am glad he is well enough to come out again, but I should think that a few weeks in the plains would soon knock him up again.

I was glad to hear that you liked the photographs: everyone out here said that they were quite good. I sent the extra one in case one of them was damaged on the way, and I don't know that there is anyone in particular to whom I want it given : perhaps Janet or Bunna would like it. You need not trouble to keep it for me as I still have one or two more left.

We had a great tennis match last evening between the Indian army officers & the British Army officers, but the British army made a very poor show. We Territorial officers stand a very poor chance against fellows who have been living in India five or six years, as of course they play almost every day and soon become really good players.

At last the war seems to be moving again and I hope the next few months will see a great difference again. If only the Russians can keep going for a bit I should think there might be a general offensive on all the fronts before long. There is a report in to-days paper that the Rommanians are being greatly impressed by the Russian offensive and that they are agitating for intervention I don't quite know yet what effect the state of affairs in Arabia will have out here, but as far as I can make out the Mohammedans of India cease to have any interest in the Turks when the Holy Cities no longer belong to the Sultan. This is all I have to write about this week for we have been working so hard ~~for~~ with the machine guns that there has been very little time for anything else.

I hope all of you are quite well

> With much love to all
> Your affectionate son
> Jim

Lauries,
Great Northern Hotel,
Agra.

7:7:17*

My dear Mother & Father.

As you see by the address I am now staying at Agra, which I am visiting on my way back from Changla Gali.

We left the latter place last Sunday morning and rode across to Murree from which we motored down to Rawal Pindi. We originally intended to go across to Murree on Saturday and stay a night there but the place was so full that we could not get rooms. We had a terrific thunderstorm on Saturday night and it was so cold that we were all sitting round great big fires, and the next night at Pindi it was so hot that we could not get cool.

It was a very fine sight going down – we gradually ~~go~~ went lower & lower & the hill tops gradually faded away in the haze. At the same time the pines were left behind and the air gradually became hotter & heavier We stayed at the station at Pindi & as our train did not leave till mid-day on Monday we had time ~~dr~~ go for a drive and look about a little. We reached Delhi early Tuesday morning, and luckily the sky was very cloudy so that it was reasonably cool and we were able to go out & see all the sights.

Of course there are very few people down on the plains now and all the best Hotels & shops are closed so that the cities all seem deserted except of course by the natives who are always present in swarms.

We saw the Fort, the great mosques, & the Viceregal Lodge, and drove through the bazaars till we were thoroughly tired. Delhi is essentially a native city and the European part is not so separate as it is in most Indian cities, and it seemed to me ~~tat~~ that it was very rightly made the capital of India.

On Wednesday morning we left Delhi and came on to Agra where we shall stay till to-morrow night. Doctor Coombs might be interested to know

---

* Should read 16

that we passed through Palwal on our way. The city is some little way from the station but we could see it quite plainly from the train situated on a bit of rising ground.

Last night we visited the Taj Mahal which really is one of the wonders of the world. it is quite impossible for me to describe it for I have never seen such a beautiful building and I am sure that none of we Europeans can quite understand ~~the~~ how fond the old King must have been of his wife to have built such a beautiful tomb for her. He built it beside the Jumna in such a position that he could always see it from his favourite tower in the Fort. On each side of it he built a mosque, and he used to come to worship in them every ~~Fr~~ Thursday. As I stood in the great gateway I could imagine the scene of the King riding up on the state elephant surrounded by all the nobles & courtiers and all the people bowing down making obeissance to the king – it must have been a magnificent sight The Taj is all of white marble which is inlaid with coloured stones to make patterns of flowers. The inlaid work is absolutely wonderful, and the workmen must have taken infinite care for it is perfect. They used agate, jasper, cornelian, malachite, black marble, jade & gold stone according to the colour they they required. The actual tomb is down below, but on the surface there is a ~~du~~ duplicate tomb over the exact spot. It is surrounded by a wonderful carved ~~screen~~ screen, made of white marble, but it is so beautifully carved & polished that it looks just like ivory.

The mosques at the side are built of red sandstone inlaid with black & white marble. The gardens are beautifully laid ~~wit~~ out and from the gateway right up to the actual Taj there is a long row of fountains between and avenue of trees.

This morning we went to see the fort which contains the King's palaces, and a mosque called the Pearl Mosque. It like, the ~~a~~ Taj is built of nothing but pure white marble which is beautifully carved.

The King's palaces are all beautifully designed & ornamented and the whole place is ~~so~~ full of historical interest. I shall try and visit Agra again in the cool weather, for at the present time it is almost too hot to move, and sight seeing is almost out of the question.

When we were coming down in the train we noticed that the country looked very different to what it did when we went up a month ago. Almost everywhere there has been some rain and instead of the bare brown appearance the country is quite green & looks nice & fresh. At Agra however it is still as brown as ever for there has ~~ver~~ been practically no rain here so far.

I missed the mails at Changla Gali so that there should be two weeks' letters waiting for me when I get back to Dinapore, and as always I shall be jolly glad to see them. I have had no news of John since he went out but I expect there is a letter waiting for me at Dinapore.

⅄ Strangely enough there is another old Sexian, H S George, staying in this Hotel. I saw his name in the book when I arrived and at once looked him up. He did not remember me, ~~but~~ for ~~he~~ I was only in Form II or III when he left, but still we had a good talk about W. A. K. & the school generally.

It is really too hot to write any more to-day – I have had the greatest difficulty to keep the perspiration from falling on to the paper

I hope you are all quite well

With much love to all

> Your affectionate son
> Jim

Dinapore

14/7/16

My dear Mother & Father.

We left Agra last Friday night and reached Dinapore the following evening feeling very tired & frightfully dirty. On our arrival I found two weeks letters waiting for me so that I at once set to work to read through them.

We found Dinapore very different from what it was when we went away – it is not nearly so hot but owing to the rains it is just like a turkish bath. I am glad to say that all the dust has gone and everything is beautifully green; but even this has its drawbacks for the grass harbours snakes which are not very pleasant neighbours. Two crites and a cobra were killed in this bungalow a few nights ago so I can assure you we always have a good look round before we go to bed at night, just to make sure that there is nothing between the sheets or ~~un~~ under the pillows.

I found Royal with his arm in a sling when I got back, he having broken his collar bone. He was riding along on one of the horses when the brute put his foot into a hole & fell over with ~~Roal~~ Royal on board.

The first part of our draft arrived to-day, and the remainder will be here to-morrow. They are Derby's recruits and look a much better lot of men than the last lot, but we shall soon find out what they are made of. They are all to be handed over to me for a time till they are fit to join the companies so I shall have quite an interesting job training them.

Colonel Clutterbuck has arrived in Bombay but he is staying there a few days to just recover from the effects of the voyage which he found very trying.

I am sending Mother a parcel containing a box made of sandal wood which I bought at Delhi by this mail & as it is packed rather carefully it should arrive safely. The box is made of sandal wood the outside of which is carved, but the edges are inlaid with ivory, ebony, silver, copper A & turquoise. It is a beautiful bit of work and I was awfully pleased with it, but I cannot keep anything of the sort out here as it soon gets spoilt by the ~~we~~ damp & heat.

Inside there is a little picture of the Taj Mahal painted on ivory and mounted on carved ebony which I also thought was rather pretty.

I bought some picture frames & rather a pretty table cloth as well, which I also intend to send home to Mother as soon as I h can get them packed up. I think they will look well in the drawing room. All the work was done by natives, and we ~~w~~ went round the work rooms & watched them doing it.

A telegram came this week asking if any of us ~~wa~~ who had done musketry & machine gun courses would like staff jobs so I sent my name up but I don't think anything will come of it for the C.O. would not recommend me – he said he could not spare me from the regt. The General was here last Wednesday but did not inspect us. He dined in the mess with us & I had a long talk to him – he inquired for both John & Andrew.

The latter has just had an attack of malaria, which is awfully bad luck as it will throw him behind with his work besides making him very weak for some time. I heard from John last week and so far he seems to be getting on very well indeed, but by this time I expect you have heard from him as well.

You seem to have had a h very bad Summer this year, I should think the hay making must have been rather a failure.

I hope you are all quite well
With much love to all

> Your affectne son
> Jim

2/4th Somerset L.I.
Dinapore

21/7/16

My dear Mother & Father.

I have been very busy training and equipping the draft which arrived last week. Three officers, besides Col Clutterbuck, and 131 men arrived and were given to me to train till they were fit to join the companies. They are a very good lot of men, – much better than our last draft: they are all very keen and there are very few unfits among them.

The Colonel seems very fit again, but I don't know how long he will last out in this climate, for although it is not so hot as it has been it is still very trying. he is perhaps a little older than before his illness, but he is as charming as ever.

Another draft of 70 is due to arrive in a few days and I believe it includes two more officers so we shall then be up to strength with both men and officers. If only we could get the Bttn together again we could do some jolly good work, but at present the men are all over the place.

The monsoon has been very strong all over India the last few days and there has been so much rain up in the Darjeeling hills that there have been several rather serious landslides which have blocked the railway. Some of our men were due to come down yesterday but they were stopped till the railway has been cleared.

I am sending Mother two photograph frames of inlaid work & a silk table cloth this week, all of which I bought at Delhi. I ought to have ʌsent the frames last week because they have been rather spoilt by the damp – the wood has warped a good deal; but if they don't turn out very well I will send ʌ some more another time I should like mother to have a good pair because when in good condition they are awfully pretty and the work is marvellous. ~~The cloth~~ I bought the cloth because I thought it rather pretty and it shows you the kind of work they do out here.

I hope the things I sent last week have turned out satisfactorily. Royal was so pleased when he saw them that he at once ~~we~~ ordered ~~an~~ pair of boxes for his mother. We lost one of our men last week from enteric fever. He had got over the worst of it & was considered convalescent when he suddenly got worse and died. Dinapore is rather a bad place for enteric and we have to be awfully careful to drink only boiled water etc, and as company officers we never finish inspecting cookhouses, latrines etc.

I heard from John this week : he wants me to send him some books so that he can start learning Persian. Rumour has it that the 1/4th ~~my~~ may be sent to Egypt to reorganise & to get fit again. I doubt if there is much truth in it but I don't think they ~~do~~ will any more fighting just yet.

The news of the British offensive is very cheering – everyone out here is awfully pleased about it & I hope we shall manage to break the German line somewhere or other. If we can I think we shall get them on the run, for they have got lots of cavalry ready behind the lines.

I suppose Bunna will soon be taking the Oxford Senior – we are fully expecting him to get 1st class honours.

I hope you are all quite fit
With much love to all

     Your affectne son
      Jim

2/4th Somerset L.I.
Dinapore

28/7/16

My dear Mother & Father.

I am again acting adjutant for a time while the proper adjutant is away in the hills. I originally took ~~over~~ it over for a few days until ⚊ Flower should return from the hills to relieve me, but when he arrived the Colonel would not let me change so I suppose I shall carry on for the next six weeks.

Another draft of ⚊ 78 men & two officers arrived ⚊ yesterday from England, and I think the men are better than the last lot, so we have now had two quite good drafts and in a short time the Regiment will be as good as it was before. Of course it is still much too hot to do any real training but as soon as the cold weather comes on we shall soon make them efficient. We had a rugger practice a day or two ⚊ ago, ⚊ as we are hoping to enter a side for the Calcutta cup in September. The men are ⚊ awfully keen and I think we shall raise quite a good side.

I saw in the casualty lists a few days ago that F D Withers of the Somersets had been killed. I am awfully sorry about it for he was an awfully nice little fellow. He was always ~~cheerful~~ cheery & as brave as a lion & I am sure he would have made a name for himself for he was awfully clever.

I am afraid we shall have very few of our friends left by the time this war is over for they all seem to get killed off.

I tried to go off to the Gulf again this week – three subalterns were called for, and although I applied, I being a Capt I was not allowed to go.

I am still doing Hindustani, but I am afraid I don't get on very fast; somehow or other I don't seem to get much time for it. John is going to take up Persian and I am sure he will get through the Lower Standard before very long.

I was very sorry indeed to hear that Aunt Ethel has been so ill, but she could not be in a better place than Park Cottage or better hands than Mother's, so I hope to hear soon that she is getting better. Fancy old Ted Drewett off to France – is he in the RAMC or the London Scottish. The Germans will get a bit of a fright if they see his old head appear above the parapet.

⚊ Royal & I both bought some little bull terier puppies two days ago – I bought two & he bought one. They can only just walk and we can only feed them on bread & milk, but they have already started to eat our shoes & play tug of war with the floor mats. Between us we have now got five dogs in the bungalow – you will probably hear next that we are keeping a ~~proppa~~ proper kennels & running the Dinapore hunt or something of the sort. They are quite sporting little dogs – I should like to be able to give one to Duffy they would be just right for him.

It will be splendid for Mary to spend her holidays at Westgate & I hope she will have a jolly time. She will be quite a traveller by the time she gets home again. Col Clutterbuck is delighted to find that we can all ride, and nothing pleases him better than to get us all out on the racecourse riding round as hard as we can go.

I have absolutely exhausted my supply of information so this will have to suffice for this week.

I hope you are all quite well
With much love to all

Your affectionate son
Jim

2/4th Somerset L.I.
Dinapore

11th August 1916

My dear Mother & Father.

The monsoon has strengthened a good deal the last three days and we have had a good deal of rain, but it has been remarkably cool and to-day I am writing quite comfortably instead of being wet through as usual. As soon as the sun comes out we shall have to pay for it I am fear, and the prickly heat will be in good form. I am getting it rather badly again but so far it is not nearly as bad as it was last year at Port Blair.

Last Monday, being Bank Holiday we chartered a river steamer & took the men for a trip on the river. We first of all went up stream as far as the meeting of the three rivers, and then came Ganges, Gogra & Sone, & then turned round & went right down beyond Patna. The rivers are all fairly full now and the Ganges here is about th two & a half miles wide here. Patna looked very picturesque from the river, with it temples & mosques : all along the river side there are bathing ghats where the people come & and bathe in the sacred river. We spent the whole day on the boat, taking food & drinks with us : I thoroughly enjoyed myself and I think most of the men were quite pleased with their trip.

I am awfully busy just now, as there is a good deal of work going on both in the office & outside. Last night we had a wire to say that another draft had arrived in Bombay for us. This being the first intimation we had received that they were are were coming, we are now very pushed to make room for them in the barracks. We shall now be very strong indeed but I am afraid we shall have to send some more to the Gulf before long.

As I was going through the barracks a day or two ago I met Henry Perett who has just come back sick from the Gulf. He has had malaria very badly and is not looking at all fit, but he will be sent to the hills before long and should then be ever so much better. E Appleby has also returned here but I have not yet seen him.

John seems to be quite fit again, and is going back to duty but the officer who went out with him is back in India again.

I am going up to the hospital to-night to be inoculated against cholera – several cholera cases have just returned from the Gulf so all the men & officers have had to be done. ~~We~~ One of our men died of cholera yesterday, but he was away at Barrackpore on detachment.

I ~~am~~ was pleased to hear that Aunt Ethel was so much better & I hope she will soon get strong again. How did Aunty Bel like Park Cottage? I don't think she had ever seen it before had she?

I hope you are all quite well

With best love to all

> Your affectne son
> Jim

Dinapore

֍ 1/9/16

My dear Mother & Father.

We have had a very busy week indeed since my last letter for nearly half the battalion ᵏˢ is moving about at the present time and it has been rather difficult to arrange things so that everything goes off correctly & up to time. The drafts to and from the hill stations are moving, & we have been changing some of the men on the detachments so that altogether we have had rather a difficult time.

There are so many officers sick now that it is very difficult to carry on, and to add to the difficulty we received a wire to say that four officers with more than one year's experience in India were to go off to Mesopotamia. I don't think I have ever seen the Colonel so upset as he was at the thought of losing four more of us, and he is going off to Calcutta to-night to see the General personally. He says that he will not let us go under any circumstances, but I think he will have to spare two at any rate. I have sent my name in because I feel that it is my duty to do so, but so far the Colonel will not hear of my going away. He says that he has lost two of us already & that he really cannot spare the third.

We have had a tremendous lot of rain lately & the Ganges is in flood. At Benares it has flooded part of the town and in other places lots of crops are being destroyed. Just opposite our barracks there is a large island formed ⟨ where the Sone joins the Ganges and usually it is about forty feet above the level of the water but now it is almost completely submerged and the tops of the crops are just visible. I think the river will rise still more yet for there is plenty more rain to come by the look of the sky.

I have just got rid of one of the puppies as they ~~were~~ are now getting quite big and are rather difficult to manage. I have given it to our Coy. Sergt. Major and ⟨ he says he is going to make it the company dog.

The news that Roumania has joined the war on the side of the Allies is splendid. She has been rather a doubtful quantity at times, but now that she has definitely decided to come in, ⟨ the end of the war should be a little nearer at anyrate. The news from France and Russia is still good and we seem to be pushing slowly on, but I am afraid that those people who thought the war would be over this year will be disappointed for it looks as if there will be another Winter in the trenches.

I suppose all the flowers etc in the garden at Park Cottage are nearly over by now but those in our garden are just beginning to come out again and the place begins to look quite nice ~~again~~. We can grow the most delightful lillies here – they absolutely scent the air in the evenings.

I am very glad you had a spell of fine weather for the haymaking & I hope it will be equally fine for the harvest. The letter ~~was~~ I received from Janet last week was awfully well typewritten – she must be quite an expert judging from that letter.

This is not a very interesting letter this week, ⟨ but there seems to be very little to write about in Dinapore – I shall be able to do better when I get my leave & go to some fresh places.

I hope you are all quite well
With much love to all

    I remain
      Your affectionate son
        Jim

~~Sept.~~ 2/4th Somerset L.I
⟨ Dinapore

Sept. 9th 1916

My dear Mother & Father.

I have still to wait for my chance of going on service. I told you last week that four officers were wanted for Mesopotamia, and I thought at one time that I might have gone, but as several of us sent in our names to go the Colonel put them all into a hat and drew for it, and I was not one of the chosen.

We are still very busy owing to shortage of officers, and ~~wth~~ with four more going away it will be worse still. During the early part of next week I shall have to be Adjutant and command a company as well. One of the senior captains is now on the sick list & will shortly be sent back to England, and another has just been appointed to a staff job so I shall now get a double company instead of being only second in command of one.

On Monday the Ganges was higher than it has been for over forty years, owing to the very heavy rains which we have had. Benares & Allahabad were flooded and here at Dinapore we should have been swimming for it if it had risen much higher. The island almost completely disappeared and most of the crops were destroyed. It has been fine for the last two or three days and the water has now fallen about four feet, so that all the excitement is over. There seems to be a break in the rains now and we are getting very hot weather again, but the nights are certainly cooler, ~~and this~~ making it ever so much better than it was a couple of months ago.

We lost another man last Monday under rather sad ~~cirsum~~ circumstances. He was suffering from enteric fever and had a very high temperature, so much so that the medical officer detailed a special orderly to watch him ~~th during~~ the whole the night. He became very delirious during the night and managing to escape the orderly ran for the river which runs just by the hospital. He was last seen running along the bank but he must have been drowned for no trace of him has since been found.

John writes very cheery letters from Mesopotamia – he seems to be quite fit now and as the weather is not nearly so bad as it was he will probably last out quite well. I have not heard from Andrew just lately but in his last letter he said he had just been made a Lce. Cpl. How is Duffy? I was awfully sorry to hear that he has had to go to bed again & I hope he is alright again by this time. Poor little fellow – that broken leg has given ~~him~~ him a jolly bad time. I am awfully glad Bunna had such a good time with Uncle Andrew – his effort coming home was similar to mine the first time I went to Scotland when I went straight through ~~to~~ to Dumfries instead of stopping at Annan.

I have only one puppy left now as I gave one to the Coy Sergt Major for a company dog. The other is growing quite well but he is getting more & more mischeivious. When I woke up yesterday morning I found him eating my slippers and my boy has just been in to complain that he has completely spoilt a pair of socks.

We are still playing hockey and tennis but I shall never be very brilliant at the latter as I put one of the small bones of my wrist out of joint several months ago and the doctor could not get it back so that my wrist is always rather weak. We beat the Battery at hockey last night and are now looking out for a side to send to Calcutta later on to play in the tournament. The rugger side is getting into training and Royal has now gone down to finish them off.

I am just going down to knock a polo ball about with the Colonel and after that we have got night operations so I shall have plenty to do till mess time.

The war news seems ever so much more cheery now – we seem to be pushing on everywhere. If only we can keep it up it will go a long way towards ending the war.

I sincerely hope you are all quite well

With best love to all

> Your afffectne son
> Jim

Dinapore

15/9/16.2/4th ~~Some~~

My dear Mother & Father.

I have two letters to answer this week, one from Father dated 14th Aug. & the other from Ted dated the 23rd. I am delighted with the photos of Bunna, Father & Ted which arrived with them – it is awfully nice to get photos of you all and I would like one of the others when they have them taken.

It hardly seems two years ago that I was in the Channel Islands with Father, and yet it is more than that now – so many things have happened since then that the time has slipped away very quickly.

I arrived at Dinapore from Calcutta this morning having been down there for to play for our side in the rugger cup competition.

The train service to and from Dinapore & Calcutta is very convenient indeed. The distance is nearly 350 miles and and by mail train you can leave either place after dinner at night and arrive at the other about 6–30 AM. It seems funny to go such a long way for one football match but out here distances are so great that this one is considered quite a small one.

I left here Sunday evening, and arrived at Calcutta about 6–30 AM Monday morning. Royal came in from Barrackpore in the afternoon and we changed together in the Hotel before going out for the match. We were drawn against the 1/4th R. West Kents and lost by 8 pts to nil after a jolly good game. They were the better side as we had awfully weak threequarters but I think our forwards were quite as good as theirs. The ground was very wet and soft & I think this saved us from a heavier defeat as of course on a dry ground we should have been hopeless against good threequarters.

I intended to go back the same evening but I received a wire telling me to stay till ~~Wednesday~~ Tuesday to attend the funeral of Capt. Bartell, one of our Captains who died in Hospital at Calcutta. The Colonel turned up the next day to attend the funeral which was a very large one, and Royal, the Colonel & I all attended together. It was awfully sad because he was a splendid fellow and he has a wife and two young children.

On Wednesday evening we played a friendly match against Lucknow, another of the sides entering for the cup. We beat them by two tries to one so we have the satisfaction of knowing that we were by no means the worst side down there. As a matter of fact we had a rather better side for the second game and the men had recovered from the stage fright which affected them in the first game.

I had quite a good time in Calcutta, and met lots of fellows whom I had previously met on courses so that there was always someone to talk to.

I have just heard that I am going up to Darjeeling for a fortnight in three or four days time and then I have to go down & take command of my company at Barrackpore where they are on detachment. I am awfully glad that I am to have a chance of going to Darjeeling for I want to see the place and I am also in need of a change having been down on the plains during the greater part of the hot weather.

I am awfully glad the things from Delhi have arrived safely and that you all like them – I think they are very pretty indeed.

From the photographs Father & Ted both look very well, the latter seems to be very fat & thriving and decidedly cheerful. Old Bunna looks an absolute lady killer – no wonder the old rascal gets on so well with the mistresses.

It must have looked very funny to see Father going off on a bicycle to buy cheese – but "these be 'mazing times" and I am only too pleased that he is well enough to be able to do it.

I heard from both John and Andrew this morning – they are both very fit and cheery.

I was not very fit before I went down to Calcutta but the change has put me right again and I am as right as ninepence now, and after a stay in the Hills I hope to be ready for anything.

I hope you are all quite well

With much love to all
Your affectionate son
Jim

Dinapore

15–9–16

My dear Bunna.

You all write to me so regularly especially you & Ted that I feel rather guilty for not writing to you more, but I usually have very little to write about ~~and~~ and little time in which to write

Thank you very much indeed for sending me a photo of yourself – it is awfully good of you and you look an absolute charmer – I must not say too much or you might think I was flattering you.

We had two jolly good games of rugger down at Calcutta and we did not mind losing to the West Kents for they played a very sporting game, and were the better side. The Lucknow people were not nearly such a nice lot and we were jolly glad that we managed to beat them for they made certain that they were going to take at least eight points off us. Congrats on becoming cricket captain – I hope you will do well yourself & get together a really good team. You really must be careful with those mistresses or we shall be hearing of Mrs Bunna.

What an event for Cary – Margy Hill putting here hair up – I suppose she is now absolutely irresistible now I am going up to Darjeeling in a few days time for a rest, & I hope a good time. It is very wet up there now but I am told that it will soon get nice and ~~co~~ fine I believe there is plenty going on next month, dances, teaparties & all that sort of thing.

I hope you are quite fit

With love from
Jim

Rugby Football

Opening of Calcutta Tournament
West Kents 8 Vs 2–4th Somersets 0
by "Half-time"

The twenty-seventh Calcutta Rugby Union Challenge Cup Tournament, for which ten teams have entered against six of last year, was opened on Monday evening under far from ideal conditions. The day had broken dull and dismal, and shower succeeded shower until late in the afternoon, when there was an improvement and during play also it kept fine, but the CFC ground, where the West Kents and the 2–4th Somersets met in the first match of the tournament, had been rendered slushy, and this was responsible, in no small measure, for the poor exhibition of "rugger" witnessed. Indeed the standard of play was so low that it was hard to believe one was watching a tournament game. As could only be expected, the game was generally confined to the forwards, who were seen more to advantage in the loose than in the scrum, which was generally wheeled. As a side, the "Men of Kent" were superior in every department to their opponents and fully deserved their win by a goal and a try (or 8 points) to nil. Had the passing among the Kent "threes" been a little more accurate than it actually was, they would easily have won by a larger score, as they kept pressing right through and it was only occasionally that the Somersets invaded their territory. There was, however, some good individual play witnessed on both sides. Large, the Kent full back, was safe and sure in his kicking and made some well-judged punts, while Capt. Norman and Allen at three-quarter, Lieut Trought, the scrum-half and Capt. Bourne, Lieut Douglas and Williams at forward also did very well, in both attack and defence. For the Somersets, Fowles shaped quite well at full-back, while Comm and Toscana were often prominent in the third line. Foster, who worked the scrum, was not well supported by Redfield. Of the forwards, Mackie, Creedy and Royal did best, though the last-named did not show a quarter of his brilliant form of three years ago, when he represented Somerset County.

The Game

Capt. Bourne kicked off for the West Kents from the Fort-end at 5–5, and after the ball had been brought out of touch, the Kents "threes" indulged in some passing, which took play inside their opponents "25," where a series of scrums were formed. It was only Fowle's good kicking that prevented the invaders scoring. A forward rush headed by Mackie saw the Somersets re-cross the half-way line and get well inside the Kent "25," where Large fell on the ball. A "free" to the attackers saw Comm attempt a drop, which missed. A loose forward rush by the Kents transferred play to the other end. Lieut Trought picking-up nicely and running straight through the defence. Lieut Swanston added the extra points (5–0). A kick and follow-up by Capt. Bourne off a "free" was returned into touch by Fowles, but the Kent halves kicking well were continually gaining ground. A dribble by Comm relieved the pressure and after some midfield play had taken place, poor passing among the Kent backs spoiled an otherwise promising movement. A punt by Lieut Swanston was followed by a forward rush by the Kents, Toscana finding touch, and with the Somersets gaining a "free," half-time was called.

Royal re-started, a scrum being ordered in the centre and from a "free" to the Kents, Capt. Bourne gained lots of ground, Coombs's return being a poor one. "Off-side" against the Kents saw Creedy take the "free," but one of the Somersets having been guilty of the same breach no advantage was gained by them. A punt by Fowles was beautifully returned by Large, and after all the Kents "threes" had handled, Goodwich got over with the second try, which Lieut Swanston could not convert (8–0). The Kents continued to press and Fowles had to touch down once. Some clever play on the part of Allen was replied to by Comm who dribbled in great style until tackled by Large, and a kick and follow-up by Goodrich compelled Fowles to touch down again. The remainder of the play consisted of forward rushes by the Kents.

The teams were:–

West Kents.–Large (full-back); Goodrick, Allen, Capt. Norman and Paulley (three-quarters); Lieut Trought (scrum) and Lieut Swanston (stand-off) (halves); Capt. Bourne, Lieut Douglas, Scantlebury, Newbury, Townsent, Jell, Ashinden and Williams (forwards)

2–4th Somersets.–Fowles (full-back); Coombs, Toscana, Comm and Carr (three-quarters); Foster (scrum) and Predfield (stand-off) (halves); Royal, Mackie, Hardinge, Creedy, Romans, Barber, Cornish and Mayles (forwards).

Referee:–A. B. Morrison (CFC).

Lucknow Vs 2–4th Somersets

The 2–4th Somersets, who lost to the West Kents in the Cup on Monday, gave Lucknow a practice game on the Police ground on Wednesday. The Somersets won by two tries to one or six points to three. C. R. Clayton refereed.

2/4th Somerset L.I.
Jalapahar

21/9/16

My dear Mother & Father.

I am now up in the clouds once more surrounded by fog and rain, sitting in front of a good fire and wearing thick English clothes, while only yesterday I was only too glad to be able to discard as much clothes as possible.

On returning from Calcutta the I found the Adjutant had returned once more, so the Colonel said that I could go off to to the hills at once for a fortnight. I had a good deal to do before I left and it took me two days to get ready and when I did make a start, I found that the line was breached by the floods and that traffic was stopped. Ҟ I had therefore to go via Calcutta which was really better for me. After I have finished up here I have to go to Barrackpore which is quite near Calcutta, and so I packed all my kit & took it down to Barrackpore and then came on here. We left ҟ Calcutta at 5–30 PM by the Darjeeling mail and had dinner on the train. At 10–30 we had to change and get into a train on the metre guage train line as the broad Guage does not run all the way to Darjeeling. A couple of years ago the broad guage used to end at the Ganges and the passengers used to cross the river in a ferry steamer & get into the metre guage train on the other side. Now there is a very fine bridge over the river and we go right on to a place called Santahar before changing. After the change we all went to bed and did not wake till 6 AM at Siliguri where we had to change again to get on to the Darjeeling Himalayan railway. The latter is an af awfully funny little arrangementҟ with its miniature engines and carriages but it is a wonderful ey engineering feat. For the first time for several days it was a fine clear day and even from Siliguri we could just see the snows, & I am told that they were wonderfully clear from Jalapahar, but the clouds had settled down again by the time I reached there.

It is awfully cold ҟ up here – there is a ҟ strong wind blowing right off the snows and it needs all our thick clothes to keep it out, but it Ҟ is delightfully fresh – quite different from the hot stuffy air down below.

I have not been at all well for several weeks, nothing wrong but feeling very done after the hot weather, and although I have only been here about one day I already feel ever so much better and have quite regained my usual appetite.

I only wish you could see the place – you would never forget it. In the distance the hills get higher & higher till at last the snows show up white and clear. The hill sides are covered with forests except where they have been cleared and there here one can see the tea gardens laid out in even rows.

We are in a delightful bungalow and there is a jolly little mess so I think ҟ we are going to be awfully comfortable. Darjeeling is now at its best, there is something going on every day and it is crowded with people who so have come mostly from Calcutta.

Of course John must have told you all about the place when heҟ was here but I hope you won't mind hearing it all again.

I find that there are quite a lot of people up here who I know and I am going to look some of them up this afternoon if it is fine enough, and then call at Govt. House & get that job over, before I forget it.

This week's mail has not yet arrived here as the boat only arrived at

Bombay to-day: ~~so~~ it will take at least three days for the letters to get up here.

The men like it very much indeed up here, they ~~all~~ have all got back their colour and look ever so fit. It is rather amusing to watch them improve ~~aft~~ when the first come up. They always come up looking white and p~~l~~ale – every one gets like that down below in the hot weather but in a few days they begin to look quite different and get as right as can be~~t~~.

I am awfully glad Duffy has got his leg right again & I hope you are all quite well

With much love to all

> From your affectionate son
> Jim

Jalapahar

27–9–16

My dear Mother & Father.

Mother's letter dated Aug 29th arrived yesterday – it was rather late, but not too late for me to say how glad I am that Mother has been asked to be a governor of Sunny Hill Girl's school and has accepted. I am sure that John & Andrew will be equally pleased when they hear about it. It is because she has had so many of us to look after that she has not been able to do these things before, but having brought us all up, no one could possibly have been chosen who ~~could~~ is so well able to say how girls or boys should be taught & looked after. I sincerely hope that it is but the prelude to many more such honours I have been up here for a week now and am thoroughly enjoying myself in fact I don't think I ᵏ ever had such a good time before. The cool weather has made me quite fit again, I have regained my appetite & have started to make up some of the weight which I lost during the last two months down below.

I am here on duty, which is much better than being on leave : ~~as~~ for one thing it is not nearly so expensive and also the work prevents us from wasting time. We have just enough to do to occupy the mornings, and then there is is plenty of time during the ~~even~~ afternoons & evenings to enjoy ourselves.

I have hardly had any meals at the mess someone seems to invite me out to almost every meal except breakfast & there there is tennis when it is fine, badmington, dancing and roller skating but the latter has not captured me at present.

I think John was very popular when he was up here – nearly all the ladies I have met have enquired ᵏ for him.

I went out to tea one day last week and much to my surprise I found Lord & Lady Carmichael (~~Gover~~ Lt. Governor of Bengal) there. I was introduced to both and as it was quite an informal party with only one or two other people besides myself there I ~~sad~~ saw a good deal of them. Lady Carmichael was an awfully nice old lady and ᴴ His Excellency ~~semed~~ seemed quite a cherry old bird. I am going to a dance at the Club to-night and I don't quite know what time I shall get back here for I have to ride two miles after it is all over, but it is Thursday to-morrow and we are having a holiday so I shall be able to stay in bed nice and late. It is awfully funny coming ᴧ up here and finding so many people ~~up~~ about again as the plain stations are quite deserted all the hot weather.

The General is coming to inspect us on Friday and we have been practising the march past etc the last few days as we want to put up a fairly good show just to prove that we are doing a little work.

Last Friday there was a tremendous cyclone at Calcutta which did a good deal of damage. It travelled up the Bay, ~~and~~ ᴧ passed right over Calcutta and then followed the ~~Co~~ course of the Ganges. The telegraphs were all destroyed and houses & trees blown down. As a result of it we have had very rough cold weather and the night before last there was a very heavy thunderstorm which seems to have cleared up the wet weather. We have had a delightful day to-day & this morning we could see the snows beautifully. When they are hidden by clouds we think this place is fairly high up, but when the clouds clear away you can see the hills towering right up above – range after range can be seen each a little higher than the other, till at last you get to the snows. I have not yet seen Mount Everest but I hope to be able to do so before I leave here if it gets clear enough. The cloud effects are perfectly marvellous – just at this minute we are in a little cloud and it is just like a thick fog but in a few minutes it will clear away and we shall be in the bright sunshine again. I always wish that you could come out here & see these things – you really can't imagine a finer or more wonderful sight than the everlasting snows right up on the "roof of the world."

I wrote to Cox and Co a few days ago and asked them to forward the sum of £2 to Father. Will you please give £1 each to Marky and Angus as a birthday present from us all. weᴧ are sending money because it is easier to send than a present and not so liable to get lost.

I hope you are all quite fit

With much love to all

> Your affectionate son
> Jim

Jalapahar

¥ 4th Oct. 1916

My dear Mother and Father.

I have had an awfully good time since I came up here and am now feeling quite fit again. Darjeeling is very gay just now, – the number of people here is a record and everyone seems to be pleased to be away from the plains

I have been asked out to dinner or tea nearly every evening and have been to several dances and concerts so that I have been making up for all the time I have spent in bad stations. This is the first time I have been in a station with lots of people in it since I came to India, and it is a very nice change, but I think it is very easy to have too much of A a good thing and I am sure I should get very tired of it if I were staying here very long.

I expect I shall go down to Barrackpore one day next week as I have been up here a fortnight and that is as long as I was supposed to have.

We are sending another draft to the 1/4th – I believe 200 men – but I have not yet heard whether any officers will have to go – I expect not.

It must be getting quite cool out in Mesopotamia now for John wired to me a few days ago asking to have me to send him out his thick clothes. He says they require blankets at night so that the nights at anyrate are chilly. We don't need them yet at Dinapore in fact the people there are still sleeping under punkahs.

It is still very wet and foggy up here which is quite unusual for the time of year. It seems quite unable to clear up this year but I suppose the fine weather will come some time or another.

I heard from Andrew yesterday – he seems to be doing exceptionally well. I hope he will get into the 54th Sikhs because they are it is a very good regt. and Blakely another of our fellows who passed out at Quetta is in it.

I am awfully glad Rob passed the Oxford Senior and I hope he will still go ahead & do well. What does he want to do – would he or care for a course at Reading the same as I did? I think Father's suggestion that he should become a chartered accountant a very good one indeed if he cares for figures.

I have been rather busy this morning ge sending off some men to Dinapore to go with the draft and shall have a job to catch the post with this letter. The mail closes at 2 o'clock up here which is rather a nuisance because down on the plains it always goes out at night.

I hope you are all quite well

With very much love to all

   I remain

      Your affectionate son

         Jim

2/4th Somerset L.I.
Barrackpore

9–10–16

My dear Mother and Father.

When I saw the paper this morning and saw that the "Arabia" had been sunk I was very much afraid that the letters intended for Mother's birthday had gone down and I was just off to the Post office to send a cable when I heard that the mails on board were those of October 25th, so I hope Mother's letters arrived safely.

The German submarines seem to be be frightfully active again now & we shall have to devise another method of catching them. I am awfully glad that all the passengers on board the "Arabia" were saved, although she was apparently sunk without warning.

We are having magnificent weather here now : the cold weather commenced on Saturday 4th October. On Friday evening there was a beautiful sunset and the air seemed to be cooler and everyone said the cold weather is coming at last. When we got up on Saturday morning the wind had changed round to the North and the temperature had dropped 10°. It was an extraordinary change – in the course of a few hours we passed from hot weather to cold. Of course we all began to turn out our thick clothes and everyone commenced to take down the fans and stop the supply of ice.

The cold weather on the plains of India is supposed to be the finest climate in the world – I don't know if this is really the case, – probably it is because everyone appreciates it so much – but I do know that I am feeling quite different already. When I get up in the morning I feel quite fresh and can work the whole day without feeling tired whereas only last week we all felt so tired that we hardly knew how to carry on.

The men are brightening up wonderfully, they are all turning out for games in the evening now and they seem to take ever so much more interest in their work.

All the ladies have come down from the hills now and the station is ever so much more cheery. It rather gets on your nerves in the hot weather when you go about and see all the bungalows empty but now that everyone has come home again it is ever so much more cheerful.

I am going into Calcutta to-day to see the General and I shall stay there to go to the pictures to-night as they have brought out the film on the Battle of the Somme from England, and it is very good indeed. I saw it last Saturday evening and I decided then that I really must see it again. The King's visit to the troops is also shown and when the King appeared on the screen for the first time the cheers were absolutely deafening. That sort of thing is awfully good out here as it impresses the natives, especially in Calcutta where there is always a good deal of sedition I am still very busy as one of my officers has gone into hospital with malaria and another is away on leave so there are only two of us left to carry on.

I am very glad indeed that the Centenary Services at the Chapel were so successful and I hope that the Chapel will get a good deal of benefit from them. I see in the Western Gazette that a site for the new manse has been purchased – where is it to be? Do you ~~rember~~ remember the five recruits which I got at Yarlington while we were stationed at ~~Yarlington~~ Bath? One of them Pte Fox by name is being sent home to-day to be invalided out. If you come across him when he gets home he will be able to tell you all about Barrackpore. Another of them brings my letters every day – he is the detachment postman; the other three are all in Mesopotamia I received a very cheery letter from John two days ago: he seems to have fallen into quite a good job and is quite enjoying himself.

I had my pony clipped yesterday and she now looks very well indeed – she has improved quite a lot since I have had her and in a few days I hope she will be in good enough condition for polo.

The puppies continue to afford us a good deal of amusement and ⅄ not a little annoyance.

Please thank Angus and Rob for their letters which I received last week – I always like to hear from them all.

How ~~are~~ is Grandma Mackie and the rest of the Ellesmere people – I have not heard from any of them for some time because I am afraid I owe them all letters which I mean to write every mail but never seem to make a start.

I sincerely hope you are all quite well

With much love to all

> Your affectionate son
> Jim

Jalapahar

⅄ 11–10–16

My dear Mother and Father.

I am writing ~~to~~ a few days earlier than usual this week because I have just received a wire telling me to proceed to Barrackpore at once and by the time I get there the mail will have gone.

Royal has been carrying on down there while I have been up here but he has been detailed to go to Mesopotamia with the draft which sails from Bombay on the 20th inst. I have wired to the Colonel & asked him to let me go instead, ~~but~~ because I should like to get out there with John again and I know that Royal is not keen. If I do go I shall send you a cable and you will know what has happened long before you get this letter. Every time a draft goes I feel that I ought to be doing something more than training recruits out here in India and I hope the Colonel will let me go this time.

The weather up here has now cleared up, ~~beautiful~~ and we are having delightful days, while the nights are ever so much colder. I hear that it is getting much cooler down on the plains so I ʌ don't mind going down again. We have had splendid views of the snows every day lately and they seem to get more beautiful every time you see them. I am awfully glad I have had a chance of coming up here for it is undoubtedly a place to see.

I had a treat last mail as I had two letters from home – one from Janet & one from Father, so although I got two I fear that one of them was not meant for me and that either John or Andrew did not get one. However I was very pleased to get them.

I am very glad indeed that Father is having a good year : but what a price to pay for the cheese! I wonder people can still afford to buy it. ʌ Are all foodstuffs being sold at corresponding prices?

I have been having a much quieter time this week chiefly because I wanted to have a good look at the country and have therefore spent a good deal of time walking round the khuds. it is very beautiful indeed whichever way you go. The roads usually run along the sides of the khuds which are covered in trees, & ferns, grass etc and every now & then you come into a sort of glen in which there are the prettiest little waterfalls imaginable. The little streams come rushing down and of course form a waterfall wherever the khudside is particularly steep. The bazaar down in Darjeeling is rather an interesting place because all kinds of people come in from the hills to buy & sell their goods. There are lamas from Thibet, Nepalese, Ghurkhas & the natives of this particular district and they are all a little different, so that it is awfully interesting to go down and watch them. ʌ

The Poojah holidays ended to-day and people have already started to leave Darjeeling. In a few days I expect the place will be getting quite empty although a few people will probably stay here for November.

I heard from John a few days ago and was awfully pleased to hear that he has been made a Captain while commanding a double company. I am awfully glad that he is getting on so well for he is a splendid officer & thoroughly deserves it.

Andrew is very happy up at Wellington and is still working very hard indeed. His course will soon be over and I hope he will be able to come and see us before he joins his Regiment.

Tell Duffy that my puppy – now named "Piper" – is getting on splendidly. He is getting quite big and always comes on parade with me. He is terribly mischievious and playful and I have to take good care that that none of my shoes or slippers are left where he can get at them for he takes a delight in tearing up everything he can get at.

I leave here to-morrow morning and go direct to Barrackpore where I shall probably stay for a time unless I am sent on service. It is quite a good station and I think I shall have a good time there

I hope you are all quite well

With much love to all

> I remain
>> Your affectionate son
>>> Jim

2/4th Somerset L.I.
Barrackpore

26–10–16

My dear Mother and Father.

I have had a very busy week since I last wrote, as Fortt who was here with me had to go off for a musketry course and for two days I was left all alone with 200 men to look after, but two more officers were sent here two days ago and I have not been quite so busy since.

The officer who was here before Royal was very slack indeed and the Colonel told Royal & I that we had to smarten things up a bit so we have Royal had a great time straff "straafing" everyone and I have been carrying it on. There has been a great improvement however and things are really going quite well here now. Barrackpore is entirely a sub residential suburb of Calcutta; there are no shops of any sort here and we therefore have to go into Calcutta fairly often to get anything we may happen to require.

The bungalows are all very nice and nearly all of them stand are quite detached standing in a good big garden. The club has splendid tennis courts, and a very fine golf course and I believe later on there are lots of dances.

It is quite good, there are very good playing fields, and if they want a change they can always get a pass to go into Calcutta where there is always something for them to do.

They all seem very happy here and I think one reason is that they are getting jolly good food. Two nights ago we played a rugger match against the gunners and were very badly beaten but we are going to play again to-morrow and I hope to be able to get together a better side and give them a good game.

We can get plenty of sport out of our original men & also out of the first two drafts but the Derby recruits are perfectly hopeless. They don't seem to take any interest in anything and they just do their parades because they are ordered to – I am trying hard to make them play games etc but so far I have been quite unsuccessful. They may be volunteers in name but they certainly act as if they were conscripts.

In some ways this is rather a difficult station to be in so because being so near Calcutta it is more or less in the public eye and, ~~everyth~~ if you happen to make a mistake of any sort you see a long article in the paper about it next day, and then of course it is taken up by the authorities.

We have a very nice little mess here, and as there are only four of us there are enough rooms for us to be able to live and mess in the same bungalow.

The mails have been very erratic lately, ~~and~~ with the result that I have had two letters from you this week, ⅄ the last one being from Father dated 4th October. I think some of our letters will be rather late too for the boat did not leave Bombay till Wednesday instead of Sunday this week and I think the same thing happened last week All the letters one gets nowadays tell the same sad story of someone killed or badly wounded : of course we like to hear about it but it is a terrible thing. I had a letter from a fellow I knew at Reading last week & he told me that nearly every fellow who was at Reading with me has been either killed or wounded – Passmore & Drummond are about the only two exceptions.

I am awfully glad to hear that Mary & Margaret both won prizes at School last year and I am delighted that ~~they should~~ on the same day that Mother was announced governor of the School he two daughters should have taken prizes. We are all most awfully pleased about Mother's appointment because she so thoroughly deserves it. I shall be only too pleased to send a s subscription to the Manse fund – will see about it next week as it is too late this week.

About Andrew's finances – I think he will be able to live on his pay quite well, as in the Indian army a junior subaltern draws nearly as much pay as a British army Captain. Of course one can't save much out here however much you try for with every increase of rank & pay there are extra expenses which you are absolutely bound to pay. Andrew has done very well so far, for he managed so save enough at Port Blair to pay for his course at Wellington and I expect ~~he is~~ what he means to say is, that when his course in over he will just about have spent all he has got and just at first he will be a little hard up on joining a new Regt: but you can be quite sure that we shall not let him get too hard up so that he has to get in debt or borrow money.

I had a notice yesterday ~~that~~ to say that a new charger is coming for me, as I am entitled to one now as a double company commander. Much to my delight she is a polo player so I shall be able to get some fun out of her when I am off parade.

I am very pleased to hear that Harry Bargery is quite fit again & will you please remember me to him when you next see or write to him.

I am sending some photographs this week if I can get them off in time but if not they will follow next week.

I hope you are all quite well

With very much love to all

I remain your affectionate son
Jim

Barrackpore

2nd November 1916

My dear Mother & Father.

I have been very busy indeed since I last wrote trying to push on with the training of the men. The cold season is supposed to have commenced now & that means that we have to push on with the training as hard as we can. As a matter of fact the cold weather has not set in yet & it is still very hot – I only wish it would get really cool for a bit. Everyone says that it will be quite cold in about a fortnight, but then they told us that at the end of September so I really don't know what to believe.

Strangely enough the cold weather in Calcutta is the cold weather is very bad indeed for Mosquitos. In most places they get less in the cold weather but down here they increase chiefly owing to the river. They have started to get very bad now and you cannot possibly sit down at night unless your legs are well covered up. I usually put some oil call citronella on my legs & ankles & this is quite effective in keeping them off because they don't like the smell of it.

My horse is a real beauty & I am delighted with her. She is awfully fast and takes an awful lot of riding but she is a splendid polo player & can turn anywhere & anyhow.

I often have to go into Calcutta on business etc and I can find my way about in there quite well by this time. Last week there was a big native festival called the "Feast of lights" which seems to correspond to our Christmas day. Two of us drove all down round the native streets to see the no illuminations which were really wonderful. Apparently the more lights they can produce the better it is for them, so every little hovel & hut was illuminated by hundreds of little candles which made the otherwise dirty hovels streets look quite pretty & picturesque.

I rather like Calcutta & I think it is the best of the Indian cities. As a city is is certainly much finer than Delhi but of course Delhi is really being rebuilt. The river runs right through the City and you can drive all along by the side & have a look at the ships, which seem to come from every country in the world except Germany. All the people have started to come down from the hills now and the trains into Calcutta are crowded every day. I happened to go into yesterday by the Calcutta Mail & it it was so full that I could hardly find a seat. The two big stations in Calcutta are just like English Stations except of course that they are always crowded with natives. The Howrah Station which is the terminus of the East Indian Railway reminds me very much of Waterloo.

There are some very nice people here in Barrackpore – most of them go into Calcutta every day and come back again at night. A good many of the are awfully rich just now for they are in the jute trade which since the war has improved tremendously. There are hundreds of men out here who have made fortunes out of this war owing to the fact that all the German trade has been stopped. The Indigo planters round Dinapore were absolutely smashed before the war on account of German anhiline dyes but they are doing awfully well now because the Germans are no longer exporting dyes & indigo is again in demand. Father may be interested to know that one of my officers is the son of the late Rev. Sir James Cameron Lees who was the minister of the biggest church in Edinburgh. He was is in the 4th Camerons but was out in India when war broke out and has never been able to get home. He is now attached to us. but

We have had some good games of rugger this week against the gunners – they are bett a better side than we are but our men are improving and I daresay we shall beat them one of these days.

I am enclose a poem wrtt written by a budding poet laureate now in my company. Even if his poetry is not exactly polished I think there is a good deal of truth in many of the verses.

I sincerely hope you are all quite well

With much love to all

Your affectionate son
Jim

Barrackpore

14–11–16

My dear Mother & Father.

I am afraid that this week has been rather uneventful and I have therefore very little to write about. We have as usual been very busy, and but it has been rather difficult to know how to carry on because we are shortly to return to Dinapore and the actual date of the move has already been altered twice.

𝕬 𝕿erritorial's 𝕷ife in 𝕵ndia.

1. A Terrier's life in India
   Is not what you may think,
   For I tell you I have had some,
   And above all found the clink.

2. The Second Fourth Battalion
   Of good old Somersets
   Is the Regiment I belong to,
   From Blighty you can bet.

3. Now listen, boys, awhile,
   For this it a'int no lark,
   The tale that they did tell us
   Before we left Prior Park.

4. "Now come with me," our Colonel cried,
   "To India so bright,
   And I'll guarantee that in 4 months
   In France you'll be to fight.

5. Your food it will be plentiful,
   Your money as much again,
   So cheer up, boys, and come with me,
   And bring your Country fame."

6. So out we came to India,
   Lured on as in a fog,
   And found that when we reached it,
   We had bought a great big dog.

7. We all were in good spirits
   When we left old England's shore,
   And very glad were we to reach
   That town called Bangalore.

8. We had only been there just a week,
   Then oh! what a different tale!
   For when they went to pay us out,
   Our hearts, we thought, would fail.

9. We only get five chips a week,
   That is our blooming pay.
   And if you are not careful,
   You're broke the following day.

10. Now since we've been in India,
    We've not had any toys,
    But I think we really ought to,
    For they treat us just like boys.

11. Now we get some lovely porridge,
    And bags of Household jam,
    It makes us feel like times gone by,
    When we were Mammy's Lamb.

12. Now what do you think, my hearties,
    If you were feeling bad,
    And you went to see the Doctor,
    It's ten to one you're had,

13. For seven days on defaulters,
    And you wonder really why,
    But you'll have to do as Asquith said,
    Wait and See till bye and bye.

14. Our Breakfast and our Dinner is the same,
    Which consists of bags of soup,
    And if you wish to have some tea,
    You can have it on the book.

15. From Bangalore we travelled
    To the Andamans so grand,
    And was very sorry when we reached
    That fever-stricken land.

16. It was there, whilst on these Islands,
    Our hardships again began,
    For they stuck us in Native Barracks,
    And never cared a damn.

17. We were on Active Service,
    At least, they said 'twas right,
    And we had to shine our bullets
    Before we went to fight.

18. Now the fever there was very bad,
    It made one feel quite queer,
    And the only thing that done me good
    Was "Charlie Chaplin's" beer.

19. Now what do you think of that, boys,
    For what I say is true,
    And I hope that you in Blighty
    Will come and see us through.

20. Now, boys, don't think this foolish,
    Or think it is all rot,
    For I'm sure if you were out here,
    It would drive you off your dot.

21. Now come along, my comrades,
    And do the thing that's right,
    Join up and be a soldier
    For our noble king to fight.

22. This is the time we need you.
    Yes, need you every one,
    So come and be a sport, boys,
    And on the Kaiser train your gun.

23. We left the Andaman Island
    For India once more,
    To a place that is much hotter,
    A place called Barrackpore.

24. The white folks of this country,
    Towards us, are like ice,
    They do not seem to realise
    How great our sacrifice.

25. We left our wives and children,
    And everyone so dear,
    For these hard-hearted people
    Who settle down out here.

26. We do not want ought of them,
    But only what is right,
    And that is their good manners,
    To speak and be polite.

27. Now, boys, we do not grumble,
    Whether white people, black or blue,
    If they only would respect us,
    We would stick to them like glue.

28. And now my tale is drawing nigh,
    Let's sing that grand refrain,
    God save our King and Empire,
    What we've done we'll do again.

29. And now I've told my little tale,
    Long live our noble King,
    And may he be victorious,
    And suck the Kaiser in.

GOD SAVE THE KING.

By one who's had some.

It was originally to have been Oct. 26^(th), but this was altered to Nov. 27^(th) and I heard a rumour to-night that we were now to stay here till Dec. 15^(th).

I shall be awfully sorry to leave Barrackpore as I am now getting quite settled down and if we have to move on Dec. 15^(th) it will be very awkward for I shall not be able to make any arrangements to give the men a good time at Christmas.

I had an awfully good day yesterday snipe shooting. Three of us left Barrackpore by the 7 o'clock train and went about 20 miles up the line. We then drove out into the country for about a mile and shot for about three hours. It ~~was~~ is rather cold in the early morning now and the snipe were very wild indeed so that although there were plenty of birds about we had great difficulty in getting near to them. However we managed to get 16 birds and had throroughly good fun. We were frightfully tired when we got back to the station as we had to walk about in water almost up to our knees. The snipe feed in the paddy fields and these at this time of the year are all under water. The country ~~all~~ round here when you get away from the towns is all jungle with patches of paddy flat dotted about here and there & I suppose a few years ago it was absolutely infested with tigers & panthers. The climate for the greater part of the year is very hot and moist and these are just the right conditions for the ~~S~~ growth of jungle.

I had an awful fright yesterday for I almost walked right on top of a huge great snake about 8' long. I put up my gun & was just going to shoot at it when one of the natives called out and said that there was not need to shoot as it was not poisonous. I had a wire from Andrew to-day to say that he will arrive in Calcutta to-morrow & I hope he will be able to stay here for a few days.

Since I have been here I have been playing quite a lit of tennis. There is a very good marker at the Club and I usually play with him – he has taught me ever so many new shots. We are playing on hard courts at present but the grass ones will soon be fit – they are still a bit soft after all the rain we have had.

We are going to be inspected to-morrow by the divisional director of Medical Services so we have had a general clean up to-day. He is frightfully keen on sanitation so we are getting ready lots of bowls of permangamate which we are going to put all over the place. I heard from Royal a day or two ago – he likes Pindi quite well as it is quite cold now, ~~and~~ but I expect he will tell a different tale if he happens to be there in the hot weather.

I hope you are all quite well & I hope that Mother has been able to get a servant by this time

With much love to all

Your affectionate son
Jim

P.S. Please thank Margaret for her letter.

Barrackpore

2̶8̶3–11–16

My dear Mother & Father.

It is time once more to write and wish you all a very merry Christmas and a happy New Year. I hope you will all spend a very jolly Christmas day in the old style just like we used to do before the war when we were all together. I assure you we shall follow you in our thoughts the whole day, from the time Duffy jumps up to look for his stocking to the time the Ellesmere people go away after supper ; we shall be able to see the look on Teddy's face when she finds the thimble in the plum pudding and on Angus's when he finds a doll.

Since we wrote the same good wishes last year from Port Blair lots of things have happened to us out here. John has gone to Mesopotamia, Andrew has passed through the Cadet College & will spend his Christmas day at Kohat right up on the frontier & I am com have become a company commander, which is a very different state of affairs from what it was last year.

It hardly seems two years ago that we left Southampton to for India and it yet when we think that in the mean time Janet has left school & Rob has k reached Form VI we can it seems much longer.

Andrew arrived here last Saturday looking very fit indeed, and since his arrival we have had a most enjoyable time together. He goes off to Kohat in two days time and I am sure I shall miss him when he has gone for it seems like the old Regiment to see him about again. You cannot imagine how he has improved since he came out to India – he works awfully hard at his books and he has become quite a great reader : he is very fond of his job & having been posted to one of the best Regiments in the Indian Army he is bound to do well.

We went in to Calcutta on Monday and sent off a big box of Christmas things to John, but we are not sending home Christmas presents to you all because we would rather give good birthday presents and cannot afford both.

I told Cox & Co to send the Rev^d. Parsons the sum of £5 towards the Manse fund & it should arrive about the same time as this letter : this sum is from all three of us.

I shall have a busy day to-morrow as the Divisional General is coming to make a complete inspection of the station. Now that the training season has started we are getting rather a lot of inspections for all the big people are have come down from the hills and of course they are rather curious to know what we dwellers of the plains look like after having been roasted during the hot weather. My old company have just relieved the detachment at Dum Dum which is quite close to Barrackpore so I shall have to over there as soon as I can to see them all again.

Andrew and I went into to Calcutta last night to see the water carnival in Eden gardens. With the exception of Bournmouth during the centenary fétes I have never seen a place so beautifully illuminated. The palm trees were covered with little coloured lights and every bush was hung with little electric lamps. On the lake there were illuminated water lillies ~~all~~ also lit by electric light, and large barges containing concert parties. The whole arrangement was so cunningly devised that the music seemed to come from right away across the water although as a matter of fact the lake was only about 100 yards wide. ~~The~~ It was quite interesting to sit & watch the people & contrast the English ladies in their evening dresses with the native ladies in their native costumes, which were in most cases absolutely magnificent I hope you will all have lots of parties and as much fun as you possibly can this season and ~~the very~~ I hope that ~~during~~ you will all be quite well and fit. I suppose the season for colds has ~~sent~~ set in now : it has out here. The change from the heat to the cold is always rather ~~tryn~~ trying because it is so sudden.

Once more every good wish for a Christmas
With much love to all

> I remain
> > Your affectionate son
> > > Jim

₴ Barrackpore

30–11–16

My dear Mother & Father.

Andrew went away last Sunday evening looking very fit and cheery. I went into Calcutta to see him off and we had dinner together in the refreshment room at the station, after which I had to get back to Barrackpore again.

He seems to have money enough to go on with as he has been very careful indeed and has saved quite a lot, but when he gets to his regiment he will probably have rather a lot of initial expenses as he will have to buy a pony, mess uniform etc. He has made up his mind that he will manage to pay for it all himself, but if you don't mind me suggesting it, it would be a great help to him if you would send him out say £20 or so just to start him on his way. He has been an awfully good boy since he has been out here & paid all the expenses of Wellington himself out of his savings. He did not go to College & so has practically kept himself since he left

School & I am sure if you would send him something just ~~K~~ to give him a start he will never need to ask for ~~another~~ any more help. He does not know that I have written this so that if it comes he it will be quite a surprise to him. The Brigadier General came over again last Monday but he did not give us much trouble as he came chiefly to see the battery. He told me that we were to move back to Dinapore on Dec. 11th for certain so we have not much more time to spend in ~~Dinapore~~. Barrackpore.

I ~~h~~ am sending home this week two little brooches made ~~out of~~ from the waistcoat buttons of our mess kit. The pins are only gilt, so they are not very valuable but they are rather pretty. I had three made, intending to send one to each of the girls but I am sending one to Aunty Ethel as she very kindly sends us papers nearly every week so I am afraid I must leave it to you to dispose of the other two.

I am also sending three ~~nac~~ necklaces which John bought at Darjeeling. When he went on service he asked me to take them and send them to the girls but I mislaid them and forgot all about them. I however found them again a day or two ago and am sending them on. They are rather pretty and are made from stones found near Darjeeling.

I have had no official notification yet, but I believe that another draft for us has just arrived at Bombay. I don't quite know what we shall do with so many men as we are now a good bit over strength.

I am awfully pleased to hear that Angus is able to play his violin in public now – he must be getting on very well indeed. I suppose he will soon become a member of the Cary string band.

We are working very hard indeed now as we want to do as much training as we possibly can during the cold season. We start at 6–30 every morning & go on till 12–30 with only an hour for breakfast – these are very long hours for India, as work takes ever so much more out of one out here than it does in England. The climate in Barrackpore is terribly relaxing – Dinapore is a more healthy station.

I can't think of any more this week and I have written so many letters during the last fortnight that I am quite tired of the job.

I hope you are all quite well & that you all spent a very merry Xmas together.

With much love to all

       I remain
          Your affectionate son
            Jim

2/4th Somerset L I
Barrackpore

27–12–16

My dear Mother & Father.

I received Mother's letter dated 8th Nov. this morning and was very pleased to hear that you are all well.

Before I write my next letter I suppose we shall be back again in Dinapore as we are due to leave here on the 13th. The people here, are very sorry indeed that we are going we seem to have made ourselves liked by them all and since it has been known that we are going we have had so many o invitations to dinner etc that we have had to refuse ever so many.

The only thing I fee which makes me at all glad to be going back to Dinapore is that N the strain of the work here is beginning to tell a little, and at Dinapore there is not nearly so much responsibility.

You see I have 300 men here and am absolutely responsible for, their training, the condition of the barracks; their kit, comfort, and health. Besides this I have to keep the correspondence up to date and this usually takes from 10 to 12 every day. Being so near Calcutta we have to keep absolutely up to scratch, and as we we never know when the General or some of his staff are coming out to see us.

Until last week I was also commanding the station which includes a battery of Artillery, besides the infantry; and this also made me president of the Cantonment Committee which is a takes up rather a lot of time if it is not very strenuous.

This will give you some idea of the sort of work one has to do on detachment : at Dinapore of course nearly all the office work is done by the Adjutant and the Colonel is o.c. Station so that the Company Commander has much more chance to train his men. I see by to-day's orders that Ron Vallis has joined us, so I am going to try and get him into my company if possible. At present he is acting as assistant Adjutant as owing to the arrival of a new draft of 200 men the orderly room staff are rather overworked.

I think the new just at present is as bad as it possibly can be. The Roumanians have been driven right back, German submarines h seem to be doing just what they like and now the Cabinet at home are having a row.

So far from the scanty news which has come through we have been absolutely unable to understand the cause of the Cabinet crisis. It seems to me that the ministry undoubtedly required a little stirring up but I don't think this could have been done without getting rid of Mr Asquith. M^r

Lloyd George is very good indeed to run the ministry of munitions but I don't think he his quite the right type of man to be the prime minister & I am completely at a loss to understand why Sir Edward Carson, whose only qualification seems to be that he is a fanatic, should be included in either the Cabinet or War Council. I suppose things will straighten out again very shortly but just at the present time they do not look very bright.

I cannot understand why the government do not take up the subject of India more seriously. All round here we are surrounded by jute mills many of which, on account of the bad state of the trade were, so before the war on the point of being closed. Since the war the owners of those men mills have been raking in money so fast that they do not know what to do with it and yet while the people at home are being taxed to the utmost the income tax out here has hardly been raised. and every Any one of these jute people could give £5 or 6000 to any fund you like to mention and yet they have not been touched. While every man at home has been forced to join the army there are hundreds of men in Calcutta alone, apart from the civil servants, of a military age who are doing absolutely nothing but live a life of luxurious ease.

The weather is getting much cooler now – the mornings are really cold and evening during the day it is not very hot. I am as fit as can be now thanks to the cool weather and am looking forward to the plum pudding which Mother said she you was were sending out

I took the whole company out for a paper chase yesterday and much to the joy of the men I beat them all easily as I was quite 200 yards ahead of anyone else at the finish. They were all very pleased about it for none of their previous captains were any good at sports.

I think it is time for me to wish you all a very happy New Year. I hope that the war will be over before the end of 1917 but I must admit that it does not look very hopeful just now. Still there must be better times coming and for all of you at home I wish every happiness and the best of health.

I am glad that Father is so well, and I hope Mother will have a good Winter this year.

With very much love to all

> I remain
> Your affectionate son
> Jim

Barrackpore

13–12–16

My dear Mother and Father

After receiving my last week's letter you will probably be rather surprised to see that I still write from Barrackpore. We were all ready to move when we suddenly received a ~~wor~~ wire to say that we could not return to Dinapore owing to an outbreak of cholera. I believe it has been a very serious outbreak although I have so far received no definite information but from Bttn Orders I see that there have been five deaths during the last three days.

We shall now remain here till after the Viceroy's visit and shall have to provide the guards for him. He arrives at Calcutta on the 22nd inst and will have a state entry. I am sending in some men to help line the streets. On the 27th he is coming out to Barrackpore to live, and will remain here for a fortnight going in to Calcutta every day by launch. The Gunners are going off to camp the day after to-morrow so I shall be o.c. Station while he is here which I suppose will mean that I shall have to ~~dine~~ attend some of the dinner parties at Govt. House. Of course those sort of things are an honour but they are rather terrible.

I expect we shall have a worrying time while the Viceroy is here – you would be amazed if you could see the preparations which have already been made for guarding him.

Of course the alteration of arrangements due to the cholera have made us very busy as we first of all had to get ready to move and then we had to settle down again. This practically stopped our training for a few days but we are going ahead again now.

I had a visit from the Brigade Staff on Tuesday and ~~we~~ they stayed for breakfast with us. They did not see the men as they only came over to see about the arrangements for the Viceroy's visit.

Last Saturday the Artillery held some very good Battery Sports and the officers were "at home" to the residents of Barrackpore. They gave us an awfully jolly afternoon – some of their riding and driving exhibitions were very good indeed. It reminded me somewhat of the old School Sports when all used to line up along the ropes and almost go mad with excitement.

The people here are going to hold a gymkhana on Christmas day which I think will be very good fun. I will send you a programme when I can get one & then you will be able to see what we are doing.

I am sending home a copy of "Indian Ink" this week. I don't know whether you will care for it as of course a good deal of the humour etc can only be appreciated by living here; but as it corresponds to the English

"Printers Pie" I thought you might like to see it – some of the pictures are rather good.

I received Mother's letter of Nov. 8th last week and was very glad to hear that she is at last going to get a little help with the work again – I hope the new girl will be a success.

I am sending ~~home~~ a few photographs this week which I have taken lately. My pony ʇ is looking ever so much better now than she did when they were taken. She looks very thin there but that was just after I had her – since then I have been feeding her up. Everyone admires her – now she carries herself so well.

My dogs are getting quite big now & they are much more obedient. They come round and wake us up every morning ~~by~~ if they think we have been sleeping too long. Piper always jumps up on my bed and starts to lick my face.

Ron Vallis has been posted to my company and he was to have come down to Barrackpore yesterday but ʇ as he has not yet turned up I suppose the cholera has prevented him from leaving Dinapore. I am awfully glad he will be with me for we shall be company for each other. One of my subalterns who has been here with me all the time is one of the Fortts of Bath – he is a splendid fellow and I get on with him very well indeed.

I cant think of any more to-day ~~so I hope~~ so I think I will go off to bed as I have been busy since half past five this morning.

I am very glad indeed that you are all so well and I do hope that you will all keep ~~w~~ it up during the whole Winter.

> With much love to all
> Your affectionate son
> Jim

2/4th Somerset L I
Barrackpore

21st Dec 1916

My dear Mother & Father.

After a fortnight without an English Mail the postman brought Father's letter of the 15th Nov. two nights ago, and I am now looking forward to the plum pudding & the book which Father said had been sent off. I am very fit indeed now and I am sure I shall be in very good form for the plum pudding.

This week we have spent a good deal of time rehearsing ceremonial, as ʇ 100 of my men have to take part in the Viceroy's State entry ~~to-morrow~~

TO MEET THEIR EXCELLENCIES THE VICEROY AND LADY CHELMSFORD.

The Governor and Lady Carmichael
request the pleasure of the Company of
The Officers 2/4th Somerset Light Infantry
at an Evening Party on Tuesday the 26th.
of December 1916 at 9.45. p. m.

Government House.
Mess Dress.

An answer is requested addressed
to the Aide-de-Camp in waiting.
Please show this card at the Gate.

INSTRUCTIONS
FOR THE
TROOPS TAKING PART
IN THE
STATE ENTRY
OF
Their Excellencies
THE VICEROY & LADY CHELMSFORD
On December 22nd, 1916.

Calcutta:
TRAILL & COMPANY, LIMITED,
20, BRITISH INDIAN STREET,
1916.

A Happy Christmas

For we've come up from Somerset,
Where the cider apples grow;
For we're all king's men in Somerset,
As they were long, long ago.
An' when you're wanting soger boys,
An' there's fighting for to do,
You just send word to Somerset
An' we'll all be up for you!

From CAPT. J. R. MACKIE
AND OFFICERS
of "D" Company.

BARRACKPORE.   CHRISTMAS, 1916.

into Calcutta to-morrow. They will be commanded by one of my subalterns as I have to attend at Government House for the reception. ΧHe is going to stay a few days in Calcutta and will then come out to Barrackpore for a fortnight. I have to attend all sorts of functions during the next week or two. On Saturday night I have to ~~at~~ dine at the United Service Club, as the Viceroy is going to be present there : and on Boxing day there is a party at Government House Calcutta in his honour. When he comes out here there is sure to be a dinner party & a garden party which we shall have to attend.

The men are going to have a jolly good time this Christmas : the people here are going to give them a first class dinner and then they are to have sports in the afternoon and a good tea. I am very glad indeed that so much is going to be done for them for they have worked well and deserve to be looked after at Christmas time, especially as the people round ~~have~~ here are making fortunes out of the war. Fortt and I have been invited out to dinner on Christmas day by some very nice people and I think we shall have a jolly good time.

Ron Vallis has arrived here and is looking fairly fit – he is ever so much fatter than when I last saw him ~~and~~ but he has certainly not grown taller. I was very glad indeed to see him – it is very fortunate indeed that we should both be in the same company.

Four other officers have also been sent here this week so the company is now up to strength with both officers and men : and I ~~hope~~ I shall not have so much work to do myself now.

It is ever so cold at night now : we always have to wear great coats when we go out and we could often do with a fire but unfortunately there is no fire place in this bungalow. Every day is delightfully fine and the breeze is cold and invigourating so that there is really not much to complain about just at present.

I was awfully sorry to hear that Mother had been unwell & I do hope that she is quite fit again by this time and that you all spent a very merry Christmas. How is the new girl getting on? I suppose she is better than no servant at all I was also very sorry to hear that Grandma Mackie was unwell. I hope that it was nothing serious & that she is now quite fit again.

Andrew seems to like Kohat – he says that it is very cold indeed but he seems to be getting some good shooting.

I shall have to stop now as I must be off to the barracks.

I hope you are all quite well

With very much love to all

Your affectionate son
Jim

2/4th Somerset L.I.
Barrackpore

28–12–16

My dear Mother & Father.

Thank you very much indeed for your Christmas wishes and also for the book & plum pudding. We ar have had three mails on during the last ten days and our Christmas letters arrived on Christmas day; and it was awfully nice to be able to start Christmas day by reading your letters. I have not yet had time to read the book but we are going to have the plum pudding for dinner to-night.

We had a very jolly Christmas on the whole for the people here were very good to us, and did their best to make us feel at home. One person sent us in a bunch of mistletoe but unfortunately we were unable to put it to its proper use as no female accompanied it. I spent the morning visiting the men. I first rode out to the rifle factory to see the men on guard out there, and then I came back to have a look at the men's dinner which was given by the people of Barrackpore. I have never seen a better dinner provided for a lot of men. There were six courses consisting of soup, goose, turkey & ham, plum pudding, jelly, cheese, fruit & sweets and each course was properly served on a clean set of plates. The table was properly laid and there was plenty of beer and lots of smokes. Many of the men had never had such a dinner before & of course they were all delighted. I enclose a copy of the Christmas card which we officers sent to each man in the company.

After dinner there were sports for us all which were awfully good fun. Some were mounted & some were on foot but all the events were amusing : perhaps the one which caused most fun was the bullock cart race. A bullock cart was provided for each competitor drawn by two bullocks and each man had to drive his lady partner to a certain point – you would have roared to see our frantic efforts to make the bullocks tort trot & when they did trot we could not make them go straight.

Two One of the mounted races consisted of riding your pony at a gallop past a lady who threw you a ball. You had to catch the ball & then gallop on & put it into a bucket. I went in for it but was unable to catch the ball. In the evening we all went out to dinner with some awfully nice people. They were New Zealanders and gave us are splendid evening – they set out right from the first to make us feel at home.

Last Friday the Viceroy made his State Entry to Calcutta. When he landed there was a salute of 31 guns & then he drove off to Govt House & all the streets were lined with troops & at Govt. House there were two Guards of Honour.

I was standing on the steps of Govt. House and had a splendid view of the whole show. First of all came ~~his~~ the Bengal ~~men~~ body guard followed by a battery of R.F.A. Then the Viceroy's body guard came and immediately behind it came the Calcutta Light Horse who acted as escort to the Viceroy's carriage. In rear of the whole procession was the 17th Light Cavalry. As the carriage drew up at Govt. House the ~~body~~ guards of honour gave the Royal Salute and there was another salute of 31 guns. His Excellency inspected the guards of honour and then went into the Throne room where he received all the princes & officials.

On Monday evening four of us attended an evening party at Govt. House. We went first of all into the throne room where we waited for the Viceroy. Presently he came in accompanied by his Staff & Lady Chelmsford, and they all walked down the centre of the room to the thrones where they sat down. Then the Viceroy proceeded to present medals & decorations to a few people after which we all went in to supper.

The Viceroy came out here two days ago and will continue to to live here for the next fortnight. We find a Guard for him at Govt. House and one of my subalterns has to live there & have meals with them all. He was of course frightfully worried about it at first but he says that they are all so nice that he soon felt quite at home.

Of course all this has made us very busy indeed, but everything has gone off quite well so far, and my men quite distinguished themselves for smartness in Calcutta last Friday.

I am ever so sorry that Mother did not receive her birthday letters. I should have cabled but I thought that her letters had got through safely. I hope Mother received the £5 which I instructed Cox & Co to send her.

It is awfully nice having Ron W Vallis here – he is a very jolly little fellow and we get on splendidly together. I have got seven subalterns here now so ~~we can~~ you can imagine that we have a pretty lively time. We have got a piano in the mess and I am afraid that our neighbours must get somewhat bored with our efforts when we happen to be in form.

Mother asked me in her letter if I knew of anything which John wanted for his birthday – as a matter of fact I have been wondering myself and have not yet come to any decision. I don't know a bit what he wants out in Basra so I should think something which he can keep would be best.

I am looking forward to the cheese which Father said he was sending out as we cannot get it out here. It is expensive at home now but the price ~~of~~ of it is almost double out here so it is really a great treat nowadays.

Please thank Janet, Mary, Angus & Margaret for the very pretty Xmas cards they sent me – I was awfully pleased to receive them.

I hope Mother & Grandma Mackie are both well again & that all the rest are quite fit.

With much love to all

     I remain

      Your affectionate son

       Jim

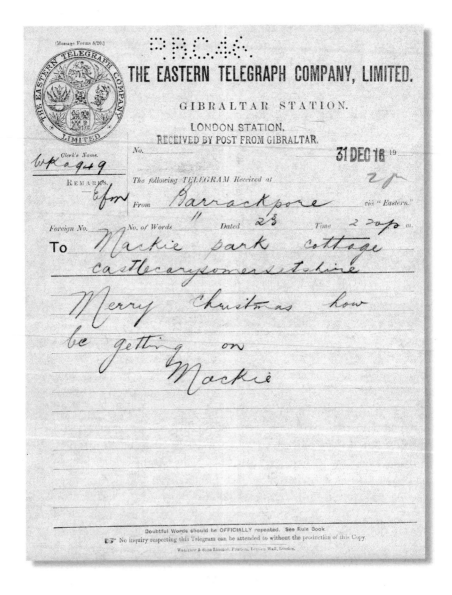

LETTERS FROM 2/4 BN. SOMERSET

LIGHT INFANTRY (P.A.) 1914–19

VOLUME III: 1917

5–1–17

My dear Mother and Father.

The last few days have been rather extraordinary in some ways for I have received a series of telegrams each one of which seemed to contradict the other. I received orders about a week ago to attend the Artillery practice camp at Kotwa on the sixth, but these were cancelled yesterday, and I was told to proceed to Lucknow at once for a course in equitation. Next I received a wire from the General to say that I was not to be allowed to leave the Station during the Viceroy's visit, so in spite of all I am still here. I am sorry I could not go to Lucknow for it is a very nice course and I should like to get a little change for a week or two.

We have been very busy since Monday fo getting ready another draft for Mesopotamia : they will sail from Bombay on the 10th and are leaving here to-morrow morning. It is awfully bad luck having to lose your men just when you are getting to know them and I wish the powers that be would arrange some other system for sending reinforcements to the Gulf.

The Viceroy gave a very big dinner garden party at Govt. House yesterday – there were 2,500 guests and we all had tea under one big banyan tree so you can just imagine the size of it.

The Govt. House grounds are very beautiful indeed : the run down to the Hughli on one side and are full of magnificent trees and flowering shrubs. All officers turned up in uniform but as usual the big natives turned up in magnificent costumes for most part made of brightly coloured materials.

If It is awfully funny how we feel the cold now : I suppose it is because our blood became very heated during the hot weather. The temperature dropped to 43° the other night and it seemed as cold as if it were freezing. I don't know what it will seem like when we come back to England again. "Piper" has not been at all well just lately – he has had a slight attack of distemper but he seems better to-day and I think he will soon be fit. X I miss him very much when he can't come on parade with me.

Ron Vallis went into hospital to-day with an attack of fever – I don't think it is very serious and I hope he will soon be out again. People get fever out here when in England they would only have a cold and the attacks soon pass off.

I was hope Grandma Mackie is better now & I also hope that Mother is quite fit again and able to be up once more.

Please thank Angus for his letter and ask Rob to remember me to M

Capt Brown when he comes back to school again. I am very glad indeed that he has at anyrate come through safely in spite of his wounds.

I hope you are all quite well

With much love to all

> Your affectionate son
> Jim

Barrackpore

✗ 18–1–17

My dear Mother and Father.

We have not had any letters from you for about a fortnight and we don't know when the next mail is due as the arrivals & departures of the boats are not being published now.

I write every week on the same day as before but we never know whether we have caught the mail or not.

We have now heard definitely that we are going off to Camp on the 24th. ~~If the~~ Unless any alterations are made at the last minute we shall leave here on the 24th and go up to Dinapore during the night. We shall then be joined on to a special train containing the remainder of the Bttn. and all ~~of~~ off us will then go to Arrah. We shall then march in stages to a place called Sassaram where we shall go into camp for a month.

I think it will be quite good fun if all goes well but we have rather a lot of recruits to deal with We were inspected on Tuesday by the Inspector General of Infantry in ~~N~~ India, General Christian, who was accompanied by Colonel Clutterbuck. They were both very pleased with us and the General congratulated me on having a very smart and efficient detachment.

Last night I went in to Calcutta and had dinner with the Colonel, who is looking very fit indeed. He is very keen indeed about the Camp, as he has not had a chance of seeing the Bttn together since he came out, and he is full of schemes & plans for making us work while we are out there.

I had a game of polo last week – at least I went down on the field to ride about, but my pony got so wild and excited that she took up all my attention and I had very little time left to go for the ball. She looked splendid, for she reared, & snorted and galloped about just as if she was wild and ~~all~~ t everyone admired her but a I admit she almost defeated me at one time. She quieted down quite a lot towards the end and if I take her out a few more times she will soon settle down to it again.

It is getting much hotter again. During the last few days we have had to start wearing thin clothes again and even at night it is not nearly so cold.

Just at present it is much colder up at Dinapore where it does not begin to get hot till February so we shall probably notice a difference when we go up for camp.

Lord Carmichael is now living out here for a few weeks – he is rather a nice old fellow and he nearly always speaks to us if we meet him out. He plays round the golf course nearly every ~~even~~ evening with his wife and it is rather amusing to watch them padding round together for neither of them are very expert.

Ronald Vallis is quite fit again now – we usually have a game of tennis or hockey together in the evenings.

We have just been playing a game of hockey – the men against the officers and NCO^s. The officers & NCO^s as usual were beaten 4–1 but we had a very close game.

I suppose all the ~~bo~~ others have gone back to school again now – has Duffy gone back again this term?

I hope you are all quite well and will continue to keep so

With much love to all

> Your affectionate son
> Jim

2/4th Somerset L.I.
Barrackpore

~~De~~ Jan 24th 1917

My dear Mother & Father.

You will be surprised to see that I have not yet moved from Barrackpore. Everything was ready for us to leave here on Wednesday evening but I had a wire from the Colonel at the last minute to say that the move was postponed till the 29th so now we shall leave here on Sunday evening in order to reach Dinapore Monday morning. I don't know why the alteration was made but I think the Brigade raised a difficulty of some sort.

Mother's letter of Dec. 20th arrived yesterday and was very welcome indeed as we did not receive a mail for nearly three weeks. I can't think why they don't send them across the Mediterranean in a cruiser for the mail boats find it very difficult indeed to get across now

I think there is another mail due in a day or two but now that the arrivals of the boats are not published we never really know when the letters are coming until they actually arrive.

I was very sorry indeed to hear that old Andrew Mackie is dead, but from what you said a few weeks ago I thought he could not live much longer.

I am so glad to hear that Mother has at last received her birthday present as I was afraid it had gone astray somewhere or other, in fact I was on the point of cabling to ask about it when her last letter arrived. I hope she will buy just whatever she likes with it, as there is no particular thing which I wish her to get. Is the tortishell table which I sent from Port Blair still in good condition? because I have heard from another fellow who sent one home that the squares have all been coming off the one he sent & that it is not much good now.

I am rather keen on seeing my men of the last draft who are still at Dinapore as I see from the particulars which have been sent down to me that there are one or two Cary men among them. I believe one of the Chamberlains and one of the Earwakers are there but I don't know which ones. If there are any more Cary men in the other Companies I shall try and get them with me. Duffy seems to be getting quite a man now – I should have liked to see him wearing his Eton collar for the first time.

I am afraid the cold weather has quite gone, as far as Calcutta is concerned at any rate, for the hot weather bird has come back again and that is a sure sign that the cold is almost over – as he corresponds to the cuckoo at home, which heralds the Summer, but his voice is not so pleasant : in fact he makes such an awful row that he is commonly known as the "brain fever" bird.

I can't think of any more news this week as we have not been doing very much outside our work. The first part of the week we were busy getting ready for our move and now all our kit is packed up and we are waiting to start. I will tell you all about the camp as soon as we get there.

I hope you are all quite fit

With much love to all

> Your affectionate son
> Jim

2/4th Somerset L I
On the trek

1–2–17

My dear Mother & Father.

We have left Barrackpore and are now on the march – I thought we should never get away for we we have had so many contradictory orders and have packed up for a move so many times that I really began to think we should stay on there for a week the hot weather.

However, we did get away last Sunday night evening and travelled up to Dinapore during the night. We arrived there about 7 AM and at once transferred our kit into the special train which was waiting for the whole Bttn. The Bttn arrived about 10 AM and we all entrained for a place called Arrah where we pitched a camp & spent the night. On Tuesday we started to march to Sassaram which is 61 miles from Arrah. We march about 12 miles a day then pitch our tents and spend the nights. It is surprising how quickly the men can pitch and strike a camp now – at first they were a little bit slow but now it all goes like clockwork. Reveille goes at 5–30 every morning and the tents are all on the carts ready to move off by 6–30. We then have breakfasts and march off at 7–30 – this usually allows us to reach the next camp at about 1 PM so that we get most of the afternoon for rest.

The country is all very flat but it is very well irrigated and cultivated. There are long stretches of flax fields in which flax is growing the chief crop & the blue flowers look awfully pretty. Here & there patches of sugar cane are growing also barley & vetches but of course as soon as the hot weather comes on all these crops will be harvested & there will be nothing but stretches of bare brown country Whenever we pass through a village all the people turn out to see us and the school children have been ordered to hold a sort of parade. A whole party of them are in the camp now having come six miles to welcome the British soldiers.

Of course troops very seldom visit this part of the country and the natives can't understand us a bit At one place when they heard we were coming they caught all the fish in the ponds round about three days before we were due to arrive in order to be ready for us. Of course the medical officer promptly disposed of it.

I had a wire from Andrew a few days ago to say that he had been selected for the Indian Cavalry in France and that he would probably sail shortly. If he does go you will probably see him before long as he is certain to be able to get some leave.

As I am writing in my tent without a table you must excuse more this week – I will write again when we get to our permanent camp.

I hope you are all quite fit.

With much love

from your affectionate son
Jim

P. S. Thank you ever so much for the cheese which has just arrived. It is a real beauty and has arrived in perfect condition. It is absolutely splendid after a long march to be able to come in & have a good piece of bread & real good cheese.

The Camp
Sassaram

7th Feb 1917

My dear Mother and Father.

We reached here last Saturday and are now very comfortable in our permanent camp where we shall stay for a month. We are working frightfully hard for we have just heard that we are to do Kitchener's test in a week's time and as we have 200 men who have only just arrived from England you can imagine what a lot there is to teach them in a very short time.

I can assure you we were very glad when we marched in for we covered 63 miles in five days and only stayed one night at any place. While on the march reveille went at 5–30 AM and all kits and tents had to be packed up and on the carts at 6–30 AM in order that the transport could get away before the Bttn as the bullocks which ~th~ drew the carts could not go quite as quickly as the men.

We usually reached the next camping ground at about 12–30 PM and the transport was so well managed that it was never more than ten minutes after the column. The men were soon very expert at pitching and striking a camp – it never took them more than ¼ of an hour to strike the tents and pack them on the carts. It is an awful nuisance however when the fatigue party arrived to strike the officers' tents just as one was out of bed for it was awfully cold dressing outside. it is ever so much colder up here than it was at Barrackpore – the nights are bitterly cold and even the days are not so hot chiefly because the air up here is very dry.

We were very lucky indeed on the march as we had it fine the whole time, ~whe~ but the day after we arrived here it rained quite hard. This Winter rain was due about Christmas time but it was very late this year. I think it is over now and there will be no more rain till the beginning of May.

The ~k~ country through which we marched was all perfectly flat but I should think it was very fertile, for everywhere there were magnificent crops of flax sugar cane, wheat & vetches. It is splendidly irrigated – we crossed small canals every few hundred yards We are now at the foot of a low ridge of hills which are well wooded and make a very nice change from the monotonous level of the Ganges plain. I rode up one of the hills this morning and you can't think how nice it was to be able to look down from above once more.

The jungle on the slopes of the hills is full of game – we have already had several duck shooting expeditions, and when Kitchener's test is over we shall go out after black buck etc, but at present we have not much time for shooting.

Ronald Vallis and I shared a tent while we were on the march but I now have one to myself and he is in the one behind mine. We had to send off a draft to-day & Ron ⴕ is taking them up to Dinapore; he may have to go to Bombay with them & if he does he will probably stay to bring back the new draft which is due to arrive shortly.

I ⴕ Thank you ever so much for the cheese you sent me for Christmas: it arrived just before we left Barrackpore so I took it on the march and was you can't think how we enjoyed it. Lots of the officers who had some of it said that it was the best cheese they had ever tasted – it really was a beauty and it arrived in perfect condition. I received an awfully nice Christmas cake from Aunt Agnes of Dornock Mains – it was very kind indeed of her to send it out.

The people at Barrackpore were awfully sorry to see us go and they all want us to go back there again but we are due to go to Dinapore after the camp is over. I shall however try to go down there one leave some time or other for everyone was very kind indeed to us.

I received Mother's letter dated Jan 10th ~~last~~ this morning and was sorry to hear that Father has been unwell also to hear ~~th of~~ of W Martins death. It is awfully sad for his wife and children and I don't wonder that ~~the~~ it cast a gloom over Cary.

I am glad you liked the little brooches – I will certainly send a button for Mother and Margaret as soon as I can get them.

Andrew is very pleased that he has been accepted for France and I am sure that it will be a good thing for him go as it will ~~se~~ be better for him in after life if he has been on ~~war~~ service. I hope he will be able to come down to see me before he goes.

My company is doing very well indeed and the Colonel is very pleased indeed with it. I hope we shall do well on Kitchener's test.

Joe Earwaker (who used to play rugger for Cary) is one of my men – he is looking very fit and seems quite happy. I have not had time to have a long talk with him since we came here.

I hope you are all quite well & that Father & Grandma Mackie are both better.

With much love to all

      I remain
        Your affectionate son
          Jim

Park Cottage
Castle Cary Somerset
England

Febry. 14th 1917

My dear Jim

It is Janet's turn to write to you but being your 21st Birthday. I am enclosing a note as well. We all write in wishing you a Happy Birthday, & very many happy returns of March 18th little did we think when you left home you would be away now but we are thankful you are all three safe & sound so far & trust you will be spared to come home again some day. We are very proud of you all & hope your health will keep good in India.

Father has sent Cox & Co £6.7.6 to be paid to your account £5. from Father & myself 10/- from the children. 10/- from Grandma & 2/6 each from the 3 aunts at Ellesmere.

Grandma still keeps poorly Aunt Dick is a little better now Aunt Jane is in bed with a very bad leg. So altogether it is not a very lively household.

The snow is going slowly but it still keeps bitterly cold. I shall be glad for the childrens sake when it gets warmer but we are I am glad to say all keeping very well indeed.

Janet will tell you all the news so I must conclude. With very much love & Birthday wishes

Ever your loving
Mother

I expect we shall reserve your birthday party till war is over things here are in too serious a state for parties.

We saw since, last we wrote, all English in India have to join up for defence in India.

2/4th Somerset L I
The Camp
Sassaram

14–2–17

My dear Mother and Father.

I have just had a wire from Andrew to say that he is sailing from Bombay on Monday and that he will not be able to come and see me before he goes. I was hoping to have just had a few hours with him before he sailed but I am afraid it is quite impossible – however I expect you will soon be seeing him ~~soon~~ for even if he is not allowed to go home before going to France he is sure to get some leave before he has been out there long. ~~We~~ Since we came to camp we have been training harder than anything we have ever done before in order to get ready for Kitchener's test which starts to-morrow. The General says that he is going to make it even more strenuous than it was last year, but perhaps when it comes to the point it will not be so bad.

I am thoroughly enjoying the camp for, although we are working hard it is all field work which I like very much indeed. My company has done exceptionally well ~~in~~ the last few days & the Colonel is very pleased indeed with it – I ~~sh~~ hope we shall keep it up during the test.

Our programme just lately has been something like this 7–0 Breakfasts 8–0 to 2–30 – Field day. 2–30 Dinners 3–30. Pow-wow & lectures and twice a week night operations in addition. The men are as hard as nails and we are all frightfully sunburnt, but it is making us all ever so fit. The nights are still very cold but we shall soon have to stop our work during the middle of the day for it is getting ever so much hotter.

I had one day off last week and went off for a shooting expedition. We sent our kit & guns out over night and early in the morning we rode out to the scene of action on our horses – a distance of about seven miles.

We had made our arrangements beforehand and the "shikara" was waiting for us with beaters etc. We were at the foot of a low ridge of hills and the whole country was covered with low jungle which was rather difficult to get through. Fortunately we did not have to go far for we soon sighted a small herd of deer on the hillside but I must admit that if they had not been pointed out to me I should never have seen them for they were exactly the colour of the rocks and even with field glasses were difficult to pick up.

We stalked them all the morning and eventually got within 250 yards of them and fired. I managed to drop two with consecutive shots but we were rather disappointed when we came up to them for one was a doe & the other was a young buck whose horns were only about 4′′ long. However we had a most enjoyable morning and I don't think I have ever discovered a more exciting form of sport. I was awfully sorry when I had shot them for they were perfect little beasts and it was an awful shame to shoot them but the stalking part of the business was simply splendid. I want to try and go out again before we leave here if I can get a chance.

My pony is in fine form now – she seems to like camp life as much as I do and she is simply magnificent on parade in the mornings. Everyone says she is the best pony in the Regiment – her coat shines just as if it had been sprinkled with gold dust.

We are still sending off drafts, but I really think we have now finished:

and now that compulsion is to be introduced into India I hope we shall be relieved to go on service. I am very glad that they have at last decided to conscript some of the people out here for there are hundreds of fellows out here who could very well be spared. Some of them came out here when the war broke out in order to escape conscription in England.

Ron Vallis is very fit except for a cold – he played football for the company to-night – we beat "B" Coy 4–1. He has just returned from Dinapore having taken up the active service draft.

I can't think of any more news to-night and I want to get off to bed as we shall not get another good sleep for about three nights.

I hope you are all quite well

With much love to all

> I remain
> Your affectionate son
> Jim

The Camp
Sassaram

22–2–17

My dear Mother and Father.

Just at the present minute I am feeling rather stiff and tired having just run in the cross country race for the Regimental Shield. For once in a way I was not my included in the "also rans" as I managed to come in third this time. My Coy. won the race easily, as securing the 1st, 3rd, 4th & 6th places and of these the 1st 3rd & 4th were officers so we did rather well. The course was a very difficult one – 3 miles long – and I admit that I had as much as I could manage to get round.

The shield competition also includes hockey, football, sports and shooting – we are running the sports on Friday and the final of the football comes Saturday while the first round of the hockey will be played off to-morrow. I hope "D" Coy. will win the competition we have got into the final of the footer and I feel sure that we shall win the hockey.

On Sunday afternoon we marched back to camp having completed Kitchener's test once more. It lasted for four days this year instead of three, and although it was frightfully strenuous only about three men fell out.

We started off with a nine mile march and an attack on a retreating enemy which lasted till about 2 PM when we had dinners. At 3–30 PM we moved out again and did an attack with ball ammunition returning to the bivouac about 6 PM. Then we received orders to picket the hills all round and make a perimeter camp, ~~like~~ similar to the ones used in frontier warfare. This camp was attacked about 9–30 PM and after we had beaten it off we were allowed to go to bed. Of course we had no tents – it was just a bivouac under the trees.

On the following morning ~~the~~ before breakfasts the General inspected us in physical drill & bayonet fighting and after breakfasts we moved out to do field firing again. It was in the latter that my ~~coy~~ company scored a tremendous success. One platoon under Ron Vallis did so well that the General said he could find nothing to criticise and he congratulated me on having such a smart platoon. Of course we were all frightfully pleased for the other companies all got badly dropped on during the morning.

At 4–30 the same day we all moved out again and took up an outpost line along the crest of the hills staying out till 6 AM on the morning of the third day when we were called in. As soon as breakfasts were over however we had to climb the hills once more and take up a defensive position which was at once attacked. We drove off the attack and then took the offensive ourselves, and in this latter operation we had to clear a ridge about 1000 feet high. I can assure you we were glad to sit down when we reached the top, but I must say the view was simply magnificent. After this we went back to the bivouac and rested till 8–30 PM when we went out to do a night attack. This lasted till about 12 midnight.

Early on the fourth day we started to march home but it was a long time before we reached our destination for we had to fight the whole way back. We were very glad of a bath and a sleep when we reached camp but were all very fit The training season is practically over now as it is getting far too hot to work in the middle of the day. The change during the last three days has been absolutely remarkable so much so that the medical officer has decided that it is too hot for us to remain in tents and we are going to strike the camp on the 26th.

My company is going back to Dinapore but I am going down to Barrackpore just to hand over to "B" company and after that I shall take a few days leave. I am very sorry indeed that we are breaking up the camp so soon for I have ~~thro~~ thoroughly enjoyed the whole of it in spite of all the hard work we have done. It came as a very welcome change from Barrackpore and I feel ever so much better for it.

The Colonel has just gone off for a tiger shoot ~~the~~ to which he promised to take me but I had to give it up at the last minute to play for the company in the hockey tournament. I was awfully disappointed at not being able to go as it is a chance one does not often get; but as I could not do both I decided to play hockey in order not to disappoint the men who like to see their officers turning out for games etc.

I have a Corporal in the company called Howe who was the captain of the Bridgewater Town rugger side for some years and he tells me that he can remember playing against Father quite well. I had a long chat with him yesterday – he knows W. S. Donne quite well.

Your letter of the 17th Jan arrived to-day. I was very sorry to hear that Uncle Will and Stephens are both ill and I hope that both are fit again by this time. Fancy Carr coming over to see you! I wish he would come out here again for he was one of the jolliest fellows I have ever met.

If you have kept all the photos I have sent back you will find Carr in one of the groups I took ᴂ coming out on the Saturnia.

What extraordinary changes are taking place in Cary lately – if many more people leave the place I fear that there will be very few left whom we know by the time we come back.

I suppose Andrew has sailed from Bombay by now – he said he was leaving on the 17th.

I hope you are all quite fit

With much love to all

Your affectionate son

Jim

2/4th Somerset L.I.

Barrackpore

1 Mar 1917

My dear Mother & Father.

You will see that we have finished our camp and that I am back at Barrackpore once more. I am not really here in an official capacity as my company is at Dinapore but I just came down to hand over the station to Capt Farwell of "B" Coy who has relieved me. I am staying with some people here called Mr & Mrs Bocquet who are easily the nicest people I have met out here and I go down to the barracks in the morning and then have the rest of the day free. In this way I am combining work with leave. This is the first time I have stayed more than one night in a private house since I left home and it seems awfully strange after living in Mess all this time but I am having an awfully nice time.

We had great excitement the last two or three days at camp playing the football and hockey tournaments, and you will be pleased to hear that my Coy won both of them. The football final against "C" coy was a great game because "C" Coy were formerly the champions, having been unbeaten for about six months: but it was a splendid game but we won in the end 1–0.

We won the hockey 2–1. The Colonel presented medals for the football & Capt Farwell presented them for the hockey, so you can imagine how keen the play was for the men always go for a game if there is anything at the end of it even if it is only a pin.

I did not leave Sassaram with the remainder of the Bttn. as I had to ~~go to~~ leave for Dinapore last Sunday in order to attend a court martial on the Monday. It was on a sepoy who had lost the bolt of his rifle – this does not seem a very big offence, ~~out~~ but out here it always means a court martial as it is very essential that rifles, or their parts should not get over the frontier.

It was rather a slow business as ~~we had~~ all the evidence was given in Hindustani and we had to have an interpreter to translate it to us before we could write it down.

~~It~~ I left ~~Barrackpore~~ Dinapore as soon as the trial was over to come down here and I have to be back there again on Monday morning It is much cooler now than it was last week for we had a good many thunderstorms last Saturday which brought the temperature down quite a lot. I am afraid that the change is only temporary however for the cold weather has quite gone now and every day is hotter than the one before it.

The news the last few days has been rather good – first of all the recapture of Kut and then the German retirement on the Western Front. I suppose it won't do to be too optimistic about the latter till we know more about it but it can't do any harm at anyrate & it sounds rather nice to be able to say that the Germans are retiring. It is over two years since we have been able to say this.

I am very sorry indeed that the camp is all over – we worked awfully hard while we were out there but it made us ever so fit and we we had a tremendous lot of instruction.

"Piper" was awfully pleased to see me again when I came back. Fortt kept him for me while we were at camp during which he has grown quite a lot. He is now quite a big dog and is not nearly so mischievious as he was.

I should love to see Ted with her hair up – I suppose it takes her about two hours to dress now so she manages to find lots of time to stand in front of the glass.

I hope Uncle Will and Stephens are better – have the "Mumps" visited Park Cottage yet? I also hope that Grandma and Aunt Dick are better they both seem to have had rather a bad time.

The last mail came in on Monday but I have not seen my letters yet as they were sent to Sassaram and I suppose they have now gone to Dinapore. They will probably arrive here just after I have left.

As I have no letters to answer and can think of nothing interesting to write about I will let this do for this week.

I hope you are all quite well

With much love to all

       Yours affectionate son
       Jim

2/4th Somerset L I
Dinapore

₸ 9–3–17

My dear Mother & Father.

I reached Dinapore once more last last Monday morning expecting to have to spend the greater part of the hot weather here but on our arrival we were greeted with the unexpected news that we were shortly to have a move.

We are to be relieved on April 10th by the 2/5th Somersets from Burma and are to preceed to Poona, which is one of the best stations in India I believe. Whether we shall make a long stay there or whether it is only a temporary halting place I don't know but from the information we have we received I should think there was going to be a concentration near Bombay and we might possibly go on service. However whatever happens I think Poona must be a better station than Dinapore.

I had a very jolly time at Barrackpore – the people I was staying with were awfully nice and I was sorry to have to come away. However it is a good thing that I did not stay any longer for I found lots of work to do when I got back here.

It is getting quite hot again now – a few days ago we had a thunderstorm which cooled the it quite a lot but is effects are nearly worn off as again. The nights are still quite nice and cool and people are beginning to sleep out of doors once more.

I have just applied for another three days leave next week to go over to Patna and stay with M^r and Mrs Mackenzie. He Mackenzie is in charge of the Govt. printing works at Patna and I met him at camp where he was attached to my company. He is volunteer officer and thinking he might learn something from us he came and stayed in camp with us for a fortnight. Both he and his wife are very nice indeed and I am sure I shall have a good time over there.

I had a terrible shock when I woke up last Sunday and remembered that it was Margaret's birthday & that I had not written to her.

I could not cable on Sunday so I sent one off early on Monday morning and immediately wrote to Cox & Co and told them to send her a present. I hope she will forgive me for being so careless – we were out at camp when it was time to write to her and were so busy with Kitchener's test that I never gave it a thought. There are two native infantry regiments in Dinapore now besides ourselves, but the artillery have gone and also the 1/4th Depot. The latter went off the Secunderabad on Wednesday.

We sent all our unfit men to Calcutta yesterday to join the Garrison Battn of the Lincolns. It was rather sad to see them go for lots of them have been with us all the way through and they felt it awfully keenly having to leave their old regiment. One of the recruits I got at Yarlington – Wilton – was among them.

Before leaving Bombay Andrew sent me a beautiful leather attaché case as a 21st birthday present. I am awfully pleased with it for it is a thing I wanted very much indeed – it was awfully good of him to get it for me. I received Father's letter dated 6th Feb. containing birthday wishes last Wednesday for which thank you very much indeed.

You seem to have had an extraordinary cold winter and I expect it has caused a good deal of suffering among the poor people for with all the prices so high they must be very badly hit.

The news from Mesopotamia and France has been awfully cheery lately – I hope it is the beginning of the end. The Mesopotamia effort is certainly a great success but it is rather difficult to understand exactly what is going on in France. Anyhow the Germans are retiring & that is quite good enough for the time being.

I am glad to hear that you are all fit now and ~~also~~ that the Ellesmere people are also better.

With much love to all

      I remain
        Your affectionate son
        Jim

Patna

15th March 1917

My dear Mother & Father.

I am staying at Patna for three days with M^r and Mrs Mackenzie – as I told you last week I met Mackenzie at Camp where he was attached to my company. He came over to Dinapore last evening to fetch two of us, and motored us back. We are staying here till Monday morning when we shall have to return in time for parade.

On our way here we drove through the new city of Bankipore where, if you remember we formed the Guard of honour to the Viceroy when he opened the New High Court last year. Since then the place has grown up in an amazing manner – the High Court ~~is~~ has been completely finished, the College has been built also Government House & the Secretariat; and bungalows for the officials have sprung up ~~every w~~ everywhere. A park has been laid out, a polo ground made and trees have been planted all along the roads. It is awfully interesting to see what a change has taken place in a year and ~~it~~ the growth of a new city is a thing one does not see very often ~~eng~~ in England. It will be another two years before the place looks really nice as of course everything looks so frightfully new, and the lawns & gardens have hardly had time to look really well yet, but when the whole place is finished it will be a very fine city.

Bankipore is of course the modern & European end of Patna and some day the name Bankipore will be dropped entirely. The native City of Patna is bounded one one side by the Ganges and ~~runs~~ and on the other by the railway and stretches continuously for nine miles. We are right in the heart of it ~~here~~ now, having passed through 6 miles of the bazaar to get here. You cannot imagine what the bazaar is like – the streets are frightfully narrow – the houses are mere huts, and the people are crowded into them like sardines. Cattle, fowls, goats, people & fleas all live together quite happily, ~~on~~ making the place smell like nothing on earth. I hope to have a good look round presently but there is really nothing very interesting to see except the particular house in which we are now staying. The latter is a survival of the old Dutch settlement and at that time was an opium factory – (Patna is famous for its opium) but it has now been converted into the Government Printing Press. It is a perfect example of an old Dutch house and tourists from all over the world come to see it. They ~~k~~ knew the way to build houses to keep out the heat in those days – the walls are about 6′ thick, the rooms are very big and high and the verandahs are wide and cool. The front of the house faces the Ganges which comes right up to the walls and a magnificent terrace about 200 yards long runs right along the front. Mackenzie has made quite an English flower garden on this terrace by means of flower pots and boxes, and he grows roses, pinks ~~panseys~~ pansies & geraniums etc.

16th Mar. There is an Army Clothing factory in Patna which I had a look at this morning. It is not a bit like an ordinary English factory as there is no big machinery or anything of that sort. The cutters don't use tables – they just spread the cloth out on the ground and squat about round it. All the sewing is done with Singer's sewing machines but the button holes are made by an awfully neat little machine which can make hundreds of them in a very short time.

We also had a look at the Govt. Survey office this morning and saw them making the maps of the district – there is ever so much more in ~~mak~~ map making than I ever imagined.

Yesterday afternoon we all went to Lady Chamier's garden party where we had quite a jolly time. It was not a bit formal – we just played tennis, ~~and ej~~ enjoyed ourselves, and had a very good tea. Lady Chamier wants me to come over again as soon as I can, but I don't expect I shall be able to do so ~~no~~ as we shall be very busy getting ready for move very shortly.

Hot weather conditions have fairly set in now – the hot wind has started to blow and all the bungalows have to be shut up all day to keep it out. The dust is awfully bad and the air towards evening gets absolutely laden with it.

Everyone has started to sleep outside again and the row of bungalows in which Ron and I are now living ~~are~~ is rightly called ~~Py~~ Pyjama alley. It is an awfully funny sight when we come back from Mess at night to see all the beds in a row along the verandahs. The white mosquito nets look just like ghosts in the moonlight.

The Mackenzies have one little boy – quite a jolly little fellow very much like Duff used to be when we left home. I am afraid I have lost the art of talking to children not having had anything to do with them for so long.

I have just finished reading "T Tembarom" the book you all sent me for Christmas: ﹨ I have had so little time for reading that it took me two months to get through it but I enjoyed it immensely. It is ﹨ awfully interesting and exceedingly cleverly written. I have now lent it to Ron Vallis and he says he likes it very much indeed.

Ron has just bought a puppy which is rather smaller than ~~piper~~ Piper was when I first had him and I think it takes him all his time to look after it There has been no mail this week but we are expecting one every day – I think it will probably arrive on my birthday.

The Mackenzies have apparently got wind of the fact that it is my birthday on Sunday and I think they are going to ~~hol~~ have a party to celebrate it.

I hope you are all keeping quite fit

With much love to all

Your affectionate son
Jim

2/4th Somerset L.I.
Dinapore

23–3–17

My dear Mother & Father.

Thank you all very much indeed for your letters containing birthday wishes and for the present you are sending. It has not yet arrived but when it does I shall try to get something with it which I can keep. There is no chance of spending it here but there are shops at Poona I believe. Thank you also for the cablegram which arrived to-day.

I spent my birthday at Patna with the Mackenzies; they somehow found out that it was my 21st and they had a special dinner to celebrate the occasion

Andrew and Colonel Waddy at a station between Calcutta and Dinapore

& of course we had to have another when I returned to the Mess the next day. I ~~never~~ never thought we should be out here as long when we left home, and I quite thought I should spend my 21st birthday at home, but looking at things as they are at present ~~I~~ we shall be lucky if we are in England again by this time next year.

I have ~~just~~ been over to Bankipore to-day with the Colonel to attend the Lieut Governor's garden party. We had quite a good time – there was tennis and dancing: ~~the latter~~ We danced on the finest floor I have ever seen: I think the wooden planks were laid on springs. Ronald was over there in very good form – he is now staying a few days with the Mackenzies.

There is a tennis tournament in progress here at present. It is quite a big one, open to the whole of Bihar & Orissa, and is lasting throughout the whole week. On Saturday, which is the last day all the finals are going to be played and we are giving an at home followed by a concert. Then we are going to finish up with a supper in the Mess to which all the ladies are ~~going~~ going to be invited.

I entered for the mens singles handicap & doubles handicap. In the former I just lost after three great sets. We both won a set & then my opponent won the last one. In the latter we reached the semifinal and then we came up against a pair who absolutely played us off the courts. ~~We~~ They completely outplayed us & we did not stand a chance right from the start.

I had three letters from Andrew to-day sent from Aden, Suez & Port Said. He seems to be enjoying his voyage immensely and after two years out here it will probably do him a lot of good.

I am awfully glad Duff is getting on so well at School – he seems to have inherited his ability at Arithmetic from Father.

I hope the play at Sunny Hill was successful. I should h liked to see Mary as "Snug" & Pussy as a fairy – must have h been very pretty indeed

Ron Vallis has just got hold of a little dog – the funniest little fellow you ever saw. I am looking after it while he is away: ~~but and~~ ⅄ he is awfully amusing. Piper looks quite a giant beside him but the little one is so fierce that he quite frightens poor old piper who usually comes to the conclusion that discretion is the better part of ~~so~~ valour.

I am sorry to hear that Aunt Jane is ill again but I am delighted that everyone at Park Cottage is quite fit They have had rather an unlucky Winter at Ellesmere I don't think there is any more news this week but I am enclosing one or two photographs. ⅄ I shall have a few more to send as soon as I can get them printed.

Once more thank you all very much indeed for my birthday present
With much love to all

> Your affectionate son
> Jim

2/4th Somerset L.I.
Dinapore

28–3–17

My dear Mother & Father.

I am writing on Wednesday this week instead of Friday for I have just heard that Ron & I have to go off to Muzaffarpur on Friday morning. I don't quite know whether we are going to judge at the Bihar Light Horse Sports ⅄ or whether we are going to ~~up~~ umpire at a field day, as I have only just received a brief message to tell us to get ready: but I am certain that we shall have an awfully good time. Muzaffarpur is the same place to which we went for the shooting competion last year & on that occasion we had a splendid time.

To-morrow Ron & I are going over to spend the day at Bankipore. We shall go over early while it is cool and in the afternoon shall go to Lady Chamier's garden party. After that we have both been invited out to dinner so we shall have a late drive home.

Our "At Home" last Saturday was a great success – nearly everyone ~~from~~ at Bankipore came over including Sir Edward Gait & Sir Edward Lady Chamier. After the tennis finals we had a jolly good concert in aid of the Red Cross Funds and ⅄ then we all invited guests back to the mess for supper.

I have never seen the mess so full before – there were over sixty people there and we had some difficulty in finding room for them but we managed it with a squeeze and everyone thoroughly enjoyed themselves. After it supper we danced and played various sorts of games most of which were suggested by the Colonel who was in great form the whole evening.

~~Sun~~ We have now been invited to so many ~~p~~ dinner parties at Bankipore that we really can't deal with them & have had to refuse them all.

The last three days have been by far the hottest we have had so far and hot weather conditions have set in in earnest now. The nights have started to get hot and all day the hot wind is blowing so strongly that towards evening the sun is quite obscured by the dust clouds in the air. There is dust everywhere and it is impossible to keep it out. The only use I can find for the hot weather is that it keeps down plague which is frightfully bad round here just now. The natives are dying off like flies and we have to be awfully careful not to let our own servants go anywhere ~~ne~~ near the infected areas. If it gets much worse we shall all have to be innoculated against it.

The mails for this week have not arrived yet – they are very irregular indeed now and we never know when they are coming.

The news is still very good from France and it looks as if the Germans are on the run. I hope we shall be able to drive them right back this time.

I hope everyone at Ellesmere is better now and I hope you are all quite well.

With much love to all.

> Your affectionate son
> Jim

2/4th Somerset L.I.
Dinapore

5–4–17

My dear Mother & Father.

Your letter of the 28th Feb. arrived a few days ago but the one for the previous week has not yet come, neither have I received any intimation from Cox & Co that the money you sent for my birthday has been received. However one must expect the mails to be delayed in these days and no doubt the missing letters will turn up some time or other. The letter in which I acknowledged the receipt of the cheese which you sent for Christmas seems to have gone astray. It arrived quite safely the day before we left Barrackpore so I took it on the march with me. It was a splendid cheese – the journey did not affect it in the least.

We had quite a good time at Muzafferpore last week. ⅄ Ron and I judged the sports which consisted of tent pegging, skill with the sword & shooting, ~~but~~ and the humourous part of it all was that neither of us knew a thing about the use of cavalry swords. However ᶜ we managed quite well and everyone was satisfied that we gave the prize to the right man. After the sports I stayed on another day in order to visit the Imperial College of Agriculture for India which is at a place called Pusa only twenty miles from Muzafferpore. We ~~wen~~ motored out ~~we~~ in the morning and had lunch with Hutchinson, the Bacteriologist. He shewed me over the College & explained his particular work to me and then after tea we called on M^r & Mrs Mackenna. Mackenna is the director of Agriculture to the Imperial Govt and in the course of conversation he said that they would be frightfully hard ~~of~~ up for men in the Agricultural department after the war & was very keen that I should ᵏ try and get in. I told him that lots of things would happen before the war ~~war~~ was over and that I preferred to wait. However he sent ~~me~~ a whole lot of papers ~~on the~~ about the department this morning for me to read. ~~A~~ The Agricultural ~~dep~~ Service out here is quite new and is not as well paid as the I.C.S or Forest Service but it will probably be greatly improved in the near future.

The College at Pusa is a very fine building and the grounds are very nice indeed. It is entirely used for research at present, ᵏ and there are practically ~~no~~ no students but the Govt. are anxious to make it into a residential College for Students.

They are at present trying a rather interesting experiment to try and improve the milking qualities of the cattle and with this end in view are crossing Native cattle with Ayshire Bulls. The first lot of heifers resulting from this cross should come into milk shortly and of course they are all anxiously awaiting the result. At present the great drawback to the cross is that the bullocks have no humps and are therefore not much good for work.

~~The M~~ A great deal of Indigo and Sugar are grown in the Muzafferpore district and as both have risen tremendously in price since the war the planters over there are all rich men now.

To-morrow being Good Friday & Saturday being "Jellalabad" day we have got a holiday till Monday so Ron and I are going up to Benares for a day or two. I am told that it is well worth seeing, so we thought we had better take our chance at once. We are going off by the night train to-night.

I am afraid it will be very hot but we shall have to see as much as possible ~~by day~~ in the early mornings, and evenings.

The Civil people out here are frightfully worried about the new defence scheme which came into force on the 1st April. By it they all have to do 90 drills in the next ~~two~~ three months which means that they will have to do about an hour a day at drill as well as their ordinary work. As the hot weather is fairly on us now I am afraid some of the fat old civilians will have rather a bad time of it before their drills are finished.

Our move to Poona has been cancelled but as the move of the 2/5th

Somersets from Burmah to Dinapore has not been cancelled yet I think we shall probably go somewhere else. If they don't make haste however it will be far too hot before long.

It will be Bunna's birthday to-morrow – I hope he will have a good time.

I am sorry to hear that mother has been ill with influenza – I am afraid it was the result of the very cold weather you had.

I sincerely hope she is better now & that as the others are quite fit.

With much love to all

Your affectionate son
Jim

2/4th Somerset L.I.
& Dinapore

13–4–17

My dear Mother & Father.

I was ever so sorry to hear by the last mail that Mother was so unwell again and I sincerely hope that she is better again by this time. I hope you will both be able to get away for a good holiday for I am sure you both need a change and rest.

I wonder if we shall be home to see you all before long – at anyrate we are leaving India very shortly, but have not yet heard where we are going.

We heard last February that we were going to move to Poona in April and then to our great disappointment the move was cancelled. We we were all frightfully annoyed at the prospect of another hot weather in Dianpore, but about a fortnight ago we were received fresh instructions. According to our last orders as soon as the Bedford Garrison Bttn arrives from England it will go over to Burma to relieve the 2/5th Somersets who will come here to relieve us. We shall then proceed to Poona to await embarkation.

We don't know a bit where we shall go but I feel sure that it will not be Mesopotamia for we h have received instructions to hand in all equipment etc belonging to the India Govt. Of course we are all speculating as to where it will be and needless to say we hope that first of all we shall be sent to England. All the chargers will have to be sent back to the remount depót in a few days time – we shall all be awfully sorry to see them go for you get very fond indeed of your animals.

I don't know what I shall do with "Piper" – I should like to have him sent home but I am afraid he would not be allowed to travel. If not I shall give him away to someone our here.

Ron and I went up to Benares last Thursday night and came back on

Saturday evening. We travelled all night and arrived at Benares early Friday morning. The best time to see the people bathing in the river is just as the sun is rising so we went to down at once. Thousands of people were bathing in what to them is the sacred river – all along the bank steps lead down to the water and the ~~bathers~~ whole way along the crowds were so thick that there was hardly room to move. We went out in a boat and watched the scene from the water. Up on the bank are the great big palaces of the Maharajahs each one of whom has a palace in Benares, and there are temples of various kinds dotted all along the top of the bank.

We took lots of photographs and had a look at some of the temples and then went back to the hotel for breakfast. After breakfast we went to the the Monkey temple, the famous Golden temple & the bazaars. Our guide took us right down into the native city through streets so narrow that people on each side could easily shake hands without crossing and we had a look at the brass market, and the Benares embroidery. Benares is famous for both its brass and embroidery so we bought a little of each just for the sake of having it. The embroidery is awfully pretty being worked with golden & silver thread on very fine silk for which Benares is also noted.

The population of Benares is mostly Hindu and most of the temples etc are therefore for the Hindu religion but there are a few Mahommedans who have a very fine temple down by the river. The bazaars were full of sacred bulls which seemed to wander about just where they liked and take whatever they liked.

The afternoon was much too hot for sight seeing so we stayed in and had a sleep but in the evening we drove four miles out to see the ruins of old Benares and the old Buddhist temple. It was all frightfully interesting and we were awfully glad to have had the opportunity of seeing it because Benares as a city is really quite unique.

On Saturday we had a look round again and went out to Ramnager to see the palace of the Maharaja of Benares and in the afternoon of caught the mail train back to Dinapore.

Monday being Easter Monday we tried to take the men out for a river picnic but we could not get a steamer so we had to try to get up some sports. They were got up in an awfully hurry but we had great fun & the men all seemed to enjoy themselves

Last night we had a paper chase for the whole Bttn which was great fun. The hares gave us rather a bad time as there false trails were so well laid that we wasted no end of time finding the right ones. In the end I came in second and Ron was fourth. It is very hot indeed now and the beastly hot West wind blows a gale every day. I wish we could get a thunderstorm just to cool it down a little and lay the dust but at present there is no sign of one.

I enclose a few photographs taken when we were staying with M^r & Mrs Bocquet and also one or two of Benares.

I do hope Mother will soon be better and that all the rest are quite fit. With much love to all

> Your affectionate son
> Jim

2/4th Somerset L.I.
Dinapore

⚑ 19–4–17

My dear Mother & Father.

~~My dear~~ Last Monday I received a letter from Messrs Cox & Co stating that they had credited my a/c with Rs 94, which is the equivalent of £6–7–6, sent out from England. Once more thank you all very much indeed for it – I will try and spend it on something useful when we get to Poona.

As far as I personally am concerned this has been a most uneventful week and there is absolutely nothing to write about beyond our usual routine work.

Dinapore goes along just the same as it has done for the last twenty years except that it gets hotter and hotter. We have not yet reached 100° in the shade but it has been 98° once or twice, which is rather too hot to be comfortable.

The Colonel has not been at all well the last few days – he ran in the paper chase last week and the effort was too much for him for he had ~~been~~ to stay in bed three or four days. He is better now and went off to Darjeeling yesterday for a change.

We had another paper chase yesterday, but I contented myself with riding round as I had a sore foot caused by hockey the night before. To-night we are going to play hockey again – the match being the Officers v the men; – I think it will be a very close game and I should not be at all surprised if the officers won.

Ron Vallis has been detailed as an instructor to the new defence Force until we leave here, so I don't see much of him now. I think he has rather an amusing time on the whole for none of the officers or men know a single thing about soldiering.

Next week it will probably be still more amusing as all the Bankipore people have to come over to Dinapore to drill including the High Court Judges etc.

I don't think the compulsory service is working out particularly well out here because there are so many men who have to be exempted. Except in a commercial City like Calcutta there are very few men who are not officials, and of course these are not available for service unless other men are found to replace them which is impossible The Administration must go on and we cannot afford to relax our hold over the country ~~that~~ by sending all the officials off on service. It looks to me as if the whole scheme was a bit of eye wash to public opinion in England and I am not sure that the new system will produce any more men than the old system of volunteers; of course there are certain men who will be raked in who had ~~never~~ no intention whatever of doing anything at all and as far as this are concerned it is a splendid idea. We are all frightfully pleased about the offensive in France – we seem to be really getting on now and it looks as if the Germans are quite unable to stop our steady advance.

I received Mother's letter dated March 14th to-day and was awfully sorry to hear about the mumps. I hope Mother is better again by this time and I hope that she will be able to take a good rest and get quite strong again. I hope all the others will manage to steer clear. An officer from the 2/5th Somersets arrived here ~~to-day~~ yesterday to start taking over so I suppose we shall soon move out. He told us that he ~~sh~~ had heard that we should probably be relieved about May 9th, but this is not official and we shall just have to "wait and see".

I hope everyone at ~~Ellesmerse~~ Ellesmere is better now – how is Aunt Jane's leg getting on.

I hope Mother will soon be quite fit again
With much love to all

       Yours affectionate son
          Jim

Dinapore

3rd May 1917

My dear Father.

Just a short note to convey my very best wishes & many happy returns of your birthday. I sincerely hope that the future will bring a maximum of happiness and a minimum of worry & trouble to you and that before long we shall all meet again in Park Cottage.

I feel sure we shall be back again to see you before this time next year for the war must come to an end: it cannot go on like this for ever.

You told me that we were not to send you anything for your birthday but we really cannot let the occasion pass without sending something, so I have told Cox & Co to send back £5, which please accept from John & I.

Our departure from India seems to be still delayed, chiefly, I ~~chrank~~ think on account of the difficulty of finding transport – I think we shall be on the move in the very near future – destination still unknown. I hope Mother is getting better by this time. She has had an awfully bad time just lately but ⟨ I hope that she will soon get quite strong again.

My company is going splendidly now – from being by far the worst Company in the Bttn when I took it over, it has become one of the best. We have just won the Bttn Ch Sports Shield having won the hockey, football & shooting competitions. The only competition we lost was the at Sports in which we were second.

I hope you are keeping quite fit & & will continue to do so. Do you ever get any of the old trouble now or has it quite gone?

Once more very best wishes for your birthday

With much love from

Your affectionate son
Jim

2/4th Somerset L.I.
Dinapore

May 4th 1917

My dear Mother & Father.

We have received two English Mails this week so our letters are quite up to date again. The most recent one only arrived a few minutes ago & I have just finished reading it. I am ever so glad to hear that Mother is better again and able to go out, but I was am sorry that Duff has also had mumps. However I am glad that he is better & I hope that no none of the other will get them. I expect Duffy looked very doleful with his face tied up in a handkerchief – tell him that I wish I could have just had a look at him.

I spent last weekend at Pq Patna with the Mackenzies and returned here Monday morning. Mrs Mackenzie has just gone off to the hills for the hot weather so I managed to persuade Mackenzie to come over to the guestni night Wednesday and stay on till Thursday afternoon. On Monday evening Ron and I were inoculated against enteric fever with the result that we spent the whole of Tuesday and part of Wednesday in bed. When we were done on our way out we had it in two doses but this time they gave it to us in one dose and did us for three diseases at the same time. Tuesday was the worst day I have ever had: we both had high temperatures & ached all over, but fortunately it only lasted one day.

We are quite fit now and I am off to Calcutta this afternoon with a party of men. Someone had to go & as I wanted to get a few things the colonel said I could go. I shall probably come back on Monday evening. It is much cooler to-day & has been raining steadily all day. This is a most unusual occurrence at this time of year – a man who had been here 20 years told us that he never remembers seeing the rain set in like this before. Usually there is no rain from about January to June with the exception of a few thunderstorms. We don't mind the rain all as long is the temperature remains low.

What an extraordinary year you have had! I was surprised to hear that the cold weather had set in again at the end of March. & it I suppose it is warmer again now as I see that the papers all say that the weather on the Western front is now fine & dry. I must go off to the mess now to get have my lunch as I have to start to march to the Station at 2–15 and it is getting rather late.

With much love to all & hoping that you have quite got rid of all the mumps.

> I remain
> Your affectionate son
> Jim

P. S. I heard this morning that Passmore had been awarded the Military Cross.

2/4th Somerset L.I.
Dinapore

10-5–17

My dear Mother & Father.

Our stay in India is nearly over now and we shall soon see the last of Dinapore. We have just received our final instructions which are, to proceed leave Dinapore on the 16th and arrive in Bombay on the 20th: I presume that we shall embark at once.

I shall try and get a letter off from Bombay if possible and after that you will probably not receive one for about a month if we go round the Cape. If however we go to Egypt you will not have long to wait for a letter.

We don't know at all where we are going: some think to France direct & others think to Egypt so that it is rather difficult to know what to do about kit. If we go to Egypt we shall require thin clothes like we use out here, but if we go to France they will be no good at all & it would be better to sell them before we leave here. I don't suppose we shall know for certain till after we leave Bombay so it is not much use to worry.

Last Friday afternoon I took some men down to Dum Dum & Barrackpore. I arrived at Dum Dum Saturday morning and had tiffin with Harford & Flower & then I went across to Barrackpore and stayed the night with M^r & Mrs Bocquet. I went in to Calcutta on Sunday evening and spent the whole of Monday shopping and ~~was~~ finished just in time to catch the mail train back to Dinapore. I bought things for nearly everyone in the Regiment and there were lots of things I wanted to get myself so I really had a very busy time.

Fortunately last Sunday & Monday were exceptionally cool days, owing to a big storm on Friday which cooled it down considerably. The weather for the last week has been extraordinary and people who have been here over 20 years cannot remember having seen anything like it before. Usually there is no rain at all till the monsoon breaks in the middle of June but during the last few days we have had very heavy thunderstorms and lots of rain. It looks as if the monsoon was coming up early this year and we are already getting the preliminary burst. If this is the case we are going to have a very rough passage as soon as we get outside Bombay harbour.

The rain is awfully nice and refreshing – it has cooled the air, laid the dust and made everything look nice and green again.

We are just getting very busy now packing everything up, collecting in stores and getting ready to hand over. It is perfectly amazing the amount of kit we have all collected in two years and I hardly know how to pack all mine up – I think I shall have to leave all mine behind to be sold after I have gone.

All the kit bags have to be painted with the company colours and we have to hand over all the barrack furniture, beds, blankets, mosquito nets. We are going to pitch a camp on Monday so that we can ~~go~~ get out of the bungalows to enable them to be cleaned out and checked. It will be very hot under canvas but of course it will only be for a couple of days.

Capt Bealy tells me that Father met his wife a little while ago & had a talk about us all – he says that he knows Father quite well but never realized that ~~I~~ we were his sons.

Colonel Waddy is not coming with us – he has now been seconded from the Regiment and will remain out here in India till after the war.

Ron Vallis will probably be coming back to-morrow as all the instructors we have lent to the Indian Defence Force are being recalled. I shall be glad to get him back again for I have rather missed him since he has been away.

I think it would be a good plan if you sent all my letters C/o G.P.O. London as I shall get them quicker that way than if they come out here & then have to be sent back again.

I hope Mother & Duff are now both quite fit again & I hope that Duff had a very jolly birthday.

With much love to you all

   I remain
    Your affectionate son
     Jim

2/4th Somerset L.I.
Dinapore

16–5–17

My dear Mother & Father.

According to my letter of last week we should be leaving Dinapore to-day for Bombay, but after having kept us under orders to proceed on service for rather over six weeks, three days before we were due to start the General Staff decided to cancel the move.

Last Saturday we received definite orders which stated that we should proceed to Egypt. On Monday morning the Colonel came on to the early parade and remarked that having reached the actual week on which we were to leave he now for the first time felt safe. On returning to the mess for breakfast he found a wire waiting to say that instead of proceeding to Bombay we were to wait till relieved by the 2/5th Somersets & then go to Lahore.

I can assure you that the language in the mess became decidedly unparliamentary and everyone swore heartily. The poor old Colonel is absolutely knocked up over it – he absolutely made up his mind that he was going to take his regiment on service at last and the disappointment has quite knocked him out. You cannot conceive the effect a thing of this sort has on a Regiment – everyone from Colonel to private is absolutely fed up & depressed. All the officers have the sold their surplus kit, and the Colonel & Capt Miles have sold their motorcars at a loss and now we are only just going to move up to Lahore.

At first we thought that it we were the only Regt which had been stopped but we now hear that the Devons have been moved back to Poona from Deolali & the date of their embarkation postponed indefinitely. It looks therefore that as if the whole division has been stopped, probably owing to submarines or mines, and we now hope that we are merely going to Lahore en route for Karachi instead of Bombay. We have not been told to relieve anyone at Lahore so it certainly looks as if our stay there is to be only a temporary one.

Of course I quite understand that you will all be glad that we are staying on out here, but it is a terrible disappointment to be stopped at the last minute for after all we deserve to get our chance after being in India for 2½ years. We all hoped that if we went to Egypt we should be allowed some leave to go home but this has also been knocked on the head now.

The 2/5th Somersets arrive here on Sunday morning and we shall leave Sunday night or early Monday morning.

Lahore is a very big station, and has a very delightful cold weather but it is terribly hot now. I think there are plenty of hill stations within fairly easy reach of it and as soon as I get a chance I shall try to go away on leave.

We arranged to have a farewell dinner on Monday night & invited all the ladies in the Station, but we were all so annoyed about having the move cancelled that we decided not to have the dinner. We shall probably have it on Saturday instead.

Father's letter dated 11th ~~March~~ April arrived this week, I am glad you all enjoyed your trip on Easter Monday & I have never been to Wookey caves ʎ but from your description I should think they must be very fine indeed. What an extraordinary Winter you have had! It seems almost incredible that the wintry weather should have extended right into the middle of April. Please congratulate Rob & Janet on getting prizes in the Scripture exam and also Mary Angus & Margaret for passing 1st ʎ class. I am very pleased indeed that they all did so well especially as they did not get very much instruction this year.

I am very glad Margaret received her birthday present quite safely and was very pleased to receive a letter from her.

I am very sorry indeed that Mother has again had to spend a few days in bed and I do sincerely hope that she is now getting strong again.

Ron came back to the company last Monday – I was very pleased to see him again for I missed him while he was away. I think he saw quite enough of the Indian Defence Force while he was away & he certainly does not want to go back again.

With much love to all

I remain

Your affectionate son

Jim

P. S. Please send my letters to Cox & Co again.

2/4th Somerset L.I

Lahore Cantt

May 25th 1917

My dear Mother & Father.

I think our fate is sealed now for I doubt if we shall get out of India during this war. We reached Lahore yesterday morning and went straight into barracks, ~~as~~ so that our hopes of a concentration of troops to be despatched later have been dispelled and we have almost come to the conclusion that we are here to stay.

We were to have left Dinapore last Monday but at the very last minute the move was again posponed twenty four hours and we stayed on till Tuesday. The 2/5th Somersets arrived at the station about midday ~~Tuesday~~ Monday and we left barracks at 5 P.M. the same day passing them on the way down.

We worked till about 11 P M & then we got into the train & slept in the carriages. ~~We~~ The loading was all completed on Tuesday morning and we left at 7–30 P M. After a very hot journey we ~~go~~ reached Lahore at 2 A M Thursday morning. Fortunately they did not try to make us start unloading at once and we were able to go on sleeping till 5 A M but then we had to set to work to get the unloading done as quickly as possible for it gets too hot to work after 9 A M.

We took over the barracks as quickly as possible and sent off the 24th Rifle Brigade (who we relieved) last evening. I think that there are several reasons why we were not allowed to proceed overseas and the ~~imediate~~ immediate one is that there is a ~~show~~ fight going on up on the frontier. The General Staff at Simla are I believe rather worried about it as it may spread all along the frontier, ~~but~~ and they decided that no more troops must leave India for the time being at anyrate.

No definite news has yet come through as to what is taking place although we already know a good deal which is at present to be kept secret. I understand that one division has already gone out & that another is in reserve at the base.

As we only arrived yesterday we have ~~had~~ not had much time to look about but from what I have seen I have come to the conclusion that Lahore City itself is very beautiful indeed but the Cantonments are ~~a~~ beastly. The latter are five miles from the city; the bungalows are very old and dirty; the ground is very bare and dusty and therefore gives off a very bad glare when the sun is out; and altogether the Cantonments are rather depressing.

I drove in to the city last night and there it was very different. There are trees, green grass, and gardens everywhere, there are hotels, churches, clubs just as in a European city and some of the shops are very fine, but of course I only just had a glance at the place last night & I will tell you more about it another time.

Besides the European part there is of course the Native City which I have not yet seen but which is intensely interesting.

I think we shall like it here on the whole: it is frightfully hot now and no Indian City ever looks at its best in the hot weather ~~but~~ but I know that Lahore is noted for its cold weather season.

The men have electric fans in their bungalows – they were put in after that discussion in the House of Commons on the subject last year – but they have not yet reached the officers' bungalows. However we are fairly comfortable already and in a day or two we shall have settled down completely.

I hope you are all quite well now – I am afraid you must have been a very sick household with Mother Janet, Mary & Margaret all ill at the same time. However did you manage to get along?

With much love to all

> I remain
> > Your affectionate son
> > > Jim

2/4th Somersets L.I.
The Fort
Ferozepore

30–5–17

My dear Mother & Father.

If I had been told ⟨a few days ago⟩ that I should shortly be commanding a fort containing an arsenal, a Coy of R.G.A. & a Coy of British Infantry I should certainly not have believed it, but the fact remains that at the present time I am doing so.

Soon after we arrived at Lahore we heard a little more about the reason why we did not leave India for Egypt, ~~and~~ (namely the Frontier Show). From what we can gather ⟨it⟩ is going to be rather a big show, but of course it may not come to much in the end as the tribesmen are rather erratic sort of people & they may go back to their homes without doing much damage.

However the Indian Govt are pushing a good many troops up to the frontier just now in case of necessity. We received orders ~~two~~ three days after reaching Lahore to mobilize for service on the frontier as quickly as possible. The first wire came on Sunday afternoon and on Monday morning we started to draw the equipment. On Tuesday we were rearmed with new rifles and then in the evening we received instructions to send two companies to Ferozepore to ~~joi~~ relieve the 2/6th Sussex regt. Pending the arrival of the 2/4th Cornwalls.

B & D Coys were sent over & we arrived here Wednesday morning (yesterday) the Sussex moving out the same evening. We shall probably only stay three or four days as the Cornwalls are being sent down as quickly as possible, but it was an awful nuisance having to pack up & come over here at very short notice. The worst of it is that in spite of the shortness of our stay we had to take over everything and shall have to hand it over again to the Cornwalls. ⟨"D" Coy are occupying the Fort, which I said contains the Arsenal. There are an awful lot of guards to find we have to be frightfully careful to see that unauthorised people are not allowed in. it is a very big fort and I can safely say that it is the hottest place I have ever been in. There are lots of walls and the place is enclosed by a high rampart which keeps out all the breeze and get frightfully hot.

Just at present electric fans are being installed and in the meantime the old hand punkahs are out of use so that the heat is almost unberable.

The station itself is quite a big one and what I have seen of it looks quite nice. There is quite a good swimming bath at the officers mess which is a great acquisition – I went along and had a swim this morning before breakfast.

I don't quite know what will happen to us when we area fully mobilized but I suppose we shall go on up to the frontier. The General told us this yesterday morning that we were to be brigaded with a Bttn of Nepalese Imperial troops which will be rather good fun for the Ghurkas are awfully jolly little fellows.

The days up in this part of India are ever so much longer than they are down at Dinapore. Down there it used to be quite dark at 7 P M but up here it remains light till 8 P M. It doesn't give no us any more time out of doors however for the result of the change is that we can instead of being able to go out again at five up here it is too hot to go out till six.

It was rather funny at first and the first night we were nearly all late for mess as we did not realize that it was so late.

Ron and I applied for leave to go to the hills for three weeks but when the order for mobilization came in all leave was stopped. We intended to go to Kasauli – I daresay we shall be able to get away later on.

Mother's letter dated M April 25th arrived to two days ago – I was delighted to hear that you are all so much better – I hope that Mother will now keep quite fit. Father seems to be very well indeed busy indeed – I hope he will not do too much and so get ill again. There is a very big native city both here and at Lahore both of which I want to see if I can for the people up here are very different from the ones down in Bihar & Bengal. They are mostly Sikhs & Punjabis and are a much better type than the Biharis. They are very fair skised skinned and much to my amnusement all the women wear trousers instead of skirts.

It is too hot to write any more this week – I on am only wearing a towel so I can't take off any more clothes – and I think I have come to the end of my news.

With much love to all

> I remain
> Your affectionate son
> Jim

2/4th Somerset L.I.
Ferozepore

6–6–17

My dear Mother & Father

You will see from the above address that we are still at Ferozepore and have not yet returned to Lahore. ~~alth~~ As far as we knew up to last night the Cornwalls were due to arrive here to-morrow morning and we were to leave to morrow night. As usual however, ~~th~~ a telegram arrived at the eleventh hour telling us to stand fast for the present. We have also been told to stand fast with our mobilization so it looks to me as if ~~the~~ we were going to stay on here and the Cornwalls got to the frontier. If this is the case it will be awfully bad luck on us but I ~~af~~ am afraid that it is going to happen.

The heat ⱶ in this part of the world is absolutely terrible just now this being the worst time of the year and the Fort is the worst ~~part~~ place of all. The walls & ramparts seem to give out heat ⱶ which almost burns the skin off your body. Troops can only stay down there a month at a time in the hot weather as it is so unhealthy. Already I have about fifteen men in the hospital with sandfly fever and others go down with it every day. If we ~~ha~~ do have to stay on here I sincerely hope that we shall be able to send some drafts to the hills. There is quite a good hill station for the stations in this district called Dalhousie and the sooner we are allowed to send men up there the better.

I received Father's letter written from Jersey yesterday & am very glad that he enjoyed his visit to the Channel Islands. I was very interested to hear all about the people I met when I was over there – fancy Donald Luke teaching in the Sunday School: he must have changed very considerably.

With regard to the ~~cutt~~ extract from the London gazette which Father forwarded you will see that everyone in the 1/4th have been made captains while we have all been made permanent Lieutenants but have lost the temporary rank of captain. I am very lucky, for I keep the rank of captain as long as I command a company. The situation is rather funny now for the 1/4th have 4 majors & about 12 Captains while we have no majors & only five captains. I don't know whether it will be allowed to remain ⱶ so, but I expect the 1/4th will send us some captains & we shall send them some Lieutenants.

I am awfully pleased that Andrew has managed to get into such a good Regiment – ⱶ if only he gets through this war safely he is bound to get on well afterwards. He seems to be quite pleased with life at present & his accounts of France ~~se~~ almost make one quite envious.

Last night we drove out to see the new Kaisar i Hind Bridge over the Sutlej which is about five miles from here. It is a fine bridge, over a mile long &

having a road running above the railway line. It is built on stone pillars which are about 30 yards apart. The river now is very low indeed but in another month after the rains have broken it will be a very fine sight indeed.

I am very glad you are all so much better now & are at last having some warmer weather.

I hope you will all continue to keep fit

With much love to all

> Your affectionate son
> Jim

Ferozepore

14–6–17

My dear Mother & Father.

There is not very much to write about this week as it has been far too hot for us to do a great deal. We have been obliged to stop all parades after 8–30 A M and we then do all the office work so as to finish for the day by about 9–30. We then have breakfast after which there is nothing for it but to shut ourselves up in our bungalows till 6 o'clock at night when we try to play hockey & tennis.

We get a violent duststorm about every three days which as a rule cools the air quite considerably for a few hours.

We have now heard definitely that we are to demobilize and on Saturday the 2 Companies here at Ferozepore are to return to Lahore after having been relieved by the 1/9th Hants.

The show up on the Frontier seems to have started but the only news we have had is that contained in letters from fellows who are up there. I believe we have started to push up into the hills but there has already been a fight of some sort.

No mails have arrived this week so far although the weekly service is still supposed to be running. I suppose we shall soon be having the fortnightly service, but I believe w the weekly service will still run from India to England.

I heard from John yesterday – he has had rather a bad attack of fever but he says that he is better again now.

We have had a terrible lot of sandfly fever among the men at the fort just lately. Last Monday I had over 40 sick out of 131. The electric fans have been started now and they are a great improvement.

Ron Vallis wh went off to Mhow last night to attend a bombing course – he will probably see Colonel Waddy while he is there for the latter commands the convalescent depòt at Mhow.

Colonel Clutterbuck is still in hospital and I am afraid he will be there for sometime yet for he is not at all well.

I hope you are all quite fit now

With much love to all

> Your affectne son
>> Jim

P.S. I am afraid this is a very short letter but I really have nothing to write about.

2/4th Somerset L.I.
Lahore Cantt.

22–6–17

My dear Mother and Father.

We are now back in Lahore again having arrived here last Monday morning. On the whole we were all glad to get back again for, knowing that our stay at Ferozepore would be a short one we did not really settle down there, and it was so frightfully hot that we could not do anything at all.

Since we came back here it has been exceptionally cool owing to monsoon storms which when they come up cool the air wonderfully. At Ferozepore the nights were so frightfully hot – for ꓵ about th four days the minimum temperature was 93° and everything you touched was hot. The storms we have had the last few days have made the nights delightfully cool, and a cool night makes all the difference.

I drove down through the native city two evenings ago, but there are all sorts of things to see and I shall have to go down again before I have seen it all. Weꓵ spent about half an hour watching a wrestling ꓵ school which most amusing. The ring consisted of a bare patch of ground covered with loose earth which apparently was soft enough to prevent the wrestlers from hurting themselves when they fell. There were three trainers, ~~and these~~ who took each of the pupils in turn and wrestled with each for about a quarter of an hour. When they began to get slippery with perspiration they threw dirt over each other so that at the end of each match the combatants were ~~abou~~ covered with a fairly thick coating of mud. Like all Northern cities the native part is surrounded by a wall and in the centre of it there is a fort in which we keep one company of British troops.

There is a very striking contrast between the ~~former~~ European part & the native part. In the former each bungalow stands apart in a large garden, the streets are wide and ~~tre~~ lined with trees, and everywhere there are gardens

& lawns. The very minute you pass through the gate into the native city you get into the bazaar in which people & houses are packed so tightly that it is difficult to understand how so many people can get into such a small space.

Lahore, being the capital of the Punjab, is a great ⃭ centre for trade etc and in the bazaar ~~you~~ although most of the people are Punjabis, yet you see almost every type of native in India. There are wild looking Pathans, Sikhs with their long black beards, Kashmiris, and every other sort of native. Needless to say the ⃭ smell is absolutely filthy but if you can put up with it, the bazaar is well worth going down to see.

I have applied for leave to have three weeks up at Kasauli commencing July 16th and it has gone up to the Brigade so I hope I shall get it. By that I time I shall be jolly glad of a change although at present I am as fit as possible.

Two mails arrived for us this week and for some reason or other Mother's letter of the 16th May reached me before Janet's letter of the 9th. However both of them have arrived now and we are right up to date again I am very glad indeed that ~~Mother~~ & you are both taking a holiday this year & I hope Mother will feel ever so much better for it when she comes home again I was awfully sorry to hear that Ray Lockyer had been drowned – he was a jolly nice little fellow. I had not heard before that Lizzie Johnston had a daughter – I expect she is frightfully proud of her. I am feeling rather stiff to-day for I went out for a ride ⃭ yesterday on one of the new ponies and he gave me rather a rough time. He is only about half broken & is as wild as a March hare and I had my work cut out to stick to him. The new horses have not been allotted to officers yet, but when they are I think I shall get him.

There is no more news now and I can't find anything else to write about this week so I am afraid that this will have to do for one more week.

With best wishes to all & hoping you are all quite fit

        I remain
            Your affectionate son
               Jim

        Lahore Cantt.

        ⃭ 5–7–17

My dear Mother & Father.

Much to our surprise we did get a mail last week after all. The mails which went down on the "Mongolia" were dated May 31st, ~~but sh~~ and as the "Mongolia" was a very fast boat she passed the boat containing the mails of the previous week on the way. These were the ones we received last week.

I was very pleased to hear that Ray Lockyer was not drowned after all and I can just imagine how delighted his people were when they heard the news.

We have had another week of comparatively cool weather owing to the monsoon. Of course we shall have to suffer for it when the clouds clear off again because the air will be so moist but we find that it is best to be thankful for what we have & let the future take care of itself.

We all sleep on the roof nowadays as there is always a little breeze up there and we can often sleep without a mosquito curtain as the mosquitos do ~~so~~ not seem to come up there.

Another of our men died this morning – he was operated upon for abcess on the liver a few days ago and was not strong enough to recover.

We are sending off a draft of 150 to the hills to-day but we have just heard that as usual the move has been postponed. I expect it will probably be cancelled to-morrow.

I went ~~don~~ down to the Fort last evening and dined there with the fellows who are stationed in it. I did not have time to see much of it but I want to go down again as soon as possible for ⟨everyone says that it is very interesting indeed.

The papers this morning contained the very good news that the Russians had at last made another advance. If only they could keep it up it would give us a chance to go ahead in on the Western Front and then perhaps there would be some possibility of the war coming to an end.

I fancy they must be making satisfactory progress against the submarines for the weekly mail service between England and India is going to be resumed shortly.

I am looking forward to my holiday in the hills & I shall be quite ready for it when the time comes for I have just started a dose of Lahore boils, which are awfully painful & uncomfortable. They are not yet very bad and I am trying to deal with them before they spread, but the only real cure is to go to the hills because the fact that they come at all is a sign that we have had too long on the plains.

We had a very quiet ~~week~~ time last week and I can't think of anything more to write about just now – the ordinary routine does not provide ~~so~~ very much of interest which can be put into a letter.

I hope Mother is keeping fit and I sincerely hope that you had a really good holiday. How are all the Ellesmere people – I have not heard from any of them for a long time, ~~but~~ but it is probably my own fault as I expect I owe them all letters.

With much love to all

> Your affectionate son
> Jim

2/4th Somerset L.I.
Lahore Cantt.

13–7–17

My dear Father & Mother

I received Mother's letter dated June 5th two days ago and was awfully interested to hear all about your holiday. I am ever so glad that you enjoyed yourselves and hope you both feel better for the change. It will be rather nice having Uncle Walter's boys down at Cary – I don't think I have ever seen either of them.

I have not been doing very much this week for I have not been quite so

No. 1 & 2.

well as usual, having had a great big abcess or boil right in my elbow joint. For several days it was frightfully painful and gave me an awfully bad time, but all the pus is out now and the inflamation has gone down so I hope the place will soon heal up. I was inoculated against boils last Wednesday so I hope that I shall not get any more. The first few days of last week

6

were very hot indeed but a very welcome storm blew up two nights ago and cooled the air quite considerably.

I am going off to Kasauli on leave to-morrow but I feel sure that I shall be recalled before I have been up there long for I think we are going to have another move very shortly. The frontier show is practically over now and the Mashuds have come to terms so I think the n move out of India which was cancelled last May will come off as soon as the cold weather comes on. In the meantime we have heard unofficially that we are going to Poona very soon. It may be only a rumour but the G.O.C Division gave us the information so I think it is probably true. Anyhow ⚡ if I only get a few days at Kasauli it will make a little change.

There must be something in the wind for we sent a draft of convalescents off to Dalhousie last Sunday and we have just heard that after they had marched 30 out of the 60 miles between the railway & Dalhousie they were stopped, & told to rest for two days & then return to Lahore.

I was delighted to hear of ℞ Rob's success at cricket – I should think 8 wkts for 6 runs was almost a school record. I am glad he did it against Shaftsbury for they always used to beat us when I was at school.

I am sending a few photographs this week and I shall probably send some things which I got at Benares next week. I should have sent them before but I was afraid that they would be sunk on the way: I think I shall risk it now.

Hoping you are all quite well

With very much love to all

Your affectionate son

Jim

Photographs

1.&2.) **Views of the barracks at Dinapore. No 1 is one of the bungalows occupied by my company.**

3. **The officer's mess Dinapore**

4. **My bearer with "Piper". Taken at Ferozepore.**

5. **My "bhisti" or water carrier with his skin of water**

6. **The well in the garden of our bungalow. The bullock going round causes the wheel marked x to revolve. ~~The~~ To the latter is fixed a continuous string to which little pots are tied. ~~A~~ These come up from the well full of water and are emptied as they revolve with the wheel.**

Kasauli

20—7—17

My dear Mother & Father.

Father's letter of June 13th and Janet's of the 20th both arrived last night so I had quite a treat. I am ever so glad you had such a good holiday and am delighted to hear that Mother is feeling so much better as a result of the change.

I am now in Kasauli on three weeks leave and am absolutely delighted to feel cool once more. I left Lahore last Sunday night just in time to prevent my going into hospital, as I was covered with boils which were frightfully painful. I arrived at Kalka on Monday morning and then rode the nine miles to Kasauli on a pony. It was rather a difficult job for I could hardly sit down even on cushions, but I managed quite well by riding a little & then walking & so on. When I reached Kasauli I met Mrs Bocquet: (who I knew in Barrackpore) her husband is now in Mesopotamia & she is staying with some friends of hers (M^{r} & Mrs Cowan of the I.C.S.). The latter sent across and invited me to to come and stay with them ʎas long as I liked and of course I accepted. I am now having an awfully good time – they are awfully nice people and they absolutely insist that I should stay with them during the whole of my leave. Of course it is much nicer than staying in a hotel.

I suppose Andrew told you all about Kasauli when he was up here last year. It is quite a nice little place, awfully pretty and fairly cool. It is not as big as Darjeeling and it is much quieter, but it suits me quite well. There are lots of awfully nice walks and plenty of tennis. The tennis courts are all on sand, which is not quite so nice to play on as grass, but they are quite good and we get plenty of fun out of them.

I feel quite different now to what I did when I came up – the boils are all going and so is the prickly heat. By the time my three weeks are over I shall be quite ready for the rest of the hot weather. I think the nights should begin to get cool by the ~~be~~ middle of September and by the middle of October the real cool weather should have set in. I rather hope to be able to just go across and see Simla while I am here but now that I ~~was~~ am staying with other people I may not be able to get away.

These hill stations in India are awfully pretty – I do wish you could see one of them. After you get up to 5000′ nearly all the plants – birds etc are English ones. About here there are crowds of wild ~~daliahs~~hliahs which make the place look awfully nice now that they are in flower. The pine trees also start at about 5000′ – you have no idea how pleasant it is to smell the pine trees for the first time as you ride. They are rather stunted here as Kasauli is only between 5000 & 6000 feet high, but when you get up to 8000 & 9000 feet they are absolutely magnificent.

There is a signalling class going on up here now & when I see them at work I always think of Andrew sweating away up here last year.

I had a letter from him to-day – he seems to be ever so happy out in France & he is undoubtedly getting on very well indeed.

I suppose by this time Rob has ~~won~~ heard the result of his scholarship – I do hope he managed to get it. I am very glad indeed that he has been doing so well at cricket and I hope he will be able to keep it up all the season.

I can hardly realize that Lovell is old enough to join an O.T.C. ~~he seemed such~~ it seems such a short time ago that I saw him as a school boy. It wonder what Aunty Madge will say when he joins the army.

Piper is enjoying himself up here – he like his master is jolly glad to feel nice & cool. He is a great favourite with everyone.

I hope Janet enjoyed her holiday at Frome & Nunney – it was rather bad luck that she could not go down to stay with fat Phyllis.

I hope you are all quite well

With much love to all

> Your affectionate son
> Jim

2/4th Somerset L.I.
Dove Hall
Kasauli

26–7–17

My dear Mother & Father.

As you see from the above ~~dr~~ address I am still up at Kasauli and from the reports we get of the temperature down at Lahore I am jolly glad to be up here. I am feeling quite fit now – the prickly heat & boils have both disappeared and I can now sit down again without having to build a foundation of cushions.

The only drawback to the hills at this time of the year is that it is nearly always raining. In about two months time the rains clear away and then I believe the climate is absolutely perfect. The people up here all say that the winter is perfectly delightful. Every day is very cold, clear & frosty, there is no rain and you have to wear furs the whole time.

If by any chance we should stay up in Lahore during the cold weather I shall certainly try to come up here just to see what it is like. However I don't think it likely that we shall stay there very much longer. I have heard that ~~we~~ trains are being arranged to take us to Deolali instead of Poona. The latter is a rest camp where troops concentrate before leaving India, and if we do go there it is almost certain that we shall go overseas.

I have had some awfully nice walks since I have been up here – the views are simply magnificent. We are on the first high ridge off the plains and we can see the latter quite plainly on one side. On the other side the ridges get higher & higher till you see the snows. ~~The~~ Simla is on the next high ridge to this & we can see it quite clearly when there are no clouds.

For the most part the rain has come in the morning so that we have been able to play tennis nearly every afternoon. After the grass courts the hard ones are rather difficult to play on but ~~w~~ they are quite nice when you get used to them.

I am having an awfully good time with the Cowan's – they simply won't hear of my going to stay at the Hotel and insist that I shall spend the whole of my holiday with them, which of course I am only too pleased to do.

No English mails arrived this week as we had two last time – I suppose we shall have two more next week.

I heard yesterday that Eric Vallis is in India on leave, and that he is going down to Ceylon. When I last heard from Ron he did not mention this so I don't suppose he knows about it. I wonder that Eric does not come up to see him, for if it is too hot at Lahore they could both go to the hills together.

You would be amused if you could just ~~look in~~ come to one of these small hill stations and hear the people talk. The ladies have absolutely nothing to do – the husbands of a good many of them are in Mesopotamia and those of a good many of the others are in the plains – and they just sit and discuss one another. I just laugh at them, it is so awfully amusing – every new dress or new hat which is produced is carefully criticised – every new person who comes up no matter whether male or female is carefully discussed and then everyone is ~~qu vere~~ on alert to see which particular set he or she joins. If ~~sh~~ the newcomer joins a set ~~a~~ which consists of the wilder spirits then of course the others all say that he is no good & vice versa.

The centre of the whole place is the club and on a fine day everyone in the station wends their way to it about 4–30. Everyone is of course going to attend ~~someoneel~~ else's tea party and these little parties are made up months ahead. Tables a placed on the sort of terrace overlooking the tennis courts and then the whole station proceeds to have tea – the meal lasting from about 4–30 to 7–30 P.M. ~~The te~~ Those who do not play tennis go steadily on the whole time but the tennis players have a little respite when their turn comes to play.

In this station there are four available courts and usually about eight sets ~~have to~~ wish to play on them. In order to prevent fights they have devised a system by which as soon as a set is finished one of the players dashes off, even before ~~k~~ he knows whether he has won or lost, to sign his name on a board. other players do the same when their sets are finished & so you go on again in the order in which the names are put up. Now just imagine the little scene – two sets finish about the same time – a player from each dashes off to sign up. They both reach the board at ~~appro~~ approximately the same minute, both very hot & dishevelled. They look at each other & then the bolder of the two signs the board, the other follows suit when the first has finished. Result – if they are two men nothing much happens – if a man and a lady the latter decides that the ~~latter~~ man has no manners – if two ladies a deadly ~~faud~~ feud.

While the tennis is in progress as I said before those who do not happen to be playing eat tea & discuss one another and talk scandal. As soon as it is too dark to play the station moves into the club or sits in the compound outside it. As soon as each group is installed drinks and hot potato chips are brought and the conversations which were interrupted by the move are resumed. At 8 P.M. most people begin to go home to dinner and I presume that they still talk about each other when they sit down to their own dinners.

You would laugh if you could only see & hear them and after the war I should love to be able to bring you out and just ~~wat~~ visit all these places again. I have been rambling on and I am ~~not~~ doubtful if you will be interested ~~wi~~ by all this but of course in England it is never necessary to send all the ladies off to the hills & so things are rather different, but it is amusing when they really are collected together. Owing to a landslip down on the railway we have not yet had to-day's papers but yesterday the news from Russia was very disappointing. They seem to have retired without putting up a show and let the Germans right into their lines.

I hope you are all keeping quite well although you must find the hot weather rather trying after such a hot cold winter.

With much love to all

I remain your affectionate son
Jim

Dove Dell
Kasauli

1–8–17

My dear Mother & Father.

I am writing two days earlier than usual this week as owing to the fact that I am going up to Simla early to-morrow morning I shall probably not get a chance to write if I leave it till Friday as usual. Simla is about 50 miles from here by rail and if I leave here about 9–30 A M I shall get there about midday. I shall spend to-morrow afternoon and Friday morning there and then return here Friday evening, having just had time to have a look round.

After I get back I shall only have three more days leave XX as I have to get back to Lahore on the 6th Aug. – however the Cowan's have invited me to come up again in September so I shall try to get ten days later on X if we are still at Lahore which is rather unlikely. I thought I might have to take another three weeks here whether I wanted to or not for Mrs Cowan's dog was taken ill a few days ago and everyone thought it was going to have rabies. However it has been under supervision for the last three days and no further symptoms have developed so I suppose it is alright. Had it gone mad we should all have had to undergo a course of treatment at the Pasteur Institute.

The last few days have been very wet indeed and we have not been able to play tennis so we have had to take long walks to make up for it. We usually get wet through but that doesn't matter as long as it is cool. There has also been some rain down on the plains and they have had it a little cooler in consequence. I hope that by the end of August the nights will begin to get cool as the days are already getting a little shorter. At present the days are so long that the nights do not have a chance to get cool.

Owing to the rain there has been a land-slide on to the railway somewhere

3

4

Lahore

5

down below and our letters and papers have therefore been very late during the last few days. There was no English mail last week so I hope we shall get one two this week – they should be here in a few days. I heard from John yesterday – in spite of the excessive heat he writes very cheerily and says that he is keeping very fit.

Andrew seems to be awfully happy at Rowen – has he had his leave yet?

Ron Vallis and Royal hope to come up for a few days commencing Aug. 3rd so I shall just see them before I go down. They have not yet heard whether their leave has been granted as it seems that we may be moved very shortly.

The regiments are coming in from the Frontier as quickly as possible and the Depót of the Sussex, who are going to relieve us, has already arrived – the remainder of the Regiment will follow as soon as possible.

I enclose a few photographs of Lahore City which I took the day before I came up here. Two of us drove all down through the native City and managed to x take the a few photographs.

I suppose the boys are just going back to School after the Summer holidays – tell them to remember me to W. A. K & Mr Brown when they go back.

I hope you are all quite well now

With very much love to all

I remain

Your affectionate son

Jim

Photographs

1. **One of the gateways to Lahore. The city is surrounded by a wall & these gateways come every few hundred yards.**

2. **The main street. I stood in the gateway shown in No 1 to take this picture.**

3. **One of the temples on Lahore. In order to get this one of the natives allowed me to go up on to the roof of his house. In the foreground are little booths which act as refreshment rooms.**

4. **This was taken from the same roof as No 3 only is x further to the right & shows the street running under the archway.**

5. **Another temple. This one is just outside the fort.**

2/4th Somerset L.I.
Lahore Cantt.

9–8–17

My dear Mother & Father.

This week has slipped away quickly and I was quite surprised when I realized this morning that mail day had come round again. I have no letters to answer, for although two should have arrived last Monday for some reason or other they did not turn up. I received the Western Gazette and the School Magazine but no letters so I expect they have gone astray & will turn up late. Cox & Co have probably made a mistake and sent them out to John.

Last week I wrote from Kasauli where I was thoroughly enjoying myself, but I am now back in Lahore again, my leave having expired on Monday. Last Thursday morning I ~~run~~ drove over the Dharampore station from Kasauli and went up to Simla. Instead of going in the train I went by the rail motor which is an awfully good way of travelling. It is is just like an ordinary motor but it runs along on the rails and it is much nicer than a stuffy train. The railway is an awfully jolly little show – it winds its way up the sides of the spurs and turns & twists in a most amazing manner, and in the motor one was able to get an awfully good view of the hills. I was absolutely delighted with Simla: it is built along the top & sides of one of the ridges which is thickly wooded with cedar trees. From the top of the ridge on one side you can see the snows & on the other Kasauli & Dagshai. As it was very wet while I was up there I was only able to see the snows once, and then I ~~jut~~ just had a glimpse of them from my bedroom window early in the morning.

There are lots of shops – all the big firms of India have shops up there and it was awfully nice to see all the European people walking about & shopping in the middle of the day just like they do in England. I only stayed one night as Mrs Cowan wanted me to come back & spend as much of my holiday as possible with them. I came down in the motor & the journey was really quite thrilling. We simply whizzed round the corners at a tremendous pace & I can assure you we all held on to the sides as tightly as possible.

I left Kasauli on Monday evening and walked down to Kalka. I ~~wa~~ did not want to go down into the heat a bit, and the Cowans pressed me to try & get some more leave, but it is very bad form to apply for extensions so I ~~decid~~ promised to try & get another 10 days later on.

I don't know whether I was spoilt by living in a private house up at Kasauli but it has just dawned on me how really fed up I am with this business out here. ~~We~~ For nearly three years we have been out here doing the same old things every day and there seems very little prospect of anything different yet. I am very fond of India and am quite happy out here, I like my Company & my Bttn but as I don't intend to stay in the army the whole thing seems to be so futile.

Both John & Andrew have got a profession to work at, & incidentally although I joined the army first they are both drawing more pay than I am, but although I am twenty one I have no profession and nothing to really go for. By this new promotion scheme no matter how you work in the army you can't get any further, ~~as~~ for all promotion is now strictly by seniority and fellows you passed over before because you were more efficient than they were have now become senior again

I am not complaining a bit – I joined up to do my share and am only too willing to do it but I should like to feel that I was doing some good for myself & that I had something to work at, like John & Andrew.

I am learning Hindustani slowly but surely; ~~and~~ it keeps my brain from stagnation and I daresay it will be very useful to me in the future. If we could go on service we should be~~x~~ able to feel that we were doing something more than just sitting out here. Please don't think that I am complaining, or am unhappy or anything of that sort – on the other hand I am thoroughly enjoying life, but as I said before it all seems so futile and as I have been thinking about it rather a lot lately I thought I would just like to write it down.

I am ever so pleased with my company now – we can beat any other company at all games & sports, the men shoot well & drill well & the keenness ~~a~~ & esprit de corps among both officers & men is splendid. More than half the Bttn hockey & footer sides come from my company & when I came back from leave I found that two of my platoons were in the semi final of the platoon football competion. Ron Vallis' platoon is one of them & I think he will probably win it. He is now having 10 days leave at Kasauli with Flower & Royal – I am expecting him back to-morrow.

With regard to the Cowan's with whom I stayed at Kasauli it may interest you to know that Mrs Cowan's father is Colonel Campbell I.M.S. who is in charge of the war hospitals at Brighton. He received a knighthood in the last birthday honours for his work there.

Since I came down it has been fairly cool here ~~and~~ and we have had a little rain, but the worst of the damp air is that it is very bad for prickly heat.

We are going down to Lahore to-night to play a hockey match against the North Western Railway side. They are one of the best sides in India so I am afraid we shall get rather a bad licking.

I was delighted to see Rob's name appear so many times in the School

Magazine – he has done well there & old W. A. K. will have reason to be pleased with the Mackie family by the time he has finished.

I hope all of you are feeling quite fit now – I am in splendid condition after my holiday.

With much love to all

>I remain
>>Your affectionate son
>>Jim

2/4th Somerset L.I.
Lahore Cantt.
Lahore

15–8–17

My dear Mother & Father.

Just after I sent off my letter last week we suddenly received instructions to the effect that the Regiment must be ready to move within 24 hours notice any day after the 20th inst. The wire ∝ which brought these instructions also said that we should proceed overseas. We had started to pack up and get ready for the move when we were told that as the 2/6th Sussex would be here on the 19th we should move out the same evening. Yesterday however we were told to stand fast as owing to the heavy floods the railways had been breached and the Sussex could not move. Toda day the we received the information that we shall proceed to Poona en route for overseas next Wednesday i.e. 23rd inst so that they are evidently getting the λ lines mended again quite quickly.

We have heard from the Devons in Poona and they say that we shall go into camp when we get there – apparently they got the camp ready for us three weeks ago expecting us to arrive then, bec but of course we could not get away till a relief could be found. After so many false alarms we are all rather doubtful whether we really shall leave India after afl all, but at present everything looks quite satisfactory. I am awfully pleased that we are going to see Poona before we leave the country for everyone says that it is one of the best stations in India. It is quite cool there now and I believe that it is ever so pretty.

The news that we are likely to do get a change for the better has bucked everyone up wonderfully and now that there is a chance of doing something our work has assumed quite a different aspect. We now have something to work for and this has made us all keen again.

Last evening three of us visited the Shalamar gardens which are about three miles. You have probably heard of them before for they are fairly well known. They were laid out by one of the old kings years ago & although they are not so fine in these days as they were then, they are still kept up to a certain extent by the Government, and are still very beautiful. There are rows of fountains going out from a central lake in all directions, and the lake is covered with water lillies. When the fountains are playing the effect is awfully pretty. The beds & lawns between these rows are all nice & green & well kept and there are pretty little pavillions dotted about in which in old days I suppose the ladies used to sit.

We ~~w~~ went inside what were formerly the ladies quarters. They contained lots of baths & fountains and the walls were very gaudily decorated, but of course the whole thing is rather faded in these days.

To-day is the first hot day we have had since I came down from Kasauli – one day during a storm the temperature dropped as low as 89°F. The rain now seems to have cleared away and if it has we are in for another very hot spell, and for a few days the air is sure to be very moist.

Colonel Waddy is staying in my bungalow to-day. He has left ~~now~~ Mhow and is on his way to Murree to join the Garrison Bttn of the Somersets. I rode into this morning to meet him at the station and just had time to speak to Mrs Waddy & her daughters before they went on to Pindi. We are awfully pleased to see the old Colonel again for we missed him sorely when he first left us. He is not looking quite so fit as he used to do and I think the country is trying him for he is over 70 now, but he is as full of life as ever and talks as if he were not more than 40.

Colonel Clutterbuck is quite fit now and was passed fit for service yesterday so he will be able to come with us. We were afraid at one time that he would be unable to do so.

Ron Vallis' platoon has reached the final of the platoon football competition & I have great hopes that he will win the cup. The final will be played to-morrow & Ron is coming down from Kasauli to play.

I hope you are all keeping quite well

Ronald W.H. Vallis
Cousin of Geraldine Mackie
(Mother of James R. Mackie)

With much love to all

> Your affectionate son
> Jim

CLUB OF WESTERN INDIA
POONA

26–8–17

My dear Mother & Father.

We arrived in Poona late last evening after four days in the train, and we were all glad to be able to stretch our legs again. It was dark, and raining hard when we arrived and we had rather a job getting into camp as the ground was awfully wet & we had very few lamps. However we eventually managed to get all the men in & left all the baggage till this morning.

It has been wet all day but it ~~is~~ is ~~diligh~~ delightfully cool cool and we have very nice big tents so we don't mind.

The journey was very interesting indeed. We went from Lahore to Delhi and intended to come down the main line from there but owing to a breach in the line we had to make a wide detour. The country between Lahore & Delhi is as flat as ever but after Delhi as we came South it was absolutely delightful. By the way we came there were hills on both sides of us nearly all the way and a good deal of the country was covered with jungle. By that I mean that sometimes it was thickly wooded, & sometimes covered with low bushes & sometimes by long grass but it was all waste. The only cultivation was just around the villages. I expect there is some awfully good shooting all down through Central India. As we came near Poona we had to climb up the Western Ghats – these are not very steep on the Deccan side but they are higher than the general surface of the plateau.

Poona itself is a very beautiful place right on the top of the Ghats. At this time of year the climate is very much like that of the English Autumn – there is a good deal of rain but it is quite cool.

~~We~~ At present our orders are that we shall only stay here eight days and then we shall go on to Egypt. As far as we can make out one Brigade is being sent to Mesopotamia & one to Egypt & at present we are included in the latter but of course it may be changed in the next few days – ~~we~~ we have to be ready for anything in these times. The Colonel says that ⅄ he feels sure that we shall go this time because we have ⅄ at last dropped into a really good station.

This is a very short letter but I will write again in a day or two & by that time I hope to have received three mails from you.

With very much love to all

      I remain
            Your affectionate son
            Jim

Please address letters C/o G.P.O.

2/4th Somerset L.I.
Poona

30–8–17

My dear Mother & Father.

I sat up very late last night because when I got back from dinner I found three English mails waiting for me, and it took quite a long time to read them. I was awfully pleased to hear from you again for it is just a month ago since we last heard, and we were beginning to think that the letters had all been lost.

I was delighted with Janet's photograph – it is an awfully nice one & it is the first one I have seen of her since she put her hair up. She ~~looks~~ appears to be in fairly "good condition" and as she says ~~so~~ herself she is as round as ever.

We are still in camp at Poona and there is no news as to the date of our departure. The ~~Cin-C~~ C-in-C while inspecting the 1/4th Wilts the day before we arrived here told them that we were now waiting for the Naval people to make arrangements to transport ~~us~~ us & that we should go as soon as the latter were ready. The general opinion here seems to be that we shall go about September 8th but no-one really knows much about it.

Poona is a delightful spot, but just at present is rather wet. There should be a break in the monsoon very soon & then we shall get some nice fine weather. It is quite nice & cool – we need a blanket at night and can wear English serge ~~at nights~~ in the evenings although the latter is really a little too warm.

We have been playing rugger nearly every day for we want to get up a team to play the 2/6th Devons who won the cup here a few weeks ago. I had an accident while playing the day before yesterday & had one of my front teeth knocked out again. I went to the dentist yesterday to have it put right and stayed there about an hour & a half, but he could not finish the job so I have to go back gain to-day. I am afraid it will be rather an expensive job this time as the root of the tooth was damaged & he could not put on an ordinary crown so he had to make a composite one having a gold back & a porcelain front.

I was ~~ak~~ asked to ~~play~~ go down to Bombay on Saturday to play for the Poona club against Bombay but I don't think I shall play again for a few days.

~~We~~ As our stay here will probably be very short we have not started a mess. Instead, we are having all our meals at the Western India Club of which we have all been made honourary members. It is one of the finest Clubs in India, the only one I have seen which is better is the United Services Club at Calcutta. Ron and I took a drive round last evening, but there is nothing much to describe. The Bazaar & the European part are very much like those of any other city out here but the women's dresses etc are very brightly coloured and make the place very picturesque.

It is quite the best station we have had since we left Bangalore, and there is no doubt about it that Southern India is much more pleasant than the North, but there is something rather fascinating about the latter. There is no doubt about it that up there it is a case of the survival of the fittest – the weakling gets a very poor chance. ⅀ For this reason down here there are lots of beggars & blind people etc in the streets but you see very few up in the North, ~~for~~ as they just die if they cannot compete with the rest. Similarly the race of people in Northern India is much finer than that of Southern India.

I enclose a few photographs taken by one of the officers – he lent me the films to get some prints made. I am so glad that Angus & Rob had such a good time at Camp and came back looking so fit. Please thank them both for their letters & tell Angus that I am delighted that he is able to ride a bicycle. I did not think he would be able to do so with his lame legs.

With regard to Rob joining the Army I will look up the exact proceedure & let you know next week. I believe that no direct commissions are given now – every man has to first serve in the ranks & ~~is~~ if such is the case the best thing he can do is to join an O.T.C. and get a commission from it. However I will find out for certain

I have just received a delightful letter from an officer who has just left my Company to go to the Machine Gun Corps. He ~~wrote~~ writes to thank me for the good time he had with me & he says some awfully nice things. I am awfully pleased with it as I am certain that he means every word of it.

I am sorry Mother has lost her Servant and I hope she will soon be able to get another, although I suppose they are very scarce indeed now.

I hope the rabbits are going on well – tell Duffy not to forget to feed them, ~~as~~ for that is what we used to do. Do you remember a poor unfortunate dove which eventually died of starvation?

I am glad you are all keeping well & sincerely hope that ~~this sta~~ you will all continue to do so. With very much love to all

> I remain
>> Your affectionate son
>>> Jim

2/4th Somerset L.I.
Poona

6–9–17

My dear Mother & Father.

We are still in camp here awaiting orders to move off. Our latest orders are that we shall leave India as near the 15th as possible. The boat which is to take us away is supposed to be due in at Bombay on the 10th and then she will have to coal etc before she can leave again with us. The 2/6th Devons leave here for Mesopotamia to-morrow.

Of course now that we have got as far as this we want to get away as soon as possible, but ~~x~~ if we have to stay on we could not wish for a better station. We are working very hard indeed for it is cool enough to be able to work after breakfast, but we don't mind working under the right conditions. It is far better than having to spend the whole day shut up in a bungalow. India is a country in which you must have plenty of work to-do – when you have nothing much to do you begin to think about yourself and then get demoralized. We were all feeling a bit like this when we were at Lahore so we are quite pleased to be able to ~~to~~ have lots to do again. We are playing lots of rugger – Royal & I get up a game nearly every other evening and we are getting quite a good side together. We are going to see what we can do against Poona Gymkhana on Saturday.

I went down to Bombay last Saturday to play for Poona after all, for I really could not resist the prospect of a jolly good game. We had a very scratch side but it turned out awfully well and we beat Bombay by 3 tries to nil. It was about the best game they have seen in Bombay this season in spite of the fact that part of the ground was under water. We had an awfully good time down there – they gave us lunch & ~~tiffen~~ dinner at the Yacht Club which is one of the best clubs in India and after dinner we all went to the theatre.

The railway journey down to Bombay from Poona is perfectly delightful for you go right down the Western Ghats, ~~where~~ which here are about 2000′ high. The last time we travelled over that bit of line was the first day we were in India when we set out for Bangalore and it was rather interesting trying to remember all the places again. Having been down to Bombay I have now completed the circle all round India and it is a strange thing that in three years we have seen nearly all the big cities in the country. Lots of people who spend their whole life out here don't see as much as we have seen, ~~in a so~~ and I am very pleased indeed that I have had the chance of seeing so much.

The news from Russia is very bad again – they seem to have completely collapsed now and it really looks very doubtful if they will ever be able to give us much help ~~now~~ again. If only they had done their bit the war might have been nearly over but as it is it ~~look~~ seems as if we shall have another year of it.

From to-day's paper I see that there has been another bad air raid – I sincerely hope that they will never be able to get as far as Somerset.

There is another mail due from England to-night but I shall have to get this letter off before it comes, so I shall not be able to answer it.

I hear that my little "Piper" is awfully popular up at Kasauli. He seems to have quite settled down in his new home, and is quite happy but I wish I could have brought him away with me.

I enclose a 1 Rupee stamp for one of the boys – they are not very common and one of them may have a place for it in their collection.

The little farm seems to be quite profitable nowadays and you must be deriving quite an income from the hens with eggs at such a price. Father's price for the pig was awfully good.

I hope Mother has been able to get a servant and is keeping quite fit.

With very much love to all

> I remain
> Your affectionate son
> Jim

Poona

14–9–17

My dear Mother & Father

Just a short note to tell you that we are leaving here this evening for Bombay. We shall arrive there early to-morrow morning and I suppose we shall embark at once, as the ship is in the docks waiting for us. We have not been told where we are going but presumably it will be Egypt although there is a rumour that we may be stopped at Aden which I don't think is true. I will send a cable when we do reach our destination if I get a chance.

I don't quite know how the letters will work out, but if we go to Egypt you will not have long to wait, in fact you may get one from Suez before you get this one.

Everything has now been packed up and is already on the train and we shall all march down to entrain in about an hour. It seems rather funny that we really are leaving India at last for we have made so many starts, and it is also rather remarkable on looking back to see the changes which have taken place in the Regt since we landed here. There are only about eight of the original officers left and only about 60 of the original men, but in spite of all the changes we still have a very nice lot of officers & a jolly smart Regt.

I hope to get one more mail from you before we leave as there is one due in Poona to-day and I have wired to Cox's to send mine on board.

I had a letter from Andrew telling me all about his holiday last mail which was awfully interested. He told me about all the changes he saw in everyone & I came to the conclusion that by the time I get back I shall hardly recognise some of the younger ones. He was frightfully pleased to be able to see you all again & seems to have thoroughly enjoyed his leave.

I have no time for any more now but will write again as soon as I get a chance.

With much love to all

> I remain
> > Your affectionate son
> > > Jim

2/4th Somerset L.I.
HMT *Kashmir*
Red Sea

23–9–17

My dear Mother & Father.

To-day is Sunday and we are spending it on the P & O "Kashmir" in the middle of the Red Sea. We left Poona a week ago last Friday and arrived at Bombay early Saturday morning. As soon as we reached the docks we started to embark & and the 1/4th Wilts who arrived about an hour later did the same. The very minute everything was on board we moved off so we did not get a chance of seeing Bombay again. As a matter of fact Harford & I had permission to go & see Messrs Cox & Co and we just had time to finish our business & get back to the ship.

The "Kashmir" is not one of the best of the P & O Ships & there is very little deck space on here. There are 1800 troops on board so we are very crowded up – in order to give the men any deck at all the officers have had to crowd into a little space 25 yards long so it is quite imp impossible to get any exercise. The cabins are quite nice & are supplied with fans so there we really must not grumble for one does not expect much comfort on board a troopship.

For the first 50 miles out of Bombay we all had to wear lifebelts but after that we were considered safe till we reached Aden so we were able to put them away.

The first day out was quite smooth but half way through the second day we ran into a real good monsoon storm which lasted for two days and gave us a very rough time. I was not the least bit seasick but Royal who is sharing a cabin with me was awfully ill.

We reached Aden last Friday morning and remained there about six hours as we had some a draft for the Regt stationed there. We were allowed to go ashore but most of us were glad enough to get back to the boat again and we were more than pleased to know that we were not going to stay there. It really is a terrible place. It is always hot and it pl practically never rains there so that there is not a vestage of anything green. You just have bare brown rocks – there is not a single thing to relieve the monotony. The only water in the place is distilled sea water and this is an issued every day as a ration

We could see the Turkish trenches through our field glasses and the Colonel went out in a car & visited our trenches. The Artillery who came out on the "Saturnia" & the 26th Cavalry who were at Bangalore with us are both stationed there. They have a fight with the Turks every morning & evening & the latter almost captured Aden once but I think we have them held now.

The first four days of our voyage were delightfully cool but it is awfully hot now here in the Red Sea – however we are fortunate in having a head wind which is a great help.

We arrive in Suez Tuesday night and as far as we know shall disembark on Wednesday morning & after that we don't know a bit what will happen to us. I shall post this letter there. It will probably come go on in the same boat as the last letter I wrote from India as we passed the Indian Mail boat at Aden.

It was exactly three years ago today that I was first gazetted – I wonder wet whether we shall still be fighting next year at this time.

I don't suppose I shall hear from you for some weeks as I expect s the letters will go on to Cox & Co, but if you write C/o G.P.O London I ought to hear from you in about three weeks time.

I wonder if any of us will get a chance of gett having a little leave in England – I should think there was more chance of getting back from Egypt than from India. There are one or two officers on board who are going back to England & I can assure you there is not one of us who does not envy them their luck.

I hope you are all quite well

With very much love to all

    I remain

        Your affectionate son

        Jim

Egyptian Expeditionary Force

Sunday 30–9–17

My dear Mother & Father.

We arrived at Suez late last Tuesday night but did not start to disembark till Wednesday morning When we arrived we had no idea what was going to happen to us next & you can just imagine how anxiously we waited for the embarkation officer to come on board & enlighten us a lit bit. When he did come he told us that as soon as we could get everything off the ship hd we should move move up by train to Kantara. We worked hard all Wednesday morning & left Suez at 4 o'clock in the afternoon.

One of the Staff officers at Suez is a man called Rawlings who used to play rugger for Cary. He said that he knew father but he did most of his playing under Uncle Will. I had a long chat with him and of course he wished me to send his fondest regards to Father & Uncle. Strangely enough, he before the war he was indigo planting at Mazafferpur so of cau I was able to give him lots of news about that district. He also told me that Mr Templeman's son is at Suez in the Eastern Telegraph Office.

You would have been amused if you could have seen set off in the train for we were in open goods trucks & we looked just like a sot lot of sheep being sent off. We reached Kantara about 8–30 PM crossed the canal & went into camp tents in the base camp. Our camp is the farthest out into the desert & on one side we are right on the edge of the salt lakes. This is awfully nice for we are able to bathe every morning & evening. but The water is so salt that you cannot possibly sink in it – you can lie on your back & float without moving a muscle & if you happen to ᶃ take in a mouthful of it ——indescribable!

We shall probably stay here untill we are fully fitted out & then I suppose we shall move up the line. The country consists of nothing but sandy desert. There is a little cultivation near the canal but except for that there is sand everywhere. We are only allowed to take 35 lbs of kit up the line & can only leave 100 lbs here so we are sending the rest into Cox & Co at Port Said to be stored. I am going into Port Said myself to-morrow to get a few things & it will be interesting to see how it has change since I was there three years ago.

Bartlett was in there last Friday & I got him to send off a cable to you. I said on it that our address was C/o G.P.O. London but I have since heard that we ~~shold~~ shall get our letters a little quicker if they are addressed 2/4ᵗʰ Somt. L.I. Egyptian Expeditionary ⅄ Force.

The climate is delightful now – hot during the day but the nights are pleasantly cool. The sun does not seem so powerful as in India but it makes us much more sunburnt & we are all beginning to ~~feel~~ peel nicely.

I am awfully fit – this sort of open air life suits me splendidly, & it is awfully nice to feel that we are at last on active service even if we are still at the base.

I hope you are all quite well

With very much love to all

Your affectionate son

Jim

Extract from:

The Somerset Light Infantry 1914–19

It has already been stated that the capture of Beersheba was the preliminary phase of the Battle and that the attack on the Hareira-Sheria line and Gaza could only be carried out if Beersheba fell into British hands. Therefore, although there were two other Battalions of the Somerset Light Infantry – 1/5th and 2/4th – engaged in the operations, they were with the 75th Division which, with the 54th and 52nd Divisions, were holding the line in front of Gaza from coast to (and including) the Mansura and Abbas Ridges. The part taken by these two Battalions will be described later.

Egyptian Expedg Camp

7–10–17

My dear Mother & Father.

I think everyone in the camp was heartily glad ~~that~~ when he woke up this morning to know that it was Sunday morning, for we have all been so busy this week that everyone is tired out.

We have been issuing & changing equipment, training Lewis gunners & bombers, reorganizing the platoons & learning the use of gas masks, and the net result has been that we have hardly had any time to ourselves.

We have almost completed the equipment part of the business now and as soon as we are ready we shall move up the line – I think we shall go up in about three days time and I suppose we shall go straight up to form our division

Ron Vallis has not yet joined us – he went into Hospital at Suez with fever & is still there I have not heard from him but I am expecting him to come on any day I want him rather badly for one of my officers has been made Bttn Transport officer & another has been made Bttn Lewis gun officer & I am rather short handed. The cooler weather has done the men a world of good and we are not getting nearly as many sick as we did in India. The rations are very good indeed – we officers eat exactly the same as the men – but our appetites have increased so enormously that we always seem to be hungry, although the issue is quite enough to live on. We are quite close to the canal, and it is awfully interesting to watch the ships go up & down. The Indian mail boat went through a few days ago & I suppose she had our letters on board as only a few of our men received any & these were addressed G.P.O. London.

One job we have to do now is to censor the men's letters & parcels. One of the men brought in a parcel for me to censor a few minutes ago and noticing that it was addressed to someone in Portishead I asked him if he lived there & he told me that for two years before he joined up he was in charge of the lake there & just before that he was Mrs Jamieson's gardener. He said that he knew Grandma & Aunty quite well.

Several of our officers went off to Cairo last night for the weekend. I was too busy to go this week & hoped to be able to go next time but of course if we move up I shall have to wait, & get leave later on. I shall probably appreciate it more in a week or two.

I sent Mary & Angus 10/- each yesterday & if they don't get another 10/- each from John I hope they will let us know as we quite intend them to have £1 each, only I don't know whether John is expecting me to send it.

I hope you are all quite well & I also hope everyone at Ellesmere is quite fit. Please give them all my love when you see them as I have not time to write many letters now. Has mother been able to get any servant yet.

Would you mind sending me out a luminous wrist watch. I want one very badly indeed & cannot get one here. I would send in to Cairo but everything is so expensive in Egypt that and it would be a sheer waste of money if I did so. If you will kindly let me know what it costs I will tell Cox & Co to send pay you.

With very must much love to all

Your affectionate son
Jim

My dear Mother & Father

We have had another very busy week & are now absolutely complete: we have been wondering all day when we should have to move up the line & to-night we have just heard that we are goi to entrain early Monday morning. For this reason I am writing to-night (Saturday) instead of Sunday as I usually do as we shall have a very hard day to-morrow.

Our horses arrived the day before yesterday and the Colonel allotted them at once. Everyone says that mine is easily the best in the Regt and I was rather lucky to get her. The fact is she is very fresh & highspirited and none of the others cared about riding her so the Colonel said that I could have her if I could ride her. I do wish you could see her – she is an absolutely gem even better than the one I had at Barrackpore. I will try & send you a photograph of her one day.

We ĝ are all glad to be moving on for we want to get a bit nearer the front & also to see a bit more of the country. This place gets rather monotonous after a time for it is only a very large camp stretching from the Canal out into the desert. The more I see of it however the more amazed I become at the way we British do things when we once set out to accomplish something. I don't whether it is because we have just come from India & have not seen much of the war or what it is, but the arg arrangements & the way things are done ever here seem absolutely marvellous.

Except for my evening bathe I have hardly left the camp this week. We have been getting up at 5–30 A M & working steadily till dark then we are as a rule glad enough to have dinner & go off to bed. I managed to get a day off to go in to Port Said again on Wednesday as I had several things to do in there. I arranged to have a supply of food sent up every week from one of the shops, so with our rations & these extras we shall do awfully well. After the rations the men used to get in India the ones which are issued here are excellent – quite enough to keep one fit & well. The men are very pleased indeed with them. On service we don't have a big Bttn officer's mess: the officers of each company mess separately & we draw our rations from the just like the men do & then make our own arrangements for any extras we happen to require.

I have come to the conclusion that it is no easy job to be a Company Commander on service. One's responsibilities were fairly big in India but many of them were more or less nominal. On service the Coy Commander is absolutely & solely responsible for everything concerning his own men

& if ~~anyonce~~ anyone has to be slated it always seems to be some unfortunate Coy Commander.

Personally I love this sort of life, we get the open air & delightful weather, plenty of work, plenty of sleep & good food. I am now about twice as fit as I was in India & I have grown ever so much fatter since I have been here. The great problem now is to decide exactly what kit to take. In addition to what we can put ~~on~~ in our packs – all officers carry packs like the men – we are allowed 35 lbs, but as a valise & two blankets weigh 23 lbs there is not a very great margin for other things. There are so many little things that we want to take that it is rather difficult to know what to leave behind.

Ron Vallis rejoined on Wednesday evening, but as he was still looking weak & pale ~~he~~ the Colonel sent him off to Port Said for a couple of days, he came back again this morning & is now feeling ever so much better. A mail arrived from India yesterday & brought me your letters of August 15th & 22nd. I was delighted to hear that Mother has been able to get a servant again & I hope she will be a success.

I was sorry to hear that Rob had the bad luck to miss a Senior Scholarship because I sure ~~the~~ he must have been disappointed as I know he worked awfully hard. I am ever so glad that he is going to Reading – he will get on well there & it will do him a lot of good. From the idea one gets from the papers it looks as if Agriculture is going to be run carefully by the Govt after the war and there should be plenty of openings. The little farm still goes strong – it is a jolly good example of what can be done with a little field if it is carefully looked after.

I don't think I can find anything more to write about to-night and I am writing in a rather uncomfortable position by the light of a candle I am getting a bit tired.

I sincerely hope that Mother is stronger & fitter than she was & that all the others are quite well.

With very much love to all

> I remain
> Your affectionate son
> Jim

E. E. F.

19–10–17

My dear Mother & Father

I have lots to write about this week so I had better start at the beginning that is to say where I left off last week. I finished my letter to you last Saturday evening and immediately went off to bed to get a good sleep. We were up early on Sunday & had a very strenuous day getting all the spare kits into the dump & completing our preparations. On Sunday night we were able to just lie down in our clothes & get a few hours sleep but it was not a very satisfactory sleep as we had to be up at 2 o'clock on ~~Sunday~~ Monday morning to march off to the station. We left Kantara at about 5–30 A M & reached Belah at 11–30 P M having been travelling all day. It was not exactly a luxurious journey ~~we~~ for we all had to travel in goods trucks which were not over well provided with springs. It was quite good fun however & we were a very jolly party indeed. The worst part of the show came when we reached Belah, which is the rail head, for we were all getting rather tired by that time & we had to do the worst march I have ever had to do in my life. Thanks to the Y.M.C.A. we all had a cup of cocoa & a piece of cake before we set out & then we started to march three miles across the desert to a place called Surat. The men all had full packs & the sand was ankle deep & when we marched in they had all had about enough. We had nothing with us except what we had on so we just slept where we were and a very sound sleep it was too.

The railway up from Kantara to Belah is of course a new one built by the military people since this campaign started. It runs across the desert accompanied on one side by the water pipe on which we all depend for our water supply. The whole way up, the country is just bare rolling sand hills with here and there an oasis of date palms & a few huts. Just before El Arish the line turns & follows the coast line within about 100 yards of the sea.

The sandy shore is absolutely straight for miles, but what a place it would make for children – mile after mile of beautiful white clean sand an a ripping ~~bule~~ blue sea – Duffy would absolutely love it

Quite close to the railway runs the old caravan track – the same one that Abraham & ~~other~~ the other old people used when they went down into Egypt & I daresay ~~it~~ is the same road as Joseph & Mary took when they fled into Egypt.

On Tuesday we remained at Surat till about 4 A M & then we marched up to ~~the~~ join our Brigade. We had to go up by companies so that the Turks should not know that a whole Bttn was moving up. Mine was the last company & we did not get in till about 10 P M as our guide lost the way & took us much further than he need have done. It is awfully difficult country to find your way in as there are absolutely no landmarks ~~by day so~~ & of course by night it is much more difficult ~~by night~~. ⅄ We always have to take a compass whenever we go any distance from the camp. When we arrived we found that we were occupying some old dugouts in the side of ~~the~~ a hill but we were all so tired that we did not waste much time on getting to sleep.

All day yesterday & to-day we have been improving our ~~a~~ dugouts and making ourselves comfortable. We are about 1500–2000 yards behind the front line but by no means out of range of the Turkish guns, & we had a very sharp note from the Division ~~yesterd~~ this morning because our ~~our~~ men had been standing about on the skyline thereby inducing the Turks to plump a few shells in our direction. The great difficulty up here is to get water. It all has to be brought up on camels & all ranks are allowed one gallon per day for all purposes. This has to do for everything – washing drinking – cooking etc. We don't waste very much I can assure. We use about a pint every morning to wash, shave & clean our teeth in & then this water is ~~a~~ used by our batmen to wash socks etc in before it is thrown away. We can't afford water to wash our plates in but sand makes a very good substitute & you can get them as clean by rubbing them with sand as by washing them in water. As a matter of fact they don't want much cleaning for we clean them fairly well with bread before we finish our meals for even a drop of gravy is too valuable to ~~to~~ waste. Our rations are quite good when we can get them up, & I have arranged with a firm in Port Said to send up a box of extras like tinned fruit & vegetables, tinned fish etc for the company mess every ~~day~~ week. We mess by companies – ours is a very jolly little party – just five of us. You would roar with laughter to see us eating a tin of fruit – we pass the tin round & each dips his spoon in & takes one out & so on ~~ut~~ untill it is empty. Pears are rather difficult by this method but we manage them somehow or other.

We go to bed very early because we cannot use oil lamps ~~owing~~ as there is no oil to be had & candles are too scarce to waste. We are usually quite ready to go for the open air life makes us awfully tired at night, & we always sleep soundly enough ~~ins~~ in spite of the hardness of the ground. Ron & I & Bartlett are all in one dug out & we have made it quite nice & comfortable.

Would you mind arranging ~~to~~ with some firm or other to send me out a battery for my electric lamp once a month. I want an Ever Ready Battery No 295 for it & I have tried Port Said, Alexandra & Cario but cannot get one in either place. If they will send me the bill I will pay each time & if if I send a wire to say I am a casualty & anything of that sort will you kindly stop the order as I should ~~re~~ not require them in hospital.

If you could send ~~one~~ some we should be awfully grateful for a bit of cheese. Those truckles which came out to India were an absolute godsend & as there are only five of us in our mess one of them would last quite a long time. We are getting plenty to eat but anything extra like that is no end of a treat.

20th

We have not had a very busy day to-day – just ordinary parades & a few odd jobs. I had a little adventure this afternoon. The Colonel & I set out to ride to headquarters of the next Brigade on our left but as it began to get dark we decided to go home across country instead of by the track. We were both riding quietly along letting our horses find their own way when suddenly there was a tremendous bang in front of us and no end of a flash The Colonel's horse took absolutely no notice of it, but mine was absolutely scared. She swung round & galloped off as hard as she could leaving me a spectator on the ground. Luckily she ran into some artillery horse lines & was caught so I did not have to walk all the way home. It appears that we rode almost on top of a pair of big guns & when they went off we were only about 10 yards away.

While we were having supper we heard that we were all going up to the trenches to-morrow.

21ˢᵗ

We were told officially this morning that we were going up to the trenches to-night to be attached to another Regt for a few days before taking over the line ourselves.

22ⁿᵈ

We marched up after dark last night and each company went to its own part of the trenches.

I have been busy to-day learning the routine & finding my way about. The Turks have not worried us a great lot – ~~we~~ they put a few shells over ~~&~~ our front line this morning but they were nothing to talk about. Now I must stop to try & get some sleep for we don't get a very long night and every little ~~bt~~ bit helps. I am glad we are here at last for I wanted to see the real thing. I don't profess to like the shells a bit & I was in no end of a funk when the first one pitched in front of me this morning but one soon gets more or less used to them & there is a great ~~sa~~ satisfaction in knowing that we are doing some good work at last.

The English Mail came in yesterday & brought me the Western Gazette posted on Oct. 1ˢᵗ. I suppose I shall get some letters next week.

I sincerely hope that you are all quite fit

With much love to all

> Your affectionate son
> Jim

E. E. F.

24–ⅹ10–17

My dear Mother & Father

I was delighted this morning to receive two letters from you dated 21ˢᵗ &

4th October. They were addressed C/o G.P.O. London and therefore came direct. The last I had came back from India & was dated July 27th so I was awfully pleased to hear from you after such a long time.

I was also very pleased indeed to hear that Rob has passed the London Matric and has gone to Reading. It is a jolly good start and I am sure he will be able to keep it up.

I am now writing from a dug out in the trenches. In We moved up up last Saturday night and were attached to another Regt for instruction, but they have now gone out & we are left to ourselves. We have had an awfully strenuous time getting settled down and taking over but I think it will be much easier now, although one never has much time to spare at this job. The worst part of it is the night work – one officer always has to be awake and then there are patrols & all that sort of thing.

Things are very quiet just now. Both sides put over some shells every day & there is a certain amount of aeroplane work but there is nothing very much to worry about. I think it is the lull before the storm.

Ron is quite fit again and is acting adjutant for a few days as Ingram has got a touch of fever. As a matter of fact the health of the Bttn is remarkably good now and the men are all finding the benefit of the change of climate.

27th I am feeling awfully pleased to-day for I had lots of letters to-day. There were three weeks letters from you sent back from India and several from the various friends I made in India. Among the ones from you was one containing Mary's photograph whi with which I am absolutely delighted. The only other one I have of Mary is the one in the group taken the day before we left home and she has changed ever so much since then. Andrew told me that she had grown into a very pretty girl but I didn't realize the extent of it till I saw her photograph.

Yesterday morning I had no end of a fright … I woke up suddenly & heard an most appalling row – the ground shook & you could not hear yourself speak & I made sure that we were being attacked. We always sleep in our clothes so it did not take me long to get out and when I did I was quite relieved to find that we the noise was caused by our guns & not those of the Turks. We were fairly straafing the Turkish positions & as it was quite dark it was rather a fine sight watching the shrapnel bursting over their lines. We are giving them a very bad time to-day, and but they will get it a good deal worse before very long.

These trenches are fairly comfortable but they are absolutely infested with fleas. A short time ago they were occupied by Indian troops & since then the fleas have been almost unbearable. As an example of what they are like I had to get up & undress twice last night and between 8 PM & 5 AM I killed 12 fleas in my clothes. You could hardly put a sixpence on my body without putting it on a bite.

I am awfully glad you received the parcel of Benares stuff safely as I wanted you to see it. It is very lucky that it was not spoilt in spite of the oil on the outside I got a letter from John to-day but I have not heard from Andrew X since I left India – I hope he is still getting on alright in France.

Passmore has won a bar to his M.C. – his mother wrote & told me about it. As you can imagine she is frightfully proud of him.

My man has just brought my tea and it will be time to "stand to" very soon so I will make this my excuse for ending this week's letter. I don't write the whole letter in one day like I did in India – I just write a little bit whenever I have time & I think this will make them more interesting.

With much love to all

> Your affectionate son
> Jim

The Fall of Gaza

Meanwhile Gaza had fallen.

The date of the attack at Gaza had been left open till the result of the Beersheba operations was known. It was intended that the former, designed to draw the enemy's reserves towards the Gaza sector, should take place from twenty-four to forty-eight hours previous to the attack on the Sheria position. After the Beersheba operations had proved successful, reports were received at G.H.Q. that an ample water supply would be available in the town and hopes were entertained that it would be possible to attack Sheria on 3rd or 4th November. The attack on Gaza was, therefore, ordered to take place on the morning of 2nd November. Later reports showed that the water situation was less favourable than had been reported, nevertheless it was decided not to postpone the attack. The objectives of the attack were the hostile works from Umbrella Hill (2,000 yards north-west of Gaza). The front of the attack was about 6,000 yards and Sheikh Hasan, the farthest objective was some 3,000 yards from the British front line. A preliminary operation against Umbrella Hill was to be made on the night of 1st November, four hours previous to the main attack on Gaza.

This preliminary attack was made at 11 p. m. on 1st by a portion of the 52nd Division and was completely successful, though it drew a heavy bombardment, which lasted for two hours, on Umbrella Hill and the British front line. The hostile shell fire ceased, however, before Zero hour for the main attack, i.e. 3 a.m. on 2nd November, and the troops formed up for the attack without interference.

The official despatches show the British troops forming the XXI Corps in front of Gaza at 6 p.m. on 1st November, in the following order: 75th Division on the right, 54th Division in the centre and 52nd Division on the left, with its left resting on the coast-line. The right of the line ran from about El Mendor north-east to Sheikh Abbas, thence turned sharply round the Abbas Ridge, north-west to the coast.

The ground over which the attack was to take place was mostly sand dunes, rising in places to a height of 150 feet. The sand was deep and heavy going. Several lines of strongly built trenches and redoubts defended Gaza, the most important of which lay south and south-west of the town. Of these Middlesex Hill, The Maze, Outpost Hill and Umbrella Hill were well garrisoned and protected by thick barbed-wire entanglements.

At 3 a.m. on 2nd the main attack was launched and all objectives were reached "except for a section of trench on the left and some of the final objectives in the centre." Sheikh Hasan fell into the hands of the 52nd Division. The enemy apparently suffered very heavily from the preliminary bombardment by the XXI Corps, losing a third of their men in one division, so that a fresh division had to be moved up from their general reserve. This was part of the object of the attack, i.e. to prevent the Turks reinforcing their right where the Beersheba operations were in progress.

From the Diaries of the 75th Division neither the 232nd nor 233rd Brigades were actively in this operation and the 2/4th Somerset Light Infantry of the former and the 1/5th Somersets of the latter were therefore not employed in the attack. The 232nd Brigade was in Corps Reserve in the Wadi Simeon area, and the 233rd Brigade held the left sub-sector of the Sheikh Abbas sector. The 2/4th Somersets were at Paisley and the 1/5th Battalion at Queen's Hill and the Slag Heap (south of Burnt Tank).

The Somerset Light Infantry 1914–19

The 2/4th Battalion, Somerset Light Infantry, had taken no active part in the operations. The Battalion remained at Paisley from 1st to 6th November, but at 12 noon on 7th was sent up to Ali el Muntar, arriving at 6 p.m. Here the Battalion bivouacked.

The 2/4th Battalion at Ali el Muntar had been turned out at 1 a.m. to take up a line of outposts on Middlesex Hill and Outpost Hill at 3 a.m., but at 8 a.m. they returned to El Muntar and similarly spent the remainder of the day in quietude.

As a whole, the 75th Division, after occupying the Beer Trenches, Tank Redoubt and Atawineh, evacuated by the enemy during the night 7th/8th, had been able to link up with the left of the 10th Division. The Composite Force; however, relieved the 75th Division during the afternoon, the latter having been ordered to push on to Beit Hanun.

By the 9th the operations had reached the stage of a direct pursuit of the Turks by as many troops as could be supplied so far in front of railhead. Indeed, it was now a question of supply rather than one of manoeuvre. Water and forage were the two great difficulties.

Early on 9th the 232nd Brigade received a message from Divisional Headquarters which stated: "You will march to Beit Hanun as early as possible. Every man will take two days' rations." The march began at 11.45 a.m. in great heat. The Brigade set out in the following order – 2/5th Hants, 2/3rd Gurkhas, 2/4th Somersets, 1/5th Devons, 229th Machine-Gun Company, and marched via The Quarry and Chaytor Hill. Beit Hanun was reached about 3 p.m., but contrary to expectation the water supply was found inadequate for watering the troops, and it was decided to push on to Dier Sineid, units leaving their water transport behind for refilling. About 5–45 p.m. the Brigade reached its destination where all units bivouacked for the night.

During the evening of 9th November there were indications that the enemy was organizing a counter-attack from the direction of Hebron towards Arak el Menshiye, but as it was obvious that this attack could only be made by troops who were very much disorganized and had lost heavily, the threat was ignored and orders from G.H.Q. gave instructions for the pursuit to continue as early as possible towards Junction Station with the intention of cutting off the Turkish Jerusalem Army: the Imperial Camel Corps was ordered to move to the neighbourhood of Tel el Nejile where it would be on the flank of any counter-stroke from the hills.

It is impossible from the Battalion Diary of the 2/4th Somersets to gather anything of the enormous difficulties which confronted the advance at this stage. Even the Brigade Diary, though it does, here and there (in copies of messages and orders), tear aside the veil and show something of that great effort and wonderful march across the desert, is all too brief in its description of the following up and ultimate defeat of the entire Turkish Army in Palestine.

The first order received from Divisional Headquarters on 10th November by 232nd Brigade Headquarters stated:-

"232nd Brigade will march to Es Suafir el Gharbiyeh 13 miles north-north-east of Deir Sineid on main road … The object of this march is to give the enemy no chance of recovering, and all ranks must be prepared to undergo considerable hardships and privations. Rations will be got to you this evening and if possible, on the following evening. Battalions may be thinned out to 500 if you wish men weeded out, leaving their rations with you and being marched to Mansura ... Move to be completed by 18.00 (6 p. m.)."

Perhaps it was because of the frank statements in this order (that all ranks must be prepared to suffer privations) that every one responded so splendidly to whatever call was made upon them. No men were sent back, but each British battalion of the 232nd and 233rd Brigades left behind at Gaza a percentage of officers and men, and these details were organized into a column of about 400 men with about 15 officers, which followed up as hard as it could go after the Brigades, and rejoined its various units at Latron on the day the attack on Saris and Enab was made.

At 8 a.m. the Battalion left Deir Sineid and about 5 p.m. arrived about one mile due west of Es Suafir el Gharbiyeh where a line of picquets was put out facing north. Brigade Headquarters then reported to Advanced 75th Divisional Headquarters that it had relieved the 2nd Light Horse Brigade (less one squadron) which remained to cover the right of the 232nd. The Turks were holding Beit Duras and villages about one mile in front of the Brigade and the 2/3rd Gurkhas were shelled while taking up the position allotted to them. But again the water question was acute, for the Diary reports: "Can water men, but do not think horses or mules. The latter in most cases have had no water for thirty-six hours. Going was very bad." Such was the report sent to Divisional Headquarters. Poor, faithful animals: they, no less than the troops, had responded nobly to the calls made upon them, for the Brigade Diary states: "The animals at this time were beginning to show signs of exhaustion, but had done extremely well, despite being without water for so long. The R.E. materials were quite inadequate to obtain a quick supply of water from the wells." But that was not the fault of the gallant sappers, they could only issue what materials were available and could be brought up. On the morning of 11th information was received at 75th Divisional headquarters that the enemy was holding the ridge north-east of "S" in Es Suafir el Gharbiyeh and Beit Duras. During the previous evening British Cavalry had captured 1,500 prisoners and 13 guns. The 52nd Division had advanced troops in Esdud but was concentrated at Mejdel. The 232nd Brigade was ordered to hold the line Es Suafir el Gharbiyeh-Beit Diras inclusive: the 233rd Brigade was to move to the neighbourhood of Julis, and the 234th Brigade troops to neighbourhood of Eijeh. These moves were to be completed by 16.00 (4 p. m.).

At 2.30 p. m. on 11th the Somerset piquets were withdrawn and the Battalion (in Brigade) moved forward according to orders, Brigade Head-quarters reporting to Divisional Headquarters: "Beit Duras occupied by our troops, Turks having retired before our mounted troops, who captured two guns. Am advancing my left to Jewish Colony, not marked on map, at D. 24a. at 14.00 to-day." The 2/4th Somersets were apparently on the left, for their Diary records that at 15.45 (3.45 p. m.) the Battalion reached Jewish Colony and two picquets were put out facing north-east.

Both on the 10th and 11th the operations had showed that the enemy's resistance was stiffening in the general line of the Wadi Sukereir with centre about El Kustineh, but the threatened counter-attack from the direction of Hebron ended in an ineffective demonstration, and the enemy retired north-east, prolonging the Turkish line towards Beit Jibrin. This increased resistance, taken with the fact that prisoners from almost every Turkish unit had been captured, pointed to the fact that the British advance was no longer opposed only by hostile rear-guards but practically by the reminder of the Turkish Army, which was making a last effort to arrest the pursuit south of the Junction Station – a position of importance.

The 12th November was accordingly spent in preparations for an attack on the enemy's position covering Junction Station, though the 4th Royal Scots of the 156th Brigade (52nd Division) on the left of the 232nd Brigade (75th Division) made a very gallant, but unsuccessful attempt to capture Brown Hill. The Hill was finally captured by the 2/3rd Gurkhas and 2/5th Hants of the 232nd Brigade, the 2/4th Somersets covering the right of the Brigade connecting with 233rd Brigade, the 1/5th Devons being in reserve. On this date (12th) the only entry in the Diary of the Somersets is: "12.34 (12.34 am). Put out piquets 200 yards north-east of Jewish Colony. 14.30 (2.30 p. m.). Moved up to support the guns 500 yards to the north and bivouacked there."

By the morning of 13th November the enemy had sprung out his force on a front of about twenty miles from El Kubeibeh, on the north, to Beit Jibrin to the south. The right half of his line ran approximately parallel with, and only about five miles in front of, the Ramleh-Junction Station Railway, his main line of supply from the north: his right flank was already almost turned. On this flank he had been forced into this position by the rapid movement along the coast and the maintenance of determined pressure on his read-guard.

The country over which the attack was to take place was open and rolling, dotted with small villages surrounded by mud walls, beyond which were plantations of trees. The most prominent feature was the line of heights, upon which were the villages of Katrah and El Mughar. These two places stood out above the low flat ground which separated them from the rising ground to the west on which was another village, Beshshit, about 2,000 yards distant. The Katrah-El Mughar line was a very strong position and the Turks were expected to put up a stout resistance, seeing that their right flank was threatened.

The first objective of the 232nd Brigade of the 75th Division was the line

Yasur-Kustineh,* the formation of the attack being: front line – 2/4th Somersets on the right, 2/5th Hants on the left; second line – 2/3rd Gurkhas on the right, 1/5th Devons on the left. The 233rd Brigade was on the right of the Somersets.

The Somerset Light Infantry 1914–19

The 2/4th Somersets (232nd Brigade) moved to Abu Shusheh on 16th, and similarly remained in this place throughout the actions of 17th. On this date Lieut-Colonel Clutterbuck, commanding the Battalion, was evacuated sick to hospital, and Major Dundas of the 2/3rd Gurkhas assumed command.

The Battle began on 17th with an advance by the Yeomanry through the hills direct on Bireh, by Annabeh, Berfilya and Beit ur el Tahta. By the evening of 18th a portion of the mounted troops had reached the latter place, and another Shilta, but beyond Annabeh the route was found impossible for wheels.

On the 19th the infantry advance began. The 75th Division was to advance up the main road as far as Kuryet el Enab, with its right flank protected by Australian mounted troops and, in order to avoid fighting in the close neighbourhood of the Holy City, was to strike north towards Bireh by a track leading through Biddu. The 52nd Division was to advance through Berfilya to Beit Likia and Beit Dukka, and thence support the movements of the 75th Division. Orders from Divisional Headquarters, issued during the evening of 18th, stated that the Division was to concentrate about Amwas on 19th as a preliminary move. The situation at this place was then unknown, as the Australians were still attacking it. Units were warned that it might be necessary to attack the Amwas-Latron line (both villages inclusive), in which case the 233rd Brigade was to be on the right with its left on Latron inclusive, and the 232nd Brigade on the left. As soon as these two places were occupied and the Division had concentrated, the 232nd and 233rd Brigades were to march to Kuret el Enab, the 232nd leading. Strict orders were issued that the tombs from Latron to Enab were to be guarded and all ranks warned that they were on no account to be approached: also "no officers or other ranks will enter Jerusalem or country within a radius of 6 miles of it. Any officer or man found in the town is liable to be shot."

At 7.30 a.m. on 19th the 232nd Brigade left the Abu Shusheh position and occupied the Latron-Amwas line without opposition. Preparations were the made for the advance along the Jerusalem Road. At 11 a.m., covered by

---

* Kustineh (exclusive)

Vaughan's Rifles, the 232nd Brigade moved forward in the following order towards Rab el Wad: 1/5th Devons, S.A.F.A., 2/5th Hants and 2/4th Somerset Light Infantry. No opposition was met with, though the Brigade was under long-range artillery fire, causing a few casualties. Just beyond Rab el Wad the Brigade entered the Pass of Bethoron and the heights on both sides of the road were therefore picketed. But now progress became terribly slow. The difficult nature of the ground and the heavy weights of the men's packs prevented anything in the way of a rapid advance. At about 1.30 p.m. the O.C., Vaughan's Rifles, reported that he was in touch with strong enemy forces and two companies of Devons and one company of Gurkhas were sent up the heights on the right and left of the road, respectively, as reinforcements. The enemy was, however, in strength and little or no further progress could be made after 5 p.m. Rain began to fall and a stormy evening followed, darkness setting in early. Under these circumstances the 232nd Brigade bivouacked on the position occupied on, and north and south of, the road. Throughout the night the enemy was active, especially on the left of the road, but he was successfully held off.

At dawn on 20th the advance was again continued, the 232nd Brigade still leading, the 233rd in support and the 234th back at Latron. The 2/5th Hants (less one company) of the 232nd Brigade were pushed out on the right of the road, joining up with 58th Rifles. About 7.30 p.m. the 1/5th Devons were sent up on the left of the road to fill the gap between the Gurkhas' right and the road, and the 2/4th Somersets were brought up from the rear along the road. A general advance then took place. but progress was very slow: the country was extraordinarily difficult and the Turks were in force covering not only Enab, but defending Saris, which would have to be taken before any advance on the former village could take place. On the right especially the Turks held obstinately to their positions, and more than once counter-attacked, but were easily repulsed. About 11 a.m., however, the O.C., 2/4th Somersets, reported that the enemy's resistance in front of Saris showed signs of weakening and the Battalion was therefore ordered to attack the village. Supported by the fire of the L.A.M. Battery the 2/4th Battalion dashed forward and, at the point of the bayonet, captured the village and drove the Turks back on their Enab position: about thirty prisoners were taken by the Somerset men. A Battalion of Gurkhas from the 233rd Brigade (having been lent to the 232nd Brigade) was sent up and, moving forward, occupied the strong ridges about half a mile east of Saris, driving the Turks still farther back and capturing many prisoners. Brigade Headquarters then arrived and began immediately to organize an attack on Enab, the 1/5th Devons and 1/4th Wilts to carry out the assault. By this time (it was late afternoon) the troops of the 232nd Brigade, who had been marching and fighting all day, were dog-tired, but fortunately two more battalions of the 233rd Brigade were placed at the disposal of the Brigadier of the 232nd: these battalions were the 1/5th Somersets and 1/4th Wilts: they replaced the 2/4th Somersets and 1/5th Devon, who were much exhausted.

The Somerset Light Infantry 1914–19

Egyptian Expeditionary Force

2nd Nov. 1917

My dear Mother & Father.

Since I last wrote we have seen a good many of the realities of war and I must say that in spite of the terribleness of the whole show they are very impressive. Although we are put on our honour not to write anything about the actual military plans etc I suppose there is no harm in my saying that the advance out here in Palestine which we have been preparing for for months has begun, for even now the capture of Beersheba is in all the English papers and to-morrow you will see that we have made considerable progress towards the capture of Gaza.

I am awfully glad that we are in it too – there are lots of hardships etc but I think they are worth it for there is no end of satisfaction in feeling that we are at last doing our bit with the rest.

We have known what for a long time that we should soon begin to attack & for the last five days the Turks have had a terrible time. We have bombarded them incessantly night & day – during the attack last night it looked as if their positions were all on fire so intense was our bombardment. We were relieved from the trenches last Monday night in order to make us available for the forthcoming operations and we marched back to so and occupied some positions in the rear. It was awfully nice to be out of the trenches again for the constant night work when you are in the line is an awful strain and one felt ever so safe as you marched back from the front. As a matter of fact we learnt next morning that we were anything but safe for the redoubt which my company is occupying had no end of a shelling. The enemy had the range to a nicety & shell after shell pitched right on the trenches. We lay very low indeed & were very lucky not to have any casualties. Bartlett & I had a very narrow squeak – we were standing up on the top having a look round when a great H E shell suddenly burst within five yards of us. I can't think why we were not hit it was pure luck for we might easily have been blown to pieces. The shell seems to have burst forward entirely & as we were to one side of it we just escaped.

We get a straaf like this every morning of about five but we are ready for it now & when the first shell comes over we get down in the bottom of the trenches as quickly as possible. Our Brigade is in reserve for this show so we may not get much fighting but on the other hand we may come in for quite a lot of dirty work.

3ʳᵈ Nov:

I received a letter from Father to-day dated 16ᵗʰ October so it only took about a fortnight to come. This is ever so much quicker than it used to be be in India. I don't suppose I shall come across either the Dorset or the Ayrshire Yeomanry for a bit for all the cavalry are out on the right ‹ at present – however I may come across them this week.

During the last two days the weather which ha was previously so delight-fully cool has suddenly become very hot. Instead of the sea breeze there is a very hot wind blowing across the desert which almost brings back recollections of Lahore. The nights are still cool so we do not feel it so much. I am glad to hear that Andrew is still well & happy although I am not surprised that he wants to doing something more than just living at the base. I have not heard from him for quite a long time but I expect some of his letters have gone out to India.

When we move off from here I shall have to leave Bartlett behind as the O. C. Coy & his second in command are not both allowed to go into action together. He I shall be awfully sorry to have to leave him here for we have lived and worked together continuously for over a year in fact ever since I got my Company and previous to that we were together when I was at Calicut just after ~~I cam~~ we came out to India. I hope he will be allowed to join us again before long.

Ron is now assistant Adjutant so I don't see so much of him as I did, in fact I have hardly seen him at all for about four days. He sent across just now to say that he intended to come over to see us presently, and I suppose he will bring us all the latest news. We are almost on detachment now for for we are occupying two redoubts which are both about two miles from Bttn head-quarters. I usually go over once a day but otherwise we are quite on our own.

I shall be very glad indeed of the socks which Mother says she is sending, for it is absolutely impossible to replace anything which is worn out up here, and I find that my socks are already showing signs of wear. I am afraid you will think that I ask for something every week nowadays but we can't get a thing here and I can get things from home almost as quickly as from Cairo. I ordered a box of food to be sent up from Port Said every week but they take nearly three weeks to come up, as all available transport is being used for military purposes.

I hope you are all quite well & also that Mother will have a very jolly birthday
With very much love to all

Your affectionate son
Jim

Egyptian Expedy Force

16–11–17

My dear Mother & Father

I have not written to you for a fortnight but I am sure you will forgive me when you hear the reason. During the last fortnight we have hardly had an hour's rest, we have had nothing to eat but bully beef & biscuit & very little of that & we have suffered terribly from thirst. In addition we have been into action, and I believe did very well indeed, and as a result we arrived here to-day (not far from Jerusalem) in a state of complete exhaustion. We have been promised a week's rest & by that time we shall be ready for anything.

Ron had to go back after the second day of the advance so I asked him to write to you & I have no doubt that he did so.

I will try & give you some sort of connected account of what we have been doing although we have been so absolutely done that some of it I hardly remember. You will know more about the whole show than we do for we had very little news and only know what has really happened on our own bit of front.

We really started two days before the capture of Gaza as we were then expecting a counter attack by the Turks which did not come off. However we had to stand to almost the whole time while the Turks shelled us rather heavily. No one knew exactly the day of the intended attack on Gaza 'till the actual day of assault but we knew it was coming for the bombardment we gave the Turkish positions was literally like hell let loose. It was so intense that the Turks cleared out and we had parctically no opposition on our part of the line.

After the capture we bivouaced there for a day and then it was decided to follow up the Turks as quickly as possible. We took two days rations with us & set out. We were told at the start that we should be on half rations ~~but we~~ so we knew what to expect more or less.

I will just describe the three days during which we had our fight & they will give you some idea of how things went.

We left our bivouac about midday with a little food & a bottle full of water & marched out in time to just come in for the tail end of an action. As soon as it was dark we advanced our positions and then dug in for the rest of the night. At dawn we were withdrawn & just had time to fill our water bottles before marching off again. We had no time for food as we were wanted to attack at once.

We advanced to within about 1000 yds of the enemy's posn & then had to lie there for five hours while the flanks came round. We were lying right in the open & the enemy were occupying a position in the hills so they could see our every movement. The result was we had a most appalling time for their guns got our range exactly and deluged us with HE & shrapnel. How any of us escaped is absolutely miraculous for he searched systematically along along our lines & if we got up to move he followed us. The men were magnificent, as steady as could be, & the General said he never saw men stand a shelling better. About 1–0 PM we were told to advance to attack ~~gun~~ a position which was strongly held by machine guns & I am glad to say we carried it sucessfully & received lots of praise from the General for the way we did it.

Our casualties were wonderfully light 3 killed & somewhat over 50 wounded – we were very lucky in not having the whole Regt wiped out everyone thought it would be. My company lost rather heavily 4 Sergts & 8 others wounded out of about 50 who went into action. I cannot speak too highly of the men they just did splendidly. The shelling was a terrible experience but they went on to the attack afterwards as if they were on the parade ground in India. I am glad to say that I came out ~~so~~ without a scratch. ~~and I tried to~~ After it was over I had an awfully pleasant experience for a deputation came from the men to say that they were proud to be in my company and that they had every confidence to go wherever I took them. It was awfully nice of them and I was ever so pleased about it.

After sunset we had to ~~dg~~ dig in & put out outposts. We were absolutely parched with thirst & as hungry as could be but there was no water or food to be had, so we had to make the most of it. Water arrived at dawn next morning but we got no food till 11 A M as we had to start off again on the march at 7 A M.

However we are going to have a few days rest now and we are already feeling better for ~~it~~ the thought of it.

17th I took my boots off to-day for the first time for five days and managed to secure a quart of water to wash in. Three of us have already bathed all over in it and they are still washing socks in it.

Lack of water & sleep were our two greatest troubles and knocked us out more than anything else. We nearly always had to go the whole day on a water bottle full of water and a pint of cocoa in the morning or evening. We could get very little sleep for we had to dig in most nights & if we were not digging it was too cold to sleep. The days are very hot & the nights bitterly cold & these two extremes are awfully trying.

The men ~~sufferred~~ are all crying out for tobacco & cigarettes – there is hardly a match in the Bttn but these thing will all come up if we stay here for a few days. All the transport has been bringing up guns & ammunition but it will soon be available for bringing up other supplies. We are all in jolly good spirits and of course we are frightfully pleased that our first action was a success. I would not have missed it for anything but I don't mind how soon the end of the war comes now.

Most of the inhabitants are Arabs but dotted about in the most fertile places there are model Jewish villages. We were always very pleased when we could bivouac near one of these as there was always a good water supply in them and they make quite good bread which we bought from them. With a ~~truly~~ the true generosity of a Jew they charged us 10/- a loaf but we would have paid 30/- if they had asked it.

I have not heard of a single case of looting by our men, in fact we pay well over the market price for everything. On two occasions our Brigadier commandeered a flock of sheep but the owners received the full value for them. Boiled mutton – what a luxury! I have never eaten anything more delicious ~~that~~ than the mutton which came from those two flocks of sheep.

Poor Ron was awfully sick when he had to go back – he had a boil lanced the day we started and the doctor would not let him go on.

We are all hoping to get some letters up in a day or two and I hope some arrangements will soon be made for us to ~~send~~ post some ~~off~~. I shall get this one ready & post it at the first opportunity.

I hope you are all quite fit
With very much love to all

> Your affectionate son
> Jim

Egyptian Expeditionary Force

28th Nov. 1917

My dear Mother & Father.

Yesterday was a great day for us – we received the first letters we have had since the advance began nearly a month ago. I received one from you dated 23rd Oct. & thank you very much indeed for it – I don't think any letter was ever more welcome.

I have lots to write about and hardly know where to begin but I had better take this opportunity of wishing you all a very Merry Christmas as we may not be able to write again for sometime although I think we shall be able to send off our letters fairly regularly again now. I hope that in spite of the war conditions you will all spend the brightest & happiest of Christmases. I wish I could be home to spend it with you, but I am afraid that it is impossible this year although I think that the war will be over next year & then we shall all be able to come home again.

When I last wrote about a fortnight ago when we were resting for a couple of days but was unable to send the letter off till a few days ago as nothing at all has been sent down the line.

We are now resting again and this time I think it will be a long one as our division has been relieved from the line. The whole division has gained a splendid reputation and our own Bttn has done splendidly. Ours has been the leading division in the chase from Gaza to within six miles of Jerusalem & for a good deal of the way ours was the leading Brigade.

We have been into action twice since I last wrote and have done awfully well. We were congratualted by the C in C for our on the occasion when we captured Saris a village called Saris and lots of outside peole have congratulated the C.O. on having such a fine Bttn.

Poor old Harry Marsh who used to work for Mr Drewett was killed during the attack on Saris. He was close beside me when he fell & I think he died amost at once, but I could not stop to see. When we marched down the line after having been relieved I had a look at his grave. The day after we lost Capt. Harford & Capt. Bealy. The latter died of wounds but I think Harford will get fit again in time. Both were knocked out by the same shell. For the first time in my life I have known what it is to be really miserable & I will try to describe the circumstances.

We moved out from our rest camp on a Monday M morning and advanced steadily all day. Just as night fell it started to rain and kept going steadily all night. We had nothing to cover us so we got absolutely wet through, but as we managed to keep a fire going we kept up a certain degree of warmth. Next morning we went on again climbing up into the hills all the time – during the day we captured Saris. After the fight we had to march another three miles and we did not move off till after dark. We were then about 20 2800 feet high & it was bitterly cold & raining in torents torrents. We reached our bivouac area about 8 PM & then had to spend the whole night walking about to try & keep warm. The rain hardly ceased the whole night and by the morning we were absolutely sodden & chilled to the bone. I confess that during that night I felt thoroughly miserable but the sun came out in the morning & nd under its cherry influence we soon became quite happy again.

Our relief came as quite a surprise. We marched into position about 6 PM & fully expected a hard action in the morning as we knew the Turks were in force in front. At 7 PM we sent in our fighting strength – (ours was 207 out of 600) and went to sleep. At 9 P M we were all roused up & told that we were going back down the line for a rest. We were delighted I can assure you for we were all feeling absolutely exhausted & the prospect of a fight in the morning was not a bit attractive.

We marched back 5 miles that night, rested a day & then did a march of 16 miles. Now I think we have reached a more or less permanent place for a time at any rate, and already we are beginning to get some food again. For days we only had a tin of bully & a handful of biscuits each with a little cocoa or tea & sugar, but of course things improve every day up there now.

It was perfectly amazing as we came down the line to see the changes which a few days have brought forth. Villages which we captured only about a week ago are now enormous dumps where stores are being collected, the railway is creeping up and motor ambulances are dashing about.

We are now getting cheese & jam as well as our bully & biscuit and cigarettes & tobacco should arrive soon. The men felt the loss of tobacco & cigarettes more than anything else and for two or three days officers & men smoked tea leaves.

It is nice to feel safe again and to know the when you go to sleep that you will not have to wake up & move off in the middle of the night.

I am glad that I have seen some fighting at last but I have now had quite enough & I don't care how soon the war comes to and end.

Since we came down we have been absolutely stuffing ourselves with Jaffa oranges which grow everywhere round here – we are bivouaced in an orange grove now. We can get six great big oranges for 2½ᵈ and they are absolutely delightful. I shall be delighted to see the socks which mother is sending – the ones I have here are getting very worn & thin.

I am glad Rob is getting on so well at Reading. It seems very familiar to hear about all the people at the College again.

Once more I wish you a very very happy Christmas & I hope you are all well & fit.

With very much love to all

        Your affectionate son
        Jim

On the 10ᵗʰ the 229ᵗʰ Brigade concentrated and, after bivouacking for the night below Beit Hannina, the Somersets settled down for a few days at Beit Iksa. And here, for a moment, it is necessary to leave the 12ᵗʰ Battalion and turn to the doings of the 1/5ᵗʰ and 2/4ᵗʰ Battalions during the capture of the Holy City.

Although continually in reserve or support and occasionally taking over front-line positions from other units of the 232ⁿᵈ Brigade as it advanced, the 2/4ᵗʰ Somersets do not appear to have been involved in any fighting with the enemy during the latter part of December. On 11th, while other units of the Brigade took Midien, Zebdah, Budrus and Sheikh Obeid Rahil, C and D Companies were attached to the 2/3ʳᵈ Gurkhas, D Company going forward and occupying a hill on a line between Haditheh and a point midway between Sheikh Obeid Rahil and Budrus, the attack passing right and left of (and being covered by) D Company's position. In successive stages the Battalion moved forward to Mukam Iman el Aly, Sheikh Obeid Rahil, Bornat and Horse Shoe Hill. It was at the latter place that that the 2/4th were relieved by the 1/5th and moved back to bivouacs at Surafend. The Battalion was now under the command of Lieut-Colonel E. B. Powell, who had arrived on 18th December and taken over from Major L. K. Bunting.

The Somerset Light Infantry 1914–19

Egyptian Expeditionary Force

2nd December 1917

My dear Mother & Father.

Since I last wrote we have had a comparatively quiet time and have been able to think things over a little. The predominant feeling with all of us I think is that we are jolly thankful to be alive. It is very different fighting out here to what it is in France. Since we left Gaza there has been no trench warfare – when we attacked we had to advance across the open & there is no doubt about it the Turks know the way to use machine guns under such circumstances. For th about forty miles above Gaza the country is rolling open down land which seems to be exceedingly fertile. Then you come to the hills & even now I shudder to think of them. Jerusalem is surrounded by hills & this accounts for the extreme difficulty of the present operations. The hills are bare & stoney – you can imagine the effect of shrapnel on such country in fact one Bttn which had rather heavy casualties a few days had more men knocked out from stone wounds than from actual bullet & shell wounds.

At present although we are supposed to be resting we do a little marching most days. We are now not far from Jaffa. If all goes well I hope we shall spend our Christmas down here more or less in peace. The great event of the last three or four days has been the arrival of the mails. All the back ones have come up & I think I had more letters than I have ever had at one time since I left home. You can't think how I appreciate them – one wants to be on a show of this sort to realize the real value of letters. I have received three from you dated 23rd & 30th of Oct & 6th Nov. so I think they are right up to date.

Dec. 3rd Another mail arrived last night but the letters have not yet been sorted. I am looking forward ever so much for the various parcels which are on the way for me. The books which you are all sending will be invaluable for untill the mails we ~~hav not~~ hadn't a single thing to read. The papers etc which are now coming keep us going more or less but it will be a real pleasure to have a book to read again.

I heard from Ron yesterday – he is down at Belah having quite a good time and is fairly fit again.

Now I have a bit of good news to tell you. Since I last wrote I have been recommended for some sort of award in connection with the recent fighting. Of course I may not get anything at all, but still there is quite a lot of satisfaction in having had ones name sent up. I had two letters from Andrew last mail & he tells me that he has gone up to the line at last. I do hope he will do well & come out of it quite safely.

I was sorry to hear that Mother is suffering from R̶h̶ rheumatic again this Winter & I do hope that she will take great care of herself during the damp cold weather.

I hope you will all spend a very happy Christmas & that you are all quite fit. With much love to you all

> Yours affectionate son
> Jim

E. E. F.

2–12–17

My dear old Rob.

Many thanks for your letter which I received a day or two ago. You can't think how pleased I was to hear all about the old Coll and the people I used to know up there.

So you have made the aquaintance of Ma Jones – not a bad sort when you know her – Miss Eales & D̶o̶ Dʳ Cole have you. The latter two are quite good sorts although old Cole is a bit gruff at times.

Fancy Miss Chell being at Reading! You needn't trouble to give her my love for I only met her once or twice at dances when she came up to visit her brother. I mean to write to Chell again when I have time for I owe him a letter.

Fancy our old Bunna learning to dance! I hope you will get on with it for you will find it awfully useful when you leave Reading and dances are awfully good fun. I should like to be able to go to one now.

We are now having a rest which I can assure you we were very much in need of. We turned the Turks out of Gaza & then followed them up to within six miles of Jerusalem. By that time those of us who were left were nearly dead with fatigue & want of food and we were eventually relieved.

We had a good deal of fighting – our Bttn went into action three times, but in addition to this we got shelled almost every day. the Turkish Gunners

(I believe they are Austrian) are very effective indeed – anyhow when they did open fire they always managed to do us some damage.

Are you taking the degree course or the Diploma Course or both? In Whichever you are taking I suppose you have been out to the farm & made the aquaintance of Mr Pennington. I wonder if you have met Miss Little who resides chiefly in the Dairy – she is rather a terror.

If you have to join the army you are quite right in going for a corps like the Artists rifles but when you apply for a commission I should try to get into the gunners if I were you. If you possibly can keep clear of the infantry. They are the worst paid arm of the service, they do all the dirty work & they have to footslog the whole time. If I were joining up again I would go for gunners every time.

I must stop now & write some other letters but before doing so I wish you a very happy Christmas & a very bright new Year. I hope you will keep fit & have a very brilliant career at Reading.

With best wishes

        Your affectionate brother
        Jim

E. E. F.

12–12–17

My dear Mother & Father.

We suddenly discovered while talking together that this morning that we left England exactly three years ago to-day. It does seem a long three years doesn't it – we have seen & done so much & such changes have taken place that it seems as if we left home ages ago.

I have been unable to get a letter off since I wrote on Dec. 2nd but I hope to be able to get this one off to-morrow. We were then resting behind the line but as usual our rest did not last long for we came into the line again last Sunday. This time however instead of being up by Jerusalem we are within a few miles of Jaffa, in fact our rest consisted of marching from one part of the line to another by easy stages.

There is no doubt about it campaigning like is is entirely a fine weather job; in wet weather it is absolutely beastly. We had an experience of the wet last weekend which will last us quite a long time. It started to rain on Friday evening and on Saturday morning we had to move into Ramleh. It simply poured all day & by the time we reached our bivouac area we were soaked & the area itself was three inches deep in pure slush. There was nothing for it but to try & erect a shelter of some sort & lie down in the wet. It was bitterly cold & we spent a very unpleasant night. The next day was stormy but we had some fine intervals which absolutely saved us for we were able to dry ourselves a little. I don't quite know why we did not all get ~~rhumatic~~ rheumatic or something of the sort, but ~~we~~ you can seem to stand more ~~an~~ when you are on a show like this than you can at ordinary times.

The weather is awfully cold now – quite like English winter weather. Even in the middle of the day thick serge clothes are none too warm & at night we are glad enough of two or three blankets.

I am awfully glad that Jerusalem has now been captured. We all expected that we should get it before long but the country all round there is so difficult ~~that~~ for fighting over that the Turks might very easily have hung on for quite a long time. The country all round here is very hilly & stony but the hillsides are covered with narcissi which are just coming into flower. It seems funny to be able pick them just like we do primroses or cowslips at home. We have not yet been able to get up any ~~parcels~~ of the parcels which have been sent out to us. Letters are now arriving fairly regularly but so far no parcels at all have come up. We are all looking forward to their arrival for we are very tired of bully & biscuit & if only we could get all that is on the way we should be doing very well indeed. Last week we twice had an issue of white bread & fresh meat both of which were great luxuries, and now that the cold weather has set in we get a very good issue of cheese every day.

We had a bit of a show yesterday, as we were advancing our line to a better position in front. My Coy was the only one of ~~ours~~ ours in it and I had one man wounded but it was not a very difficult operation.

I expect this letter will reach you somewhere about the New Year so I will wish you all a very happy New Year. I sincerely hope that during 1918 you will all enjoy the best of health and that before it ends I shall be able to come home to see you all once more.

I hear that Ron Vallis is on his way up with another draft and I expect he will arrive during the next few days. I hope things are going well in France – we get very little news of any sort & what we do get is mostly rumour. We did hear yesterday that the Germans had been finally turned out of East Africa which I suppose is the last of their colonies.

I am still very fit, in fact except for a sore heel & a cold I have had nothing the matter since the advance commenced.

There is news of another mail this evening – I hope it is true.

With very much love to all

> I remain
> Your affectionate son
> Jim

E. E. F.

🗡19–12–17

My dear other & Father.

Since I last wrote I have received the wrist watch which Father bought for me and I am delighted with it. ʎ A ʎ watch is an absolute necessity at this game and it is a great boon to have one which will keep good time again.

I could not write last Sunday as we were very busy all day road making. We had another show on Saturday & advanced our line to some commanding positions in front so of course we had to spend Sunday consolidating etc. We had quite an easy time on Saturday as we were in reserve this time and the objectives were gained without much trouble so we were not called upon: We had one casualty in my company namely my horse. She was very badly wounded by shrapnel so we she had to be shot. I was awfully sorry to lose her for she was a beautiful animal, – I think I told you about her when I was at Kantara – and besides it is very awkward indeed being without a horse, for you can carry all sorts of things on your saddle.

On Monday evon evening Ron Vallis rejoined us bringing with him a good large draft which we badly needed. He had a very strenuous march up but in cam is looking very fit. We were albte all very pleased to see him for again – it is rather nice to get someone new fresh to talk to as we have exhausted all topics of conversation among ourselves.

Two nights ago we took over a fresh part of the line which has been recently captured and we have to spend our nights consolidating and putting it into a state of defence. We just have to be quiet all day in our dug outs as if we move about & show ourselves we get badly shelled.

It is still very cold and the last two days have been wet again. The rain out here ʎ seems to last for three days at a time so we are rather hoping that it will be fine to-morrow so that we can get everything dry.

To-day has been quite a red letter day for us as we have had a full ration of fresh food, bread, meat, bacon, cheese & jam – the first we have had since the early part of November. You can just imagine how pleased we were to see it come up & how much more so to be able to eat it.

We have great hopes that our other parcels will be up by Christmas & if they do come we shall have a great time

23ʳᵈ

I have had no chance of sending off this letter yet but I have great hopes that a mail will go out to-morrow. We have not been able to move since we took over this part of the line except at night as we held are holding a salient which is shelled from every side during the day. We go in to our dug outs at dawn & have to stay there without moving till dusk. There has

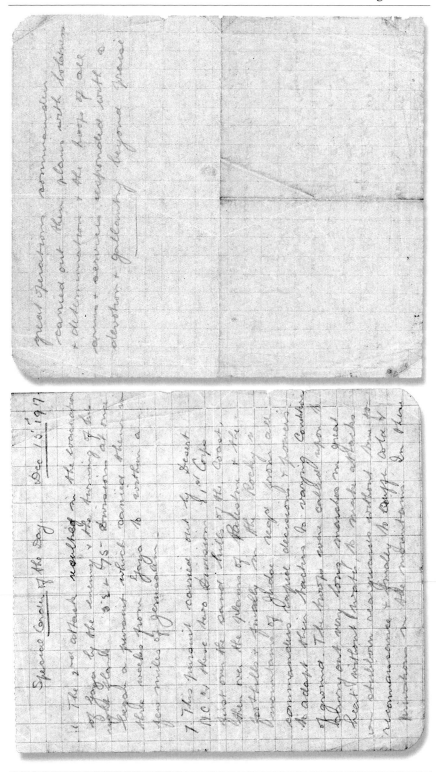

been a big show on our left to-day & the Turks have had to retire so we are able to ~~go~~ move out ⟩ a bit this afternoon.

My ⟩ Christmas letters arrived last night and I had a most enjoyable morning reading them. Please thank Mary, Angus, Margaret, Malcolm & Janet for the Christmas cards – ~~ar~~ they bring quite a Christmas feeling with them. I shall think about you all on Christmas day I can assure you & I do hope you will all spend a very jolly day. I am looking forward ever so much to the time when we shall all be able to get home again & be a jolly party just like we were before the war.

Thank you very much indeed for the battery which you sent: It also has arrived & has been almost invaluable the last few days. The other parcels have not yet come but things are beginning to come up now and I hope they will be here before long.

I think we really must write that book about the adventures of the family along the Bruton Road – I think it would be awfully funny to read. I am sorry that the last adventure had such a disastrous effect on Margaret's nerves but am awfully glad that there was no real damage done.

I had letters from both John & Andrew to-day & both seemed to be quite fit although I fancy John has been rather over-working himself. I am sorry Andrew did not get his leave because I know how ~~much~~ much you look forward to his visits: however he is sure to get it when his Regt. gets a rest again.

I sincerely hope that you are all keeping fit, although I suppose it is rather a job to keep free from colds at this time of the year.

With very best wishes for the New Year & best love to all

> I remain
> Your affectionate son
> Jim

LETTERS FROM THE 2/4TH BN. SOMERSET

LIGHT INFANTRY (P.A.) 1914–19

VOLUME IV: 1918–19

In the meantime the 1/5th and 2/4th Somerset Light Infantry of the 75th Division had been involved in the local operations in Palestine.

The 2/4th Somersets were in Corps Reserve at Surafend on 1st January, moving to new bivouacs, three-quarters of a mile east of the Ramleh-Ludd road, on 7th, thence on 18th to Haditheh. On 19th the Battalion took over the Dathra sub-sector of the front line. Patrol work began immediately, Rentis being visited frequently. The Battalion Diary of the 2/4th says of February that "little of interest occurred during the month," and it was not until 3rd March that anything of importance is recorded. On this date, however, the Battalion advanced from Dathra to a new position, and on the 12th, when a general advance by the 75th Division was carried out, the 2/4th were allotted Eb Diurah as its objective. This attack was successful, A and C Companies forming the firing line, and D Company being in support. By 8.15 a.m. Ed Diurah was seized with the loss of only two N.C.O.'s wounded. At 12 noon the Battalion was relieved, moving back into Brigade Reserve, and on the 18th into Divisional Reserve at Beir Dakleh for the remainder of the month.

Early in April (on 7th) the 75th Division again received orders to advance to the general line Berukin-Kh. Fakhakhir-Sheikh Subih-Rafat-Point 839 (V. 7. a.). The advance was to be carried out by the 232nd Brigade on the right, and the 233rd Brigade on the left, the 234th Brigade pushing forward its right to north of Wadi Bullut to cover the left of the 233rd Brigade. The attack was to take place in two phases.

The Somerset Light Infantry 1914 – 1919

E. E. F.

1–1–18

My dear Mother & Father.

To-day is New Year's Day so & I hope to get a few minutes to myself to write my weekly letter to you as everyone seems to have realized that the occasion demands a few hours respite from work.

I have tried several times lately to write a letter but have had absolutely no chance. Our Christmas was not very cheery, but we made the best of a bad job & did tr our best to have a good time under rather trying circumstances.

On the 23rd we gave the Turks such a bad time that they absolutely cleared off and allowed us to move forward to a new position without resistance. This meant that we ~~hard~~ were hard at work on the 24th and 25th consolidating the new line. We spent the whole of the night of the 24th building sangars, wiring etc & did the same on Christmas night. These had to be built owing to the fact that in that part of the line it is impossible to dig trenches owing to the rocks.

We should not have minded a bit had it been fine, but it started to rain on the 23rd & continued steadily till the 26th. We all got wet through of course on the first day & had to remain wet till the sun came out again to dry us. When I woke on Christmas morning I found that I was lying in 6$''$ of water and we spent the whole day trying to get warm. In spite of the weather we managed quite a good dinner which made us quite cheery. We got a fresh meat ration of Australian Rabbits which made an excellent stew – then we followed this up with plum pudding & cheese. The plum pudding was a great stroke of luck. Col Clutterbuck sent us two from Cairo and the Coys drew for them. I was lucky enough to draw the largest so we had quite a good share each. We also had a ripping cake which Col Waddy sent us from India and we ate this sitting round the fire after we had finished work at night.

The parcel mail was the cause of great excitement. There were quite a lot of parcels from home but not the ones intended for Christmas. Those received should have arrived weeks ago. I was lucky enough to receive two from Port Said containing chocolates etc. I ordered them ages ago & had quite given them up for lost & it was a great stroke of luck getting them on Christmas day.

Our Regt was relieved from the line on Boxing Day and I can assure you we were glad enough to march back especially as it was a nice fine sunny day. It is only when you are absolutely wet through & chilled to the bone that you realize wheat a godsend the sun is.

We are now well back behind the line not far from Ramleh & Ludd. The former is the Arimathea of Biblical times & the latter used to be Lydia. The last few days have been delightfully fine but it is raining hard again to-day. Fortunately we are on sandy soil and it dries very quickly so we shall not get very wet this time.

We are frightfully busy training the new men & making roads. Discipline is inclined to get very lax when we are actually fighting or in the line & we spend most of the time that we are out of it drilling and smartening up generally.

There were lots of rumours about peace at Christmastime, but as none of them have been confirmed I don't suppose they are true, although it looks as if people were beginning to think seriously about it. I don't know what the feeling in England is but all our men think that ~~we~~ the war will soon be over. I hope so at any rate, but cannot see much sign of it yet.

2^(nd) Jan I could not finish yesterday as I was called away for some other job. We ~~h~~ managed to have a very cheery dinner last night to celebrate the occasion. ~~W~~ There is a little Jewish colony about two miles away which can boast of a capital little ~~res~~ hotel. We ordered dinner there, and eight of us walked over and spent a most enjoyable ~~dinner~~ evening. It was nice to be able to sit down to a proper dinner with a nice white cloth & china plates, and although we all got wet through coming back it was well worth the trouble.

We heard a few days ago that the Colonel had sailed for England, and yesterday Major Bunting left us ~~to~~ in order to go home. We now have a new Colonel – a regular ~~X~~ who has just left the staff. Of course he will make for the efficiency of the Battn but we do miss the old Colonel for he used to make the Bttn feel almost like your home and he was such an absolute ~~gentleman~~ "sahib" as they say in India.

I hope you are all keeping fit – we have had no mails since I last wrote but are expecting one every day now.

Has Mother ever received her~~s~~ birthday present? I told Cox & Co to send it off but they have never informed ~~X~~ me that it has been sent and I am rather afraid that the letter ~~has been to~~ was lost. Also has John sent his share for Mary's & Angus's present – if not I will do so at once.

I am as fit as ever and am getting awfully fat, ~~X to~~ chiefly owing I think to the cold climate & the fresh air.

With very much love to you all

> I remain
> > Your affectionate son
> > > Jim

E. E. F.

6–1–18

My dear Mother & Father.

To-day is Sunday, and we are supposed to be having a holiday to celebrate our Christmas day which we spent while up in the line but it has rained so hard the whole day that we have not been able to leave our shelters. However we have bought up some sheep and vegetables and hope to be able to give the men a good feed to-night if only the rain stops long enough for us to get the fires going. Luckily our bivouac is on sand and all the water quickly drains away, otherwise we should be well under water by this time.

We have just heard that £12000 worth of turkeys had to be destroyed down the line as owing to the wet weather at Christmas they went bad before the transport could get them up. I understand that our Christmas pudding ration is still down there, and as this will keep I hope we shall get it up sooner or later.

I had two letters from you dated Nov 28th & Dec 4th and was ever so sorry to hear that Mother had been ill. I do hope she is better now and I hope that her week at Bournemouth will do her lots of good. Andrew is awfully lucky getting 14 days leave, ~~&~~ and I know you must be delighted to have him ~~for~~

8th Jan

I had to stop writing on Sunday owing to the fact that my bivouac was completely flooded out, and I could not continue yesterday as we were moving to another bivouac area. We have been in luck's way the last two or three days for the ration carts brought us another English mail this morning and I received Janet's letter dated Dec 11th.

I had a good laugh over the picture which Father described of Janet & he making brawn – I expect the result was absolute perfection There was great excitement yesterday over a circular which came from G.H.Q. about home leave. One C.O. from every Brigade is going to be allowed to go home on leave shortly also two officers from each Bttn may send in their application, but as these latter will only be granted under very exceptional circumstances I am afraid I have no chance as the married officers can always raise a much better case than the single ones. However now that leave has been opened again I may get a chance next time.

I was awfully sorry to hear ~~about~~ that Wilfred Barber had been killed & his brother wounded & I can quite imagine that his parents were dreadfully upset.

How is little Duff now? I do hope that he is better by this time. I expect he was awfully pleased to have Andrew home again.

~~&~~ There are some things ~~on this~~ about war which are awfully pleasing in spite of all that is beastly. I have just experienced one of the pleasing things & it has bucked me up quite a lot. Some of my wounded NCO[s] & men have begun to return and it is ~~most~~ frightfully pleasing to see how ~~&~~ delighted they are to see one again. Nearly all of them bring me back chocolate or something of the sort from the base and one Sergt carried a ~~&~~ huge box on his back the whole way up ~~up~~ although he had to throw away some of his kit to do it. They are splendid fellows all of them and their confidence in one's ability to lead them is perfectly extraordinary.

The wet cold weather still continues but it is sunny and warm to-day and after all one fine day makes up for a good many wet ones.

Our rations the last few days have been awfully good – very different from what they were a week or two ago. You must think ~~& do~~ that I ~~am~~

always write about food: but food, ~~and~~ peace & home leave are about the only things we talk about up here.

I enclose a few photographs which I took at Kantara – I have only just had a chance to get them developed, but they have come out quite well.

I do̧ hope that Mother & Duff are quite fit now and that all the others are keeping fit.

With very much love to all

> Your affectionate son
> Jim

E. E. F.

13–1–18

My dear Mother & Father.

I wrote my last letter last Wednesday and it is only Sunday to-day so I really have very little to write about, but as we shall probably be moving back to the line during the next few days, ~~I thought~~ and shall therefore be very busy I thought I would just get off a few lines at once. I received Janet's letter dated Dec 11th ᴋ a day or two ago & I rather expect another one from home to-night as one from Uncle will dated 14th Dec arrived last night.

The news of the capture of Jerusalem seems to have caused some excitement in England. We were not "in at the Death" although untill we were relieved our Battn was the nearest one to it. I will try and write out an exact account of our share in the campaign one day as I think it will interest you.

I enclose an extract from the Special Order of the Day which deals with the work of our Division & also a copy of the Divisional Order which thanks us for our efforts as I thought you might like to read them both.

Ron Vallis went down the line to-day for his Lewis Gun course at El Arish after which he will be able to have ᴀ seven days leave in Cario – lucky man.

I hope Janet & Mary enjoyed their visit to Frome – Ron says that their cheery visits do Uncle & Aunt no end of good. Uncle Will says that Hugh McKenow is getting married very shortly. He is rather young for the effort isn't he? Makes one feel quite ancient.

I have just got hold of a new horse to replace the one which was killed. She has been with us ever since we left Kantara but up to the present no-one has ridden her as she was supposed to be quite ~~unridable~~ unrideable. My groom took her in hand a week or two ago & she is greatly improved. I rode her for the first time the day before yesterday & she gave me no end of a toss but I mean to stick to her and I shall be ready for her next time.

We have had a very wet cold day to-day, rain, sleet & hail but it seems clearer now & I hope it will be finer to-morrow I was ever so glad to hear that Mother & Duff were better & I hope that they will both continue to get quite fit again very quickly.

Hoping all the others are quite well
With much love to all

> your affectionate son
> Jim

E. E. F.

31–1–18

My dear Mother & Father.

You will be surprised to hear that I am now in Cairo thoroughly enjoying 10 days leave. It came as quite a surprise for the day before I left the Regt. I was told that my application for leave had been refused for the second time. I was rather disappointed I must admit for it seemed as if everyone could get away except about three of us who had been right through in all the fighting. Next morning at five o'clock I telephoned the "all clear" to the Adjutant as usual and I was just about to hang up the receiver when he said that I could go off on leave at once and take a party of 15 men with me. It did not take us long to get ready I can assure you, & I have rarely in my life felt so happy as I did as I marched down the line, with thoughts of a bath & clean sheets & clothes, and good food. The men all felt the same too, so we were a very cheery party. We had quite a long march to the rail head but it only took us one night to get down to Kantara. We travelled at night so could not see the country, but I hope to see something of it when we go up again as it will be interesting to see the changes which took place have taken place since we first marched up.

We got to Kantara at 5 A.M. and at once dashed off to the Dump to get some clean kit out of our boxes and then crossed the canal and caught the Cairo train. Kantara is perfectly amazing – it has grown enormously since we left it (& it was big enough then). It is now quite a city built almost entirely of tents.

A thing which strikes one most forcibly on coming down the line is the number of men who have comparatively safe & easy jobs at the base. I should think there were quite three men behind the line for everyone one in it & yet they are not nearly so cheery as the men in the line who have all the fighting to do and all the hardships to put up with.

The journey from Kantara to Cairo was very pleasant as the trains are very comfortable indeed. There was a tremendous crowd of us and it was difficult to find a seat but none of us would have minded if we had been obliged to stand the whole time.

On arrival at Cairo I at once went to Shepherds Hotel and got a room & then a bath. Think of the luxury of it – a real hot bath & the first for four months. I soaked for about an hour and during that time I got rid of inches of dirt.

At first I thought I should have rather a dull time for I did not know a sole in the whole place and one felt most frightfully lonely, but I discovered that Ron Vallis & Bartlett were staying ʰ in another hotel, so I at once rushed off and found them out & since then we have had a top hole time.

I think we have almost seen all the sights now for we have been going steadily ⱦ during the last three days. Everything is frightfully interesting but I was a bit disappointed with the pyramids, chiefly I think because we have seen so many pictures of them that there is nothing new when you see them in reality. I was fascinated by the Sphinx – there is something frightfully impressive about his face and when you think of the thousands of years during which he has sat there and looked out upon mankind with the same expression on his face it makes you feel very small & insignificant. If only he could talk he could tell some wonderful stories.

Cairo is a very fine city indeed & very different to what I imagined. I thought it would be something like all Eastern towns – a few European streets & shops mixed up with native ones and all the rest a huge bazaar. Instead of this it is a typical Continental town well laid ~~with~~ out & quite clean & modern. There are countless cafe's & eating houses ~~where the people~~ outside of which the people sit & talk & drink just like they do on the Continent I am told. We visited the Zoo yesterday afternoon & this morning had a look at the Citadel both of which were very interesting. We have also been down round the bazaars where they sell most beautiful embroidery, carpets, & gold & silver ornaments, but one really ~~wnts~~ wants lots of money if you start buying all that sort of thing.

Cairo is the most expensive place I have ever been in: everything is a terribly high price and money disappears like wildfire. It may not be so bad in peace time; I suppose things are expensive everywhere now.

I do enjoy sleeping in a bed again – untill previous to coming here I had not slept with my clothes off since last October so you can imagine how nice it is to be able to undress and get into a nice soft bed.

We have had no letters from home for a long time, but I think there will be some waiting for us when we get back to the Regt again and we shall be pleased enough to see if they are there.

Bartlett & Ron have to go back to-morrow but I shall have a couple of days left and I expect I shall find plenty to do getting some things which I want to take back with me.

I hope Mother is better and all the others are quite well

With very much love to all

Your affectionate son

Jim

E. E. F.

6–2–18

My dear Mother & Father.

My leave is over & I am now on my way back to the Bttn; of course one never wants to come away when he is having a good time but all good things come to an end and I feel much better in every way for the change. I spent lots of money, for Cairo is frightfully expensive, but in a job like this where it is all work & no play money spent on pleasure when you get a chance is never wasted. I feel much more cheery than when I went down, and that is a great thing for I always find that you must be cheery yourself if you want to keep the men in good form.

We reached railhead yesterday afternoon and went to Ludd to be dis-infected to-day. This is done to everyone who goes up or down the line in order to prevent the spread of disease. After that we came to the rest camp at Ramleh where we shall sleep to-night. I hope we shall be able to go on up to the line to-morrow morning. While I was at Cairo I met two Cary people both of whom recognized me, ~~before~~ I although I should not ~~of~~ have known either of them had they not spoken to me,

The first was a man called Powell who in peace time is in the Bath City police. He said that he remembered me as a little boy when I used to go to Sexeys. The second was Jack Hunt who used to live down by the Horse pond. He has improved wonderfully and is now a very smart little fellow. He speaks awfully well and looks ever so fit & I forget what Regt. he said he was in. I expect his people would like to know that I have seen him. I was delighted to see both of them for it made one feel much more at home.

There were lots of fellows from other Regts. down there on leave and it was awfully interesting to hear the part they all played in the last show; they all spoke awfully well of us.

7th Feb. I was not allowed to go on up to-day as there are some more men on the way up for us & I have to wait & take them up. I am not a bit sorry either for it has been raining in torents the whole day and had I set out t̶o̶ from here I should have been soaked, whereas I am now in a nice dry tent.

There is one r̶e̶a̶s̶o̶n̶ thing I am very anxious to get back for & that is to get letters again for I am sure there must be quite a lot up there for me as I have not had any for about a month.

I had a very interesting journey up the line as I was able to have a look at all the places which we took when we advanced for the first time. The changes which have taken place since then are perfectly amazing. I was awfully struck by one place in particular; when we first occupied it we marched in at night right on the heels of the Turks. and It was then nothing more than a collection of huts but now there is a large railway station there and stack upon stack of supplies etc. also a huge camp of white tents.

The country is very beautiful now indeed now. The fields have all been cultivated and the green corn is coming up everywhere. The country which was bare & brown when we came up first is now covered with grass, and as we have given the natives every encouragement they have brought back their cattle & sheep which are to be seen everywhere now. The plantations of almond trees are all in blossom and they look very beautiful indeed. They make one think of Somerset when the apple trees are in blossom.

I hear that Royal has gone off to England at last. He has been expecting to go for a long time – I just missed seeing him for he was coming down as I was going up & we must have crossed in the train.

There are still very persistent rumours that our Division is to be sent back to England but I am afraid they are too good to be true.

How is Andrew getting on? – I have not heard from him for a long time
I hope you are all keeping fit
With very much love to all

        Your affectionate son
        Jim

E. E. F.

10–2–18

My dear Mother & Father

I arrived back in the line the day before yesterday after a very tiring journey. It has rained hard for the last five days with the result that the plain between Ramleh and the hills is almost unpassable and all the little mullahs and ditches are now absolute torents. We had to tramp through this for about eight miles & when we had finished we were covered in mud from head to foot.

When I got here there was no end of a treat awaiting me in the shape of four English Mails – we have now had all our letters up to the beginning of January. I am delighted to hear that Mother & Duffy are both better and also that Mother is taking things easily and staying in bed to breakfast. I hope she will soon be quite strong again. Your letters are all awfully topping & I simply love reading them – they buck one up no end when things seem a bit dull.

Nothing came of ~~my~~ the recommendation which was sent up for me & I hardly expected anything myself, but the men are all awfully sick about it. It was quite a small incident but they were rather pleased about it. Since you ask I will tell you what happened. We were advancing across the open towards the Turkish position and when we got to within about 250 yards we got into a ditch which gave us good cover. It was no good staying there so I got together a party of 12 & tried to take them on. The Turks had marked us down however & as soon as we got up to move they got three machine guns on to us & fairly pelted us with bullets. ~~So~~ We dropped down at once & tried to hang on, the men using their packs as head cover. Six men were knocked out at once two being killed outright – the two men on either side of me were hit & it was only good fortune which saved me. I saw one of my sergts at the other end of the line get badly hit in the stomach & as he ~~went~~ rolled over he got two more bullets in the wrist one of which cut an artery. As he was obviously bleeding to death I could not let him lie there without doing anything to help him so I just went along & bandaged him up more or less & then carried him in to the ditch where he was under cover. After that the Turks it made it so hot for us that we all had to get back under cover & wait till their flank was turned. From what I have heard these M.C.s etc are just put into a hat & drawn for out of the names which are sent in so it is more or less luck whether you get one or not. I have managed to secure the confidence of my men & that is the great thing after all when you have to go into action with them. I have found that Somerset men are great fighters as long as you keep in front & show them where to go – they don't like to be driven on from the rear.

What are the chances of peace now? I think the war will be over this year but there is going to be some terrible fighting in France before it comes – however I think we shall beat them this time.

My servant produced a sugar card yesterday which had been sent out for him to see – we were all rather interested in it as none of us had seen one before.

I received the parcel of socks & books this week for which thank you all very much indeed. The socks are a great boon & the books will be a real pleasure to read. I was delighted with Margaret's photograph – of course she has altered during the last three years but she is now an awfully pretty little girl. Please thank her ever so much for it. I shall write to her in a day or two.

I forget to tell you that I met Whitley while he I was in Cairo & had tea with him one afternoon. He was wounded in the knee & I doubt if he will be fit for service for a long time. His wound is not a bit serious but anything the matter with a knee is always a fat long job isn't it? He is a very cheery old bird & I thoroughly enjoyed the time I spent with him.

Royal set out for England a few days ago feeling very pleased with life. I had the bad luck to just miss him for he was going down the line as I was going up & of course we must have passed each other. I expect he will come & see you sometime or other.

Andrew was very lucky to be at home when his Regt was so badly cut up, but I am ever so glad he was not there. I am afraid his he is having a bad time out there now that the weather is so cold.

I enclose a few photographs which I took in Cairo & also a few which my Coy Sergt Major took.

With very much love to you all & hoping you are are all keeping fit

      I remain
          Your affectionate son
          Jim

E. E. F.

18–2–18

My dear Mother & Father

Mother's letter dated 15th Jan arrived two days ago & I was delighted to hear that she is so much better & and able to get out again. I do hope she will take the greatest care if herself now so so that she won't get ill again.

We are all having a very quiet day to-day as the whole of my company including myself was inoculated against cholera yesterday. When we first went out to India there used to be awful trouble over inoculation – 50% of the men used to refuse to be done. It is very different now however – the whole of the company was done yesterday without an objection of any sort, so the men evidently realize that is is a good thing. Cholera inoculation is a very mild one, but I think we are going to be done again for enteric next week and that is a real beast. It usually lays us out completely for about two days.

I have been living all alone for the last five days, all my officers being away on courses or leave. The last survivor went down to Cairo on

Wednesday to join the R.F.C. Most of the other companies are ~~the~~ also very short just at present. Ron Vallis is ~~temporably~~ temporarily commanding "A" Coy during the absence of Flower who is away on a course – I wish I could get him back again in my Coy.

When we came in ~~from~~ at "stand down" this ~~this~~ morning we had to dash for cover among the rocks as we found that we were being shelled by our own guns. Our anti-aircraft guns were shooting at some Turkish aeroplanes & some of the shells instead of bursting in the air came right down & burst in our bivouac area. Our airmen are simply splendid in these days. A few days ago one of ours attacked six ~~of~~ Turkish ones & drove them all off – only yesterday we saw one of ours have a go at five of the enemy's. We thought he was down once for he suddenly did a nose dive down to within about 500 yards of the ground – however he righted himself and went for them again.

We have had a very fine week and it has been quite hot during the middle of the day but I think we are in for some more wet weather. The clouds have been banking up against the hills all day to-day & I should not be a bit surprised if it rained to-night or to-morrow. We are much better prepared for rain than we were say at Christmas time. I, as a Coy Commander have been issued with a tent and each man now has a bivouac sheet & a great coat. It is awfully nice having a tent in which I can stand up without knocking down the whole show & in which lay my things with being afraid that I shall come in one day & find them all wet through.

I am very sorry indeed that Mother did not get her birthday present – the letter I wrote to Cox & Co must have been lost. I will send it this time by postal order together £1 for Margaret. I cannot send it off this week as I have no money here but I shall be able to get some in a day or two & then I will send it ~~to you~~ again. I am ever so sorry that Mother has had to wait so long but I will send it as soon as I possibly can.

Janet must be having a very busy time now that she has the office all to herself but still it will all help to win the war. I think the end now depends almost entirely on the people in England. The men out here at anyrate, can manage it, & I am sure they can in France, if only these munition workers & so on at home can stick to it for these next few months. I have just taken on a small sporting bet with my Sergt Major that the war will not last four years & I think I shall win – what do you all think about it

My cheese has not yet turned up and I am afraid it must be lost – still it may come yet as things turn up in a most remarkable way out here.

I was very sorry to hear that Grandma Mullins was ill when you last wrote & I sincerely hope that it is nothing serious.

I can't think of anything else to write about now so will "continue in our next."

I hope you are all as fit as I am, for if so there is nothing much the matter as I am in tip top condition.

With best love to all

I remain

Your affectionate son

Jim

My dear Mother & Father.

I received Janet's letter dated Jan 22nd a few days ago and I was awfully sorry to hear that you had received no letters from me for five weeks. I can assure you that I write every week with the utmost regularity so the letters should arrive regularly. As a matter of fact Ron's people and everyone to whom the men write are complaining of the same thing so I suppose they are all being held up somewhere. The letters which we wrote between the 15th & 24th Jan have been sunk also the ones written by you about the same time so that one mail at anyrate will never turn up.

Two days ago I received a ripping parcel from you containing shortbread, candles, battery, chocolate & thirst quenchers from Duff all of which arrived in excellent condition. Thank you ever so much for it – I love getting your parcels and the things you send are just what I want and are no end of a treat. Are you perfectly sure that the things you send out can all be spared for I know you are awfully hard up for food at home just now? After all we are getting very good rations now, that and the railway has started to bring up canteen stores so that we are quite well off. I do hope that you don't have to stint yourselves to in order to send me things. You would be awfully amused to if you could see us when the parcels arrive – we behave just like a lot of school boys. All o The fortunate person who receives one is soon surrounded by everyone we else in the mess all & everyone speculates as to the contents – great excitement prevails I can assure you.

After the more or less private things have been removed the eatables become common property to be shared by all the mess. Soon the signallers come to say that someone at headquarters or in one of the other companies wishes to speak. If you could listen you would hear a conversation something like this over the telephone.

"Hear you had a parcel today!"   Yes

"Anything good?"   Rather top hole

"Would you like me to come up to tea to-day?"

As a result of a conversation of this sort ~~this~~ which took place this morning I am going down to tea with Ron this afternoon as he is all alone in his Company just now.

You will understand this better when I explain how we live up here. Each company in the line has its own headquarters & the officers of each company \ mess together. About half a mile to the rear is Battn Headquarters which of course has its own mess. All the companies are ~~lik~~ linked up to each other & to Battn headquarters by telephone & the latter is worked by the Coy signallers who always live very near the Coy Commander's bivouac. They are usually very irresponsible people and in time become extraordinarily good at repartee as they spend the greater part of their time in trying to be funny at the expense of the signallers of some other company. This best time for this kind of amusement is of course at night when there are not many messages to be sent or received & it causes considerable annoyance to the Coy Commander who is trying to sleep quite close by. However it is rather a pity to stop them for they are usually a very cheery crowd and one wants people to be as cheery as possible at this game.

We have had some very wet cold weather this week and I am afraid there is more to come, but after this spell I don't think we shall get much more.

I am frightfully pleased that I am now on quite good terms with the C.O. Do you remember that I told you when he first came that he was rather a trial? He was absolutely unreasonable at first but as far as I am concerned personally the difficulty has now been overcome. He is awfully pleasant to me now and is is very pleased indeed with the work of my company. He told me one day that I could tell my men that a piece of work we had just finished was the finest thing of its kind he had ever seen. He said it was an absolute model. Of course we were ever so pleased for he is a specialist on defences and therefore is well qualified to give such an opinion.

I am going down to Kantara to-morrow to settle up some company accounts so I shall get a little change I shall try to go to Port Said while I am there to have a look at my kit & also to see Coney who is there on some sort of duty.

Janet must be awfully busy now that she has the office all to herself but I am very glad indeed that she is able to do it.

I expect Mother finds it very quiet during the daytime while everyone is at school. Fancy our home ever being quiet – it shows that the war has been going a long time and that we are all getting older.

I enclose a couple of photograph which were given to me a day or two ago – I think they will interest you.

Please thank little Duff for his present – It is awfully kind of him to spend his pocket money on me & I do appreciate the little fellow's kindness ever so much. When you next see the Shepton Montague people will you please give them my love & tell them that I have not forgotten them but I really have not had time to write. for I have not sent them a line for ages but I hope to do so before very long.

I wonder if Andrew will come out here – I should like to see him again and I think it quite possible that his Regt. will come to this part of the world unless they go back to India. When I last saw him at Barrackpore we had an awfully good time together.

Royal left me his dog when he went home – it is the same one as he had in India & which I kept for him when he I was at Barrackpore so the old fellow knew me quite well. He missed Royal a bit at first but he is now quite happy with me now. He always shares my bed with me at night and no-one dare come near my tent while he is in it.

John seems to be in very good form – his last letter was full of new schemes for developing his district so he seems to still be very keen on his work.

I hope the letters have all turned up by now – will you ask Janet to let me know if she has yet received her birthday present.

I am hoping that the postal orders for Mother's & Margaret's presents will be up here to-morrow & if they do arrive I will send them off at once.

With very much love to all & very many thanks for the parcel

> I remain
> Your affectionate son
> Jim

E. E. F.

3–3–18

My dear Mother & Father.

I said last week that I was enclosing some photographs but I am awfully sorry that I forgot to put them in – however I will try & remember them this week. I went down to Kantara last Monday night to settle up some Company accounts & had two days down there. The journey down is quite easy nowadays. You get into the train at Railhead, and put your bed out & go to sleep. At 5 A.M. you wake up to find yourself at Kantara. I managed to get my work done the same day as I arrived there, so the next day I went into Port Said & spent a very pleasant time with Coney. I then caught the midnight train back to railhead & reached the Regt in the afternoon. It was a very brief peep at civilization but it made quite a nice change & I thoroughly enjoyed myself during the few hours I spent at Port Said.

Yesterday morning a wire arrived from Baghdad asking if I could be spared to take up Civil work in Mesopotamia – re a job like the one John has, I think he must have obtained it for me.

Of course I was full of hope, that I should be allowed to go & you can imagine how disappointed I was when the C.O. told me that he had already replied that he could not spare me. I used every argument I could think of to get him to alter his decision but it was no good. – he said that His argument was that the war must be won & that he could not spare a Coy Commander just now. I pointed out that if I did not get the job someone else would & that as I had joined up in 1914 I had a prior claim for anything of that sort, but it was no good. There is no doubt about at all if you want to get good jobs in the army you must either be very inefficient or else make a nuisance of yourself, in either of these cases your Regt gets rid of you on the first opportunity. If you do your best & make things go well you are always greeted by the remark – you cannot be spared.

My men all cheered like anything when they heard that I was not going, for there is another advance coming off in a few days time & they were afraid that I should not be coming with them.

I think we shall have made a move forward before I write again but it will not be a very serious job & I don't think we shall get much opposition. I don't think we are going right on for a bit.

These hills are awfully difficult to move about in as it is awfully difficult to get the transport up – as it we can only use mules & camels.

The capture of Jericho was awfully good work, for the country on that side is much more difficult than it is here, and the weather was awfully bad at the time of the show. It will make our right flank very secure.

I hope you have received some of our letters by this time. We have not had any from you for over three weeks, but I received the Western Gazette which was sent off on Feb 4th this morning so I hope the letters will soon follow. One of your letters I know was sunk but I think the others will probably turn up later on.

Have you heard any more about Andrew coming out here – it would be awfully funny if we were to met again in this part of the world.

It will be Margaret's birthday to-morrow & I do hope she will have a good time. I sent off her present & also Mother's while I was at Kantara.

Father must be awfully busy nowadays with the business & the Food Control meetings & also in addition the Agricultural Wages Com Board. I was ever so pleased to hear of his nomination for the latter for it must be a great compliment especially as he was nominated by Mr Hobhouse.

I am still very fit indeed – one can hardly be otherwise in such delightful weather as we have had for the last three days.

I will try & write next week as usual but if by any chance we are moving & I can't manage to get a letter off you must not worry. I will write on the very first opportunity & after all as long as you don't hear you will know that I am perfectly safe for you will get a wire at once if there is anything wrong.

I hope you are all keeping well
With much love to all

> Your affectionate son
> Jim

E. E. F.

9th March 1918

My dear Mother & Father.

I have very little to write about this week but as we are having a very quiet day I thought I would take the opportunity of getting off a letter.

During the early part of the week we were very busy getting ready to move forward. All our surplus kit had to be dumped again and sent back down the line but so far we have been allowed to keep our valises and bivouac sheets, which means that we can carry 30 lbs of kit in addition to our packs & can also have some shelter from the weather, so we are quite well off this time. It is an awful job to decide exactly what kit to keep and what to send back. At first it seems as if you want everything you have, but when you start to sort it out you can usually cut it down fairly satisfactorily. The great trouble is that the days are getting very hot again while the nights are still cold so that it is rather difficult to know just what sort of kit to carry. Of course if we start to make another big advance I suppose the valises will have to be sent back.

We made our first move forward at dawn on Thursday morning – there was no opposition as the Turks retired when we advanced. Just at present we are kept busy with patrols and making roads.

We are back on our old bully & biscuit ration again but we are not nearly so badly off as we were during the last advance for each company has been issued with a donkey for the purpose of carrying th stores for the officers mess. It is an awfully good idea for one we can bring along quite a lot of extras on him.

The flowers on these little hills are simply marvellous in fact the whole country is just like one big garden. There are now white & purple anemonies as well as the scarlet ones also phlox, rock roses, orchids, tulips, cornflowers, cyclamens and lots of others. I found some bee orchids yesterday and they were so wonderfully made that I really thought they were real bees.

When we took up our new position I went across to see the Regt on my left as usual & one of the first officers I met was a fellow who used to live in the same corridor as myself at Wantage Hall. He has only just come out from England so I had lots to talk to him about.

I heard from Ray Lockyer two days ago. He is in Cairo at at present & wrote to askm me to look him up next time I get down there.

We have had no a letters this week but & I hope you have now received some from me. Ron's people had received one from him when they last wrote so I expect you had one at the same time.

I was awfully sorry to hear that mother was unwell again for I hoped that she was getting quite fit & strong, but I am glad Duff's cold is getting better

So the old pony has gone at last has he? I think it is about time for the old fellow was getting somewhat the worse for wear when I left home, and the trap was certainly almost done for. However both did us very well indeed and they t have both taken part in a good many of our adventures along the old Bruton Road. Father seems to be terribly busy in these days – I hope he won't work too hard and get ill again.

I am afraid I can't raise any more news now
so with very much love to you all

I remain
Your affectionate son
Jim

E. E. F.

14 15–3–18

My dear Mother & Father

This week I have to report that we have made another advance which was successfully carried out, captured all our objectives and Consolidated the positions gained. But what to me is far more important is the fact that the I have received two weeks mails from home containing letters from you both & also from Janet. The last one is dated Feb 5 15th.

The advance took place last Tuesday and we moved forward about three or four miles. Our share was not a very big one but we carried it out quite successfully & the General was quite pleased with us. After it was over we went into Brigade Reserve and were able to sleep with our boots off for the first time for eight weeks.

I was very pleased when I received Janet's letter to see the cutting from the gazette showing an that I have been at last given the substantive rank of Capt. We Territorials have been treated awfully unfairly all the way through and have our promotions have been practically at a standstill for ages so it is rather nice to see them going on again. I shall now be able to keep my rank & pay if I have the bad luck to be wounded or to go sick.

March 17ᵗʰ. The Colonel has just returned from Ramleh where he went to be invested with the D.S.O. by the Duke of Connaught. He was away a couple of days during which time I was in command of the Battn so that I can now say that I commanded a Bttn before I was 22.

I shall be 22 to-morrow but it does not seem a year ago that we celebrated my 21ˢᵗ birthday in the mess at Dinapore, although a good deal has happened since then & we have all been through good times & bad. I hope all the bad times will be over by this time next year and that we shall all be home again.

I am very glad indeed that Mother is better again & that her servant is a success. She will be able to get about quite a lot now that you have a new pony and trap. I am sure you must find the good of the little farm in these days of food scarcity – it is extraordinary the amount which can be produced from such a small piece of ground.

We have had a terribly wet day to-day and everyone is wet through and the men are celebrating the fact that it is Sunday evening by singing hymns round the fires. It was far too wet to have a service this morning but the padre has just held a sort one this evening. It was a picturesque little scene. We all sat ~~down on the~~ round the Padre up on the hill side under the olive ~~gro~~ trees and as it was just getting dark as he finished his sermon he very appropriately chose "Abide with me" for his last hymn. I couldn't help comparing it to those peaceful Sunday evenings at home when we used to ~~goo~~ off to chapel & then as a great treat were allowed to stay up for supper.

Things don't seem quite so hopeful now as they did a month or two ago do they? The Germans have forced Russia & Rumania to sign peace and it looks as if they have got the best of it so far. I suppose we shall win in the end but I am afraid the end is rather a long way off.

I am very glad Janet received her present – I will send Mary & Angus 10/- each to make their present up as soon as I can get some P. O.ˢ·

I am glad to hear that Grandma Mackie still ~~keeps fit, but I am very~~ sorry indeed that Grandma Mullins keeps so unwell. I hope she will be better when the warm weather comes along .

I am afraid Andrew has been getting a rough time but still he is quite safe so far & that after all ~~is~~ is the great thing.

I hope you are all now quite fit – I still keep very fat & well.

With the very best love to you all

> I remain
> Your affectionate son
> Jim

E. E. F.

25–3–18

My dear Mother & Father.

We had a very strenuous week last week doing intensive training, and we had to spend the greater part of each day scrambling up & down the hillside, the result being that we got very fit & considerably increased our appetites (not that they were by any means small before).

I received a letter ~~you~~ from you about a week ago dated Feb 20th & two days ago I heard from Andrew who ~~now~~ is now in this country too, so I sent him your letter to read as I did not know how long he had been on the way. I am delighted that he has come out here & I have great hopes that we shall meet each other before long. It will be ~~fu~~ topping to see him again, because he will be able to tell me about all of you having seen you so recently. Did he get leave before he left France? I last saw him at Barrackpore just before he left Wellington & we then had a great time together.

I am now down in Ludd getting my company fumigated. We marched down yesterday, the fumigation was done to-day and we shall go back Friday to-morrow. I think a good deal of livestock was killed during the process for everyone gets very very dirty up the line. The men only have the kit they stand up in and are never able to bath or get a change so it is impossible to keep clean. I have been awfully lucky in this respect – I have not had a single crawler so far.

When we started yesterday it was beautifully fine but when we got about half way it started to rain in torrents and on reaching our destination we had to pitch our bivouacs in an absolute quagmire. However we have had to do it before and we all got fixed up eventually but during the night it rained so hard that we all got flooded out and we had to finish the night on our feet. It has been very stormy all day to-day but I hope it will be fine to-morrow for we have a very long march in front of us.

I was very interested to hear about the Govt. taking over the cheese business & I hope Father will do well out of it. I should think the Govt. would be only to glad to get his services.

It was very good indeed of Major Bunting to write to you. He left us soon after the New Year and I don't suppose he will ever come back. They have no ~~yu~~ use for old men in these days. Only the young & fit can stand the sort of fighting we do out here – it is a case of the survival of the fittest.

I dined at Brigade Headquarters with the General the night before I came down here & had quite a good evening. The General is awfully nice t when one goes to visit him & it is a treat to have a good dinner nicely laid out.

The food is no better than to our's but is is nicely served & you sit down to a table with a white cloth on it & have a clean plate for each course – just the little things make all the difference.

We have a very pleasant bivouac area up the line now; the only drawback is that the Turks can just reach us with their shells & they occasionally amuse themselves by dropping over a few. Just by the our area one of our subalterns has discovered the remains of an old Roman temple. He was digging a hole for some reason or other and came across a beautiful mosaic pavement which he carefully cleared. it is a wonderful bit of work & the colouring sand is beautifully preserved. There are several of other old temples in the district some of them having been built by the Knights of St. John.

I hope Grandma Mullins is better now & th I also hope that Mother is now fit & strong.

With very much love to you all

       I remain
            Your affectionate son
            Jim

E. E. F.

31ˢᵗ March 1918

My dear Mother & Father.

Janet's letter dated March 5ᵗʰ arrived last evening and I was sorry to hear that the letters I wrote thanking you for your parcels had been sunk. I

My Sergt. Major and two others sitting on the top of a tomb, which they excavated. The stone they are sitting on closed the entrance

A working party building a sangar

received all the parcels sent off by you except the cheese, which I am afraid is absolutely lost, and they were all in good condition. I am now looking forward to the one you sent for my birthday ~~it~~ and I think it will arrive at a time when we shall greatly appreciate the contents for we are moving off again in a very few days on a new show & that means bully beef & biscuit.

We have had a quiet week on the whole, although we have been very busy training the men & so on, but we have had our nights in bed, which of course is the great advantage of being in reserve.

I am glad you went up to Bath & saw Major Bunting. I heard from him last night & he said he was awfully pleased to have had the opportunity of seeing you. I expect he told you all about what we have been doing, how we live and so on but I should not believe quite all he told you for he usually ~~exagera~~ exaggerates a good deal. ~~He is~~ I am sorry in very many ways that he has left us for he was a very kind old fellow and was deeply interested in all of us and ~~them~~ Regt always had a very homely feeling when he & the old Col were there but of course as far as fighting is concerned we are much better off with the new Colonel, with whom by the way I get on very well indeed now.

A good many fellows went off to courses yesterday & they will rejoin us later on; ~~but to show~~ this leaves myself the signalling officer & the quartermasters the sole survivors of the officers who started off from Gaza on the last show. This will give you some idea of the changes which take place in a Bttn on Service.

I expect Grandma was delighted to have Uncle Andrew & Agnes home

The Colonel

The arrival of the day's water supply

Campbell, one of my subalterns – has now gone to the RFC

Fortt, Clutterbuck (Colonel), Myself (J.R.M.)

at the same time and I am delighted to hear that Agnes is so much better. I suppose she will have to be very careful for sometime yet won't she.

It is Easter Sunday to-day & I hoped that my men would have had a holiday to enable them to go to service but late last night I received orders to send my company out on a working party to push on with the road. It is very bad luck on them for they have worked splendidly lately & they like to get a holiday & special days like this. It is wonderful how they keep so cheery all the time for they get a pretty rough te time on the whole.

We are all very pleased that the Germans have at last started their great offensive for it will bring the end of the war a great deal nearer. Nothing except breaking the line is any good to them now & I don't think they will ever do manage that. If they don't break it they are beaten & I believe the German people realize this. I think this will be their last effort & a very costly one too.

I have not heard from Andrew during the last few days but I suppose he is still at Kantara although I should not be surprised to hear that his Regt was coming up the line any day.

We are just being issued with our Summer clothing, khaki drill & topees & our helmets for the weather is getting very hot indeed. I am afraid we shall not find the country so healthy as the hot weather comes on for there is a good deal of malaria & fever generally out here during the hot weather.

I am very glad that you had your photographs taken in Bath & I am looking forward to seeing the result. I hope Margaret has got rid of her cold and is able to go to school again. Please thank her very much indeed for her letter.

I still keep very fit indeed & shall have to take a bigger size in clothes if I get much fatter. I sure this will please Ted.

I enclose a few photographs which I don't think you have seen.

With very much love to you all

I remain

Your affectionate son

Jim

The Spirit of Jellalabad Day

Berukin and El Kefr, and the 233rd Brigade Rafat: in the second, the 232nd and 233rd Brigades were to secure the line Kh. Fakhakhir-Sheikh Subih-Arara when Berukin and Kefr had been captured.

In phase one of the 232nd Brigade attack the 2/3rd Gurkhas were to capture El Lefr and the 2/4th Somersets Berukin: in phase two the 2/3rd Gurkhas were to advance and occupy the general line S. 20. c. 5.4. -S. 27. a. 5.5. and hold the Wadi Lehham; the 1/5th Devons were to advance and occupy the line S. 27. a. 6.5. -Kh. Fakhakhir; the 2/4th Somersets and 2/5th Hants were to be in Brigade reserve, but prepared to move as the situation demanded.

Meanwhile the 232nd had also made splendid progress. It will be remembered that the objective of the 2/4th Somersets (Lieut-Colonel E. B. Powell) was Berukin. At 4.30 a.m. on 9th the Battalion, less C Company, moved down on to the ridge south of Wadi Ballut. At 5.14 a.m. D and B Companies advanced over the ridge to attack Tin Hat Hill. For the first 250 yards of the advance the enemy mostly withheld his rifle fire, but on reaching the terraced slope of the Hill, heavy rifle and machine-gun fire met the attacking troops. The Lewis guns of A Company (in support) were then brought forward to keep down the hostile fire. By 7.30 a.m. D Company had crossed the Wadi, but B company, on the left, had been unable to do so.

The descent into the Wadi Ballut, after the first few hundred yards, was most precipitous, necessitating jumps of five or six feet from terrace to terrace which were taped by the Turks' machine guns placed on the lower slopes opposite and on the flank. With the exception of two officers, who were wounded later, the casualty list of eight officers and 50 other ranks occurred during the descent into the crossing this Wadi. Most effective assistance was rendered by the Divisional Artillery, and about 8 a.m. the Turks were seen retiring over Tin Hat Hill. The two attacking Companies – D and B – were therefore ordered to push on and, by 9–45 a.m., were on the top of the Hill. The 2/4th Somersets were then told to hang on to the top of Tin Hat Hill, whilst the Devons attacked Berukin. In the meantime C Company of the Somersets had advanced against Necklace Hill and, though all the while under heavy rifle fire, pushed on down into the Wadi Ballut and up the slopes of the Hill, capturing their objective. On reaching the summit of Necklace Hill they were able to open fire on the retreating Turks, causing the latter some casualties. During the afternoon the hostile guns heavily bombarded Tin Hat, but their fire was mostly ineffective and at nightfall consolidation was proceeded with.

At dawn on the 10th C Company went forward to take over Berukin, but the village was in the enemy's hands still, the Turks having regained it in a counter-attack. However, with the aid of some of the Devons, the Turks were again ejected and the village was consolidated.

During the two days' operations the 2/4th Battalion had lost 2/Lieuts E. L. B. Fear and G. R. Kitchen and eight other ranks killed, six officers and forty-two other ranks wounded.

On the 27th April the Battalion again went into the front line, relieving the 2/3rd Gurkhas and the right company of 2/4th Hants at El Kefr.

The 2/4th Somersets, however, had seen its last fight in Palestine. From the 11th to 28th the Battalion remained either on Tin Hat Hill or in bivouacs in support, but on the latter date was relieved by the Punjabis. On the 1st May the 2/4th reached camp at Surafend, entrained at Ludd on the 2nd and arrived at Kantara on 3rd. Here, until the 23rd, the Battalion remained, training, but on that day moved to Port Said and there embarked on the "Ormonde" for France. Marseilles was reached on 1st June.

The Somerset Light Infantry 1914–19

E. E. F.

✠ 6–4–18

My dear Mother & Father.

I had a great surprise last night for after having quite given it up for lost the cheese which you sent off last October turned up. It must have been hung up somewhere or other, but it is in still in quite good condition and we are going to start eating it for lunch in a few moments time. It has just arrived at the right time for we move off very early to-morrow morning on a new effort and as we shall have to live on bully & biscuit for the next few days the cheese will be a great help. I think we shall have some fairly hard fighting to do during the next few days if the Turks decide to hang on, but if they clear out we shall gain our objective without much trouble. There is a rumour that we are coming right out of the line for a real rest when it is all over but I don't know whether this is true or not.

There is very little to write about this week for th beyond the usual preparations for the move there has been very little going on.

Last Tuesday morning I commanded a guard of honour for the G.O.C. Division when he came up to present some medals which had been won by various people in the Brigade. One officer of the Gurkhas was presented with the M.C. & he had already won the V.C. in France during the war – luk lucky fellow isn't he?

In order to celebrate Bank Holiday we had a free day on Monday but it was very wet & cold & we could not do very much. However we had some football & sports & were as cheery as possible under the circumstances.

I enclose a photograph of one of my sergeants taken outside his bivouac & it will give you a very good idea of the kind of way we live. Both officers & men live in these little bivouac shelters which are really quite effective – they keep out the rain & cold and only take about two or three minutes to put up. Every man carries one sleep sheet in his pack.

We are rather sorry to be leaving our present bivouac area for it is an awfully delightful spot and we have had quite a good time since we have been here. By this I mean that we have been able to sleep with our boots off every night &, get a wash & shave every morning & get some canteen stores up from Ludd. It doesn't take much to make us happy in these days & in that respect we are just like a lot of school boys.

I heard from Andrew a couple of days ago – he is still down at the base & is quite fit & cheery. When he wrote he had just come back from a visit to Cairo. I may be able to get down to see him after this next show but at present all leave is stopped.

I am rather hoping that we shall get an English mail to-night – another one is just about due and there was a rumour last night that it would be up to-day. If it doesn't come to-night we shall have to wait for three or four days.

I hope Margaret's cold is better & that you are all keeping fit.

With very much love to all

> Your affectionate son
> Jim

E. E. F.

17–4–18

My dear Mother & Father.

I am afraid you will wonder what has happened to me as I did not get a chance of writing last week. However I sent a field card just to tell you that I am fit and now I am going to try & write a proper letter.

I last wrote just before we went into action again and I little knew then what we should have to go through within the next few days.

On the night of the 7th April my company did a night show and captured some high ground out in the front of our position. We tried to make a surprise out of it but when we got within about 300 yards of our objective two star shells went up & gave us away so we just made a rush for it. When we had captured the position I had to post pickets all round & that is an awful job in the dark for you can't see the ground & you can't tell a bit where you are.

The next day we rested & then early on the morning of the 9th we went over the top to attack the Turkish positions. I can't describe the action for it was absolutely terrible. The ground we had to attack over was almost impossible – (we had to cross a place just like Cheddar Gorge) but we hung on & and eventually captured the objective. My company & one other were told off for the attack, but the other went wrong somewhere & never came up & so mine had to do everything. I eventually reached the top with 25 men at about 12–30 P.M., the attack having started at 5–0 A.M. Half my company were casualties including myself, although I was not really wounded. Early in the show I fell and hurt my knee very badly. However I ~~carried~~ had it bandaged up and went on. When I reached the top I could hardly move, but and my knee got worse next day so I had to go down the line with it. We lost ~~so~~ 9 officers altogether 2 being killed.

The colonel was awfully pleased with me & said I had done awfully well & when I went away he thanked me for what I had done. The men too were simply splendid – at one time we thought we should have to retire but they hung on just like bulldogs for about four hours & then the Turks bolted over the top. The casualties were terrible – all my best N.C.O.^s were wounded some of them very badly indeed, but they were ever so cheery in spite of the pain. I absolutely hate war when I see the men getting knocked out for even a nice wound is frightfully painful.

Ron was wounded in the hand early in the action – ~~he~~ the bullet went between two fingers one of them being broken & went down the line at once.

The medical arrangements were splendid. When I went down I went

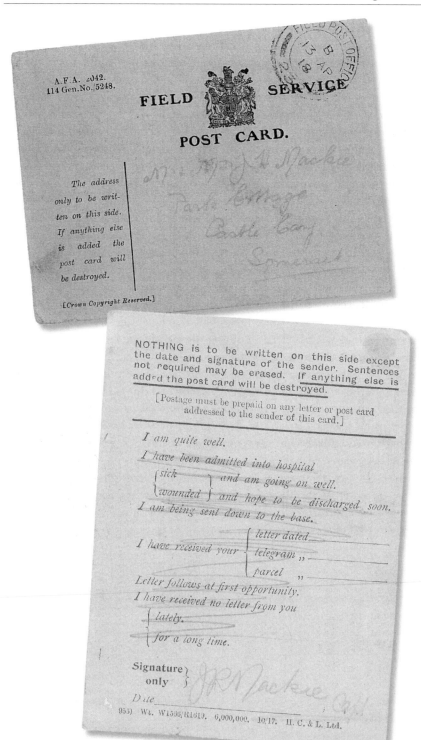

from the field ambulance to the casualty clearing station in a sand cart & from there to Ludd in a motor ambulance. I arrived there late at night but they at once put me to bed & gave me some dinner & I simply dropped off to sleep at once for I had had practically no sleep for three ~~days~~ nights as the Turks counter attacked three times. The next day we went down to El Arish in an ambulance train & on the following day we were sent on to Kantara. We stayed there one night & last evening I arrived at Nasarich Hospital Cairo where I expect I shall spend quite a long time. My knee is badly damaged & there is a good deal of fluid ~~on~~ in it but it is already getting better. If you see my name in the casualty lists you will know that there is nothing much the matter.

The hospitals are splendid ~~in you are~~ and one is looked after awfully well by both doctors & nurses. This morning I discovered that Ron ~~was~~ is also in this hospital, also Richards of our Regt & several fellows of the Hants who I know very well. Ron's wound is going on well & he is allowed to go out in Cairo but at present I am kept in bed.

I came down in the train with a fellow called Clarke who used to be at Reading with me. We were lying on stretchers side by side when we recognised each other – I had not seen him since we left Reading in 1914. I am going to wire to Andrew & let him know that I am here & I hope he will be able to come in & see me. I saw old Whitley last night – he was wandering round the hospital & I spotted him & called him in for a chat. He is nearly well now but ~~is still~~ his leg is still a little stiff. ~~N~~ I expect he will soon go back up the line.

That cheese which you sent off ~~K~~ last October is ~~was~~ a beauty – we managed to get it brought up to us after the fight on the 9th and it did go down well I can assure you. ~~We~~ It was just the very thing we wanted.

I received Mother's letter dated ~~the~~ March 19th on the 8th & was glad to hear that you were then all quite fit. I hope you are all still quite well.

With very much love to all

Your affectionate son
Jim

Secret

Copy No. 6

2/4 Batt. Somerset L.I.
Orders No. 4

Reference Map. BIDEH (C4)
1:40000

1. On April 9th the 75th Divn will secure
the general line BERUKIN - KH - ~~ARGRA~~
FAKHAKHIR - The Ridge (SHEIKH SUBIH)
- ARGRA - RAFAT - Pt 873. The 29th
Brigade will advance their line to CRAG
HILL (G 16a) Simultaneously to conform
with their movement

On 9th April 232 BDE will secure
the line BERUKIN - KH - FAKHAKHIR -
520 C54 (approximate) - 233 BDE will
operate on left flank of 232 BDE, the
dividing line between 232 BDE & 233 BDE
will be a line EL·KEFR - SERTA both
inclusive to 232 BDE

The Advance will be divided into two
phases

PHASE 1
(a) At 0505 EL KEFR will be bombarded
for 5 minutes
(b) At 0510 all artillery will lift to
Ridge running from A8a to SHEIKH

NAFUKH and 2/3 GURKHAS will secure
EL KEFR - Simultaneously 2/4 SOMERSETS
will attack BERUKIN from GHUSSANEH

(c) As soon as SHEIKH NAFUKH has
born seized 2/5 HANTS will debouch from
about G14a and attack BERUKIN

(d) One Company 1/5 Devons will follow
the attack of 2/4 Som. L.I and occupy TIN
HAT HILL (G10C00)

PHASE 2

2/4 SOM. L.I will be in BDE RESERVE & move
as Situation demands

2. The BN will be ready to leave Bivonac
area at 0430 in following order. HQ B.
D. & C. Coys + G. Mules + 1 Amm. Mule per
Coy will join Companies

3. D + B Coys will occupy TIN HAT HILL starting
from the point of assembly G15C.d at 0510
    If resistance is considerable the BN will await
advance of 2/5 HANTS against BERUKIN
    C Coy will occupy NECKLACE HILL and
link up with HANTS' right when it advances
over LOOPHOLE HILL + Conform to its movements

3.

① Coy will be in reserve in rear of BN Battle HQ

② Sig Officer will arrange communication between HQ + C Coy. HQ + Front line / watches will be synchronized at 2000 to-night.

4   1 subsection 229 M.G Co will accompany 2/4 SOM. LI as far as TIN HAT HILL (A 10 c 00) 1 section on forward slopes of SH KAUWASH. of which 2 guns will support the BN

5 After occupation of TIN HAT HILL BN HQ + RAP will be stationed there until Capture of BERUKIN + afterwards at BERUKIN.

6 Separate instructions have been issued by QM.

ACKNOWLEDGE.

Issued by runner at 1900

A. J. Ingram CAPT.
A/ADJT 2/4 SOM. LI

COPY Nº 1. BDE.
- 2. H.Q.
3. A Co.
4. B. Co.
5. C. Co.
6. D. Co.
7. Q.M
8. M.O
9.
10. } WAR DIARY
11.
12. File

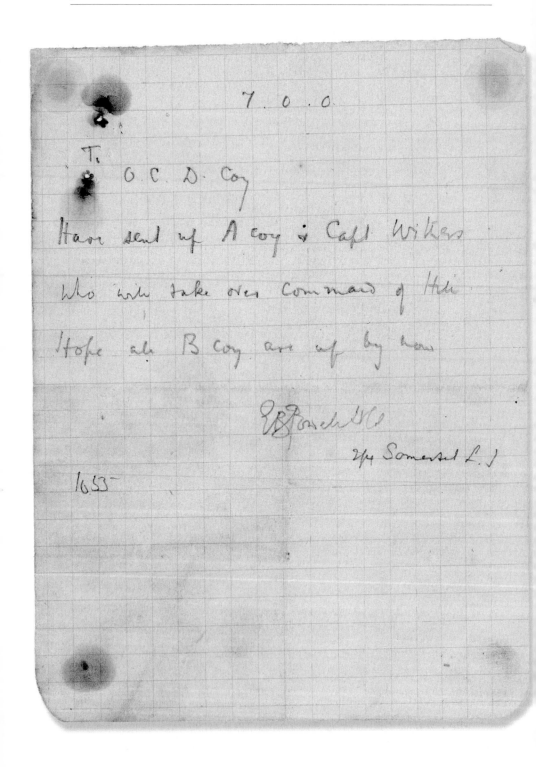

7 . 0 . 0

T.

O. C. D. Coy

Have sent up A coy & Capt Withers

Who will take over command of Hill.

Hope all B Coy are up by now

E.B.Forush &C

2/4 Somerset L.I

16.55

"A" Form
MESSAGES AND SIGNALS.

Army Form C. 2121
(In pads of 100)

No. of Message..............

Prefix .... Code ....m,	Words.	Charge.	This message is on a/c of:	Recd. at............m.
Office of Origin and Service Instructions				
....	Sent		.... Service.	Date....................
....	At ....m.			From....................
....	To.................			
....	By....................		(Signature of "Franking Officer.")	By....................

OC. D Coy.

*	...er's ...umber.	Day of Month.	In reply to Number.	A A A
		9		

D	Coy will push	on
at	once	Turks
retired	over	crest	of
~~trenches~~	HILL	aaa	
TIN	HAT HILL		

Recd 12-15

Place

Time

The above may be forwarded as now corrected. **(Z)**

....

Signature of Addressor or person authorised to telegraph in his name

* This line should be erased if not required.

(.81) Wt. W492/M1647 130,000 Pads 5/17 D.D & L. E1187

353

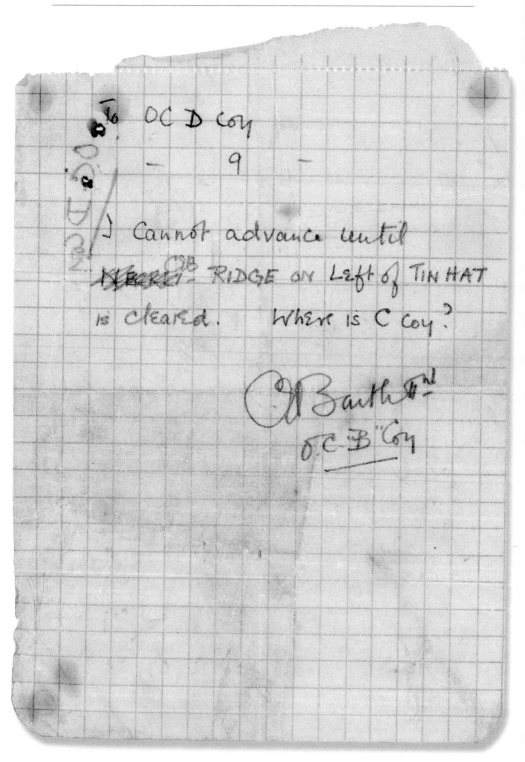

OC D coy

— 9 —

Cannot advance until
~~NEGRO~~ RIDGE on Left of TIN HAT
is cleared. Where is C coy?

Bartlett
O.C. B "Coy

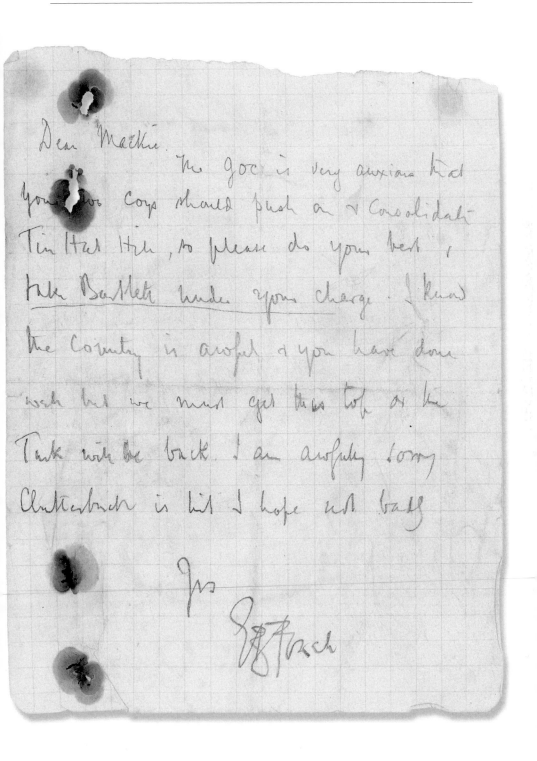

Dear Mackie,

The GOC is very anxious that your two Coys should push on & consolidate Tin Hat Hill, so please do your best, take Bartlett under your charge. I know the Country is awful & you have done well but we must get this top as the Turk will be back. I am awfully sorry Clutterbuck is hit I hope not badly

Yrs

EgbFrch

"A" Form
MESSAGES AND SIGNALS.

Army Form C. 2121
(In pads of 100)

No. of Message..............

Prefix..........Code.............m,	Words.	Charge.	This message is on a/c of:	Recd. at...........m.
Office of Origin and Service Instructions		Sent		
....	At...............m,		..................Service.	Date................
....	To....................			From................
....	By....................		(Signature of "Franking Officer.")	By....................

TO { D — Company

Sender's Number.	Day of Month.	In reply to Number.	AAA
* DF6	9th		

Have	had	no	message
from	you	since	0615
are	Pltsh	on	if
possible	are	when	do
M G	you	reported	to
be	holding	you	up
use	can so	you	want
A	Coy	up	

From	TWO	FOURTH	SOMERSET
Place			
Time		0750	

The above may be forwarded as now corrected. (Z)

.... Censor. Signature of Addressor or person authorised to telegraph in his name.

* This line should be erased if not required.
(7981) Wt. W492/M1647 130,000 Pads 5/17 D. D. & L. E1187

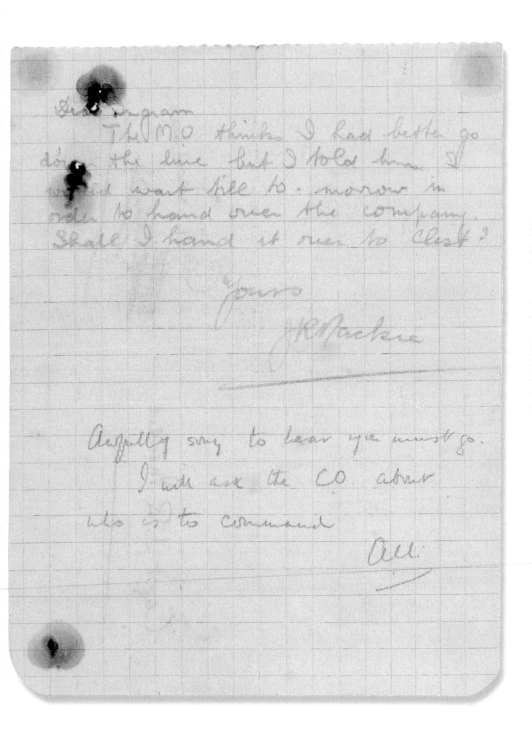

Dear Ingram
        The M.O thinks I had better go down the line but I told him I would wait till to-morrow in order to hand over the company. Shall I hand it over to Clist?

                Yours

                        J R Mackune

Awfully sorry to hear you must go.
        I will ask the C.O. about who is to command

                        All.

Nasarich Hospital
Cairo

23–4–18

My dear Mother & Father.

Very little has happened to me since I last wrote for I have been kept in bed the whole time. I am just allowed to walk out on to the verandah but that is all and I am afraid it will be another week before I am allowed to get up for my knee is still very swollen. ~~and~~ It does not pain much now except when I try to walk, but there is no strength in it at all and I cant put the least bit of weight on it.

It is rather a dull job lying in bed but I have had lots of people in to see me including Andrew. I wired to him as soon as I got here and he at once obtained three days leave and came to see me. He is awfully cheery and fit and seems to enjoy life thoroughly. He has not changed a bit since I last saw him at Barrackpore and I don't think he looks a day older. He told me all about everyone at home and it was awfully nice hearing about you all from someone who had so recently seen you.

Andrew tells me that Duff is going to Taunton when he is old enough & I am awfully glad of it for although Sexey's is a jolly good school it is not ~~one~~ the kind of school you can talk about very much, and it is awfully nice to be able to buck about your old school.

I discovered this morning that Ted Drewett is somewhere near at hand. There is a soldiers hospital attached to this one and every morning the letters are brought across for us to censor. In my pile this morning I found one written by Ted to his Mother & Father so I censored it & signed my name on the envelope as usual. I expect his people will be rather surprised when they see it.

The C.O. of this hospital used to be the Medical Officer at Sherborne School – he is quite nice ~~but~~ and comes round every morning to see us all. I think the sisters are all rather afraid of him.

We are looked after very well indeed here – the food is good & the beds nice & soft, both of which are very nice indeed after what we have had to put up with up the line. When I first came down I thought I should ~~be~~ in never want to get out of bed again for I was so absolutely tired out but I am getting rather tired of it now & shall be glad enough when I can go out for a bit

Ron's hand is getting on quite well & he had the splint taken off his finger yesterday. He was pleased to see Andrew & they both went out to tea together every evening while Andrew was here. The latter left Cairo this morning to join his Regt at Kantara as they are just moving up the line.

I hope you are all keeping quite fit
With much love to all

> Your affectionate son
> Jim.

E. E. F.

28–4–18

My dear Father & Mother.

My letter this week will be very short indeed for I have nothing whatever to write about. I have spent the whole week in bed and as a result my knee is getting on quite well. The swelling is almost gone and I can hobble about with a stick. I am going out for a a drive this afternoon for the first time.

Ron is going to have a board to-morrow and I expect he will go to a convalescent camp for a bit. His wound has healed up completely but his finger is still very swollen & painful.

Ted Drewett came up to see me two nights ago – he has got a temporary job here in the hospital. He is much thinner than he used to be but looks quite fit. We had ᴋa long talk about old times and he told me lots of bits of news which I had not heard owing to the fact that I have not yet received my last three mails. They have not yet been sent back from the Regt. I have just had a letter from Andrew written from Ludd just after he arrived there. He says that he thinks they are going across to the Jordan valley and I think this is very probable for it is quite good country for cavalry over there but I think it is frightfully hot as of course it is below sea level.

I will try & write a longer letter next week as I shall then have some letters to re answer and if I am allowed out shall be able to tell you about what I have seen.

I do hope you are all quite well
With very much love to all

> Your affectionate son
> Jim

P. S. I enclose a cheque for £3 made out to Father which is made up of £2 for Rob & £1 for Duff. ᴋThese are their birthday presents, & I should be glad if Father would kindly negotiate the cheque for them.

> Jim

ϫ 5th May 1918

My dear Mother & Father.

Two days ago two English mails arrived for me and I received the photographs which you sent me. I think they are simply splendid – I have never seen better ones of either of you and I am ever so pleased with them. I think you both look a little older than you did when we went away in 1914, but I am delighted that you are both looking so well.

Father said in his letter that he had had rather a bad cold. I hope it was nothing serious & that it has completely gone again now.

I am still in hospital but am now allowed to go out every afternoon – this is ever so much nicer than having to stay in the hospital all day. I usually go along to Shepheards Hotel & have tea on the terrace so that I can watch the people pass. One sees a wonderful collection ῍ if you stay there for a couple of hours. First of all there is the military element, British, French, Italian & ~~Grek~~ Greek & Indian officers & men & then there are the nursing sisters, in their various uniforms & then comes the civil population consisting of French, Italians, Greeks, Arabs & Egyptians. Nearly all have their own particular kind of dress but by far the most picturesque are the arabs. The native women look very quaint for they all wear a long black gown & have a white veil which covers the whole face below the eyes & they have a queer sort of wooden arrangement on their noses.

Sometimes you see the Sultan drive by in his motor. Two motor cyclists go in front of his car, one rides on each side & two come along behind. Just to prevent one forgetting that the war is a real thing a convoy of wounded in ambulance cars probably goes by en route to the various hospitals.

It is a strange scene ~~but~~ and I find it awfully fascinating – I could sit for hours & watch the ~~peol~~ people passing up and down.

Yesterday afternoon I spent a couple of hours at the museum which also is very wonderful indeed. The most ~~fascinatng~~ fascinating thing there is undoubtedly the collection of mummies of the old Egyptian kings.

They are kept in glass cases but they lie in their coffins just as when they were burried ῍ 3 or 4 thousand years ago but the wrappings have been stripped off their heads & chests so that after all this time you can see their features as plainly as the day they died.

It seems to me a very strange ~~thing~~ indeed that these great kings, some of the greatest kings the world has ever seen should now be exposed to the gaze of anyone who can afford a penny to go in and look at them.

They embalmed their bodies & built great pyramids for tombs in order that they might be in peace till the end of the world & yet their very means they used to activate this end has had the led to the present state of affairs where they are just lie in a glass case for the public to look at. Had they been put into an obscure tomb they would probably have never been disturbed – "How are the mighty fallen"! One of the mummies is that of Ramasees II who was probably the king who persecuted the Israelites. Wouldn"t he be surprised if he only knew that the reason that we are in Cairo & are therefore able to come and look at him is because we are fighting to restore Palestine to the decendents of the very people who used to be his slaves.

I shall try to go to the museum again if I get a chance for there is lots to see there – the worst of it is one feels so frightfully ignorant & you you feel that you ought to go back at once & read up all the history of Egypt.

I see quite a lot of old Ted Drewett – we had a long chat together last night. He thinks he may have to go back up the line before long.

I am sorry Rob has been obliged to join up before completing a whole years study but he has done the right thing in going to the Inns of Court & should have no difficulty in getting a commission after a bit. I hope he will be able to get into the artillery.

Ron was discharged from hospital last Friday & went back to Kantara. I have not heard from him since he went away.

I am glad Janet is enjoying here her holiday for I am sure she deserves it. I heard from Nellie Sims last mail & she says that Bert is getting on quite well. I was sorry to hear that he had been hit, but he is probably well out of it for a few weeks, for I am afraid they are still having a very bad time in France.

I herewith enclose an authority for Father to draw £3–00 from Cox & Co in case the cheque I sent last week should be lost (£2 for Rob – £1 for Marg Duff – birthday presents)

My knee is getting on slowly – it is still painful & I cannot walk at all easily yet but I get massage for it every day & I think it will soon begin to get stronger.

I hope you are all keeping quite fit & thank you very much indeed for the photographs.

With very much love to all

        Yours affectionate son
        Jim

P. S. Please do not trouble to send any more batteries for my electric torch as it was stolen from me while I was coming down the line.

E. E. F.

12–5–18

My dear Mother & Father.

I have spent another week in hospital but have been able to go out every afternoon so that I have had quite a pleasant time.

A good many of our people have been down on leave during the last few days & most of them have been along to see me. It is awfully nice to see them all again for it is an extraordinary thing how one misses the Regt when away from it.

There are very few of the old officers left there now for two or three were wounded, one or two are sick & Bartlett has left us to go to the Trench Mortar Battery. I am very sorry indeed that he has gone for he & I have been together more or less continuously ever since we left England and I shall miss him ever so much when I get back.

Will you please address my letters in future C/o Cox's Shipping Agency Alexandria for the Regt is on the move again – nearer home this time – very near in fact (I expect you can guess the rest) & it looks as if I shall have to follow on after it. In that case if my letters are addressed E. E. F. they will take a long time to reach me. Of course I may be fit to go with them & if so I will let you know at once. We may be able to get some home leave when we reach our next destination anyhow we shall all have a good try for it.

We have had some very hot weather lately – quite like India again. I must say I prefer it to the very cold weather although either is rather trying.

One afternoon I had a very jolly sail on the river – it is the best place on a hot day for there is always a nice cool breeze blowing off the river. You just go down & get into a boat & the boatman will take you out for the whole afternoon. We usually take our tea with us & then we can stay out till about half past six – we have to be back in the hospital by seven.

A very favourite haunt for Cairo people is the Zoological Garden which is one of the prettiest places I have be ever seen. It is beautifully laid out and the animals all have good big cages so that they have quite a good time on the whole. In the centre of the Garden is a big lake & they provide teas on a little island in the middle of it. I went out there yesterday afternoon.

Ted Drewett came up to say goodbye yesterday afternoon as he is being sent to a convalescent Camp before going back up the line.

I don't think I told you before that I was again recommended for the M.C. after the action on the 9th April. I did not get anything however as an immediate award but they said that I might get an ordinary award later on which I suppose is a polite way of saying that it is washed out (I have the satisfaction of being an officer in the T.F.).

I have not had a mail since I last wrote but I hope you are all quite fit. With much love to all

> Your affectionate son
> Jim

E. E. F.

19–5–18

My dear Mother & Father.

To-day is Whit Sunday and is almost ~~my~~ my last day in hospital as I am returning to Kantara on Tuesday. I shall have to go very steadily for a bit as my knee is still very weak: ~~and~~ I ought really to go to a convalescent camp and go through a proper course of exercises but as the move I spoke of last week will probably take place very soon I am going straight back to the Regt. You need not trouble to send my letters to Cox & Co after all – ~~I~~ when I asked you to do that I thought I might be left behind. The cheese which you sent me for my birthday arrived last week also the socks & battery for all of which thank you very much indeed. The cheese was simply splendid – as I could not eat it all myself I gave some of it to the sisters & they were delighted with it. I was awfully glad to get the socks as I am now rather short of them having had several pairs stolen as I came down the line.

The other parcel has not yet arrived but I hope to get it in a few days.

I have had a very pleasant time since I have been able to go out and it has quite made up for all the bad times we had up the line. The sisters are always glad to get someone to take them out & I have had several river picnics this week. ~~and~~ The river is the best thing about Cairo at present for it is so much cooler than anything else.

I enclose a ~~few~~ couple photographs which I think may interest you as they were taken a few days ago by one of the patients in the hospital.

I have just heard a rumour that two or three of our mails have been sunk, & if it is correct we shall have rather a long wait before we hear from you again. Of course it may not be true – I hope not. as I heard from John yesterday and he says he hopes to get leave in May so I daresay he is in India at present. I think he must want it rather badly. I was glad to hear that Father & Duffy are both better but very sorry to hear that Aunt Susan & Grandma Mackie are both unwell. I hope they are all better by now.

~~I also ha~~ I had not heard that T. E. A. Carr was missing – I hope he was

not killed for he was an awfully good sort. He was always frightfully keen to get to the front but if he is alive I expect he has had about enough of it by now.

I hope you are now ọu all quite fit – how is Rob's arm?
With much love to all

Your affectionate son
Jim

E. E. F.

22–5–18

My dear Mother & Father.

Just a note to let you know that I am out of hospital again & that I have rejoined the Regt.

A We shall be proceeding overseas very shortly & all our kit which was with Cox & Co. Port Said is being sent to ℞oℜ the depot at Bath. I have however just written to Cox & Co instructing them to send you my keys.

I will let you know at once when we reach our destination.

Hoping you are all quite fit

Your affectionate son
Jim

The Counter-attacks in Champagne

The Battles of the Soissonais and of the Ourco
25th July 2nd August 1918

The 2/4th Somersets, on arrival at Marseilles on 1st June, marched to the Rest Camp at Mont Fouron. Here three days were spent, the Battalion entraining at Marseilles on 4th for Berguette, reaching that place on 7th. Nearly a fortnight was spent in training for the new kind of warfare before the Battalion, then in stages the Somerset men moved north again to Bourthes (18th), Elnes (28th), Le Paradis (29th) and Wylder (30th). The 1st July found the Battalion at the latter place, but on the 2nd a move was made to Proven. Here, on the 5th, the 2/4th were inspected by the G.O.C., 34th Division

(Major-General Nicholson), and the Battalion was formed into Pioneers, D company being disbanded and absorbed by the other three Companies.

During June the 34th Division had been reconstructed and on 1st July occupied the Bambecque area, but towards the middle of the month received orders to entrain for the French zone and concentrate in the Senlis area by 18th July.

On 17th the Battalion left Proven, marched to Rexpoede and entrained for the French front, detrained at Chantilly on 18th and marched to billets at Mont l'Evecque.

The 34th Division was one of four Divisions – 15th, 34th, 51st and 62nd – which had been sent down to the French front at the request of Marshal Foch: they formed the XXII Corps. Two (15th and 34th) were attached to the Tenth French Army between the Ourcq and the Aisne Rivers, on the western side of the great salient from Rheims to west of Soissons, and the other two (51st and 62nd) to the Fifth French Army operating against the eastern side of the salient, south-west of Rheims.

On the 18th July (the enemy having counter-attacked east and south-west of Rheims on 15th July, gaining ground as far south as the Marne River) Marshal Foch launched his counter-attack between Chateau Thierry and Soissons, supporting this stroke by vigorous attacks also on other parts of the German salient. In this fighting which, on the west at least, was immediately successful, the XXII Corps became speedily engaged. This narrative, however, is confined generally to the operations of the 34th Division and particularly to the part taken in the battle by the 2/4th Somerset Light Infantry.

On 19th the 34th Division moved to Lagny, west of Villers Cotterets, the 2/4th Somersets proceeding by lorry to Vanciennes. On the night 20th/21st the Division moved again, on this occasion to the Vivieres area north of the Forest de Villers Cotterets: the 2/4th Battalion moved to Vivieres on 21st. At the latter place the Division was ordered to relieve a French division in the front line about Parcy-Tigny on the night of 22nd/23rd. The relief duly took place. The 2/4th Somersets left Vivieres at 10 a.m. on 22nd and marched into position at Min de Villars Helon, moving again at 9 a.m. on 23rd to Caves just south of Montramboeuf Ferme.

The situation on the front of the XX and XXX French Corps (the 34th Division belonging to the latter) was roughly as follows: the enemy held the line Buzancy-Villemontoire-Tigny-Coutremain-western edge of the Bois du Plessier-Le Plessier Huleu. The 34th Division attacked (with French troops on the right and left) on 23rd, with 101st Brigade on the right and 102nd on the left, but the Somersets were not engaged, indeed the Battalion Diary states that from 23rd to 26th inclusive the Battalion remained just south of Montramboeuf Ferme in reserve, moving at 9.30 p.m. on 27th to a position in the Bois de Nadon. On 28th the 2/4th Somersets were attached to the 102nd Brigade and left the Bois de Nadon at 9 p. m., marching to the Bois de Baillette, where reserve positions were occupied.

The 34th Division again took part in a general attack on 29th, the attacking Brigades being the 101st and 103rd. The attack began at 4.10 a.m., and at 11 a.m. orders were received to move the Divisional reserves to occupy the Vers-Soissons railway defence line. But the move did not take place as the attack had been held up by the enemy, who was strongly posted in Beugneux and woods to the west of that place. Soon after midday the 2/4th Somersets and 1/7th Cheshires were ordered to attack and capture Beugneux, but the attack was never made and eventually both units were ordered to consolidate the Paris Line, the line from which the attack was to have started. In this position the 2/4th Somersets remained until the night 30th/31st July, when the Battalion was relieved by the 1/4th Cheshire Regiment and marched back to the Bois de Baillette.

The position which the Somersets held in the Paris Line was no sinecure. It was exposed to very heavy shell fire, quantities of gas shell being used by the enemy, and, although the Battalion escaped with light casualties all ranks had had a hard gruelling.

Captain W. H. Miles and three other ranks were wounded during the night 28th/29th: on the 29th three other ranks were killed, Lieut M. Dat and fifteen other ranks wounded and three other ranks were missing. On 30th/31st 2/Lieut A. S. Newton and eight other ranks were killed and fifteen other ranks wounded.

On 31st the 34th Division renewed the attack, the 2/4th Somersets moving to a point of concentration along the Vers-Soissons railway. But, with the exception of having to endure heavy shell fire, of gas and H.E., the Battalion was again not called upon.

On Beugneux being captured the Somersets were moved to that place on 1st August. On the 2nd the Battalion withdrew to the Paris Line once more, north of the Bois de Montceau, remaining there until the following afternoon. Orders had been received at 34th Divisional Headquarters on the 3rd August, with drawing the Division from the French zone, and during the next few days the Division moved north again to the Second Army area, being established in the Esquelbecq area (in reserve) by the 7th August. the 2/4th Somersets were billeted at Newlands, near Eringhem.

The Diary of the 2/4th Somersets during the Battle of the Soissonais and Ourcq makes dull reading, for it is unrelieved by any incident of importance. The Battalion no doubt felt the change in status, i.e. from that of fighting infantry, as in Palestine, to Pioneers as it was now, in France.

The Somerset Light Infantry 1914–18

2–6–18

My dear Mother & Father.

As you see from the above address we have arrived in France at last and will you please address my letters accordingly.

We had a very pleasant voyage – the sea was very smooth and we had a splendid great ship but the submarines were rather a nuisance. You probably saw in the paper that one ship of our convoy was sunk just outside Alexandria on the 25th May. All the others arrived safely but we had a very narrow escape the last night on board – the torpedo just missed our stern by about six feet. Another of our ships was ⟨ struck by a torpedo which failed to explode but as we were all in bed & asleep when these things happened ⟩ they didn't worry us very much.

I have not heard from you since April 12th as two mails arrived in Egypt just about the time that we left, but I believe one mail was stopped for us here in which case we shall probably get it fairly soon.

Now that we are so much nearer home I hope we shall soon be able to get some leave. We can hardly expect it while the German offensive is still on but as soon as it is over I hope we shall be able to get away. Anyhow there is more chance of getting home from here than there was from Palestine.

I only came out of hospital just in time to come away with the Bttn. but I think my knee is fairly right now. It is still rather stiff & a bit weak but that will soon work off I hope.

Ron now commands of a Company & is therefore a Captain. I am awfully glad for he thoroughly deserves it.

Just before I left Kantara Rowland Targett came to see me. He is in an Irish Regt & happened to be in Kantara at the time. He looks awfully well.

I could have stayed on in Cairo for another three weeks but I did not want to be left behind so I came asked if I could go straight back to the Regt & I am very glad that I did so for everyone was frightfully pleased to see me when I came back.

It seems strange to be back in Europe again & to see only white people walking about but one feels much nearer home already. I never saw so many girls in my life as there are here – they seem to be everywhere. It is ever so much colder here than it was in Egypt – we noticed a great change as we came across & of course we shall notice it still more when we begin to go North.

I will write again in a few days when we know what is going to happen to us – at present we don't know a bit what the next move will be.

I hope you are all quite fit

With much love to all

Your affectionate son

Jim

P. S. Have Father & Duff received their birthday presents?

BEF

France

9–6–18

My dear Mother & Father

Since we came to this country we have had lots of letters from home. The postal authorities knowing that we were coming kept three mails for us at Marseilles. They were dated 7th 21st & 28th May respectively and last night I received a letter from you dated 5th June which is only three days ago. The mails between April 12th & May 7th must be somewhere in Egypt, but now that I have heard from you so recently I don't mind losing those.

We spent two days in Marseilles and I wrote a letter from there which should have reached you by now. While there I met a political officer from Mespot who was returning from leave & he told me that he was the person who examined John when he went up for his proficiency arabic exam at Baghdad. He spoke awfully well of John & said he was doing very good work indeed.

On leaving Marseilles whe we had a very long train journey – 2 days & three nights – and arrived here the night before last. We are now close up behind the line but not actually in it and I don't expect we shall spend a few days here in order to have some special training as the fighting out here is very different from what we have been doing in Palestine.

Don't be surprised if I am home on leave in a few days. The a There seems to be a desire on the part of the powers to do what they can for us in the matter of leave and I think we shall start to before long & if so I think I shall be one of the first. Our applications have gone in already & we hope for the best. If we don't get it we shall all be very disappointed I can assure you. It will be topping to see you all again.

We Coming up in the train we were all awfully struck by the beauty of the South of France – the Rhone valley is exceptionally pretty and it seemed awfully nice to to see how green it all was for Egypt was very burnt & brown when we left.

We came round behind Paris and at one of the stations near there some sisters of the American Red Cross gave us some coffee and ~~from~~ we wrote some postcards which they promised to send off for us.

It has been delightfully fine since we landed but it looks as if it will rain ~~to-morrow~~ to-day. We find it awfully cold especially at night but we shall soon get used to it.

The situation out here seems to have improved during the last few days & I really don't think there is much to worry about for I think General Foch has the situation well in hand. Our object is to save men & we therefore hold the line as lightly as possible. We must have a big reserve & I am sure we could stop the Germans if we used it but we want to save as many men as possible for our own offensive. I take it that it pays us better to give ground & save our reserve than to hold the Germans by using the latter. I enclose two photographs taken by one of my Sergeants. One shows the graves of the men who were killed on the 9th April & the other shows the hill down which we advanced. ~~We~~ The photograph is taken from the hill which we captured. As we came down the side the Turks had the terraces absolutely set by machine guns & when we got into the wadi at the bottom they had us in ~~enif~~ enfilade from the right.

I am glad Father likes ~~h~~ his new appointment so much – he seems to do an enormous amount of travelling. I am awfully sorry Mother had such bad luck with the ducks – it was an awful shame to have them all killed the same night.

I had a letter from Rob at Marseilles – he seems quite happy & I hope he will get on well.

I hope to see you all before long I hope you are are all quite fit.

> Your affectionate son
> Jim

BEF
France

15—6—18

My dear Mother & Father.

I have just received letters from you both dated June 9th for which very many thanks.

We have had an awfully busy week – hardly any time to ourselves – and to-morrow we are moving again but we have not yet been told our destination. We have spent a good bit of our time digging reserve lines of trenches but in addition we have had to do a lot of gas drill etc. We are living in tents and have a mess in the barn of an &l adjoining farm which is quite cheery. I am glad we are in tents instead of the little bivouacs which we had in Palestine for the nights are awfully cold & coming from a hot country we feel it more.

We have been getting a few shells over every day but they have not done much harm so far although some of them come rather too close to be pleasant. The people out here are a great surprise to me & they go on cultivating their fields just as if the war did not exist & take absolutely no notice of the shells, in fact they seem rather amused at them. Of course there are only old men & girls left & they seem to work frightfully hard for they have to do all the work in the fields. It seems rather strange to see only white people about, and one always wants to speak of them as "natives" which of course they would not appreciate a bit.

I am not surprised that Andrew feels the heat for I have always heard that the Jordan valley was a Ꝃ very hot region indeed: I am very glad to hear that he is keeping fit for I have not heard from him so for some weeks now.

We have heard nothing about any leave yet, but everyone seems to think that we shall get it before long. We are all looking forward to it ever so much & this is a ripping time of the year to come home for England must look absolutely top hole.

It is awfully funny having such a long day: it doesn't get dark till about 10 o'clock in the evening – I suppose the daylight saving arrangement has something to do with this.

I am glad Father received his birthday present – did Rob & Duff get theirs?

I shall be glad of the socks which Mother is knitting & I daresay I shall have to ask you to get me some other kit if we don't get leave for I have very little thick stuff. However don't trouble to send unless I ask for it a we are only allowed about 30lbs of kit and if I collect up too much I shall only have to dump it. We lef had to leave most of our things in a dump at Marseilles – I don't know when we shall ever see them again.

I am glad to hear that Duff is so fit again & will be able to go back to school at half term.

We I am very fit indeed – my knee is still a little weak but nothing to speak of.

I hope you are all quite fit

With very much love to all

> Your affectionate son
> Jim

B.E.F.
France

23–6–18

My dear Mother & Father.

This is the first letter I have written with a pen for over nine months and I almost forget the way to use one. Janet's letter dated the 18ᵗʰ and I have had one ~~for~~ from Angus & one from Mary during the week for which please thank them very much indeed. I love getting them and it makes one feel very near home when the letters arrive two or three days after they are posted.

We have had a very busy week indeed. As I told you last time we went right up behind the line when we came from Marseilles but now we are back in billets in a delightful little village. We marched 20 miles last Monday and another 12 the day after and arrived here very tired and with very sore feet, but the people are awfully kind and they fixed us up in some very nice billets. I am particularly fortunate in this respect for my billet is the best in the place. I am in a farm house and Madame has given me a bedroom with a nice soft bed and clean sheets, also a sitting room which we use as a company officers mess. The fighting out here is probably much worse than in Palestine but it has compensations, for you do get a certain amount of comfort when out of the line which you never even hoped for out there.

We are all feeling a bit sore about the leave question for we have just arrived from Palestine and they are not quite playing the game with us. A good many of us have had no home leave for nearly four years and even the most recently joined draft has been away from England for over nine months and yet we are only allowed to send away four people per day. This allotment has to include officers as well as other ranks so it will take about six months before everyone has been home.

Leave was opened yesterday and the first four went off very pleased with themselves. The Colonel goes to-morrow and after that an officer will be allowed to go every ~~h~~ five days. It will be my turn next ~~Fri~~ Friday but I doubt if I shall be able to go in fact I am almost certain I shall not, for another officer has submitted a special case and I think he will be given the vacancy on Friday. This will mean that I shall have another fortnight to wait as the Major & Adjutant come before me and they will go as soon as the Colonel comes back. However now that leave has started we all feel more cheery for our turn is bound to come in time. I don't think Ron and I will be able have leave at the same time – I wish we could.

It is surprising how little spare time one has in these days – I started this letter this morning but I have have absolutely no chance of continuing it till now when it is far too late to be bothered by chits from the orderly room.

We are having very nice fine weather but it is awfully cold at least that is how we find it. We are all glad enough to sit round the fire with the people of the house in the evenings and. We are getting a little more at home with French now – at first it was awfully difficult to forget Hindustani but we have improved quite a lot the last few days.

I wonder if Father would mind getting me four or five decent mouth organs – they are an awful help on the march and help to keep the men cheery in the evenings. If you will kindly send the bill along with them I will send a cheque in payment.

I hope you managed to collect enough war savings to get the aeroplane – I want to take some war bonds myself & had I known sooner I could have done so through you.

Fancy Will Donne getting married! The girl must have some pluck.

I hope the Ellesmere people enjoy their holiday at Bournemouth. I expect it is rather nice down there now: doesn't it seem ages ago that we all spent a holiday there.

I had a letter from old Colonel Clutterbuck yesterday: he says he would give anything to be back with us again. He still looks upon us as his boys and I can assure you we should all be glad enough to have him back again.

I also had a letter from Cissie of Dornock Mains a few days ago enclosing her own photograph. She has improved in looks since I last saw her. If the photograph is an accurate one she is quite a good looking girl now.

I am sorry Mother is so unwell again & I do hope that she she will soon be better. I will do my best to cheer you all up when I come home & you can't think how much I am longing to come.

I received the paper which X Father sent me, & which contained his appointment as inspector of cheese factories. He has an awfully big district to cover. Rob will writes very cheery letters but I fancy he is beginning find out the boredom of the army. It is awfully plucky of him to try & take his 1st year Diploma and I hope he will get through for he thoroughly deserves to do so.

I hope you are all quite fit
With very much love to all

>Your affectionate son
>Jim

E. F. C.
OFFICERS REST HOUSE
AND MESS
Boulogne.

17–7–18

My dear Mother.

I hope you got home safely last night – I am awfully sorry you had to travel down all alone but of course it could not be helped. I am afraid you must have had rather a dull journey for I clean forgot to get you anything to read.

After you left us we went along to Chiswick & then ↘ went back to see Aunty Hetty off. The Chiswick people were very pleased to see us but we did not see much of Aunty Ella as she was very busy. We did not go to a theatre after all for we were both awfully tired, so we just went back to the Hotel, had a quiet dinner & then off to bed.

We had to be up early this morning but we had hours of time to spare when we got to Victoria. We had a non-stop run down to Folkestone & it was raining hard when we arrived there. All people returning from leave had to wait till the afternoon boat so I had a look round & then made a splendid lunch off the Sandwiches which Father got me & a cup of coffee. The sandwiches were awfully good.

We had a delightful passage this afternoon – it was nice and fine and the water was quite so smooth, ↘ I am afraid the fishes had rather a bad time.

I got in here about an hour ago & was told ↘ that our Division had moved since I went away & that its present whereabouts is unknown so I have to report again at midday to-morrow. I shall be able to have a good look at Boulogne between this & then.

I hope you were not too tired last night for we had quite a strenuous day.

With much love to the Follies & Duff.

I remain
Your affectionate son
Jim

P. S. I was awfully glad ↘ Father came to Victoria this morning – it is much nicer to have someone to see you off.

BEF
France

Sunday

My dear Father & Mother.

I wrote to Mother from Boulogne so I really have very little to write about but as it is Sunday I thought I would just write a note. As I told you in Mother's letter when I got to Boulogne I had to wait for further instructions. I reported again at ~~R.M.~~ 12 o'clock Thursday & was told to catch the 2 o'clock train for Rouen and on arrival there to report to my depot. Just before leaving Boulogne I ~~meet~~ met Mead of Wincanton who used to be at Cambridge with John. He is now a full blown Padre and came over the day before me. I asked him where he was going & he said that he was coming to our Division & was also off to Rouen by the 2 P.M. train so we just came along together & are now sharing quarters here. I was awfully glad to meet him for he is an awfully nice fellow & I wanted some company. The worst of him is that he is an awful talker – he would leave Ted miles behind in no time. He asked to be remembered to both of you & also to David Gass.

We spent a night in the train & got to Rouen about 9 A.M. Friday. when we got to the Depòt we were told that we should have to wait till we could be sent on. The Division are still moving about & we can't rejoin till they settle down again & fix a rail head. I don't mind staying here for it is quite a good place but I do wish I could have spent the time in England instead of waiting about here. All the same I should like to get back to the Regt. for they might get into action & although I don't particularly want to fight I should not care to be out of it in spite of everything one says to the contrary.

There is a fellow here in the Depòt who used to be at Taunton School with John – his name is Cornish & there are also several of our own fellows waiting to be sent on.

I spent the greater part of yesterday going through the gas chambers & testing my mask & am very glad indeed that I am still alive.

Rouen is a delightful place – I have had a look at the Cathedral & went up to the top of the hill to see the statue of Jeanne d'arc, ~~form~~ from which you get a magnificent view of the City.

I was invited to an "At Home" given by the Nursing Staff of one of the hospitals yesterday afternoon but I did not go as I was busy with the gas but they are coming to us on Tuesday.

I don't know how long I shall have to stay here – I might go on to-morrow but I might stay here a week so I should be awfully glad if you would write me a letter direct here, ~~then~~ as I shall not get any letters till I get back to the Regt & ⅄ if I do have to stay a few days I should like to hear from you.

My cold ~~has~~ has been rather bad since I came back & I really thought I was going to get an attack of flue but it is much better to-day & I think I shall survive even yet.

I hope Father is better & that you are all keeping well. (My address here is Infy Base Depot. D. Rouen)

With love to all ~~includ~~ & and extra bit for the Follies & Duff.

> Your affectionate son
> Jim

P. S. Has Ron come back yet?

BEF
France

23–7–18

My dear Ted.

Just a note to tell you that I am leaving Rouen to rejoin the Regt. to-night. I am awfully glad to get away from here for I think there is fighting to be done & I hate being out of ⅄ it if the others are going to be in.

I have had quite a good time here & it is a top hole place but I want to get back to the Regt. Last night Mead & I ~~we~~ got a late pass & went to a French Theatre. It was quite a good show.

This Depòt is giving an "At Home" ~~to~~ this evening to the nurses of one of the hospitals & ⅄ as I don't have to leave till 6–30 I shall be just right for it.

~~Hope~~ Can you guess where our Division is – ~~he~~ not far from the fighting. Suspect us when you read of Highlanders.

Hope you are all fit

> With much love
> from Jim

BEF
France

28–7–18

My dear Mother & Father.

I left Rouen last Tuesday night, but when we set out none of us knew where we were going. However we arrived at railhead next morning and of course the first thing we did was to ask for news. We were told that the Division was up in the line and had been doing some fighting but that was all the information we could get. I took charge of all the Somersets on the train and received instructions to march them to a village about five miles away. On arriving there I found to two of our officers (Morgan & Watterson) & a party of our men billetted in the houses. They then told me that I had been detailed to take charge of the nucleus (which is always left behind when a Bttn goes into action) and that I was to remain with them. This means that I shall remain here till the Bttn comes out again unless of course they get badly cut up & reinforcements are badly needed.

We are be about 14 miles behind the Bttn but cannot get into touch with them very easily, so that I have not yet been able to get at any letters. There are qt quite a lot waiting for me when I can get at them and I suppose they will be sent back sometime or other.

Our Bttn have been in reserve so far & have had no casualties but I hope this state of affairs will continue.

Padre Mead came up in the train with me and we separated at railhead but the same evening I met him again at the casualty clearing station which is only a few hundred yards from my billet. He is staying there till he can get up the Bttn to which he has been posted.

We saw a whole lot of American troops going up towards the line yesterday – it did one good to see them for they are a splendid lot of fellows and are all ever so cheery. I rather think the Bosche is going to have a pretty bad time in the near future.

When we got here the village was quite empty as all the people were ordered ordered to clear out while the Bosche was advancing. After they left French troops were billetted here & you never saw such a sight as they left behind. They looted & destroyed everything. The Germans could hardly have done worse. I hope Angus is enjoying his holiday – as a matter of fact I expect he is having the time of his life.

Tell the Follies that they have already helped to pass away a good many dull half hours – they have provided me with quite a lot of amusing little stories while I was home. I can assure them that they are doing their bit in the great war by amusing a certain number of somewhat war weary officers.

Poor old Ron did not get his leave as leave was stopped just before he was due to go, but I think it is open again now & if this is the case he will soon be home I hope.

Have you heard from Andrew or John lately – I hope both are quite fit. I expect I shall get letters from them both when I can get to the Bttn.

The weather has been very stormy since I came back but it is not too bad as a good part of nearly every day is fine and this ~~hn~~ prevents the ground from getting too wet & muddy.

I hope Father is better & that Mother is keeping fit.

With very much love to all

> I remain x̶
> Your affectionate son
> Jim

But in the first of the great battles of the Advance to Victory fought by the British Armies no battalion of the Somerset Light Infantry was engaged. Yet, from an historical standpoint, it is interesting to note where each of the seven Battalions of the Regiment, then in France and Flanders, was located when the great Advance to Victory began on 8th August 1918. The 1st Battalion was at Censee la Valee, north-west of Bethune, the 2/4th in camp at Newlands, near Eringhem, the 6th at Hubersent, engaged in training after having arrived in France, for the Battalion had been home to England for reorganization purposes. The 7th was in Lorette Camp, Ablain St. Nazaire, the 8th west of Bucquoy, the 11th at Barly, and the 12th holding front-line trenches in the Amusoires line west of Merville.

The first of these six Battalions to be engaged with the enemy in the great drama of the closing months of the War was the 8th, which took part in the Battle of Albert, 1918: 21st–23rd August.

The 2/4th Somersets (Pioneers) of the 34th Division were in camp at Newlands from 6th to 13th August and then marched to St. Jan Ter Biezen, via Wormhoudt, where the Battalion remained until 20th. On the 29th (the 34th Division again moving up the line) the 2/4th moved to Scherpenberg, where for some time work on road repairing engaged the attention of the Battalion. Lieut-Colonel E. B. Powell relinquished command of the Battalion on 19th September.

The Somerset Light Infantry 1914–19

Capt. Mackie

Au Q. G. A., 5th August 1918.

Xe ARMÉE

ETAT-MAJOR

3e BUREAU

Au Q. G. A., le 5 Août 1918.

ORDRE GÉNÉRAL N° 343

OFFICIERS, SOUS-OFFICIERS ET SOLDATS DES 15e ET 34e DIVISIONS BRITANNIQUES.

Vous êtes entrés dans la bataille à son moment le plus rude. L'ennemi vaincu une première fois, ramenait contre nous ses meilleures divisions, en nombre plus considérable que les nôtres.

Vous avez continué à avancer pied à pied, malgré sa résistance acharnée, et vous avez gardé le terrain conquis, malgré ses violentes contre-attaques.

Puis dans la journée du 1er Août, vous avez enlevé, côte à côte avec vos camarades Français, la crête qui domine toute la contrée entre l'AISNE et l'OURCQ, que ses défenseurs avaient l'ordre de tenir coûte que coûte.

Ayant échoué dans sa tentative pour la reprendre avec ses dernières réserves, l'ennemi dut battre en retraite, poursuivi, bousculé, pendant 12 kilomètres.

Tous, Anglais et Ecossais, jeunes soldats et vétérans des FLANDRES ou de PALESTINE, vous avez montré les magnifiques qualités de votre race, le courage et l'impertubable ténacité.

Vous avez fait l'admiration de vos compagnons d'armes. Votre pays sera fier de vous, car vos chefs et vous avez eu une large part dans la victoire que nous venons de remporter sur les barbares ennemis des peuples libres.

Je suis heureux d'avoir combattu à votre tête et je vous remercie.

ORDRE GENERAL N° 343

OFFICERS, NON COMMISSIONNED OFFICERS AND MEN OF THE 15th AND 34th BRITISH DIVISIONS.

You entered the battle at its fiercest moment. The enemy, already once vanquished, again brought up against us his best divisions, considerably outnumbering our own.

You continued to advance step by step, in spite of his desperate resistance, and you held the ground won in spite of his violent counter-attacks.

Then, during the whole day of the 1st of August, side by side with your French comrades, you stormed the ridge dominating the whole country between the AISNE and the OURCQ, wich the defenders had received orders to hold at all cost.

Having failed in his attempt to retake the ridge with his last reserves, the enemy had to beat a retreat pursued and harassed for 12 kilometers.

All of you, English and Scottish, young soldiers and veterans of FLANDERS and PALESTINE, you have shown the magnificent qualities of your race : courage and imperturbable tenacity.

You have won the admiration of your companions in arms. Your country will he proud of you for to your chiefs and to you is due a large share in the victory that we have gained over the barbarous enemies of the free.

I am happy to have fought at your head and I thank you.

MANGIN.

B.E.F.
France

8–8–18

My dear Mother & Father

I was unable to write last Sunday, as I was in fact this is the first opportunity I have had for several day. I have lots of things to thank you for to-day for I now that I am with the Bttn again I have got hold of all my letters. The socks which Mother sent just before I came on leave are splendid and I am awfully glad to have them as the ones I have with me are getting very bad.

Thank you very much indeed for the cake & for letters up to the 31st July all of which I have received safely. We had the cake in the train and as we were very hard up for rations at the time it was more than acceptable. I sent Janet a field card the day I set off for to join the battn. I got a message at 12–30 at night to join the Battn as soon as possible and I set off at 5–15 A.M. so that it was rather a rush getting away. I was sent for in order that Ron could go off on leave but unfortunately all leave was stopped just afterwards and he could not go. However he will be the first to go as soon as it is re-opened again so I expect he will be home in a few days time.

I had an awful job getting to the Battn but I managed to reach them at last and just after I got there everyone the The news came through that our Division was to be relieved at once – of course everyone was frightfully pleased.

They had an awfully hard time for about a fortnight but the Division did extraordinarily well – anyhow partly as a result of its efforts the Bosche cleared out of the Marne salient very hurriedly. The Our Battn being the Divisional Pioneer Battn was mostly in reserve and id not suffer nearly such heavy casualties as the others. It did some very good work & was very highly complimented by the Divisional Comdr. & the Colonel has since been awarded the Leigin Leigion d'honneur. The fighting was very fierce indeed before the Germans really began to retreat and both sides suffered enormous casualties. I came up after the battle and there were dead lying about everywhere in spite of the fact that burying parties had been out the whole of the previous day. It was a very gruesome sight & very sad but I am afraid one gets very hardened to this sort of thing. Several C.O.s were killed and in the case of one Bttn (Scottish) there was only one officer left – he poor fellow saw his C.O. Adjutant, two Coy Comdrs Regt. Sergt Major & three Coy Sergt Majors all buried together. It was a very successful campaign for us and the Bosche suffered quite as many casualties as we did but one often wonders whether success is worth the price you have to pay for it.

We are now back again not far from where we were when I came home.

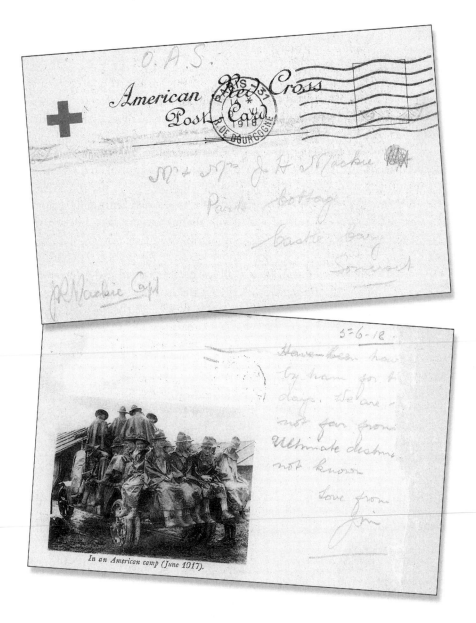

In an American camp (June 1917).

We ʌ came in last night very tired indeed after a long hot march and we are having a good rest to-day and cleaning up. We shall probably rest here for a few days while the Division is being made up to strength again. I am awfully glad Rob passed his Diploma Part I. It was an awfully plucky effort – he deserves to get through.

Fancy old Ted Drewett being home again – is he on leave or is it sick leave. What a chance for Teddy!! (My word!!) I found a letter from Andrew waiting for me when I got back. He seems to have had a trying time but he writes very cheerily and seems quite fit.

John had a very good time up in Kashmire – he says that it was a jolly nice to get a real rest & to see some different scenery again.

Buscombe is ʌn one of my officers – he isn't a bad fellow talks rather too much at present but I have no doubt that we shall cure him of that in time.

I hope Angus enjoyed his holiday – what a pity it was so wet.

Please thank Duff for his letter – I am awfully pleased with it.

With much love to all & ởɴɕ very many thanks for the cake, socks etc.

  Wɨth Your affectionate son
      Jim

BEF

11–8–18

My dear Mother & Father.

There is really nothing to write about to-day as I only ʈ wrote two days ago, but as I usually write Sunday afternoons I thought I would just send along a note. Ron left here the day before yesterday so I suppose he is home now thoroughly enjoying himself. He deserves his leave & I am awfully glad he has got it at last.

Isn't the news good the last few days – we are awfully bucked about it and I really think the war will soon be over. Anyhow it is an awful knock for the old Bosche & will nead need some explanation to the German people.

I enclose a copy of a letter the Colonel received a few days ago from one of the Brigadiers in the Division – we are very proud of it I am can assure.

I am sorry old Colonel Clutterbuck has been ill & hope it was nothing very serious. We have been getting all sorts of gifts for the men sent out by him.

We are in fairly comfortable billets now & are busy reorganizing & cleaning up – the men needed the latter very badly indeed.

The weather is delightful just now – if you are getting anything like it in England I expect the farmers are getting on with the harvest.

There isn't another thing to write about to-day

With much love to all

> Your affectionate son
> Jim

Copy of letter received by Colonel

My dear Colonel.

I wish to express to you my high appreciation of the excellent work done by you, your officers, N.C.O.^{s} , & men of the 2/4th Somt L.I. I should be pleased if you will convey my appreciation to all ranks under your command.

You were pushed into the different fights at very short notice & through the excellent handling of the Bttn both by yourself & your officers & N.C.O.^{s} you were able to carry out all orders ~~on time~~ issued to you by me actually on time which undoubtedly led to the success which was achieved by the Brigade

I cannot speak too highly of the conduct of your Bttn & sincerely hope that we shall in the near future have another occasion on which to serve together.

> Yours very sincerely
> Edward Hillman
> Bdr. General.

B.E.F.
France

18–8–18

My dear Mother & Father.

We have been on the move again since I last wrote and before I write again we shall probably be up in the line so I expect we shall have a very strenuous time ~~do~~ this week. We came here from our last place in two marches which were not very nice as it was rather hot and dusty: but we stayed the night in some top hole billets & were frightfully sorry when we had to move on in the morning. It was an awfully nice little town – the people were awfully kind & could not do enough for us, & there were lots of places where we could buy stores etc for our mess. The Divisional concert party happened to be there that night & of course we all turned up in force to see them perform. They gave us a ripping show. One fellow was acting as a girl and he was so awfully good that lots of people really thought he was a girl.

I have just heard that all our kit both from Port Said and Marseilles have turned up in Bath and I have written to the O.C. of the Depôt asking him to send it home. If the boxes don't come fairly soon I should be awfully glad if you would kindly ring up the depôt and ask about them, as I should like to have them opened.

When they arrive will you please open them & have a look at my clothes etc. There are a few odds & ends which I think Mother or the girls would like such as mats & bits of brass etc, and of course Angus can make use of anything he wants. I daresay you will be able to find something or other for Duff amongst it all.

You will find my camera & sword in my uniform case – if you would like to use the camera please do so if you can get films for it. It is a "No 2 Ensignette".

All the keys are inside one of the boxes and I left another set at Cox's but I don't know whether they sent them on. However I daresay the famous Arthur will be able to open them I think a good bit of the stuff is quite useless, as my bearer packed it up and I don't know exactly what he put in but anything which is obviously useless can be destroyed. Have you seen Ron yet? I expect he is awfully glad to be home – he said he was coming down to see you as soon as possible. I hope Ewart is getting better – was he very seriously wounded?

I rode up as far as Ypres yesterday afternoon. You can't imagine what it is like until you see it for yourself for such absolute desolation is almost inconceivable. It almost gets on one's nerves to see it.

We have had some most delightful weather lately but I think it is going to break up soon. We had one storm last night and it doesn't look a bit fine to-day although so far it has not rained.

I am glad Rob has been able to come home if only for a day and am delighted to hear that he is looking so much better. I am very keen to see Mother's new coat – you will be able to show it to me when I am home next time. The rules for leave have just been revised and an officer now becomes entitled to leave after he has been out of England 5 months. Of course there may not be a vacancy at the time but when he is due for leave he can take a vacancy when it occurs.

I must go & get lunch now for I am going up to the line this afternoon to have a look at our new quarters.

With very much love to all

> Your affectionate son
> Jim

B.E.F.
France

25–8–18

My dear Mother & Father

I have just read Janet's extremely amusing & interesting letter. It came last night & I read it through for the first time at 3 A.M. when I returned from my day's work but before answering it I had to just read it through again to take it all in.

We are in the line now – I sent Mary a field card the day we went up – and are busy working on the front line so our work really starts just as you are going off to bed. Just as it begins to get dark we all begin to crawl out of our dugouts just like rabbits & before long, where a few minutes ago ~~before when~~ there was not a soul to be seen, there are men everywhere, getting out tools, putting on equipment etc. Trains & transport begin to arrive & things begin to get very busy. The old Bosche knows this quite well so he just amuses himself by pluming over a shell or two every now and then.

As soon as we are ready, we go off to the front line where we work till ~~about 2~~ the early hours of the morning & then come wearily back again hoping all the way along that we shall not get any shelling.

Rations, letters, etc come up while we are away so when we come back after the usual cup of tea has been issued we settle down to have a look at our letters. I then write my report of the nights work & then off to bed.

We have breakfast about 10 and then I usually go out with our R.E. officer to look at the work in daylight – a beastly job on account of snipers.

This morning he started to shell us after we got back, but we are perfectly safe here against anything – we just go to earth & he can't touch us. Fortunately he doesn't do much bombing as close a up as this – the people further back get that little pleasure.

I am glad you saw Ron while he was home & I am sure Teddy had a thoroughly good time up at Frome. I expect his people were awfully pleased to see him. N Did he manage to get his extension? I have not heard yet.

The "Follies" all seem to be having a gay time & thoroughly enjoying life. I hope there have been no more black eyes over Mary.

We have had lots of fun out of some of the little stories I brought back – I expect the "Follies" would like to hear them. I hope Ron has saved up a few little incidents for us. I have just heard the good news that I am going on a course at Rouen from ~~Oc~~ Sept 7th to October 1st. It will be an awfully nice change & Rouen is a very good place to go to. It is one of the best spots in France in these days. I am sorry John has disappointed his very inquisitive sisters – never mind it will all come out one of these days no doubt.

I hope M^s Angus & Duff are both going strong – are they both back at school now?

Things are going well out here now aren't they? I do hope we shall be able to finish it off this year. If we can keep the Bosche moving now that he has started I think it will soon be over.

I am glad the little camera is a success & and am looking forward to seeing some of the photos. John & Andrew will be glad to see them too.

Give my love to Jack Mullins. I should awfully like to see him again for I have not seen him since he used to live at Melbury.

I hope Father you are all quite fit

With very much love to all

Your affectionate son

Jim

The 2/4th Somersets, the Pioneers of the 34th Division, were engaged in repairing the roads and communication trenches in the forward areas east of Kemmel, Battalion Headquarters moving to Scherpenberg on 29th September. Here and there the official despatches make brief reference to the Pioneers, but generally their praises are unsung, though in the Final Advance to Victory their work was of the utmost importance. At all hours of the day and night they laboured to put roads and communications into a state of repair. The infantry advanced so rapidly that it was almost impossible for the guns, regimental transport, ambulances, supply wagons and all the impedimenta of a moving army to go forward unless the roads were made passable, for the retreating enemy had damaged them and had blown them up.

On the 10th September Lieut-Colonel E. B. Powell relinquished command of the Battalion and on 25th lieut.-Colonel A. W. Reid arrived and assumed command. The Battalion moved to St. Eloi on 1st October and until the 16th of the month the Pioneers were engaged on the upkeep of roads.

The Battle of Courtrai, 14th–19th October 1918

Meanwhile the 34th Division had pushed on and by the night of 13th October held a line just west of Gheluwe, which place was to be attacked on the following day and the line advanced to Menin. The 2/4th Somersets moved to Zandvoorde on 13th and for the operations of 14th B Company was split up, one half being attached to each of the two attacking infantry brigades of the division.

Zero hour was 5.35 a.m. and again the attack was successful, the Pioneers following up the victorious infantry, consolidating the gains as won, and digging a support defence line. On the night of 14th the Division had gained the Brown Line which ran roughly from just west of Coucou and west of Menin to Snooker Farm, about 1,500 yards north of Menin. In the attack on, and capture of, Menin on 15th October the Pioneers were again hard at work on the defences and communications. Battalion Headquarters moved to Gheluwe on 16th, on which date half of A Company was placed at the disposal of the 101st Brigade.

Troops of the 34th Division crossed the Lys on the 17th, having fought their way to the River. By this date the British front east of Ypres ran from the northern bank of the Lys at Frelinghein to opposite Harlebeke. On 19th the Division as a whole crossed the river, A Company of the 2/4th Somersets accompanying the 101st Brigade, the Advanced Guard, C Company being attached to the 102nd Brigade in support and B Company to the 103rd Brigade in reserve. Battalion Headquarters were then established at Lauwe. On the 20th the Division became Corps Reserve.

The concluding story of the 2/4th Somersets, however, is now summed up in a series of moves. On 24th the Battalion moved to Belleghem, and three days later back to Lauwe. The 34th Division was transferred to the II Corps on 28th October and moved to the Harlebeke area, north of Courtrai, the 2/4th Somersets billeting in Deerlyck. On the 1st November the 34th Division was again squeezed out of the line by the 41st (French) and 31st British Divisions which joined hands across the 34th divisional front at Elseghem, and on the 3rd the Division marched back to west of Courtrai, the 2/4th Somersets to Wevelghem. Here the Somerset men were in training until 14th November and the Battalion was thus engaged when the Armistice was concluded at 11 o'clock on the morning of 11th November. For the gallant Pioneers – the 2/4th Battalion, Somerset Light Infantry – the War was over.

The Somerset Light Infantry 1914–19

B.E.F.
France

2–9–18

My dear Mother & Father.

I had no time to write yesterday as usual so sent a field card instead. We had a most strenuous time last week and I am feeling awfully tired now. I had a fairly good sleep last night but previous to this I only got in about

6 hours sleep in three days. As soon as I have written this I am going to bed & I have hopes of getting in about 10 hours.

A week ago to-day we had the most awful shelling I have ever seen or experienced. The Bosche must have spotted movement in the area occupied by my company so he thought he would proceed to put us out to action at once. The first shell came over about 5 P.M. & he shelled us with 9′′ shells for 2 hours during which time he put over 360 shells & all of them fell in a circule of about 100 yards radius. Fortunately we had some very deep tunnels into which we all bolted like rabbits and there were no casualties although I had an almost miraculous escape. One of the first shells pitched right into the one of the men's dugouts & a rumour went round that a man was inside wounded. One or two men ran across to see & I came up out of the sap intending to go across & lend a hand as well. Just as I reached the entrance I heard a shell coming so I shouted to the men to get under cover & the next thing I remember was being picked up at the bottom of the sap. One of these great shells had pitched not 3 yards from where I had been standing & had blown me down the steps & stunned me. Owing to the fact that I was just in the entrance none of the splinters hit me & I was soon fit again but was frightfully shaken up. I have never felt so shaken in my life & still feel the effect a little but nothing to speak of. For several days my ears were very bad & the Dr wanted to send me down the line to see a specialist, but as I am shortly going on a course I did not think it worth while.

On Tuesday we were relieved during the night & so we got away rather without any casualties. You ought to have seen us marching till we were clear of the town, there was no falling out I can assure you.,

The next night we marched to another part of the line – went back in again. It was a rotten march for the Bosche was shelling the road all the way along & we all got "wind up" very badly.

As soon as we got in we were put on to some very important work in front of the front line & worked one night at it. The next morning the Bosche had gone & we we have been after him ever since. That very night I was right up to his wire doing a reconnaissance and he seemed to be there all right at that time but I suppose it was only his rear guard.

We got in at 5–30 A.M. that morning absolutely tired out & then had to go off again to take part in the chase. It was rather bad luck but of course one doesn't mind these little inconveniences in these days for we are on the winning side now – there is no doubt about that.

We are busy pushing up the roads – most of the work has to be done at night & he tries to shell us off but we start again as soon as the shelling stops.

I go off to Rouen the day after to-morrow & shall not be at all sorry to go for I am frightfully tired and am still rather nervey as a result of the shell episode. Things are going splendidly now – of course we shall have to be careful but I should think there was quite a good chance of the war being over this year.

I have never seen anything like the ground from which the Germans have just retired – there are dead everywhere, Germans, British & French in all stages of decomposition. Many of them have been ʎ lying there since last April as neither side have been able to bury them.

I received Angus letter during the week & Father's arrived on Saturday. I was delighted with the little snapshots – they are awfully good. The group is excellent. I hope you can get films without much trouble.

I was sorry to hear that Mother had been unwell & hope she is feeling better again. Father must be awfully busy now that his work has been ful further extended. I hope he won't work too hard.

I am off to bed now & will write again in a few days.

With very much love to all

> Your affectionate son
> Jim

B.E.F.
France

₹ 5–9–18

My dear Mother &

Just a line to ʎ tell you that I am still "all correct" and to thank you very much indeed for both lots of cakes. The last lot arrived last night and are absolutely ripping. We have enjoyed them ever so much & thank you very much indeed for sending them out. The apples too were top hole. The first lot arrived when we were in the last place & I was so tired when I last wrote that I clean forgot to thank you for them.

I am glad my kit has arrived safely – I hope most of it was in fairly good condition. Will you kindly send your photograph out to me again as it was packed away by the mistake. I thought my uniform case was coming with me when we left Marseilles but it had to be left behind at the last moment & I found afterwards that the photograph had been packed in it by mistake.

Please thank Janet for her letter which has just arrived. I am quite safe at present & very busy & needless to say very tired.

Hope you are all quite fit

> Loy Your affectionate son
> Jim

R.E. Training Centre
Base. B.E.F.

My dear Mother & Father.

I arrived here this morning after a somewhat long & tiring journey, but I soon got a wash & found some very good quarters and I think I shall be quite comfortable for for a bit. It is quite good to get away from the war for a bit for although we have been in one of the quietest parts of the line we have had quite a strenuous time of late. We have been busy getting up the roads up to the front line & some of them have been so knocked about by shell fire that they are hardly recognisable. Some of the work has to be done at night in the most exposed places but we do as much as possible by day as it gets on much more quickly than at night. The Bosch knows we are busy on the roads & we have a good bit of shelling – fortunately only one or two casualties but this is entirely due to good luck. Intermittent shelling such as we have been getting is much more trying to the nerves than a bombardment for during the latter you get under cover & stay there but when the shells only come over every now & again you have to get on with the work & you never know where or when the next one will come. If I had not come down for this course I am sure I should have had to come down for a short rest for I am still feeling the effects of that shell which knocked me down that I told you about last week.

Isn't the news top hole – it is easily the best we have had since the German retreat in 1914 and the best of it is our advance is still going on. Our attacks are so carefully planned & carried out nowadays that the Bosche is forced to clear out of his strong positions & go back. We don't storm positions like Hemmel Hill nowadays & loose thousands of men we manouvre the Bosche out of them.

I wish you could see the country over which we have been advancing – such complete destruction & desolation are quite inconceivable until you have actually seen it. Even the trees are dead & one very rarely sees a bird the country is just one mass of enormous shell holes holes with here & there the remains of camps & villages. There are dead everywhere – mostly German – which have been left unburied since last April.

Thank you ever so much for the cakes & apples. I saved a few of the cakes to eat in the train on my way down here they were ripping & the apples were delicious.

The girls all seem to be having a cheery time – I suppose Ted is awfully excited about being Gwen's bridesmaid & I have no doubt that she will create a tremendous impression when she turns. I will write to her in a day or two, please thank her for her letter.

I am glad Ron has had a good time – so he thoroughly deserved his extension but the C.O. was awfully annoyed when he heard about it & cut down the allotment of officers leave. Instead of letting an officer go every 5 days he only lets one go every 8 days – it is not quite playing the game for he took his own leave quickly enough.

I am awfully glad ✗ to hear that you are all fit & hope you will be able to keep it up.

With very much love to all

Your affectionate son
Jim

R.E. Training School
~~Rouen~~ Base

✗ 15–9–18

My dear Mother & Father.

Mothers letter arrived this morning quite safely & of course I was awfully pleased to get it.

We have had a most interesting week which I have thoroughly enjoyed. The work has been very hard and we have had very little spare time in fact I have only been into Rouen about twice but one can just put up with any amount of work down here where there are no shells flying about. War at the base is not a bad job and those people who get permanent jobs down here have a jolly good time. The funny part of it is that they grouse far more than we do. We have done a good deal of field work & have been learning how to make dugouts, concrete pill boxes etc. Our evenings are taken up by drawing maps & sketches for the field schemes & writing notes. It seems quite like old times to settle down to notes after dinner & reminds me of Reading days. It is really rather nice to have to use your brains again instead of having to do mere routine work.

Last Thursday we all went off in ~~mort~~ motor lorries to do a scheme some miles out. It rained in torrents but all the same it was awfully good fun. We drove all through the forests which are very thick all round here and eventually came out on the high ground overlooking the river. We all paid a good deal of attention to the blackberries – there are lots of them everywhere & they are jolly good.

We are just near the ~~Ind~~ old Indian Cavalry Base and do a good deal of our work in the "Bull Ring" where Andrew used to learn riding & jumping. I have not met many of his lady friends yet but in his last letter he asked me to go & call on some of the nurses if I was ever in Rouen. The mess is very nice indeed and we get excellent food which is a great treat. It reminded me of India when we had a mess guest night a few days ago.

There is a tennis court here also & I must try & get a few games since before I go away for I have not had a game of any sort since I left India.

I am ever so glad you have been able to make use of the brass, mats etc you found in my kit. Although I used them myself in India I really bought them for you. The curtains always used to hang in my room.

Duff can have the breeches you spoke of for they are rather too thin for the Winter out here I think & I have 2 pairs with me now.

Will you please send me out some a few handkerchiefs and some a couple more pairs of socks. I have enough clothes at present but when it begins to get really cold I shall have to get you to send me out some warm things. It is no good to have them till I want them as I cannot carry too much & I am going to send back some of the thin stuff.

Have I any more flannel shirts – I can't remember as if not I shall have to get some more. I can get anything like that from the Army Ordnance Dept ever so cheaply and excellent quality. They supply clothing to officers at specially cheap rates.

I hope Margaret will enjoy her holiday at Portishead – it will be a nice change for her.

The war is still going well isn't it? I should not be a bit surprised if peace came along before the end of the winter for the Bosches are getting pretty fed up & the Bosche people will have to realize that the Americans are going to make all the difference to us.

I have been back nearly 2 months now – shall be due for leave again at the end of five.

I heard from Uncle Andrew yesterday – he is going to try and come to Rouen to see me. I hope he will be able to do so for I should like to see him again awfully.

I hope you are both keeping well – I have not been quite as fit as usual the last few days & had to see the Dr on yesterday. He gave me some medicine & excused all duty for a couple of days & I am feeling much better to-day. There is nothing much the matter – just a little chill or something of that sort.

W give my love to Duffy & the others

               Do From you affectionate son
               Jim

R.E.T.S.
Base

19–9–18

My dear Father.

I enclose a cheque for £77–10–0 & will you kindly invest it in war bonds
for me as we arranged when I was at home. I have just received my balance
from Egypt and may be able to invest a little more before long.

Janet says you had a very busy week last week – I hope you will not
overdo it. Did you find the people in Scotland all quite fit. I expect they
were awfully pleased to see you. When you are next in London would you
mind sending Andrew a leather Attaché Case for me. I promised him one
for his 21st birthday & forgot to get it when I was home. I don't know a
bit what they cost but I rather fancy they are something between 2 & 3
guineas. Anyhow I should like to give him a fairly good one as he gave me
a beauty for my 21st I hope this will cause you much ≀ trouble for I know
how frightfully busy you are.

I am feeling quite myself again now in fact fitter than I have been ever since
I left England. I am having quite a good rest & thoroughly enjoying the
course. I hear to-day that my solution to one of the schemes was read out to
the R.E. officers to-day as an example of how these things should be done.

I hope Mother is better & that you are keeping fit
With love to all

        your affectionate son
         Jim

R.E.T.S.
Base

My dear Mother & Father.

Hasn't it been good news again the last few days? The Palestine show is
one of the best of the war. They have done what we tried to do last April
but then we tried to break the ≀≀ Turkish centre whereas now they have
turned the flanks. I expect Andrew has been right in it & I do hope he is
safe – I ≀ see that the casualties have been particularly light. The Serbian
show has been a good one too – althogether I should think the Bosche is
really ≀ getting worried. I rather think we are up against it out here now
& there will be some jolly hard fighting before we get the Hindenburg line,
but all the same we are doing well. I see that the 74th Divn has been doing

well – they are one of the Divns. which came back with us. Our course is going along steadily & I am thoroughly enjoying it. I am ever so fit now – feeling very different from what I did when I came down.

Last Friday night the Lena Ashwell Concert party gave an awfully good show in the Y.M.C.A. here. It was a great treat to have it all in English for all the shows in Rouen are of course French. I think they are going to give another show next Friday.

One of the officers of my Coy – Parkes was down here on leave last week & he said that the Col had gone to another Regt. I don't know if he has gone for good but anyhow I don't think many people in the Regt will be sorry. Personally I always got on very well with him but I can't say that I liked him a bit.

I am glad Mary & Margaret both enjoyed their holidays – it was a nice change for them both but it must have been awfully quiet at home while they were away. I hope Janet received ~~here~~ her parcel safely. I can see she is going to be no end of a swell when she is fully togged up.

I had one or two games of tennis last week – the first since I left India. We have a court belonging to the mess here and it is top hole to be able to get a game sometimes. I absolutely out of practice and wasn't much good, but it was jolly good fun. The worst of active service is that it is all work & no play & that is why we get so stale at times. A few games make all the difference.

I received Father's letter on Saturday & was awfully sorry to hear that Mother is still unwell. I expect the colder weather has something to do with it & I hope she is better now.

Will you ask one of the girls ~~to make~~ to make me a couple of pairs of draught boards to wear on my coat sleeves. The draught board is our divisional sign & we all wear it just below the shoulder. I have enclosed a little drawing to show the size & ⟨the position of the black squares.

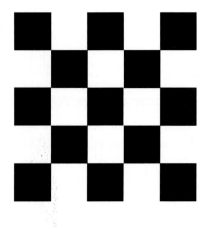

I wrote once or twice last week so there is absolutely nothing else to say now.

I hope you are all quite fit
With much love to all

Your affectionate son
Jim

L. S. M.

ROADS FOR THE GUNS.

A Pioneer Battalion must be capable of playing many parts. Not seldom it has to adopt the rôle of the roadmender. Think of men hurrying in the night time; of a ruined landscape weird in the pale light of the moon; a road scarred and torn as only a road that was once in No Man's Land could be, and the heavens hot with the rush and scream of countless shells.

For there has been a successful "push" or the enemy has retired "according to plan." In any case the Boche is farther back and the cry of the moment is for roads. Ration transports must get nearer the line; guns of all calibres must keep in range of their targets; everything, in fact, must move forward if the gain is to be made good and the infantry enabled to hold the new line or make a further advance. Hence the hurrying figures in the night time, for the roads are still too dangerous to work upon them by day.

Do not think, however, that the pioneer's job is merely to "chuck stuff" into a hole. Filling a shell-hole or making a mine-crater passable is something more than that. More in sorrow than in anger do we think of the unknown men who, in their zeal to make a track of some sort, filled a shell-hole with three mattresses, a chair, a clock, a few bundles of straw, and a barrow full of earth.

To remake a good road requires that water, if any, should be removed from the hole, a good bottom made, the hole filled alternately with bricks and stones, rammed earth, and finally the metalling, which a generous C.R.E. may provide. Happy are the pioneers whose work lies handy to a ruined farm or village, for then may be found bricks and timber in plenty, and the task proceeds apace.

The speed with which roads may be made passable depends, of course, on the nature of the country, the extent of the advance, the possibility of work by day, and the number of men available in a forward area for putting on the task. The unimaginative ones who sit at home and prate impatiently about the slowness of our troops in following up again would do well to think of these facts. Let them remember that there are no short cuts across country, that heavy transport and guns must keep to the roads, and that a careful enemy sees to it that such roads are well mined even if they have not been continuously shelled. Until these roads are made good, progress must inevitably be slow, for the infantry cannot advance without rations —Napoleon's maxim still holds good that "An army marches on its stomach"—and troops cannot hold what they have gained without artillery support.

And so the humble pioneer comes into his own and right loyally does he fulfil the task imposed upon him. W. M. P.

Newspaper cutting

R.E.T.S. ~~has~~
Base

My dear Mother & Father.

There is only one subject which one can possibly write about this week and that of course is the war. I suppose this last week has been the best week since the outbreak of war and I am not sure that the next few days will not be better still. The news has come through this morning that we have captured Courtrai and I think it is almost certain now that the Bosche will have to clear out of the Hindenburg line. I don't think our people have been really in it so far but the army to which we belong kicked off yesterday so it looks as if ~~we~~ our division will be for it during the next few days.

What a splendid show they have done out in Palestine! I expect they are having an awfully rough time of it. I know what ʏ an advance means out there – long marches, very little water & bully beef & biscuits. Have you had any news of Andrew? He is quite safe if you have not for they always wire to the next of kin ʏ even a fellow is only slightly wounded. I think we have had a lot of casualties out here – the motor ambulances are running to & from the station night & day almost continuously, but of course everyone is frightfully cheery.

It is a great sight to see the people dashing after the paper boys & the French get ever so excited when the news in good & there are always crowds of people round the paper stalls.

I received the parcel of socks etc quite safely & also Mother's letter for both of which many thanks. I am awfully glad to hear that Duff has been promoted to a higher class & can quite imagine that the little man is ~~awfully~~ extremely pleased. I sent Mary & Angus a birthday present each yesterday & hope they will get them safely. They are rather early but I thought I had better get them before I left here. Did Janet receive the things I sent her?

Our course ends Tuesday and I suppose we shall go back almost at once so I think you had better write direct to the Regt. again.

We have had some beastly weather the last few days and it begins to feel a bit Wintry. There was a thick white fog when I woke up this morning. I shall be glad of the scarf & helmet as soon as I get back to the Regt for the nights are getting very cold indeed.

I have just had a letter from Ron and he says that things are going fairly well up yonder. He has sent in his application for the I.A. and thinks he will probably get away fairly soon. He is frightfully keen that I should go with him & he uses such powerful arguments that really sometimes I think I should be wise do do so. It is certainly a way of increasing one's chances of getting out of the war with a whole skin and as he says we could always transfer to the political department, but I am not keen on the army as a profession and somehow it doesn't seem quite playing the game to go for it just as a means of saving you skin.

I heard from Col Clutterbuck yesterday – he is still trying to get a job out here but I don't think he stands much chance.

I am in fine form again now – the course has been a great rest from the point of view of being away from the war I am going to see the dentist to-morrow just to get a little stopping done & let him have a look at my teeth before I go back up the line.

I hope you are both better & have got rid of your colds & that all the others are quite fit.

With much love to all

> Your affectionate son
> Jim

R.E.T.S.
Base

4–10–18

My dear Mother & Father.

The course ended last Tuesday and to-day is Saturday but I have not yet left here. My teeth took longer than I expected and I ~~have not yet~~ were only finished this morning so I have had four days holiday which I did not expect. I think I shall probably leave here to-morrow night. I don't know where I shall find the Regt as I expect they have gone forward with everyone else – I suppose I shall catch them up somewhere or other.

The weather has turned ever so cold the last few days and I have been obliged to think about warm kit already. Will you kindly send me out one of my thick tunics, and my slacks. I think one of the tunics & the slacks match each other & I thnk it would be best to have that tunic. I should also be glad of the helmet & scarf which you have made for me. So far I don't kn need the vests yet but if it gets much colder I shall have to get you to send them out too.

I hope Janet made a successful bridesmaid at Gwen's wedding I expected she was too excited for words.

Salisbury Donne's wedding was a great event for Cary I suppose. The news is still good and all the wounded fellows coming down here seem very cheery indeed in spite of all they have had to put up with. I think the fighting in front of Courtrai has been some of the hardest of the whole war.

I heard from John yesterday – he says he is very fit & is absolutely full of his work. He couldn't possibly have found a job which would have suited him better. Is there any news from Andrew yet?

I see Col Armstrong who commanded the Wilts when we were in Palestine has died of wounds & several other officers of our old Division have appeared in the ~~calu~~ casualty lists including the Staff Capt of our old Brigade.

Tell Angus to tell Mr Brown when he next sees him that I met Lt Smith at the Club yesterday. He used to be the Regtl Sergt. Major of the 7th Somersets & helped to bandage Brown up when he was wounded.

I was looking at the Times yesterday and saw Andrew's gazette to the Indian army. His original gazette is dated July 1st 1915 and his promotion to Lt. July 1st 1916.

I can't think of anything else now but will write again as soon as I get back to the Regt.

I hope you are all quite fit

With much love to all

> Your affectionate son
> Jim

Base

9th October

My dear Mother & Father.

Just a line to tell you ~~I am~~ that I am leaving here to-day to return to the Regt. I have had a week's holiday so have not done badly and am now as fit as can be.

I have had no news other than this & my batman is waiting to pack up my things so I must not keep him waiting any longer.

Will write again when I get to the other end.

Much love to all

> Your affectionate son
> Jim

B.E.F.
France

13–10–18

My dear Mother & Father.

I am back at the old game again now but feeling very different to what I did when I went away. I am in tophole form now and have managed to raise quite a lot of new zest for the job.

I left Rouen last Wednesday afternoon and arrived at railhead on Thursday evening where I stayed the night at the Divn rest camp. Padre Mead was there too having just come down from the line to get some cigarettes etc for his men. I was glad to see him again and enjoyed his company. The next day I rejoined the Bttn.

We are having a day's rest to-day as we are expecting a busy time next week but it is not a very good &t day as it been raining steadily since last week. The mud is getting very bad indeed – I hope it will clear up again before long for if we get too much rain it will stop our advance. We are not in very decent quarters at present as we are living on what used to be the Bosche area and one gets some idea of what our shell fire must have been like for you cannot go 3 yards anywhere without stepping into a shell hole.

We have been doing some rather dirty work the last few days but our quarters are fairly safe and when we get back. I found Ron looking very fit, and but I think he was glad enough to see me again.

I found several letters from you waiting for me – thank you ever so much for writing so often – I can assure you I am glad enough to get them. I also found the parcel containing the scarf, helmet & apples waiting for me and as it is still very cold I am very glad of the two former at night. The apples were delicious – not a bit damaged – we enjoyed them very much indeed.

The little draught boards are just what I wanted and they look very nice indeed on my coat. I gave one pair to Ron and should like one more pair for the coat which you are sending out if you would kindly make them for me.

Thank you very much indeed for investing the money for me – I shall probably send back some more when all my allowances have been paid up.

The snapshots which Angus enclosed were awfully good – the little camera seems to be giving excellent results.

I heard from Andrew yesterday but his letter was written &t before the show – he seemed to be in very good form just then.

My batman went off on leave this morning and he says he wants to try & come up to see you but I don't think he will be able to manage it as he lives at Bridgewater & it takes such a long time to travel about by train. He was awfully anxious to do something or other for me so I asked him to take back some of my thin clothes which I don't want now. If he does not come up he will probably send them on by post. I am glad Janet had a good time at the wedding. I saw a very good account of it in the Western Gazette. It was very strange that Father should have met Buscombe – I heard to-day that he had just got an extension. He is not a bad fellow at all – wants a bit of breaking in but is very willing to work.

The new C.O. is a topper – I like him immensely. His is a very good soldier but is also a real "sahib" and is awfully nice to us all. It is a great change after our old one.

Ron is in fine form this afternoon – he has just been entertaining us with ↘ little love stories taken from his own life – Imagine us – Ron, Myself, Speed, Carpenter & Church, in a very small dug out made of concrete kindly left behind by the Bosche with a fire in the middle round which we are sitting. We are all smoking our pipes and telling those amusing little incidents collected ↘ up while we were on leave. It might be a good deal worse.

I hope you are all quite fit
With much love to all

> Your affectionate son
> Jim

Frogmore House
Westonzoyland
N^r Bridgwater

18–10–18

Dear Madam

As I was coming home on leave I offered to bring with me and send to you the enclosed articles of kit belonging to your son Captⁿ J. R. Mackie, as they were of no further use to him now that the cold weather has come upon us. They consist of the following

1	Thin khaki shirt
1	P^r ′ ′ Slacks
1	′ ′ green hose tops
1	′ ′ White cord riding breeches

also 2 keys, the larger one is a duplicate one to fit the long brown suit case, and the smaller one is the one that fits the lock of the kit bag that was sent from France to Bath, and I think is now in your possession.

Am afraid the articles I am sending you are in a very unclean condition owing to the fact that myself and everything I had was socked through and through with rain.

Am pleased to be able to tell you that Captⁿ Mackie was in splendid fettle when I left him, no doubt owing to his being able to go to Rouen, and being out of the line for some time, and I think has quite got over the slight shell shock he received at Ypres.

I have rather delayed sending the parcel as I have been rather unwell since being in England.

My respects to Mr Mackie, yourself, and the rest of your family hoping you are all enjoying perfect health.

> I remain
> > Yours Sincerely
> > > Percy D. Madge

(Letter from J.R.M.'s Batman)

B.E.F.
France

20–10–18

My dear Mother & Father.

We are having a most interesting ~~time~~ war just now for we are advancing steadily over quite new country, and it is really rather good fun. All the old fighting area is left behind and ~~and~~ we turn up at some village or other every night and get jolly good billets. The people are delighted to get rid of the Bosche and can't do enough for us. Some of them say that they have had no meat for three years having lived on potatoes & so on. To-day a shell killed some of our horses and the people ~~had~~ all came round & cleared off with the meat in no time. It is awfully amusing to see them jeering at the Jerry prisoners as they are marched back through the villages. I suppose they think they are getting their own back. All the villages are bedecked with Belgian flags which have been hidden away.

I hope things are going well elsewhere – you know far more about it than we do for we have had no news at all for about four days.

My coy is attached to one of the Brigades as a more or less independent unit. I have my own transport and am quite self contained. We occasionally get into touch with Bttn Hq. but often don't know a bit where they are. I like this arrangement for we are a cheery crowd and get along quite well.

Ron went off to a course two days ago. He will probably be away for five weeks so it is possible that he may not come back again if his I.A. stunt comes through. I always miss him when he is away for he is an awfully good little fellow.

I got Janet's letter Friday night – was awfully sorry to hear about the trouble with her teeth & hope they have been put right again now.

Please congratulate the two junior follies on getting so many prizes – I am so pleased to hear that they have done so well.

I hope Rob will be able to get his leave – my turn will soon be round again now – only another two months. Please give my love to little Mr Duff and tell him that I will write him a letter as soon as I get time.

I hope you are all quite fit

With much love to all

> Your affectionate son
> Jim

B.E.F.
France

30–10–18

My dear Mother & Father.

I am sorry I have not written for the last few days ~~with influenza~~ but I have been ill with influenza. Fortunately the day it came on we rolled up at some jolly good billets and I was able to go to bed & stay there for two days. I am much better now but don't feel up to the mark yet. The worst of it was we had to move yesterday and on arrival at the new place only had bare huts to go into which are not very comfortable and awfully cold.

I can't keep warm anyhow, in spite of the fact that I am wearing almost everything I possess. Will you kindly send me out some warm vests & pants as I really want them badly now.

Carpenter & Fortt went to hosp. yesterday with this beastly flue but I don't think I shall have to go for I have no temperature now and my appetite is beginning to return.

Thank you very much indeed for your letter containing the draughtboards which are just right.

Please excuse a very short letter this time. With much love to all

> Your affectionate son
> Jim

B.E.F.
France

4–11–18

My dear Mother & Father

I was unable to write yesterday as we were on the move again, but we were not moving forward this time for a change. We came back to rest billetts yesterday afternoon and are now looking forward to a quiet week of training undisturbed by the Bosche. We weren't a bit sorry to leave the place we were at for although we had made ourselves fairly comfortable it was not at all a healthy spot for it was bombed every night while we were there. One night in particular we all had the wind up for the Hun started bombing the village as soon as it got dark & kept it up without cessation till about 4 o'clock in the morning & just to make the din a little more effective he added a few long range shells.

We are in fairly comfortable quarters now – I have secured quite a good billet with a decent bed & most of the other officers have done equally well,

I am still feeling rather washed out but otherwise very much better. This

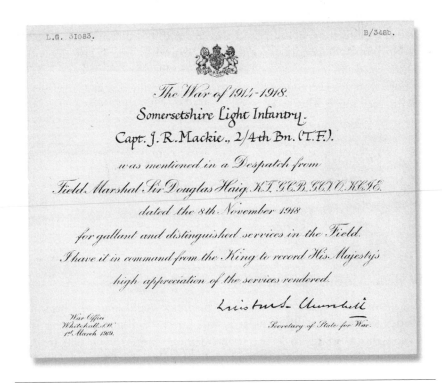

influenza is a beastly thing – two of my officers went to hospital with it and I only just managed to keep out, but as I say I am better now except for the fact that I have almost lost my voice.

I have received letters from you both during the last ƙ two days & thank you very much indeed for them. I was intensely amused over the little incident regarding Cecil Sims which Mother told me about. I think it is too funny for words.

I hope Father will like his new appointment and I am so glad ƕ you are not going to give up Park Cottage for it really is the most delightful little spot in the world.

I have just had a letter from Chell asking me when my next leave will come for he wants me to be his best man. He is going to marry a girl who used to be at Reading with us and I must say I should awfully like to go to the wedding.

I am ƨɋ now 6th on the list and we usually send an officer about every four days so I should be due about the end of the month. Will Father be more or less free about that time

Last time I wrote I forgot to thank Duffy for the postcard he sent me – will you please do so now. He is quite right – the end is very near now we shall soon all be home again. I am trying to write to you & at the same time talk to a young Belgian whose room I seem to be occupying – at present he is awfully interested in the scarf which you sent me – he thinks it very magnificent.

We are still getting awfully good weather and it is difficult to realize that it is November. It is cold of course but beautifully fine – just the sort of weather we want.

I hope you are keeping well – is there much influenza in Cary?

With very much love to all

> Your affectionate son
> Jim

B.E.F.
France

10–11–18

My dear Mother & Father.

I said in my letter to Mother that herɛ birthday would mark the beginning of better times & I really think it ƕ will for we had an officer over from Division this morning to lecure us on demobilization & he said that the latest news was that the Kaiser had abdicated that the Crown Prince had renounced his rights to the throne. The Bosche has to say yes or no to our a armistice terms by 11 o'clock to-morrow & in view of this I don't see how he can possibly refuse.

We are already preparing to have a Bttn dinner to celebrate the occasion. It is rather sad that Farwell & I will be the only survivors of the ~~old~~ original Battn present – I wish Col. Clutterbuck & some of the others could be with us for it will be a truly historic occasion. I expect England will go quite mad if the Bosche does accept our terms.

We are still resting & it is quite probable that we shall never have to go up to the line again to fight. I must say I should rather like to be up there just to fire the last shot at a Bosche or at anyrate across no man's land.

I hope you are all having a cheery time to celebrate Mother's birthday to-day – I shall drink her health at mess to-night & I know that John & Andrew will do the same.

Please thank Mary very much indeed for her letter which arrived yesterday afternoon. I am glad you have had Bunna home for a few days – it looks as if he will never be called upon to come out here & I sincerely hope he will not for it is not a very desirable place under war ∞ conditions. The first part of the week was beastly & wet but yesterday & to-day have been delightful – very cold but clear & frosty I hope you are all keeping clear of influenza for it is a beastly complain – makes one feel so rotten afterwards. I have quite got rid of my attack but I am still getting little attacks of fever in the evenings which I am almost sure is malaria. I have just had a note from Padre Mead – he was passing our Hqrs so just left a note for me. He is quite close to us now & I must try & go across to see him to-morrow. I called at his Hqrs a few days ago but did not see him although I heard that he had just had an attack of influenza.

I should like to get some news from Andrew – I expect he has been on the move all the time & was probably in the column which went right up to Aleppo.

I shall probably be able to get away on leave at the end of this week or the beginning of next. Of course I could wait & arrange to have it just at Christmas time but I think I will come as soon as I get the chance as it is a rotten job waiting when you know you are due & also it puts one lower down the list for the next time.

I hope Father is taking things steadily & will have a holiday before he takes over his new appointment. By the way did he send Andrew an attaché case if so I should be glad to have the bill so that I can pay for it.

Hoping you are all quite fit

With much love to all

> Your affectionate son
> Jim

B.E.F.
France

2 13–11–18

My dear Mother.

During the last two or three days I have received two parcels & two letters from you for all of which thank you very much indeed. The cakes & apples were topping and we enjoyed them very much indeed and the vests & so on were just what I wanted. It has become so much colder of late that warm clothes have become an absolute necessity.

Your letter of Nov 8th has just arrived and I was awfully sorry to hear that you were unable to have your holiday. I am sure you must both have been disappointed for it would have been a splendid change for you.

I was awfully sorry too, to hear that Uncle George of Dornock Mains is so ill – I do hope he will get better for as you said they will miss him terribly if he does not live.

I hope Violet will be the only one at Park Cottage to catch the flue – as it is extraordinarily infectious and makes one feel an absolute washout.

Poor old Rob seems rather vexed about the turn of events, and had the war gone on it would have been bad luck indeed, but I don't think he need worry now. The war is undoubtedly over at last and he will soon be able to discard his uniform for good. I am very glad indeed that he did not have to come out here & fight for it is a the latter is not a pleasant job by any means.

Well Mother, can you realize that the war is won & finished? I am afraid I can't quite grasp the situation just yet – one still seems to have the idea that we shall be going back into the line in a few days time.

I suppose there was great rejoicing when the news was published in England. We were terribly excited when we heard about it. We knew that the Bosche had 72 hours in which to decide & had settled down to wait for the result. When the news came, we were just playing cards in the mess before going to bed. Suddenly my batman opened the door & said that the Divisional despatch rider had just brought the news that the armistice had been signed. Of course we all got up & cheered for all we were worth – then all the men took it up & there was no end of a row. The band turned out & marched up & down the road – we fired off all our S.O.S. signals & wherever you looked there were rockets & fires & flares of every kind. It is a wonder some of us were not killed for the men started firing their rifles in the air for pure joy & bullets were flying about all over the place.

We are having a Bttn dinner to-night to celebrate the end of the war &

Copy N°. 1

SECRET.

WARNING
OPERATION ORDER No. 25.
by
Lt. Col. A.W.Reid M.C.,Commanding
2/4th. Somerset L. I.

Ref Maps 1/100000. TOURNAI. BRUSSELS

In the Field.
17th. Nov.1918.

1.   In accordance with the terms of the Armistice, the occupied
portions of FRANCE, BELGIUM, and LUXEMBURG are to be evacuated
by the enemy by the 26th. November.
    The country to the German frontier has been divided into 3
zones, and the enemy has been instructed to be clear of each zone
on the day preceding the commencement of the march of the Cavalry
into that zone, i.e., 2 days before it is entered by the leading
Divisions of the 11 Corps.

2.   The Second Army consisting of the Cavalry Corps (less 1 Division
II, III, XII, and Canadian Corps will begin its advance to the
German frontier on the 17th November 1918.
    The Cavalry Corps will cover the advance and be followed by the
Canadian Corps on the right and II corps on the left, one day's
march in rear.
    The III and XXII Corps will follow at a later date

3.   On the 17th November the Cavalry Corps will advance through the
present outpost line.

4.   On the 18th November the II Corps will begin its march and will
move in the following order :-

1st Echelon	- (41st Division	- Left.
	(29th "	- Right.
2nd Echelon	- 9th "	- Left.
	(34th "	- Right.
3rd Echelon	- II Corps H.A.Group.	

5.   The 102 Brigade Group will march tomorrow to FLOBECQ & WODECQ -
To be clear of ELLEZELLES by 10.00hrs.

6.   Lorries to be East of Roman Road LAHAMAIDE - FLOBECQ by 08.00

7.   Further instructions as to use of additional transport will be
issued later.

8.   ACKNOWLEDGE.

Invatteson
Capt a&qm
for O.C. 2/4th Somerset L.I.

Issued at 12.00
17/11/18.
    Copy No 1 O.C. "A" Coy.   Copy No.5 Quartermaster
        2 O.C. "B" "   6 Transport Officer.
        3 O.C. "C" "   7 File.
        4 O.C. Headquarters

also the 13th Nov as it was exactly a year ago that we first went into action & it was certainly more by good luck than good judgement that we came out of it. I ~~do~~ may not get away on leave just yet after all for we are off to Germany to-morrow & I may not be able to get off. However I shall get it later on & ~~the~~ if it is put off for a week or two I shall probably be home for Christmas which will be top hole. I may not be able to write for a day or two if we are on the march but there is no danger now – the day of bombs & shells is past & we just do quiet little route marches.

I am feeling quite fit again now & I sincerely hope that you are all quite well. ~~I~~ Garland's informant was quite wrong when he said that I had gone away on another course – I don't suppose I shall do ~~anymo~~ more courses during this war. Ron is still away & I think he still has another three weeks to do.

With much love to all & very many thanks for the parcels.

> I remain
> Your affectionate son
> Jim

B.E.F.
France

17–11–18

My dear Mother & Father.

Since I last wrote we have been on the march every day, and I suppose we shall continue to march for some little time for we are on our way to Germany and it is some little way when you have to do it all "a pied". We are now completely beyond the area where there has been any fighting and last night we marched into a little town in great style – there were flags on every house & the people all came out to cheer. When it came to billeting the difficulty was not to find billets, but not to disappoint the people by not giving them any soldiers to look after. I am in the nicest billet I have ever struck and the people are absolutely delightful – can't do enough for us. All day to-day we have been a sort of "merry Andrew" show and all the neighbours have been invited ~~into~~ in to have a look at us. They just come in to the mess, shake hands all round and then go away. We as it were stand in state and hold a reception.

We had a great evening yesterday. After dinner to the great joy of our hosts we all went out to the kitchen and started off by singing and playing the piano, then we danced & eventually finished up by playing games – musical chairs, kiss in the ring and all that sort of thing. There are three

"In hoc signo vinces."

34th DIVISION.

FRANCE.   PALESTINE.   BELGIUM.

A Form of Thanksgiving on the signing of an Armistice between the Allies and Germany.

ORDER OF SERVICE.

(FROM ARMY PRAYER BOOK).

Hymn 84, "*O God, our help in ages past.*"
General Confession (Page 1. To be said by all).
Absolution.
Lord's Prayer (To be said by all).
Psalm 23 (Page 4. To be said in alternate verses).
Lesson. Rev. XXI., v. 1—5, 10 and 20 to end.
Hymn 99, "*Rock of ages, cleft for me.*"
Apostles Creed (To be said by all).

PRAYERS.

On the sounding of "Cease Fire" on the bugle, the Division will stand in silent prayer of Thanksgiving for Victory.

After the sounding of the "Last Post" the Division will stand in silent prayer of Thanksgiving for the Example of the Glorious Dead.

The pious dead, the stars by day
Not seen by mortal eye,
Are not extinct, but hold their way
In glory through the sky.

Hymn 24, "*Crown Him with many crowns.*"

ADDRESS.

Hymn 39, "*Hail to the Lord's anointed.*"
General Thanksgiving (Page 9. To be said by all).
Te Deum (Page 7. By Choir only).
National Anthem.
The Blessing.

Please watch the conductor during the singing of the hymns, so as to keep the time.

or four girls in the house & I can assure you they thoroughly enjoyed themselves (& so did we).

This morning the whole Brigade paraded & held a thanksgiving service – it was rather impressive especially when ~~they played~~ the "last post" for our fallen comrades was played by the massed bugles.

Owing to this march all our leave has been suspended for the present but I shall get home later on. As a matter of fact I am rather keen on this little effort and don't want to miss it for it is awfully interesting seeing new places and new country.

Bttn orders have just been issued and they say that the censorship regulations have been relaxed and we can now say where we are, so it may interest you to know that we are to-day staying in a town called Reniax in Belguim. For several days last week we were in the Courtrai district and we have marched from there to this place, so you will be able to more or less to follow our route. The country so far has on the whole been flat but there is a little rising ground on this side of the Scheldt & the Bosche intended to make use of it to hold us up. It is picturesque in its way – all the roads are lined by long rows of poplars and of course the windmill is a great feature of the landscape.

The Bosche blew up all the bridges over the Scheldt & by cutting the dams managed to flood a good deal of the country but we have made fresh bridges & repaired the roads & traffic can now get through quite easily. Another restriction which has just been relaxed is that regarding the use of cameras. May I trouble you to send me out my Ensignette with a supply of films & please do let me know the cost of films and postage. I am afraid my ~~x~~ parcels must cost an awful lot in postage & if you would give me some ~~of~~ idea of the amount I should like to repay you.

The Belgians are awfully struck by the quality of our clothes & our general turn out as they ~~Germ~~ are so much better than those of the Germans.

The post is just going out so I must buck up & finish.

I am quite fit now – have quite got rid of my cold & I hope you are still keeping clear of the influenza.

With much love to all

> Your affectionate son
> Jim

B.E.F.
France

24–11–18

My dear Mother & Father.

I was so sorry when I received Father's letter to hear that everyone except you had gone down with influenza and I hope all the patients are by this time getting fit again.

Since I last wrote we have not moved from Wodecq as there has been some difficulty in getting up supplies to the forward divisions, as of course they are getting farther & farther from ~~raith~~ railhead. We have been spending our time training and playing football etc. Training goes on just as if we

Award of Belgian Croix de Guerre:

were still at war, for peace has not actually come yet and we must keep up the efficiency of the men.

We had rather an amusing game of football yesterday – the officers got up a side and played the Sergeants & beat them 2–0. I turned out & played for the first time since I hurt my knee & now I am so stiff that I can hardly move.

We have had rather variable weather this week – last Sunday it snowed then for two days we had thick, cold fog, but ~~sun~~ it is bright and frosty again now.

Everyone in England seems to have been very excited about the armistice – out here, with the exception of ~~the~~ a bit of a dust up on the first night,

~~wen~~ it was taken very quietly indeed. Even now I don't think any of us realize that it is over and that we shall not have to go back into the line again.

~~To~~ Two days ago we were inspected by the G.O.C. Division – he was quite pleased with our turnout and congratulated the Colonel on the smartness of the men.

I enclose a photograph which I had taken while I was in Rouen as all the officers in the Company wanted me to give them one. If you like it ~~it~~ I could get some more copies and let you all have one: ~~of~~ if you don't care about it I could have another taken sometime or other – perhaps when I come home on leave. I am trying to arrange my leave so as to be able to spend Christmas at home & won't it be topping if I can. We'll have a real peace time Christmas.

I had a long & most interesting letter from Andrew a few days ago – he must have had an awfully trying time but I am jolly glad to know that he is safe.

I had an awfully nice present last week in the shape of a beautiful silver cigarette case engraved with the Regimental crest, from one of ~~x~~ my former officers who is now in England unfit. ~~W~~ He wrote ~~ax~~ ripping letter with it saying how much he had enjoyed the time spent in my Company.

We have been getting up concerts for the men the last few days and have two most successful ones. I created a record last ~~nag~~ night by getting on to my hind legs for the first time in my life.

I hope you will both keep fit and that everyone will soon be well again. With much love to you all

> Your affectionate son
> Jim

> B.E.F.
> France

> Dec 2ⁿᵈ 1918

My dear Mother & Father.

I don't know whether I told you last time I wrote that I have applied for the leave vacancy which comes on Dec 13ᵗʰ in order that I may be able to spend Christmas at home. I think I shall get it, and I have also obtained the Colonel's permission to apply for a short extension so I hope to be able to have three weeks or a month at home instead of 14 days. I hope Rob will be home as well – if so it will be quite like old times. I am sorry you have ~~x~~ all been so ill – when I heard that Violet was ill with influenza I was afraid you would all get it as it is so extraordinarily infectious. I heard from John yesterday and he said that it had spread to Mesopotamia and that the natives were dying off like flies.

We gets lots of football in these days in fact there us a game of some sort every afternoon. My company are doing rather well just at present. We have won the inter platoon competition and I think we shall manage the inter company one as well. I had a game of rugger three days ago – the first since I we left Poona. It was awfully good fun but I found I was awfully out of condition.

We are still at Wodecq, but there air is full of rumours that we shall shortly be moving on. There has been a rearrangement of corps & divisions and I I don't quite know what formation our division is in now.

I am sorry to hear that Uncle John has had to have an operation and I hope he is going on satisfactorily. I am very glad indeed that Father has taken up his old appointment again if he did not like the new one – I guessed from his last letter that he did not care much about it.

My camera and socks have just turned up & thank you very much indeed. I am so sorry to give you so much trouble but I thought it would be rather nice to have it with me.

The Election seems to be definitely decided upon but I don't think many of us out here know very much what it is all over. Is Mr Morland the only candidate in our Division? I saw in the Western Gazette that he was had been accepted as the Liberal Labour candidate but I sa am not very clear what that means. Is he also the Coalition candidate and does he support Lloyd George, or does he run more or less on his own.

I think myself that Lloyd George is the right man & that he is sincere, but I am not quite clear whether the coalition is equally sincere. I am rather inclined to think that it is a sort of advanced Toryism under the name of Coalition but I admit I don't know much about the business at all. I wonder if Father would mind letting me know his views on the subject.

I hate the idea of women getting into Parliament & hope none of them will manage to do so – if they do I am afraid the dignity of our old Parliament will be gone for ever.

I do hope that you have by this time all recovered from the flue & are quite fit again.

With much love to all

       Your affectionate son
       Jim

B.E.F.
France

✗ 8–12–18

My dear Mother & Father.

I left the Regt the day before yesterday to go down to Calais on leave. They were just starting off on a very long march that is why I left so soon as I am not due to embark till the 13th. I am now at the Rest Camp at Courtrai and I expect I shall go on to Calais to-morrow, where I shall stay at the officers club till I can get across. As a matter of fact I shall try to slip across a day or two early if I can.

I shall stay the first night in London the same as last time if I can get a bed & shall come on down to Cary the next day – anyhow I will send you a wire to let you know that I am coming.

My leave will expire on the 28th so that I shall just be able to spend Christmas Day with you, but ✗ if I get an extension, as I hope to do, I shall probably get in New Year's Day at home also.

Courtrai is rather a dull place at present – it was knocked about a little by the fighting and things have hardly resumed their ordinary course yet.

It is a beautiful day to-day – cold, clear & frosty – I hope you are getting similar sort of weather at home – it makes one feel so much fitter than the dull wet weather. Ron is very well in these days – he was rather sick when he saw me going away as he is awfully anxious that his leave & mine should come together. He asked me to give his love to you all.

I had a couple of hours at Flobec on my way down, waiting for the lorries to start so I just called in on Padre Mead & had coffee & cake with him. He also has hopes of getting home for Christmas & says he will come across & see us if he does.

I do hope you are all feeling better now & have completely got rid of influenza. I am afraid you must all be awfully weak as a result of it.

I will write again when I get to Calais as there is no more news to-day.

Tell the Follies to pull themselves together for we must have a really jolly Christmas this year. With much love to all

Your affectionate son Jim

The 2/4th Somersets was the only battalion of the Regiment to join the Army of Occupation in Germany. When the Armistice came into Force the

Battalion was at Wevelghem in Belgium. In January 1919 the 2/4th proceeded to join the Army of Occupation and were stationed first at Bonn and then at Troisdorf. Eventually the time came for demobilization and all men who could not be demobilized were transferred to the 15th Hants and the cadre left for England, disembarking at Tilbury on 27th May 1919. The cadre arrived in Bath on 2nd June and were accorded a welcome no less enthusiastic than that accorded the 1/4th.

Extracted from *The Somerset Light Infantry 1914–1919*

B.E.F.

Tuesday 7–1–19

My dear Mother & Father.

I got back to the Bttn last Sunday afternoon and found them in some very good billets near Namur. When I reached London on the 1st I had lunch at the Norfolk Sq & then went out to St Albans. I got out there about 4 P M and stayed till~~&~~ about 9.30 so that I had quite a good evening. Uncle did not seem at all well, in fact he had spent the previous day in bed. The D^r says that there is nothing the matter except want of rest & I am sure he will have to take some rest before long. Aunty seemed very fit indeed.

I left ~~Dover~~ Victoria by the 7.30 train on the 2nd but when I got to Dover the sea was so rough that the boats could not cross – however late in the afternoon they decided to let one go so I managed to get on board. It was an exceedingly rough crossing but that didn't seem to affect me in the least – I didn't feel at all ill. I slept the night at Calais & then went down to Boulogne on the 3rd ~~cau~~ and caught the Cologne Express from there ~~on~~ the same evening.

The latter is a train reserved for officers returning from leave and is very comfortable indeed being an ambulance train which has been transformed into a passenger train. Everyone gets a bed and a blanket and one can also get refreshments. We should have arrived at Charleroi the next morning but owing to a ~~break~~ breakdown on the railway we were 27 hrs late. We travelled through St Pol, Arras, Douai, Mons, Chaleroi, Namur, and it was awfully interesting seeing the old no-man's land etc.

I had no difficulty in finding the Bttn as I got into a tram outside Namur station and was taken right to the door of the mess. We are about 5 miles out of Namur right on the banks of the Meuse, and we all have excellent quarters as the houses mostly belong to people who live in

Brussels in the Winter & just come down here for the ~~Winter~~ Summer. The river is in flood just at present and its rather fine as it runs through a great gorge here and travels at a tremendous pace. This must be a delightful spot in the Summer as the country is very hilly and is well wooded and I should think the river was delightful. We are running a Bttn mess now and ~~we~~ it is a great success so far as we have found a house which is just right for it.

Yesterday I rode into Namur with the Colonel & we had tea in there. It was a very nice tea but just to give you some idea of the prices one has to pay for things we we charged 8½ᵈ for a small wafer.

This afternoon I went out to a sort of party at the Colonel's billet – we danced and played cards & had quite a good time. They are awfully nice people & are all out to give us a good time but it is rather trying having to talk French all the time.

We have been holding boxing competitions the last two nights and have had quite a good show. I started this morning to have a few lessons from a sergeant of the Army Gymnastic school and if we stay here shall try to keep it up as it is topping good sport.

Ron seems quite fit but is rather worried about his future now that his I.A. stunt has failed. He is going off on leave on Thursday so you will probably see him before long.

The cheese which I brought back is a beauty and everyone is thoroughly enjoying it.

I suppose Rob is at home now – I hope he will enjoy his holiday as much as I did mine. I imagine that the Follies are having as good a time as ever – parties every night & so on. I hope Janet's eyes will not have disappeared completely by the time I come home next time.

It is getting very late & I must go off to bed or I shall not be able to get up to-morrow morning.

I hope you are all keeping fit

With very much love to all

       Your affectionate son
       Jim

B.E.F.
France

✗ 10.1.19

My dear Father.

Just a note to tell you ✗ two little things which I think will interest you.

The first is that I̶ my name appeared in yesterday's routine orders as having been awarded the Croix de Guerre (Belgian). I have not yet seen the ribband but will send you a piece when I ̶g̶ can get hold of a bit. Secondly, all students and teachers are to be released from military service at once, in fact the ones from this Bttn are due to leave here to-morrow. I of course come under the student class, and in view of my decision to go back to Reading, ̶a̶m̶ could leave also. The Colonel is however very short officers just at present and as he has been exceedingly kind to me I felt the least I could do was to offer to stay on till ̶I̶a few of them come back from leave. He was awfully pleased about it & asked me to stay till Ron Vallis comes back, which I have consented to do. I shall of course miss this time at the College, but I am doing a good deal of reading here and I think you will agree that this offer was the least I could do in return for the C.O.ˢ kindness to me.

I shall write to Reading to-day & tell them that they can expect me some time in Feb as I shall be ready to go there as soon as I have had a few days at home. The more I think about it the more certain I am that I am doing the right thing in going to Reading. I have not yet heard from John, ̶b̶u̶t̶ and of course when I do I may think I want to go out there, but as I have now made up my mind about the Reading effort he will have to produce something really powerful to make me alter it.

We are shortly going to Germany – I hope it will be before I leave the Bttn as I should like to get there before I leave the army.

We are having quite a good time here – will write again Sunday.

Hoping you are all quite well much love to all

> Your affectionate son
> Jim

B.E.F.
France

13.1.19

My dear Mother & Father.

As I wrote only about two days ago there is not very much more news.

The Bttn is very shortly going on to Germany but the date has not yet been fixed. In the meantime we are very comfortable indeed and none of us are in a great hurry to move on, although of course most of us are rather keen to just get to Germany before we clear out.

Of course I was awfully glad to hear about the Croix de Guerre – it is not at all a bad medal to have – better than nothing at all.

I have just heard that my official record is as follows:

Palestine   Twice recommended for M.C.
Recommended for Leigon d'honneur

For these I was mentioned in despatches

France –   Recommended for a decoration & received
Croix de Guerre (Belgian)

Please don't pass this on, as I should not have mentioned it only I thought you would like to know.

I had a letter from John yesterday and he says that while he was in Baghdad he did his best to get the authorities to apply for me again and that he thinks that they will do so He gives me lots of instructions re learning Arabic and says that it will be better for me "doing a job of work in Mespot than wasting my time out here". (Wonder what he thinks we have been doing).

We had some awfully good fun two nights ago, several of us went to a dance & party at the Colonel's billet. His people are very well to-do Belgians & are sort of leaders of society in the district and they did us awfully well We g (My pen had just run dry) We are going there to dinner on Wednesday night. Our men are creating an awfully good impression in Belgium as they are exceedingly polite & are always so smartly turned out. A lady asked me the other night if we taught them to be polite.

Demobilization proceeds very quickly and we are losing lots of our best N.C.O.s & men very rapidly. My man, Madge, goes to-morrow I am and I shall be ever so sorry to see the last of him as he has been a splendid servant and a good friend. My groom, Hatch, will also be going in a few days.

Father's letter is the only one I have had so far, Mother's has not yet arrived – the letters are taking ever so long to reach us up here.

I shall be writing to Janet for her birthday in a few days time. I suppose all the follies have been going to parties every day just lately and are by this time quite tired out.

I went for a long ride this afternoon along the hills overlooking Namur. The town stands completely in a basin and the Rivers Meuse & Sambre unite right in the centre of the town. The Meuse has been in flood just lately and we thought that the whole Country would be flooded a day or two ago, but there has not been any rain for the last two days & it has gone down considerably.

I hope Mother is keeping fit that all the others are quite well
With much love to all

Your affectionate son
Jim

P. S. Mothers letter has just arrived – thank you very much indeed for the blue book – I forgot all about it till after I left home.

B.E.F.
France

16.1.19

My dear Teddy.

Very many happy returns of your birthday & every good wish for the future. I thought I might have been at home to wish you many happy returns personally but I as I am staying on a little longer shall not be able to do so.

I am going to give you the usual present but cannot send it to-day as I have run out of cheques; and I shall probably be going into Namur presently and may be able to buy you a present of some sort there. If not I will send you a cheque as soon as possible.

We shall probably leave here on Saturday or Sunday to go to Germany – I believe to Bonn – so I may not write again to till we get there. It will be rather nice to just be able to have a look at the Bosches before I clear out.

I had a very strenuous day yesterday. Started off by running in a 6 mile paper chase across country – then changed, got on my horse & rode 10 miles to see the Bttn play a football match again the R.E.s in a cup competition (the result was a draw 0–0) & then rode back again. After that I just had time to change again & go out to a dinner par party where we played games etc till midnight. It was a very jolly evening I can assure you. I suppose Rob is at home now & having a great time – I mean to write to him in a day or two.

I hope you are all having a really good time & I hope you will have a very jolly birthday

With much love & best wishes

Your affectionate brother
Jim

B.E.F.
France

23.I.19

My dear Mother & Father.

The 2/4th Somersets have crossed the Rhine at last and we are now billeted on the inhabitants of Germany. We left Namur at about 7. o'clock last Sunday – for once in a way we had a decent carriage ~~for~~ as it was one of those taken over from the Bosche and as a result the journey was not nearly so bad as we had anticipated. We reached Cologne about mid-day on the Monday but did not stop there. Instead we crossed the River by one of the bridges and went down the other side to Beual which is just opposite Bonn. We detrained there, then marched back across the Bridge through Bonn to our billets on the far side of the town.

We are all very comfortable now – the men are in a big building which was to have been a museum but is not quite finished, and we are ~~in~~ living in the houses. They are awfully fine houses too being the ~~Best~~ best in the town. We have all got a bedroom, sitting room & bathroom and we can practically demand anything we like.

When we first crossed the frontier in the train it seemed very strange to feel that we were really in Germany at last & what seemed ~~str~~ more strange still was to see all the Bosches about and not having to try to kill them. When we crossed the Rhine one felt as if one really was part of a conquering army and it did seem a fine thing to be an Englishman. This feeling increases daily, not that the Bosch is an inferior sort of being – far from it – he is easily the best type of man I have seen in other parts of the world and one cannot help admiring the efficiency of his machine; his cities are fine, his houses are beautifully ~~blt~~ built, his bridges are wonderful structures and everything is solid and clean: – the latter in contrast to Belgium is very marked. The net result is that the more you see & the more you admire the more you feel what a splendid achievement we have made in beating him.

Fancy having Bosches billeted in our houses or sitting at the tables in our hotels & restaurants – think we should feel it an awful disgrace.

The extraordinary part about the people is that they show no signs whatever of hostility, on the other hand they do very much the other thing. They can nearly all talk English and they cannot do enough for us in their houses. Of course this is partly explained by the fact that they are afraid of punishment – the C.O. can levy a fine of 5000 marks or 6 months in prison for insolence to an officer, but there is now no doubt in my mind that ~~the~~ it is part of a policy. We arrived prepared to be full of hate but he has taken the wind out of our sails by being excessively polite and by conforming to all our orders &

regulations without any trouble. I believe his object is to make us say that
~~The~~ "The Bosche is not such a bad fellow after all – the people were not
responsible for the war, this was brought about by their rulers so we may as
well be friendly with ~~us~~ him again". He hopes in this way to get back into
favour with us & to open up trade relations & friendly intercourse the very
minute peace is signed. I am told that his factories are already starting to make
goods intended for the English market. In one billet I was in they asked me
out to a dinner party the very day after I got there in fact it is only by
constantly thinking about the devastation of Belgium etc that one can possibly
retain any hate at all. Bonn is quite a nice clean city. It is of course noted for
its University which is quite a fine show, and there is also a very fine old
Minster. In the Kaiser Platz there is a big marble statue of ~~W~~ Emperor William
I in ~~its~~ uniform, so the Canadians from whom we are taking over, when they
arrived decided that there should be no armed Bosches in the place as long
as they were in it and they accordingly attacked the statue & removed the
sword and crowned the Emperor with a jerry. Yesterday Padre & I went in
to Cologne. There is a special tram service of fast trams between Bonn &
Cologne ~~so it~~ and it takes about 45 minutes to go from one place to the other.
They are the finest trams I have ever seen.

Cologne is a very fine city and the cathedral very beautiful indeed – it is
well worth seeing. The bridge over the Rhine where General Plummer
watched the army pass when we first entered Germany is also very fine
indeed. It is wide enough for three railway lines a road & a pavement and
is about ~~500 +~~ 500–600 yards long. British sentries now guard both ap-
proaches to all the bridges.

To-morrow the ~~W~~ whole Bttn is going up the river on one of the river
steamers which we have chartered for the purpose. It is quite a free trip –
we don't pay for anything of that sort nor for our trams or trains.

We hope to go up beyond Königswinter & may get as far as Coblentz
if we push on fairly quickly. It is a wonderful chance of seeing the Country
and we mean to make the most of it.

I heard from both Mother & Janet to-day the letter being dated the 17th
Jan. I am awfully sorry ~~to heard~~ that Mother is unwell ~~again and~~ sincerely
hope that when I get the next letter I shall hear that she is better again. I
am also very glad indeed to hear that Uncle John is better. Have you seen
anything of Ron this time – I shall be coming home as soon as I can after
he returns here.

This is a long letter & although there is lots more I could write about I
think I had better stop & get to bed.

With very much love to all

>   Your affectionate son
>   Jim

B.E.F.
France

26.1.19

My dear Mother & Father.

It is Sunday again to-day so here goes for a letter although I told you most of the news when I wrote last Wednesday.

We are seeing as much of the country as possible while we have the chance of travelling at the expense of the Bosche and on Friday we chartered a big river steamer and took the whole Bttn up the river as far as Coblentz. We had an hour ashore to have a look at the place and then came back. Of course to see the country at its best one wants to do the trip in the Summer when the trees have their leaves as it all looks rather bare just now. Still, even now it is very beautiful and one thoroughly enjoys seeing fresh places & things. Königswinter is a very pretty place and is the starting plac point for tours in the Drachenfells which are seven hills just close by and seem to be a rather noted for their scenery. All up the river there are castles & country seats perched up on the tops of the hills: some are still used & others in ruins but all of them have their own particular legends & stories. The castle of the Bethmann – Hollweg family stands on a high cliff overlooking the river at Schloss Rheinech.

Coblentz is not much of a city but is greatly frequented by tourists because it stands at the juction of the Rhine & the Moselle and tours for both of the valleys start from it. It is in the American zone and the Yanks seem to have dug themselves in very successfully.

Bonn is certainly the nicest of the German cities which I have seen so far – Cologne is bigger but not so pretty and dignified. I want to make another trip to Cologne as soon as I can as I didn't have much time there when I last went.

Our job so far has been to keep the Canadians in orders and the men have all been out on patrols & pickets every night but the Canadians have nearly all gone now and things are quieter. The men are out to-day to look after the civilians as there is an election taking place – so far it has gone off very quietly and the people who with whom I am billeted say that it is going quite well by which they mean that the Bolshevists & extremists are getting beaten. The husband in this house says that Germany must always be a republic now & seems to think that Ebert & Schiedermann will pull things round successfully but his wife is all for the Emperor. She sa Both say that the Kaiser was a very good & honest man but very weak and attribute all the war & everything which was bad to the polititians. Neither have any use at all for the Crown Prince.

I don't think they realize yet how badly they were beaten & seem to think that because the army remained more or less intact that they are still in a position to treat with us. I fancy they will have rather a shock when the peace terms are settled.

There is no doubt that they think that Germany will resume her old position as a world power in two or three years time. They say they like the English best of all the troops in the armies of occupation and the girls in Cologne & the other places are simply throwing themselves at both officers & men, but one can't help thinking that it is all part of the policy. It is rather too sudden as only two months ago they hated us for all they were worth.

I think they are thoroughly afraid of us at present – one daring fellow tore up a union jack in the square here a few days ago and he was promptly fined 5000 marks & had 6 months in prison. That sort of thing keeps them in their place.

I am very glad that the "Follies" are still having a good time – I expect they thoroughly enjoyed their visit to Frome. I shall hear all about it from Ron when he comes back.

It is awfully cold here – does not rise above freezing point all day – everyone seems to expect a good deal of snow before long. I think the dry cold is very healthy for we are all keeping awfully fit.

I have not heard anything official about Mespot yet but I wrote to John yesterday and told him that I did not intend to come out at anyrate till I had been back to Reading. I doubt if he & I would make a very successful combination as I am afraid we should both want to have our own way too much to do much good.

I do hope Mother is better again – I hope she will keep warm & take life easily till she gets rid of the neuritis. How is Ted Drewett now – I hope he is better.

With very much love to you all

Your affectionate son
Jim

M.S.4.T.

9/13/

12.58 A.

D 5A

SIR,

I am commanded by the Army Council to inform you that in consequence of the demobilisation of the Army you have been disembodied as from the

8/7/19

inclusive.

You will receive a further notification of any gratuity to which you may be entitled.

You should report any change of permanent address to the :—

Secretary

War Office, Whitehall S.W.

I am also to take this opportunity of conveying the thanks of the Army Council for your services to the Country during the late war, and for the excellent work you have done.

Cpt J.R. Mackie

2/4th Somerset L.I

Park Cottage

Castle Cary

Somerset

I am,

SIR,

Your obedient servant,

R.H. Brade

(1077) W8153/RP3616 5,000 12/18 Cax.P.Ltd. H2824

"A" Form.

MESSAGES AND SIGNALS.

Army Form C. 2121.
(In pads of 100.)

No. of Message..............

Prefix............Code............. m	Words.	Charge.		Recd. at .... m.
Office of Origin and Service Instructions.			This message is on a/c of :	Date...............
W. O. F.	29./2 15.8	/8950 (6)		From...............
	Sent At..........m.		Service.	
	To............			By...............
	By............	(Signature of " Franking Officer.")	

TO: G H Q Fce

| Sender's Number. | Day of Month. | In reply to Number. | |
| B 5077 | | | **A A A** |

M S 6 Demobilise Capt
J R Mackie 1/4th Somerset L. I.
forthwith in accordance with army
demobilization regulations a a a
order to report to Indian Office
Political Dept for duty

Military Secy.

Certified true copy.

[signature]
1/4 Somerset L. I.

From............

Place............

Time............

The above may be forwarded as now corrected.   **(Z)**

....
Censor. Signature of Addressor or person authorised to telegraph in his name.

* This line should be erased if not required.

(5796.) Wt. W 492/M1647. 650,000 Pads. 5/17. H.W. & V., Ld. (E. 1187.)

REGENT PALACE HOTEL
PICCADILLY CIRCUS
LONDON W.1.

⚡ 7.2.19

My dear Father & Mother.

I crossed over to-day and am now a civilian once more as I completed my demobilization this afternoon. I took a hotel card and managed to secure a bed in this place. ~~but a~~ I was due for demobilization as you know through being a student but the day before I left a wire arrived from the Military Secretary G.H.Q. saying that I was to be demobilized at once and to report forthwith at the India Office for duty. I suppose John's efforts have been successful and I shall call there to-morrow to hear what they have to say but I shall not accept anything unless it is particularly attractive. I shall try & go down to see Uncle Robert to-morrow & may stay a night after which I shall go down to Reading & then home. I shall arrange to go back to Reading at half term as I want to get the interim grant of £35 out of the Govt. if possible.

I will write & let you know for certain when I am coming down – I shall not stay longer than I can help here for London is not to nice just at present as nearly everyone is on strike I am very fit indeed & I hope you are also

With very much love to all

Your affectionate son
Jim

---

185 Kings Road
Reading

27.4.19

My dear Mother & Father

We have practically settled down here now and as far as I can see we shall be fairly comfortable. The billet is not as good as one might have had, but we shall only be here one term and I don't think it worth while to change. Bunna & I share a bedroom and there is a common sitting room which we all use – there are 14 of us here. Of these 3 were were in the College in 1914 namely Penaluna, Hancock, & Webber. I did not know the two latter very well but Panaluna & I were in the same block at Wantage Hall and I last met him by accident in in Palestine when we were on outpost duty. Drummond is back & also Bevan & Low so that there are just a few of the old rowing men to carry on the good work.

Lewin is there too as well as Brown (our old Geography master) and I expect all these will be back next year. Wantage Hall will be open then so I expect we shall have some cheery times. then

For the first time since I was demobilized I can more or less see my way clear and I have more or less made up my mind to go all out next year & try first of all for the National Diploma in Agriculture, then for the College Diploma & then in October have a go at the degree. The latter is terribly stiff in these days & seems rather a forlorn hope but I mean to see what can be done. It will mean an awful lot of work for you can't conceive how much I have forgotten, but I hope and it is very difficult to really settle down to study especially in a place like this where you can't get a room to yourself. After all I am better off than some fellows. Bevan, Low & Joule are a & Drummond are all over 25 now so I have 2 years grace even now. There are not a great many other men back yet but they hope to have the full number next year.

Passmore has not turned up & there is a rumour that he is not coming back after all – I fancy he must have got hold of a job of some sort.

I didn't mean to do very much outside my work when I came up but they have attacked me from all sides to try & get the rowing going again, so I think I shall do something to it this term at anyrate. One can't very well come to a place of this sort & st keep aloof from the various societies etc – if everyone does that it lets down the tone of the place so badly.

I seem to have forgotten to pack in my sh rowing shorts – anyhow I can't find them in my kit – would you kindly send them on if they are knocking about at home. I should also be rather glad of those very old tennis shoes with the rubber bottoms if I am going to row for my the pair I have here are good ones & they will soon be ruined if I use them down on the river.

I have This work this year is awfully interesting as we have given up pure science completely now and are doing Agricultural subjects entirely. I have asked to be allowed to put in some time in the dairy and I think I shall try to do a month there at the end of the term if they can make room for me. They are absolutely crowded out at present but I am going to try and get hold of Todd & Miss Little next week and see if I can get them to take me in. It would be a great help if I could get in there for a bit.

I tried all over Reading yesterday to get a trouser press but there are none to be had at present – everyone is hoping to get some in before long but they seem very scarce. I wonder if Father would mind trying to get one in London or Bristol as we want one rather badly. I am so sorry that Angus had such a bad time with the dentist. I can't think how he stuck to it without anything at all to help it out for it ʆ is a beastly business at the best of times.

There is a fellow here in the billet doing Agriculture who was out in Palestine in the R.F.A. & strangely enough he was in the crowd who were supporting our Brigade. I never met him personally but he knew our Bttn quite well and used to live at our Hqrs when he was doing duty as Fort Observing officer.

The weather is beastly – it had been cold & wet ever since we came up. It is raining hard now but I hope it may clear up after this.

I hope the ~~follies~~ Follies have all recovered after all their Easter excitement – I suppose Beckey is in great demand by all the local dramatic societies.

I am glad to hear that Eric is home and looking fit – I hope to see him when we come back at the end of the term.

I hope Grandma Mackie is better, although I am afraid she has not had much help from the weather.

With very best wishes & hoping you are all quite well

> your affectionate son
> Jim

Baghdad

29.5.19

My dear Jim

I was awfully glad to get your letter of April 18th which by the way was heavily scented and makes me suspect that you had been nearer the fair sex than you ought to have been.

Thanks so much for fixing up the silver wedding present. I think you did splendidly, and I had a short note from mother last week saying how pleased she was with it. I am enlosing a draft on London for £20. Out of it I want you to take what is necessary for my share of the present, pay father £3.10.0 which is what I owe him for getting me a Persian dictionary and keep the remainder to allow yourself to get a bit of a holiday somewhere or other in the summer, or to make use of in any other way you like. Do not be afraid of asking me for help if you find the channel running a bit dry.

The hot weather has now come and we have reached 108 in the shade so we have only about another 12 degrees to go. I am however awfully fit and getting on splendidly. Last week the Revenue Secretary was laid up and so I had the Revenue destinies of this country in my hand for a day or two. On Sunday he is going away on tour for a fortnight to take his wife to Bannah en route for the Himalayahs so I shall be busy again. He is going on leave to India later in the year and I may have to officiate for him while he is away.

I see from Reuter that county cricket is on again and that Somerset having begun by ~~playing~~ taking a good licking from Surrey played a tie with Sussex, a change for them to score points so early in the season as this. Do let me know who plays for Somerset. I wish I was at home for some cricket as I might have managed to get a look in. I am sorry that S.S.N. Poyntz is captain again as he is not a good captain. I do not however know anyone who would be any better and Jack Waite has his bowling to do and does not want any more responsibilities. I might be home for some in August next year as I hope to get six months leave in England next year and by arriving home towards the end of July to get in a months cricket, some rugger, and also be home for Xmas and for Janet's 21st birthday. You had better not hold any very strong hopes about it at home as things in the leave line are very uncertain.

How is old Bunna doing at Reading? well I hope and continuing to be destructive with that leg break of his.

Well old man cheerio best of luck to you and Bunna and all

> Your affectionate brother
> John

Cheque from John. Never cashed

PROMOTION.

SUBSTANTIVE		ACTING		
Rank	Date	Rank	Inclusive	
			From	
2nd Lieut.	Sept 25ᵗʰ 1914			
Lieut.	July 1ˢᵗ 1916			
Captain	Nov 11ᵗʰ 1917	Capt	April 2ⁿᵈ 1917	
Bvt. Major				
Major				
Bvt. Lt.-Col.				
Lt.-Col.				
Bvt.-Col.				

6

PROMOTION.

	ACTING		
dates		Authority	Signature of C.O. or of a Brigade Commander in the case of a C.O.
To			
Nov 2ⁿᵈ 1917			

7

SERVICE.

AT HOME			ABROAD				Wounded (date)	Sick (date)
Unit	From	To	With an Expdy. Fce.		Elsewhere			
			From	To	From	To		
2/4 Somerset L.I.	25·9·14	9·12·14	Palest. 9·9·17 France 1·6·18	1·6·18	INDIA 9·12·14	9·9·17		Cairo 9·4·18

8

9

Official Record of Service

Certificate of Service

Certified that Captain James Richard Mackie 4 Som L.I.
served from 23 September 1914 to 8ᵗ February 1919 and
that he served overseas in India, Egyptian Expeditionary force,
and British Expeditionary Force, France as follows:-

India 20.12.14 to 14.9.17

E.E.F. 15.9.17 to 23.5.19. (Enroute to U.K. 24.5.18 to 31.5.18)

B.E.F. 1.6.19 to 31.1.19.

Captain
~~Major~~

For Officer i/c No. 2 Infantry Records, Exeter.

Exeter 9/2/20

C O P Y .

War Office,
London, S.W.1.
27.9.21.

9/13/2145 (M.S.4.T.).

Sir,

With reference to your letter No.S.C.3/27611 (S) dated 28.7.21. I am directed to inform you that the undermentioned resignation has been carried out and the following announcement appeared in the London Gazette of the 20th September 1921.

4th Bn.Somerset L.I.

Capt. J.R.MACKIE resigns his commission and retains the rank of Capt.

I am to add that the grant of the retention of the rank of Captain does not confer the right to wear uniform except when attending ceremonials and entertainments of a Military nature and on accasions when the wearing of uniform would appear appropriate.

I am,
Sir,
Your obedient Servant,

(Sd) C.W.G.INCE Major,
for Lt.Gen. Military Secretary.

The General Officer
Commanding-in-Chief,
Southern Command.

2.

Captain J.R.MACKIE.

The above copy of W.O.letter is forwarded for your information and retention.

Bath.   Major,

4.10.21.   Adjutant 4th Bn.Somerset L.I.

James R. Mackie (Jim) – 1946
Enjoying retirment at Hazelbury Plucknett, Somerset

Ross Island from Port Blair, the island is now covered in jungle

Ross Island: Ruins of the Officer's Quarters

Ross Island: Ruins of the Bakery

The Garrison Church, now roofless and taken over by jungle

Ross Island: Ruins of Government House

Ross Island: The steps leading to Government House, where the officers of the 2/4th Bn. were photographed in 1915. The author sits where his father sat in that group

Corbyn's Cove, Port Blair. A Sandy beach where companies bathed

The cellular jail. 698 single cells. Completed in 1906, Now a National Museum in Port Blair

Appendix I

Family Nicknames

I n common with many families, the children of J. Hugh and Geraldine Mackie used nicknames for their brothers and sisters. It may help current readers and future generations to be privy to these.

Christian Name	Nickname(s)
John	Buller
James	Jim, Jas
Andrew	Pud, Squeak
Robert	Bob, Bunna, Rob
Angus	Gilbert
Malcolm	Duff, Duffy
Janet	Ted, Teddy
Mary	Molly
Margaret	Puss, Pussy

The origins of these nicknames are not known to the Editor! They are in regular use throughout this correspondence.

John Mackie

Appendix II

The Editor in Military Days

Operation Question, During the Emergency in Malaya
August 1953 – at Sungei Pelek, Selangor

Left to Right:

Lt. Col. J.L. Brind, D.S.O.   C.O. 1st Bn. Somerset L.I. (P.A.)

Brigadier W.H. Lambert, C.B.E.   Commander 17th Gurkha Independent
                                 Infantry Brigade

Lieut. J.H.F. Mackie   I.O. 1st Bn. Somerset L.I. (P.A.)